Tradition and Christianity

Studies in Anthropology and History

Studies in Anthropology and History is a series that will develop new theoretical perspectives, and combine comparative and ethnographic studies with historical research.

Edited by Nicholas Thomas, The Australian National University, Canberra.

Ben Burt

Tradition and Christianity

The colonial transformation of
a Solomon Islands society

 harwood academic publishers

Australia • Canada • France • Germany • India • Japan • Luxembourg
Malaysia • The Netherlands • Russia • Singapore • Switzerland

OPA (Overseas Publishers Association) N.V. Published by license under the Harwood Academic Publishers imprint, part of The Gordon and Breach Publishing Group.

First published 1994
Second printing 2001

Amsteldijk 166
1st Floor
1079 LH Amsterdam
The Netherlands

LIBRARY OF CONGRESS CATALOGING-IN-PUBLICATION DATA

Burt, Ben.
   Tradition and Christianity : the Colonial transformation of a Solomon Islands society / Ben Burt.
      p.   cm. -- (Studies in anthropology and history : v. 10)
   Includes bibliographical references.
   ISBN 3-7186-5449-0
   1. Kwara'ae (Solomon Islands people)--Missions 2. Missions--Solomon Islands--Malaita--History. 3. Kwara'ae (Solomon Islands people)--History. 4. Kwara'ae (Solomon Islands people)--Government relations. 5. Christianity and politics--Solomon Islands--Malaita. 6. Malaita (Solomon Islands)--Politics and government. I. Title. II. Series.
   DU850.B87   1993
   995.94--dc20   94-23801
                                                                         CIP

DESIGNED BY   Maureen Anne MacKenzie
                 Em Squared, Main Street, Michelago, NSW 2620, Australia

P75691

Contents

v

List of illustrations

The author, date and source of each plate is given in the caption whenever the information is available. Maps and drawings are by Ben Burt.

MAPS

DRAWINGS

Preface

This book results from an association with the Kwara'ae people which has now continued for about fourteen years, and it could not have been written without the continued co-operation of those among them who wish to see their culture and history recorded. They have not given up this knowledge lightly, so I am the more grateful to those who showed their trust and support by providing information and persuading others to do the same, in spite of a longstanding suspicion of Europeans which has sometimes made this very difficult for them as well as for me.

A number of people have made particularly important contributions to the book. My 'father' Paramount Chief Adriel Rofate'e Toemanu is the main authority for much of what I have written, and he and his wife Bethel Buru'abu and their family have made me welcome in their homes, including Stephen Binalu and George Bako who also assisted with the research, and their wives Betty Arufala and Rosie Buana. My 'brother' Michael Kwa'ioloa has played a particularly important part in mediating with some of the foremost authorities on Kwara'ae traditional culture and contributing his own knowledge, encouragement and friendship, with the support of his wife Bizel Fanenalua and their children.

Besides many of the Kwara'ae people listed below, friends who gave valuable practical help and hospitality in Solomon Islands include Lawrence Foana'ota and Ellen Safina, Jimmy Olosua, John Freeman and Alison Worsnop, Graham and Evelyn Baines. The staff of the National Museum and National Archives in Honiara, including Lawrence Foana'ota, Alec Rukia and George Gwá'ilau, have been helpful and supportive in many ways, and access to the South Sea Evangelical Mission archive was kindly facilitated by Tim Fulbright, Ross Carlyon and Brian Marsland.

Research in Solomon Islands was carried out with the permission of the East Kwara'ae House of Chiefs, the Kwara'ae Area Council, the Provincial Government of Malaita and the National Government of Solomon Islands. Visits to Solomon Islands in 1979 and in 1983–4 were supported by the Horniman Fund of the Royal Anthropological Institute, in 1983–4 by the Social Science Research Council, and in 1991 by the Nuffield Foundation.

Of those who have contributed to the writing up of the research, David Akin of the University of Michigan has been a particularly valuable colleague, sharing information and ideas from his own research in Kwaio as well as important archive material. At successive stages from initial research through the writing of a PhD thesis for London University to the preparation of the final manuscript, the book has also benefited from comments and advice from Roger Keesing in Solomon Islands, from Bruce Kapferer and Phil Burnham at University College London, from Gordon Griffiths of the South Sea Evangelical Mission, from anonymous reviewers for the Smithsonian Institution and Harwood Academic Publishers, and from Michael O'Hanlon at the Museum of Mankind. I am obliged to a number of individuals and institutions for providing photographs, as acknowledged in the plate captions, and to Harry Persaud and the photographers at the British Museum for help in preparing them for publication. The encouragement of my colleague Penny Bateman of the British Museum is also much appreciated. Most of all I want to thank Pauline Khng and Annette Ward for their essential moral and practical support during this long project.

Many of the people who provided information for the book are mentioned in the text but, because many others are not, I would like to thank by name all those who made a personal contribution through interviews, conversation or correspondence, in many cases also with hospitality and other assistance. They are listed here in alphabetical order, with apologies to anyone I may have missed out:

David Akin, Othaniel Aifa'asia, Abraham Akalonia, Samuel Alasa'a, Eriel Aofia, Ariel Arini, Arumae, Thompson Atoa, Ishmael Augwata, Graham Baines, George Bako, Ben Banaudoe, Bauko'oru'ute'e, Robert Bera, Stephen Binalu, Rosie Buana, Marcus Bualimae, Busuakalo, Kath Crouch, Jonathon Didi'imae, Eriel Diki, Diosi, Patterson Sui Dufu, Edward Ekea, Fa'ale'a, Billy Farobo, Jeriel Fiku, Jesriel Filoa, Lawrence Foana'ota, Richard Folota, John Freeman, John Gamu, Justus Ganifiri, David Welchman Gegeo, Leslie Gereniu, Gordon Griffiths, Andrew Gwa'italafa, Dick Horton, Iniakalo, Eriel Jimi, Timmy John, Malakai Kailiu, Betty Kalianaramo, Kedeola, Roger Keesing, Timi Ko'oliu, David Kosionami, Michael Kwa'ioloa, England Kwaisulia, Haniel Kwale'unga, Nelson Kwanabako, William Kwari, George Laekalia, Jeremel Le'anafaka, Malcolm Le'anafaka, Lebefau, Moses Lebekwau, Jeriel Leote'e, Lovea, Jack Mae, Dickson Maefa'iakalo, Maefatafata, Maerora, Pierre Maranda, Maunu, Jemuel Misialo, Nemuel Nakisi, Michael Ngidu'i, Arnon Ngwadili, Ngunu, Shemuel Ofa'i, Ofota, Paul Oge, Jesriel Olosua, Jimmy Olosua, Onesmas Omani, Clement Maletege O'ogau, Aisah Osifera, Jack Ramosaea, Ramosala, Johnson Rara, David Reri, Taeman Rikimani, Riomea, Robert Riria, Alec Rukia, Tom Russell, Ellen Safina, Father Nelson Safu, Philip Sale, Hamuel Salole, Nelson Salole, Sande, Silas Sangafanoa, Francis Sisimia, Zebulon Sisimia, So'ai, Andrew So'ai, Samuel Sosoke, Rocky Tisa Sugumanu, Takangwane, Taeman

Timi, Zenas Toaakalo, Adriel Rofate'e Toemanu, Tolo'au, Daniel Tolosau, Wilson To'oga, Frank Ete Tua'aisalo, Philip Udua, Ukasina, Amasaia Unumaliu.

In their own ways, many of these people recognise anthropology as a colonial enterprise. The relationship between Third World local people and First World researchers poses difficult ethical questions which are constantly raised by Kwara'ae and other Solomon Islanders and Melanesians, if less so by anthropologists. It has not always been easy to understand exactly what Kwara'ae expect from my research, and even less easy to meet some of the requests they actually make. Kwara'ae for their part often misunderstand my motives and purposes as an anthropologist, but rightly assume that I receive some personal advantage from their help and should recognise obligations in return.

As long as people want to see their culture and history documented but lack the training or opportunity to do it themselves there is still room for co-operation between local people and foreign researchers, but whether this continues may depend on what the subjects of the research think of its results. This book does not fulfill all my obligations to my Kwara'ae friends and acquaintances, but it does document a lot of information recalled by Kwara'ae elders, many now dead, which might otherwise be lost. I apologise to readers who may have difficulty following an anthropological study in a foreign language, but I hope the book will return to the Kwara'ae people something which may be of value to them and their descendants in the future.

PLATE 1   *Adriel Rofate'e Toemanu of Gwauna'ongi , Paramount Chief and authority on Kwara'ae tradition. (Photo by Ben Burt, 1983).*

FIGURE 1   *A shell pendant, engraved with frigate birds and fern shoots, once worn by the priests of 'Aimomoko.*

CHAPTER ONE

Introduction

This is an ethnography and history of the Kwara'ae people of Kwai, a district of the island of Malaita in Solomon Islands. It describes a people fiercely attached to the tradition of their ancestors, who have adopted with equal conviction a new religion which contradicts some of the fundamental values of this tradition. The object of the study is to document and explain how and why this Pacific Islands people have transformed their society by changing their religion.

Kwara'ae history during the last hundred years has been dominated by their confrontation with the Europeans who colonised their country and introduced from the opposite side of the world a new cultural tradition which was probably as alien to Kwara'ae as another culture could be. The tribal social order and religious world view which Kwara'ae inherited from their ancestors informed their attempts first to resist and later to compromise with this colonial domination. In a long and continuing struggle for self-determination, they have reorganised their society, their spiritual as well as their human relationships, by becoming Christians and creating the new social order through which they now participate in the wider social systems of Solomon Islands and the world. But within their Christian society some serious contradictions remain unresolved, representing the contradictions of their own colonial history.

This study derives from a longstanding curiosity as to why so many colonised peoples in areas such as the Pacific have apparently jettisoned their traditional culture and religion of their own accord, to adopt that of their European colonisers. Finding myself trying to research 'traditional culture' among Kwara'ae fundamentalist Christians who evidently believed that this had been the right thing to do, I wanted to understand how they themselves viewed the transformation of their society. In case I was in any doubt, they clearly saw themselves as active agents in this process, but it soon became clear that Kwara'ae understandings of colonialism and Christianity were rather different from the ones I had developed as a sceptical member of the colonising society in Britain. These Kwara'ae perspectives are the central concern of this book. In order in explore them we begin with an analysis of their traditional society and culture, which then helps to explain the Kwara'ae role in more than a century of colonial history and the way this has shaped their present day Christian society.

THE COLONIAL TRANSFORMATION

An underlying premise of the study is that, for a people with a strongly spiritual or religious view of society and the world, conversion to Christianity represented an adaptation to the new social circumstances of the colonial order which traditional spiritual relationships had proved inadequate to predict and control. The question is how 'the social reality of religion', as Peter Berger (1967) has described it, led social change in Kwara'ae to be accomplished by religious means. It is hard to improve on Berger's explanation of how people continually create and are created by their social and cultural world through the dialectic process of "externalization, objectivation, and internalization" (1967:14). The products of people's activity, external to themselves, acquire an objective reality which imposes itself coercively back upon them through the relationships which socialise them to internalise it as subjective reality.

This dialectic is quite transparent in the way Kwara'ae created relationships of authority and power, which extended beyond the living to include the ghosts of the dead. Through these relationships, their traditional society participated in a cosmic order of spiritual power which provided a religious legitimation for the social order by transcending, and denying, its human construction. However, Kwara'ae seem to acknowledge the role they themselves play in maintaining and empowering this religious reality through faith and the observance of ritual rules, and recognise that the deities responsible for instituting their society and religion were their own human ancestors. Kwara'ae society was so effectively integrated into what Berger terms its 'sacred cosmos' that the very distinction between human and spritual domains entailed in treating the spiritual as 'sacred' was obscured. As we shall see, Kwara'ae culture comprehends spiritual power by concepts which, unlike sacredness, are grounded in human rather than spiritual relationships. In particular, rules upholding the principle of tabu emerge as central to Kwara'ae social structure and religion, being the idiom in which they conferred power upon one another and upon the ghosts of their ancestors.

An understanding of how Kwara'ae conceived of human and spiritual relationships and sought to organise and control them through an institutionalised ritual system lays the ground for an explanation not only of why they became Christians, but also of how they did so, and how their traditional society was transformed in the process. We continue with the premise that the particular circumstances of a people like Kwara'ae can best be understood by looking at their colonial history from the perspective of the traditional religious world view through which they themselves tried to understand and respond to events. To Kwara'ae, the political crises caused by colonial domination appeared also as crises in the relationships of spiritual power which supported the traditional social order and its resistance to colonialism. From this perspective it is not difficult to see how they were obliged to change their spiritual allegiances to come to terms with the new human relationships of the colonial order. In Berger's terms, colonial domination threatened the social, particularly the political, "plausibility structure" which supported the Kwara'ae world (1967:54), so that the traditional religion lost its power for them and over them as more and more people found a new source of spiritual support and protection in Christianity. The change of religion involved constructing the Christian social order as a new 'plausibility structure', and the efforts of each religious community to maintain and defend its own religious world inevitably became a political struggle between them.

By recognising the relationship between religious and social activity as dialectic in these terms, the political struggle and theological debate between Kwara'ae traditional religion and Christianity can be seen as contributing to the process of social change rather than being simply determined by it. This interpretation of Kwara'ae history recognises what Marshall Sahlins calls "The great challenge to an historical anthropology ... not merely to know how events are ordered by culture, but how, in that process, the culture is reordered" (1981:8). As Sahlins demonstrates in his studies of Polynesian history (1985), people react to events according to the structures of cultural significance they attach to them, which are realised and hence reproduced in these events. So in recognising the cultural structures of their own past in events of the present, people may find themselves transforming these structures as they attempt to deal with new circumstances by re-enacting old history.

But this should not obscure the agency of the colonisers. Although the present study does not attempt to explore their side of the colonial relationship in depth, the dominant power of the Europeans does emerge as a central Kwara'ae concern. In contrast to the early colonial 'heroic history' which Sahlins traces for the aristocratic states and military alliances of Polynesia, this dominance ultimately denied Kwara'ae the opportunity to re-enact their own history. The political autonomy of their small, feuding local communities eventually collapsed in disorder in the face of organised pressure from the colonial government. Like Sahlins' Polynesians (1981:59), Kwara'ae attempted to reproduce the traditional structures of the past by continuing to fulfill the roles and relationships established by their ancestors, but the obstacles they met eventually obliged most of them to renounce this past. Perceiving the colonial encounter in terms of their own cultural experience of human and spiritual relationships, ritual congregations came to question the power of their ancestral ghosts and sought alternatives, with far reaching consequences for the reproduction of their 'sacred cosmos' and of the entire social order to which it belonged. But, since the past was inevitably renounced in terms of its own underlying cultural premises, Kwara'ae religion as such was not so much abolished as transformed, to be reproduced in new forms in Christianity.

However, although anthropological and historical theories illuminate Kwara'ae history and culture, the underlying concern of this study is not to explore theory for its own sake so much as to attempt an understanding of how Kwara'ae themselves perceive their own culture and to explain their history in terms of some of their own cultural premises. As Fernandez recommends for the study of African religious movements, the analysis attempts the discovery of concepts embedded in local religious images, rather than "the application of imageless ideas exported from the West." To paraphrase Fernandez, the intention is to illuminate a Melanesian "struggle to maintain the integrity of their worlds in transitional circumstances" rather than "simply to fuel Eurocentric dialogues and disputes" (1978:215, 230).

WRITING ABOUT TRADITION

This approach requires the detailed account of Kwara'ae traditional culture, particularly of religion, which occupies Chapters 2 and 3 of this book. The study benefits from a long history of anthropological research on Malaita, beginning in the 1920s, which now makes it the best documented major island in the Solomons, with comparative material available from most of its twelve or so language groups (see eg. Ivens 1927 on Sa'a and 1930 on Lau, Hogbin 1939 on To'abaita, Russell 1950 and Guideri 1980 on Fataleka, Maranda & Maranda 1970 on Lau, Ross 1973 on Baegu, Cooper 1971 and 1972 on Langalanga, de Coppet & Zemp 1978 and de Coppet 1981 on 'Are'are). Particularly important is the work of Roger Keesing on Kwaio, immediately south of Kwara'ae, whose prolific writings have addressed a variety of issues, cultural, historical and theoretical, which are directly relevant to this study of Kwara'ae. Although a number of articles have been published about Kwara'ae (eg. Burt 1982, 1988, Watson-Gegeo and Gegeo eg. 1986, Maenu'u 1981, Alasia 1987), the present account is their first general ethnography. As such it has a perspective of its own which may also shed new light on the culture of other parts of the island.

The documentation of 'traditional culture' in a rapidly changing society raises a number of questions about the concept of 'tradition' itself, particularly among a people like Kwara'ae who have now nearly all taken the symbolically important step of abandoning their traditional religion to become Christians. 'Tradition' has been chosen to translate the Kwara'ae word *falafala*, which means 'culture' or 'way of life' and implicitly distinguishes the distinctive way of life followed and handed down from the past by their ancestors from the ubiquitous colonial culture of the wider world in which they now live. This is what Kwara'ae mean when they translate *falafala* by the Pijin word *kastom*, or English 'custom', but 'tradition' more accurately conveys the crucial value of cultural practices founded on ancestral precedent. In Kwara'ae usage, 'tradition' refers both to the 'tradition of the past' (*falafala ma'i na'o*) when their ancient way of life was still unaffected by colonialism, and to ideas and practices which have apparently continued from that time. For a people who often use religious affiliation to characterise their whole way of life, 'tradition' stands in particular for the social order governed by the ghosts of their ancestors. Hence it seems both appropriate and convenient to characterise as 'traditional' the non-Christian social order as it was, or might have been, in the past. It also seems appropriate that those who maintain a crucial symbolic commitment to the 'tradition of the past' by following the religion of their ancestors in the face of the Christian alternative should be referred to as 'traditionists' (as distinct from 'traditional'). While they are content to refer to themselves as 'heathen' (*hiden*) and writers may describe them more euphemistically as 'pagan', the pejorative nature of these terms in English usage makes them difficult to accept, as educated Islanders now point out.

But for Kwara'ae themselves the images evoked by the 'tradition of the past' inevitably reflect their preoccupations with the present. In some circumstances, as we shall see, 'tradition' may represent a threat to the spiritual support and protection of Christianity and in others it may stand for local self-determination and resistance to external domination, among various other things. Any description of a society derived largely from people's recollections has to take account of the ideology which informs their images of past and present, and the Kwara'ae accounts used to construct the present model of their 'traditional society' are inevitably coloured by these and other symbolic images of 'tradition'. But once such images are recognised for what they are, they can provide valuable guidelines for the construction of an anthropological image. Kwara'ae understand their own culture more thoroughly and subtly than any Western anthropologist, with insights which are particularly valuable for a study seeking to explain why and how they have transformed what they regard as tradition, and developed these images of it in the process. Of course the anthropological description of this tradition is informed by its own ideological and theoretical priorities, which makes it very different to the Kwara'ae version. Hence the present study acknowledges, as the Kwara'ae model would not, that all representations of a culture are as much the product of particular social and historical circumstances as the culture itself. This is not necessarily to claim more or less authenticity for either model, but to recognise that Kwara'ae 'traditional culture' is accessible only through images constructed for ideological purposes. The debate over how people construct descriptions of their own culture, and how anthropologists construct descriptions of them doing so, will not be pursued further here (but see Linnekin 1992 for a more detailed discussion). This account of Kwara'ae traditional culture claims only a certain explanatory power to illuminate the historical transformation of their society and the constitution of their Christianity. It acknowledges insights provided by the symbolic images of tradition which Kwara'ae have constructed for purposes of their own, but offers its own model of the traditional social order on which these Kwara'ae representations are based.

In the sense that it will be used in this study, 'traditional' implies, like the Kwara'ae image of 'tradition', indigenous as opposed to colonial or Christian, but not necessarily timeless or unchanging. It is important to remember that the pre-colonial society which Kwara'ae concepts of tradition evoke is now actually well beyond recall. Even people with personal experience of the traditional religion cannot remember what it was like before Kwara'ae first encountered Christianity, and the two religions have now co-existed for so long that in many respects the traditional religion described in this study should be recognised as one theme within a pluralist religious culture, rather than a picture of a culturally more homogenous pre-Christian past. Since the social order which this religion supported has to be reconstructed largely from present day recollections of various times in the past rather than from observations of actual behaviour, it cannot be firmly tied to a precise historical period. It should only be borne in mind that from about 1920 the imposition of British colonial rule drastically undermined the traditional Kwara'ae social order by preventing the killing which was the ultimate sanction for political authority. As a functioning political system, the traditional society to be described here thus derives largely from memories of the previous twenty years which, as we shall see, was not so much a pre-colonial or pre-Christian period as a period of anti-colonial and anti-Christian resistance. But these memories, and the present study, also draw both on more ancient stories and more recent experiences, as Kwara'ae continue to evoke and re-enact many of the cultural images and precedents created by their ancestors.

COLONIALISM AND CHRISTIANITY

This reconstruction of the traditional social order introduces the historical account of the colonial period which follows in Chapters 4 to 8. This traces the Kwara'ae experience of colonialism and their reactions to it, explaining the development of their Christian society from a perspective which raises certain questions about previous accounts of Christianity in Melanesia.

European colonisation of the Pacific was accomplished by the triple agency of trade, government and missions, but in the present study explanations focus on political and religious relationships, rather than economic ones. In the political turbulence of the 19th and early 20th centuries, missionaries and their converts often followed commercial interests into the more accessible coastal areas and islands but soon came under the protective shadow of colonial government and played an important part in the creation of the new colonial political order, as the Kwara'ae case will illustrate. The religious consequences are most striking for societies with relatively centralised political structures. By the mid 19th century whole populations of Polynesians had been led into the churches by chiefly rulers seeking colonial wealth and power in pursuit of their own political ambitions, whether as powerful kings, as in Tonga (Lātūkefu 1977) or as competing local chiefs as in Samoa (Tiffany 1978).

But in much of Melanesia mission objectives were not so easily accomplished by religious alliances between local leaders and colonial forces. In Fiji the acceptance of Christianity assisted the rulers of coastal and eastern states to consolidate political power with the support of Europeans and Christian Tongans, but it was only by using this power to conquer the independent peoples of the interior that they completed the conversion of Fiji in the 1860s and '70s (Sahlins 1985:39–40, Kaplan 1991). In politically more fragmented parts of island Melanesia mission work was only beginning to make an impact in the 1850s and '60s, not until the '70s and '80s on the coasts of New Guinea, and later still in the New Guinea Highlands where Europeans only penetrated in the 1930s. With so many independent local communities the spread of Christianity often proceeded a village or a clan at a time, in ways as diverse as the local political structures based variously on different modes of descent, ritual hierarchies and cults, graded societies and exchange systems, warfare and sorcery. There were long periods of delay and some even longer lasting pockets of determined resistance, which have continued for more than a century in parts of Vanuatu (Jolly 1982, Lindstrom 1982), as in Malaita (Keesing 1989a).

General explanations for why Melanesians have become Christians often agree in emphasising a pragmatic concern to change their relationship with the colonial world, to acquire Western goods and technology, knowledge and power, to substitute an ideology of peace for traditional religious values, and perhaps to bring about a social transformation under spiritual inspiration (eg. Belshaw 1954:50,54, Guiart 1962, Tonkinson 1982:307, Trompf 1991:155, Whiteman 1983:188–189). But although the spread of Christianity has been widely documented, the detailed local studies needed to substantiate such assertions are few and far between.

A closer look at Solomon Islands, as one part of the vast and varied Melanesian region, suggests a range of possible circumstances for the acceptance of Christianity. The people of Gela, a small and militarily vulnerable island group where the colonial government of Solomon Islands first established its headquarters, converted during the 1880s after a local leader was defeated by a British naval attack and reasserted his political authority under the protection of the Christian God (Whiteman 1983:140–142). Zelenietz (1979) suggests that the people of New Georgia abolished headhunting and feuding at the turn of the 20th century because it was obstructing colonial trade, later accepting government and Christianity as an appropriate ideology for the new social order which resulted. For the many independent clans of Choiseul, Scheffler (1964) says that Christianity provided a rationale for the way of peace imposed by the colonial government but considers that gradual conversion during the first half of the 20th century was promoted by expectations of receiving European goods and education. For north Malaita in the early 20th century, Hogbin describes local districts converting from a desire for Western knowledge and 'eternal life' or disillusionment with the power of ancestral ghosts (1939:179–184), and for Longgu on Guadalcanal he suggests a desire for protective spiritual power and the knowledge associated with European wealth (1964:91).

But until now the only island where the history of Christianity has been documented in depth is Isabel, where Geoffrey White's study (1991) enables interesting comparisons to be made with Kwara'ae on the neigbouring island of Malaita. Both islands were first visited by Anglican missionaries in the 1860s but by the early 1900s, when Christians were only beginning to gain a foothold on Malaita, the whole of Isabel had joined the Anglican church. Regional chiefs organising resistance to headhunting raids from Western Solomons had employed the spiritual support and ideology of peace of Christianity to consolidate their own authority by bringing their followers into the church. By contrast, in Kwara'ae the leaders of autonomous local communities opposed Christianity precisely because it promoted peace and weakened their resistance to government. Those who allied themselves with the spiritual and military forces of colonialism were dissidents who opposed the existing political establishment in its unusually vigorous resistance to colonialism. In Kwara'ae widespread conversion was eventually precipitated by the forcible imposition of government control.

But there are few other studies of Christianity in Melanesia, let alone in Solomon Islands, to broaden such comparisons through historical explanations of how and why particular societies were converted and transformed by Christianity. Most of the literature focuses on the role of the various missions operating in the region (eg. Belshaw 1954 Ch. 5, contributions to Boutilier, Hughes & Tiffany 1978). Solomon Islands features in histories of the Catholic Marist Mission (Laracy 1976), the Anglican Melanesian Mission (Hilliard 1974, 1978) and the most influential mission on Malaita, the South Sea Evangelial Mission (SSEM) (Hilliard 1969). Such research provides essential information on the formal organisation and the regional and global systems and processes shaping indigenous Christianity in the Pacific. But, as Barker points out (1990b:9), this may be at the expense of relegating the local religious reality to little more than a by-product of colonialism and conversion.

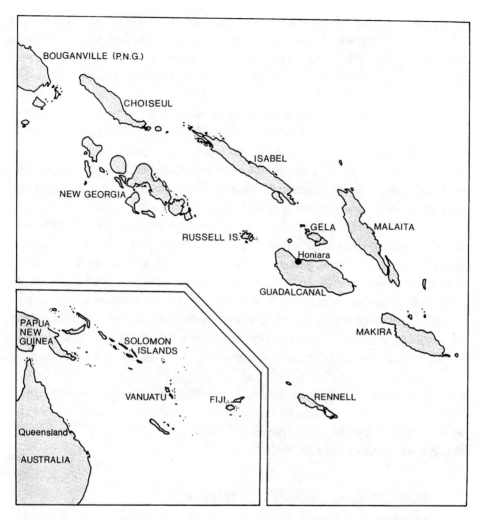

MAP 1   *Solomon Islands and the south-west Pacific.*

Studies deriving from the missions themselves, which dominate the literature on Pacific Christianity, may reflect this local experience rather better. However, the insights they gain from empathy with Melanesian Christians are often compromised by commitment to the Western religious world view which they are ultimately concerned to promote. Mission writings on Malaita, such as the histories of the SSEM by its founder Florence Young (1925) and by Alison Griffiths (1977), are often more anecdotal than analytical, with a strong theological perspective unsympathetic to Melanesian culture which often clouds historial understanding. There is also a long history of mission anthropology in

Melanesia focusing on traditional culture, especially within the Melanesian Mission, beginning with Codrington (1891) and including Iven's early work on Malaita (1927, 1930). But even when such research informs a sympathetic appreciation of local forms of Christianity, as in Tippett's wide ranging study of their development in Solomon Islands (1967), it cannot transcend a basic ideological opposition to traditional religion and a rather colonial concern for "the winning of Solomon Islanders for Christ" (Tippet 1967:43). In addition, mission research often relies upon questionable anthropological stereotypes of Melanesian culture perpetuated from Codrington's time (such as the concepts of tabu and *mana* to be discussed in Chapters 2 and 3), which inevitably distort its analysis of both traditional religion and local Christianity.

The mission perspective also tends to cloud perception of the relationship of the missions to other agencies of social change, particularly when it emphasises mystical theological explanations as in Tippett's case. In a more sociological vein, Whiteman (1983) builds upon Tippett's study to attempt a general theory of Christian conversion which emphasises the role of Melanesians as the active agents of 'culture change' responding to missionaries as advocates of Christianity. But in failing to examine how this process depended on the colonial relationship between Melanesians and Europeans in general, he risks reducing the dynamics of change to little more than an intellectual exercise in reinterpreting and blending cultural traditions. A similar neglect of the political forces which required such changes to be made detracts from Trompf's study of *Melanesian Religion* (1991), which again views the development of Christianity in terms of ideological changes and institutional histories.

LOOKING AT CHRISTIAN HISTORY

But the present study does agree with these and other anthropological commentaries on the 'colonial impact' (Jolly & Macintyre 1989:11, Lātūkefu 1978:460) that, rather than regard Pacific Islanders as passively colonised and converted, we should see them "as active participants in their own history" and as "the ultimate makers of their own religions", as Barker has argued (1991:22). This is no novelty to Kwara'ae, whose Christianity was introduced and spread mainly by the efforts of local evangelists, although they would also agree with the mission studies in emphasising the crucial role of God's spiritual power. This approach is not to underestimate the agency of colonial forces including, as the Kwara'ae case suggests, the impact of political subjugation as well as the work of the missions. Rather it requires a focus on indigenous perceptions of these forces in preference to the colonial perspective too often reflected in mission studies and histories, and this entails a close examination of the local scene.

Explaining the conversion of local communities and the development of

Christian society in these terms for a politically fragmented, and fractious, people like Kwara'ae requires the kind of detailed, intensive study of local history which has seldom been attempted in Melanesia; a region where local studies may need to be very local indeed. The diversity of experience among peoples living under tribal modes of social organisation is well illustrated by an island like Malaita, where each of a dozen local ethnic groups of different languages and cultures would once have included dozens more autonomous local communities, small even compared to other islands in the Solomons. The history of a district, and ultimately of the Melanesian region as a whole, belongs to each of these local groups who may know a great deal about their own past but very little about anyone else's. The stories Kwara'ae tell are of the lives and struggles of individuals, families and small communities, and only from these can an understanding of broader historical developments be painstakingly assembled. Although colonial records and the histories written from them are essential reference points for comparison with this oral history, they have to be interpreted from Kwara'ae perspectives informed by an understanding of Kwara'ae culture.

Kwara'ae occupy a zone across Malaita from coast to coast, but the present study concentrates mainly on Kwai district on the east side of the island. Events in this district in particular are documented in detail from the first encounters with Europeans in the 1870s to the 1980s, using recent recollections combined with contemporary written reports mainly from government archives and mission journals. What emerges is a history of resistance and compromise by a people seeking to retain their self-determination while accepting the perceived benefits of colonialism, for whom conversion to Christianity represented both the defeat of the old order of tradition and the hope of regaining control of their own lives under the new order of colonialism.

Previous research on Malaita provides some useful comparative material for this Kwara'ae history. Hogbin's account of To'abaita in North Malaita in the 1930s is an important early local study of what he called "the native side of Christianity" in Melanesia (1939:191), portraying a situation very much like that in Kwara'ae at the time. However, his perspective is that of the colonial order, endorsing the current paternalistic policy of 'indirect rule'. While describing how To'abaita had adapted Christianity to their own purposes and explaining the distintegration of the traditional political system under the new religion, he shows rather less insight into the politics or the theology of conversion, which could have been illuminated by a more detailed study of local colonial history. In Kwara'ae the kind of events which Hogbin missed can still be pieced together fifty years later in a colonial history which now has double the timespan. The situation in Kwara'ae and To'abaita fifty or sixty years ago is also illuminated by Keesing's accounts of Kwaio up to the 1980s (1967, 1989a), where the Christian population is separated spatially, ritually and politically from traditionist neighbours still resisting the subversive spread of the new religion.

Research into the development of Kwara'ae Christianity is also assisted by a large body of published work on two crucial periods in Malaitan history in particular; the 19th century labour trade which introduced the colonial period (eg. Corris 1973, Scarr 1973, Moore 1985), and the Maasina Rul movement which followed the Second World War and foreshadowed the eventual political independence of Solomon Islands (eg. Laracy 1971, 1983, Keesing 1978a). But apart from a brief account of 'pacification' (Boutilier 1979), the equally import-ant processes of political and religious colonisation between these periods have been documented only for the dramatic career of District Officer William Bell (Keesing & Corris 1980). For the period since the Second World War there are studies of the role of tradition as *kastom* ideology in the continuing Malaitan struggle for self-determination (Burt 1982, Keesing 1982c). But this has been only one theme in the development of Kwara'ae society since the war, as Malaitans have gained increasing local control of church and government and Solomon Islands became an independent state in 1978.

CHRISTIANITY AND TRADITION

From the perspective of Kwara'ae colonial history, the book concludes in Chapters 9 and 10 with an assessment of their contemporary Christianity and its ambivalent relationship to the traditional religious culture from which it devel-oped and which continues to exert a powerful influence over the future. Until recently anthropologists have not shown a great deal of interest in Pacific Christianity, regarding it perhaps as a product of colonialism rather than as authentic local culture. This probably accounts for the lack of research in Kwara'ae, long the most Christian of all the language groups of Malaita. But there is a growing recognition that, just as colonisation does not necessarily rob people of all self-determination, so they are quite capable of appropriating Western culture on their own terms and for their own purposes. If this is true of the apparently immutable material objects exchanged in trade (Thomas 1991), how much more so of religion. Anthropologists are now providing an increasing number of studies (notably contributions to Barker 1990) showing that Christ-ianity does not herald the end of cultural distinctiveness in the Pacific, and also that Western researchers should not assume they can understand Pacific Christ-ianity simply by virtue of their own Christian backgrounds.

Kwara'ae still have a distinctive local religion, but one which employs insights from both Western Christianity and their traditional religion to come to terms with a rapidly changing world. Their Christianity, and the society in which it plays such an important part, now has a Western mode of institutional organisation, linking local churches with national, regional and global organisations, which as Barker says, has "brought the world to Pacific Islanders and encouraged their entry onto the world stage" (1990b:21). A wide range of church denominations are represented in Kwara'ae and other parts of Malaita (see Ross 1978b), and the final chapters of this book focus particularly on the largest of them, the South Sea Evangelical Church (SSEC), now an autonomous Solomon Islands and particularly Malaitan church. But as Barker also points out, a superstructure of Western church institutional and ritual forms like that of the SSEC may not tell us a great deal about the infrastructure of local indigenous religious activity and experience which it serves. Although Kwara'ae Christianity is profoundly influenced by the institutions and global links of the SSEC and other churches, it is this popular religion, retaining many of the insights of traditional religion, which gives the SSEC its vitality. Through this church in particular Kwara'ae participate in a widespread movement in Melanesia to develop independent and indigenous churches and ecstatic or charismatic Christian movements (see Barr & Trompf 1983, Barr 1983). By such means they and other Melanesians are reworking their religion in the continuing development of a distinctively Melanesian Christanity.

At the local level of popular religion, continuities between Melanesian traditional religion and Christianity seem to be found wherever researchers decide to look for them. But although Christianity is probably everywhere regarded as transforming traditional culture rather than destroying it, Melanesian societies, or their researchers, vary in choosing whether to stress the continuities or the contrasts. Kwara'ae are not alone in finding analogies between the beliefs and practices of their old and new religions, or in tracing traditional precedents for their Christianity (see for instance Chowning 1990, Smith 1990, Kaplan 1990), but this has not resolved all the contradictions between them. Jolly draws an interesting comparison between Vanuatu where, as in Kwara'ae, "Christianity and colonialism are seen much more as a rupture with a heathen past" and Fiji, where they seem to be "flowing continuously from ancestral practices" (1992: 330). White's study of Isabel (1991) shows how the oppositions involved in such a 'rupture' can be resolved in the construction of new cultural identity through particular representations of traditional culture and its historical transformation by Christian conversion. These and other contributions to a growing literature on the politics of tradition in the Pacific (particularly contributions to Keesing & Tonkinson 1982, and to Jolly & Thomas 1992) demonstrate how in different societies different images of traditional culture are continuously constructed and reconstructed, usually in opposition to various aspects of colonialism, according to issues arising from particular colonial histories.

Kwara'ae is one of those Pacific societies where Christianity has played a major part in the construction of such images in the process of constituting itself, as this study will explain. To judge from Jolly's accounts of South Pentecost in Vanuatu (1982, 1989), Malaita may not be quite alone in Melanesia in actually segregating traditionist and Christian communities. But for many Kwara'ae the opposition between the new ways and the old seems to be much more important than it is for other Melanesians. Many Kwara'ae Christians would find it hard to accept the kind of reconciliation between Christianity and tradition represented by Vanuatu's attempts at cultural revival (Tonkinson 1981, Lindstom 1982: 323). They are even further removed from the easy co-existence between traditionists and Christians reported, for instance, of the Papuan Maisin (Barker 1990c), and from the nominal church affiliation which enables the Kove of New Britain to incorporate Christianity into a traditional religion modified by cargo ideology (Chowning 1990). Nor have Kwara'ae moved as far from the attitudes of their early European missionaries as the Kragur of East Sepik where, despite an iconoclastic past, only 'purists' now avoid mixing Christian and traditional religious practices (Smith 1990). Many Kwara'ae Christians still seem to take an unusually narrow view of what in their traditional culture is compatible with Christianity, which evidently reflects the fundamentalist ideology of the South Sea Evangelical Mission (SSEM). The question is why so many Kwara'ae should have joined this mission in particular, and continue to endorse its fundamentalism in their now independent church (the SSEC). The answer seems not unconnected with the traditional religion they have rejected and, as we shall see, the values and insights of that religion are actually reflected in their Christian opposition to it.

KWARA'AE: PEOPLE AND RESEARCH

Before going on to explore the 'colonial transformation' entailed in Kwara'ae 'tradition and Christianity', a few more preliminary explanations are required, about who the Kwara'ae people are and how their history and culture has been researched.

Kwara'ae are now citizens of the independent state of Solomon Islands, but for most people national identity means less than the fact that they are Malaitans. Malaitans are known in Solomon Islands for their pride in a strict ancestral tradition which they uphold with aggressive independence, and their culture as well as their numbers makes them a force to be reckoned with in national politics today. In a country of more than 286,000 people, Malaita is the most populous island with more than 80,000 people (Solomon Islands 1987). Within each major island the peoples of Solomon Islands are generally named for their localised languages and dialects, of which there are more than eighty in the country as a whole. Malaita alone has at least twelve languages and dialects representing different local culture areas. Kwara'ae, with more than 19,000 speakers, is the largest language group in the whole of Solomon Islands and the most southern of a group of six or seven closely related languages and dialects spoken in the northern districts of Malaita. The Kwaio language immediately to the south is more distantly related to Kwara'ae, but closer to the northern languages than to those still further south. (The distribution of these languages is shown on the map below).

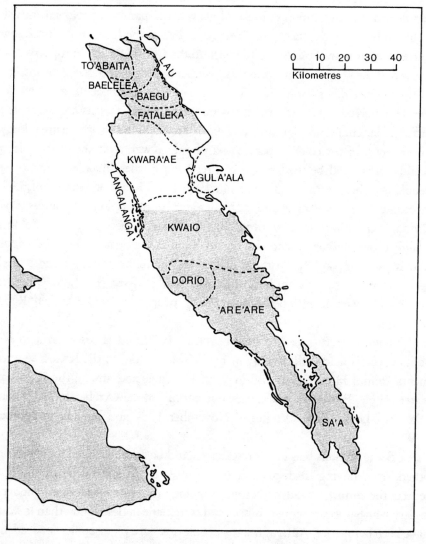

MAP 2   *Malaita, showing Kwara'ae and other language and dialect groups. The unshaded area is that covered by the map on pages 82–83.*

Like most language groups of Malaita, Kwara'ae occupy a zone from coast to coast across the island, but most live on the western side, where the Kwara'ae zone reaches from Fauābu to Bina. The people of East Kwara'ae among whom this study was researched occupy a much smaller area, bounded by the Auluta river to the north and the Kwaibaita river to the south and extending up into the mountains. Here in the central bush are the ancient places from which Kwara'ae on both sides of the island trace their origins, uniting them in a common Kwara'ae identity. Whether this identity is as old as these origins is another matter, but Kwara'ae today in both East and West regard themselves as one people sharing a common culture. However, the pattern of colonial intrusion seems to have divided East and West Kwara'ae as the focus of political power shifted from the traditionists of the bush to the Christians and Europeans of the coasts and the world beyond, and this makes it appropriate to focus the historical study on one side of the island. The people of East Kwara'ae have always been closely involved also with their coastal neighbours, a 'saltwater' people of different language and culture, and both are included in the district known during most of the colonial period and since as Kwai, after one of the offshore islands. Kwai will be used here when referring to these mainland and coastal people together. In the latest census in 1986 Kwai had a population of 3,910, including 3,183 Kwara'ae and 727 saltwater people (Solomon Islands 1987), although there are also hundreds living abroad, especially in the Solomon Islands capital Honiara, who also regard Kwai as their true home. The population is growing rapidly, so these figures are far higher than for most of the period covered by this study and double that of sixty years ago, when the whole of Kwara'ae numbered only 9,657 people in 1931 (Annual Report 1931).

The research presented here began in 1979 and is based on a total of about a year's fieldwork, mainly in East Kwara'ae and in the Kwara'ae settlements around Honiara but also in West Kwara'ae and among the Kwai saltwater people. Fieldwork was carried out during July to October 1979, October 1983 to March 1984, October to November 1987 and January to February 1991.

Some obvious bias in the research should be acknowledged if only to save others from having to discover it for themselves. In general terms the book reflects the common tendency of anthropology to create an idealised model of society which appears more coherent and systematic in description than it would have been in practice. Although some people do take a philosophical or academic interest in their own culture, most are concerned first of all that it works as a system they can live by, and for this they do not require the systemic overview which anthropologists attempt. Besides, cultural knowledge is unequally shared among the members of a society and its distribution reflects both the "political economy of knowledge" and the personal circumstances of individuals, as Keesing points out (1982a:3–5). Anthropological research must expect to meet ambiguities, inconsistencies and contradictions in cultural systems and in individual minds, reflecting priorities and perspectives differing with positions in society and the situations in which the ideas are expressed, including relationships with the researcher. In attempting to make a coherent description of a society, a search for coherence in a people's own views of their culture always risks 'finding' something which may not be there. This is particularly the case when attempting to reconstruct an earlier way of life which now exists in people's memories rather than in ongoing relationships.

As this implies, a great deal of information on Kwara'ae culture was obtained through interviews and discussions rather than from observing the activities described. This research was conducted mainly in Pijin, the common language of Solomon Islands which most Kwara'ae including many small children rely upon to speak with people of other languages, although they seldom use it between themselves. But recorded texts and documents in Kwara'ae language were also consulted for historical and cultural information, as well as to clarify concepts and usages not adequately conveyed by Pijin.

It also has to be admitted that the people who contributed information are not a representative sample of Kwara'ae society. Like the researcher, nearly all of them are men, for the conventional reasons which reflect the male domination of both Kwara'ae and British society as well as the difficulties for a male anthropologist in researching among women. Equal attention to women's perspectives would provide a rather different view of Kwara'ae history and culture, especially since the relationship between men and women played a central part in traditional religion and politics. Many of the men who have contributed are regarded as particularly knowledgeable on matters of tradition and some of them have been working for many years to systematise and codify tradition for their own purposes. This may have led to a rather over-coherent and possibly legalistic view of Kwara'ae tradition which others may acknowledge as authoritative without actually sharing themselves. Furthermore, even on matters of traditional religion, almost all informants are Christian. For those who do still follow the traditional religion today it represents a resistance to colonialism which usually extends to anthropology, so that the traditional social order, insofar as it still exists, is difficult for an outsider to observe directly and has to be researched largely from verbal accounts. Many Christians can speak from their own past experience of the traditional religion and even some who have been Christian from birth may be excellent informants on the subject, but all alike may be influenced by Christian perspectives of which they and the researcher may be unaware. Lastly, there is the fact that research into Kwara'ae culture, traditionist and Christian, was mostly conducted in East Kwara'ae. If, as Kwara'ae themselves insist, there is no significant cultural difference between East and West, generalisations about Kwara'ae culture can apply to both sides of the island, but even they acknowledge some variations, which are not accounted for here.

A NOTE ON LANGUAGE

For the sake of clarity and since the language of this book is English, an attempt has been made to find a suitable English gloss for all Kwara'ae concepts which occur regularly in the text, and Kwara'ae words are given wherever possible for reference only. Where there might be a risk of confusing such a gloss with a more general English meaning, the Kwara'ae meaning is explained when it first appears and the gloss may later be written in inverted commas. This applies also to other words which are used with a particular limited meaning, including kin relationships when they are used to describe persons who may not be related in the limited sense usually implied in English usage. Hence 'father' includes father's brothers, 'child' includes a child of a man's brother or of a woman's sister, and so on. Kwara'ae may make the distinction by adding *fafo* (eg. father's brother is *ma'a fafo*) but more often this is unspoken.

As for the Kwara'ae language itself, the spelling used here follows conventions established by Gegeo for his work on a Kwara'ae dictionary (not yet available), as set out by Simons (1977). In this system a glottal stop is shown by an apostrophe (') and lengthened vowels are shown by a macron (¯), which distinguishes them from double vowels which result from compound or reduplicated words (eg. *ā* from *aa*). For example, in the word *fa'aābua* ('make it tabu') the first and second *a* are separated by a glottal stop and the second and third *a* form a double vowel as a result of adding the prefix *fa'a* to the word *ābu*, which begins with a lengthened vowel (*ā*). (However, this use of the macron is under debate; see Keesing/Burt 1990).

It should also be noted that the language is not usually pronounced as it is written, since Kwara'ae speakers habitually shorten words in a regular pattern by which a normal vowel (ie. not lengthened or a dipthong) at the end of a syllable switches places with the preceding consonant. In addition, *f* is interchangeable with *h*. Hence, for example, the word *fera* ('men's house') is usually pronounced *hear*, *fataābu* ('priest') becomes *hatāub*, and the name of the language itself is shortened to *Kwar'ae*. This mode of speech can be quite difficult to follow even for speakers of related North Malaitan languages, and the practice is said to have been started by young people not many generations ago to confuse their elders.

But in recognition of the original mode of speech, Kwara'ae still generally use the underlying original form of words for clarity, for singing or for writing, if not always strictly according to the spelling conventions used here.

FIGURE 2   *A shell pendant, with worn frigate bird engravings, made by an ancestor of the Mānadari clan and inherited by their priests.*

PLATE 2   *Aisah Osifera of 'Aimomoko (and grandson) with the magical staff which is said to have guided Bilitigao, the first man to settle in Malaita, on his migration towards Siale in the central Kwara'ae bush (Photo by Ben Burt, 1984)*

CHAPTER TWO

Land and People,
Relationships and Rules

K̲wara'ae culture is founded upon what they now think of as a 'heathen' tradition, and the first step towards explaining how and why they have created the Christian society of the present is an understanding of this 'tradition of the past' (*falafala ma'i na'o*). In accounting for it themselves, Kwara'ae refer back to the time when their ancestors first settled and claimed the land where they live today and established the rules governing a social order which was passed down by the living, generation after generation, and upheld by the ghosts of the dead. This Kwara'ae perspective will help to explain a system of local community organisation based on ancestral ties to the the land, in which relationships of authority were created by exchanges of goods and persons. An overview of Kwara'ae society in these terms will lay the ground for an analysis of the power structure, at once political and spiritual, with which they confronted the European intruders and which they have tried to adapt to the new realities of the colonial order.

As Christians, Kwara'ae have banished the ghosts of their ancestors but retained much of what they have inherited from them, and for this reason an account of their traditional culture can draw not only on the recollections of those who have seen it change under the authority of God and government, but also on the way people live it today. In some respects what Kwara'ae regard as the 'tradition of the past' is still very much alive, not only among those few who still follow the traditional religion, but also in Christian society. Hence it is important to remember that much of the account which follows does not describe any precise historical period, while bearing in mind that the political system which shaped the 'tradition of the past' was thrown into disorder by the suppression of feuding and the imposition of colonial government from the 1920s onwards.

THE FIRST ANCESTORS

Since Kwara'ae have very definite ideas about the origins of their society and culture, we can begin with their own story of how Malaita was first discovered and settled when their ancestors arrived from overseas. The story has great symbolic importance in Kwara'ae as an explanation of tradition (see Burt 1982), so it is worth recounting at some length. The following account (heavily abridged) comes from Andrew Gwa'italafa of Ubasi, who has tried to summarise some of the different versions he has heard:

> I really come from a man called Bilitigao. At the beginning of our history he came and settled at a place called Ruafatu on Guadalcanal. Then he came on a raft and landed at a place called Su'ufau in West Kwara'ae. So after this man had settled there for a while he took off into the bush and lived in several different places. Then when he looked down towards the sea he saw it was nearby and he was afraid in case people might come after him and kill him. So he moved further up into the bush and when he reached the central bush he looked and there was no sea around him and he looked up at the hills concealing him and he started to clear a settlement there. He named that place Siale. Siale is right in the centre of Malaita. When Bilitigao settled there he had some children and a big group who had come with him. I know that I come from the line of one of his children, Umarara. He had others who I don't know, but the clans which derive from Siale know which child came from which man and if he was really born of Bilitigao and his wife Miriaba. So they settled there for a long time and my grandfather told me that a big northwest gale broke everything down and then they started to move away. Then another story I heard is that Bilitigao killed his grandson and it was that which made the settlement at Siale split up. Yet another story I heard from my grandfather is that someone defiled the stream at Siale and that was why Bilitigao was angry and they began to split up.
>
> I also heard from my grandfather that this man had about three children. He used to sacrifice and his children didn't know what kind of sacrifice it was; maybe to the bones of his ancestor or to the true God whom we worship today, we're not sure. While they were there they used to have one language and if I'm correct, maybe it was none other than Kwara'ae. Well, maybe when their father died and they started to spread out, one went to West Kwara'ae, one to North Malaita, one to 'Are'are, one to Kwaio, they began to forget their original language. My ancestor Umarara went with his wife up to 'Aimomoko, quite close to Siale, and begot the people of 'Aimomoko. They began to wonder what they would pray to. "We saw our father sacrifice pigs and we saw him pray; maybe we should just go back and sacrifice to him". So then, the traditional religion began, Umarara took his father, he cooked sacrifices to him and so starting from that we worshipped any man of ours who died who was powerful among us.

This story is well known throughout Kwara'ae, although people often disagree about its details and there are clans who claim different origins. But for most Kwara'ae today the story proclaims their identity as a people, the descendants of a common ancestor inheriting the land he first claimed and following the way of life he established as their 'tradition' (*falafala*). This common identity is largely a development of the colonial period and, as we shall see, the ancient origin story has become a symbolic statement of concerns which have developed in Kwara'ae and other parts of Malaita during this century (see Burt 1982, 1983). So, conscious of the religious alternatives introduced by Christianity, people use this story, as Gwa'italafa does, to explain the development of their traditional religion, under which they sought support and protection from their dead ancestors through prayer and sacrifice. Concerned for the changes in norms and values under colonialism, some also tell how the first ancestor instituted the 'tradition of law' (*falafala ana taki*) which governed relationships among people and their ancestors. But first of all the story explains the relationship of the Kwara'ae people to their ancestors and to their land, the foundation of their whole way of life.

MAKING A LIVING

Throughout the changes Kwara'ae have experienced during the last hundred years or more, their relationship to the land is one thing which has provided stability and continuity. As a farming people, land continues to be the basis of Kwara'ae material existence, even as they have ventured into new ways of making a living from the capitalist economy. But more than this, the Kwara'ae relationship to their land is the foundation of their relationships with one another, of their social identity and of their traditional culture. As Adriel Rofate'e explains, "The land is our father and our mother".

Like other peoples of the Malaita mainland, Kwara'ae are a 'bush people' (*to'a ni tolo*), who produce most of their own food in gardens cleared from the forest and meet many of their other needs from the forest itself. As in other tropical forest environments, the land is fertile enough to bear only one or two crops before it has to be left for the forest to regrow and replenish the soil. In the past most of Kwara'ae was covered with dense secondary forest recovering from or waiting for cultivation, broken only by clearings for temporary gardens and settlements. If gardens are short lived, many settlements are hardly more permanent, for people often take the opportunity to move elsewhere when their houses rot and have to be rebuilt after perhaps four or five years.

Everyone works the land, but men concentrate on clearing the forest and women do most of the tending and harvesting. Between them they cut the trees, clear the ground and burn off the vegetation, then mark out plots with poles and plant with digging sticks. Their main crops are root vegetables planted from cuttings, in the past taro and yams, with greens and bananas. New crops introduced in recent generations include sweet potatoes, now a staple food, tapioca and various vegetables and fruits. Food trees, particularly coconuts and *ngali* nuts (canarium almonds), are also planted around gardens and settlements but as time passes they may be gathered in the forest. Gardens support both the people and their pigs and women prepare most of the food for both, with scraps going to the chickens and dogs. But meat is an occasional luxury and people live mainly on vegetables. Where the forest is not being farmed it supplies vital resources such as poles, leaf thatch and rattan for buildings, wood, bark and leaf for tools, weapons and utensils, bamboo for containers and plants for medicines and magic. There are also wild foods, including greens, roots, fruit and mangrove seeds. In the past there was an important source of protein in wild creatures such as frogs and insects, birds, bats, cuscus and lizards from the forest, and fish, prawns and shellfish from the streams and estuaries.

As farmers of the forested hills, the Kwara'ae bush people have alway had dealings with the coastal 'saltwater people' (to'a ni asi) who speak different languages and make a living largely by fishing and trade. In the east there are saltwater communities of the Gula'ala language on the offshore islands of Kwai, Ngongosila and Leili and sometimes on the nearby shores. In the west there is a much larger saltwater population on the islands and shores of the Langalanga lagoon. Saltwater and bush people exchange fish and sea products for vegetables and forest products at regular markets on the shore, and the saltwater people also supply shell and shell artefacts which in the past were essential to the technology and economy of both areas. The most important of these at present are strings of 'shell money' beads, used as a standard of value and exchange. In the last hundred years or so both bush and saltwater people have gradually become involved in the world economy, selling their labour and, in more recent times, cash crops and raw materials to obtain imported industrial goods. During that time many of these goods have become necessities, particularly steel tools, which long ago replaced stone adzes, and Western clothing. More recently, imported foods such as rice, flour and biscuits, tinned meat and fish have become an important part of the diet. But most food still comes from the people's own lands and seas, and so does an increasing part of the cash income which brings the benefits of Western style development. For the bush people, the land they inherit from their ancestors is the foundation not only of their traditional way of life but also of their hopes for economic development and growing prosperity in the future. Kwara'ae rights in their land are now of greater concern than ever before and this is one of the themes underlying the story of their first ancestors.

CLAIMING LAND

Like Gwa' italafa, people usually approach this story as the history of their own line of descent, which is also the history of their land. These histories are passed down as genealogies which imply that the first ancestors arrived from twenty to thirty generations ago, counting as Kwara'ae do from their youngest children. Although the genealogies remembered by different clans often disagree on how they are related to one another, it is none the less generally acknowledged that all Kwara'ae, if not all Malaitans, are descended from one man whose sons and grandsons dispersed from their home in the central bush to the lands which now belong to the Kwara'ae people. Their claims to this land today are traced back to the time when these ancient ancestors discovered areas of virgin forest which they settled by clearing land for villages and gardens. The lands they claimed extended beyond their own settlements to include virgin forest which was subsequently cleared and claimed by their descendants or by others to whom they gave permission. Some men moved out of the Kwara'ae area altogether into other districts, and others moved in from neighbouring language areas to claim land in the same way. Some also moved out to the offshore islands, where their descendants became saltwater people, and although there is no garden land on these islands, village space and fishing grounds on the reefs were discovered and claimed in the same way.

The settlement and burial sites of these men (for it is the men with whom Kwara'ae are most concerned), were dedicated to them as 'tabu places' (*kula ābu*) by their descendants, and the names of these places were given to the surrounding areas and the communities that lived there. In some of these places they built shrines (*feraābu*) where the ghosts remained in continuing association with the land. These were monuments of earthwork and stone walls with burial places, houses for skulls and other relics, and hearths for sacrificial meals (as confirmed in archaeological surveys by Rukia, 1988). In a country where people often move their settlements and the forest soon covers all signs of human habitation, 'tabu places' are the permanent signs of rights in land established by notable ancestors

PLATE 3   *Clearing forest for a garden. Ash from the pile of vegetation smouldering around a tree stump will be spread to fertilise the ground. (Photo by Ben Burt, 1983)*

and inherited by their descendants to the present day. Genealogies give the impression that all the main districts of Kwara'ae were settled and claimed within about the first four or five generations. But later generations of settlers continued to disperse until the whole landscape was occupied, dotted with tabu places and portioned up into areas by boundaries following natural features such as ridges, streams and certain trees. Kwara'ae often refer to such an area simply as a 'land' (*ano*), but it is also a 'home' or habitation, *fanoa*, a word which covers any inhabited space from a village to the whole of Kwara'ae or Malaita.

The land a man claimed is inherited by his descendants who, being of 'one blood' (*ta'i gwa'i 'abu*), may in theory all make use of the land to 'establish things' (*fuirūa*) such as gardens, settlements and useful trees, and gather wild foods and raw materials. Kwara'ae are similar to other North Malaita peoples in inheriting rights and relationships through what is in effect a cognatic descent system, as studies by Hogbin (1939:26–27), Keesing (1970), Ross (1973 Ch. 8) and others show. But they also emphasise seniority of descent in the male line, as reflected in a book on land rights by the Kwara'ae author Maenu'u (1981). On the basis that men are senior to women and that heirs descended through men have priority over those descended through women, those in charge as 'senior' (*fa'i na'ona'o*) or 'leaders' (*etaeta*) for the land should be men descended in the male line, headed by the line of firstborn sons. In English, Kwara'ae usually call them the 'owners' (Pijin *ona*), but this misrepresents their role as managers of land held in common by those of 'one blood'.

The priority of the male line is deeply rooted in Kwara'ae social organisation. Local communities are usually based on groups of fathers, brothers and sons who normally take wives from other family groups to live and raise children with them, while they give their sisters and daughters in marriage to other families elsewhere. In return for their wives, men and their families give shell money as bridewealth, which also ensures that the children belong first and foremost with their 'fathers' and 'brothers' (including their real fathers' brothers and their sons) as part of a family group descended from the same ancestors in the male line. Kwara'ae call such a group *fū'ingwae*, which conveys the idea of people joined by common origin to their ancestors and their land. Although they usually translate this word as 'tribe' (Pijin *traeb*, eg. Maenu'u 1981:39), 'clan' seems a more appropriate English alternative to the technical description 'descent group' (as used eg. by Keesing 1970:755).

CLAN ORGANISATION

A Kwara'ae 'clan' can mean a group of hundreds of people tracing descent from a common ancestor ten or twenty generations ago. But those who live together in the same neighbourhood may amount to no more than the families of two or three 'fathers', 'brothers' and 'sons', as a local sub-clan descended from the same father or grandfather. Kwara'ae distinguish these more or less inclusive groups only as 'big' or 'small' clans. In the past extended families of the same local clan would have formed separate small settlements (*fanoa*), hardly large enough to be called villages and probably seldom larger than two or three households each. In 1984 the remaining traditionists in East Kwara'ae included about thirty adults in seven settlements, similar to the pattern described by Keesing (1982a:18) and Ross (1973:99) for the larger traditionist populations of Kwaio and Baegu. Many Christian villages are much the same size today but some are much larger, and the saltwater people have always lived in larger settlements on the offshore islands of Kwai and Ngongosila. But both bush and saltwater communities, Christian and traditionist alike, are usually based on groups of men descended from the same ancestors in the male line.

Men of a clan, particularly those who live together, normally have a strong sense of solidarity and identity, not only with the living but also with the dead ancestors whom they replace generation after generation as heirs to the land. They often describe the adventures of these ancestors as if they were their own; 'I came from such a place, I settled here, they buried me there' and so on. As a clan they are usually named for places inherited from these ancestors, where, in the past, the men sought spiritual support and protection by sharing sacrificial meals of pigs and vegetables with their ghosts at shrines marking the land they claimed. The greatest of these sacrifices were periodic festivals (*maoma*) in which large numbers of pigs were sacrificed to all the ancestors of the clan while feeding and entertaining relatives and neighbours from far and wide. Although people could sacrifice to any of their ancestors, they generally expected most from those they were descended from in the male line. The priest (*fataābu*) whom the ancestors chose to mediate between them and the living was ideally the firstborn man of the senior line, so that the list of principal ancestors through which the clan traced its descent would often be conceived as a list of successive priests who were also the leaders for the land. Priests were the main experts on the genealogies, mainly lists of fathers and sons, which they had to recite during sacrifices.

This relationship between clans, their ancestors and their land can be illustrated by an example which will help to explain Kwara'ae traditional political and ritual organisation. The following brief history is based on research by Adriel Rofate'e into the origins of his own clan of Gwauna'ongi.

About seventeen generations ago 'Aitakalo, a grandson of the first ancestor of Kwara'ae, left their home at Siale and went to settle at a place above the headwaters of the Fiu river, which flows down to the west coast. When he died his sons buried him nearby at Gwauna'ongi, which is the name given to the area of land around, and to his descendants. 'Aitakalo's firstborn son lived and was buried at their new home but six younger sons moved to districts far away, where they are remembered as the founding ancestors of new local clans. In the next generation the firstborn son went to live nearby at Faureba, where the firstborn son of each generation lived and was buried from then on. This meant that the Faureba people were senior among the Gwauna'ongi clan, with a claim to be leaders for all the land 'Aitakalo first discovered, and their priest was responsible for the shrines for him and his senior descendants. Meanwhile, from the third to the fifth generation after 'Aitakalo, several more junior brothers and their sons moved out into the area around Faureba, occupying or perhaps extending the area he first claimed, and another four left for places far away. The descendants of these men were buried in their new homes at new shrines, where their descendants offered sacrifices to them and were buried and sacrificed to in their turn.

These events of long ago are remembered as explanations of the recent past. In about 1920, when the Gwauna'ongi people became Christians, they included four or five more or less distinct sub-clans, named, like Faureba, for places with Gwauna'ongi as a whole, and amounting altogether to probably little more than twenty families. Ten other independent clans further away were also regarded as in some sense belonging to Gwauna'ongi. Each of these clans would sacrifice to their own ancestors at local shrines and hold sacrificial festivals for them every few years. But all of them, even those living far away, would also maintain links with the land and people they had 'emerged from' (*saka ana*) by sending back occasional sacrifices to the ancient common ancestors cared for by the priests of Faureba.

CLANS AND COMMUNITIES

Gwauna'ongi is only one of several places in the central bush from which groups of local clans in East and West Kwara'ae trace their common origins, remembered through genealogies and reaffirmed through sacrifices sent back 'up' to their ancient ancestors. But these major clans did not in themselves form local communities. Kwara'ae histories show how, as clans continued to disperse generation after generation, they settled not only on vacant land but also on land already claimed by other clans, to produce a pattern of clan-land relationships of bewildering complexity. Since men should not marry their clan 'sisters' or other close relatives, the local branches of different major clans were linked into local communities of relatives and neighbours by networks of marriage and kinship, renewed from one generation to the next.

Although women usually left home to marry they did not found new clans as a result, so clan histories usually tell of men moving away, often to escape from trouble at home. They were most likely to go somewhere where they already had a claim to the land, with their distant clan 'brothers' or in-laws or the clans of their mothers and earlier female ancestors, where they could expect support from

PLATE 4   *An East Kwara'ae village. Na'oasi is a large Christian village*
                where several branches of the Gwauna'ongi clan now live far from
                their ancestral lands in the central bush. This is the village
                referred to in Chapter 9, viewed from a garden on the site of the
                village of the same name mentioned on page 141.
                (Photo by Ben Burt, 1984)

both the living and the dead ancestors to whom they offered sacrifices. Although they would not be leaders for the land, they could live in security as welcome additions to the community. In pre-colonial times, when the land a family could use was limited by the amount of work they could do and the amount of food they could eat or feed to their pigs and give away, there was more to be gained by welcoming newcomers to share the land than by keeping them out. Newcomers added to the political influence and military strength of a local community and the leaders for the land might be willing to let even strangers, that is non-relatives, live and garden as guests. However, guests or their children usually seem to have married into the host clan, so giving their descendants the security of inherited claims to the land.

It was also possible for newcomers to obtain land in ways which are now regarded as legitimate reasons for giving leadership of land from one clan to another. Sometimes this amounted to little more than approval for a new-comer to settle and claim an area of empty land, but within a settled area a 'piece of land' (afu ano) might also be given to return some kind of debt or obligation. Most commonly a piece of land was given to a woman of the clan to be used by her and her husband and inherited by her children. This can be seen as a way of encouraging the husband to join and increase the strength of her clan, and it meant that his descendants would gain leadership for a piece of land where their claim would otherwise be based only on descent from the woman. Many other cases are also remembered of pieces of land being given instead of the shell money, pigs and food usually presented to fulfil certain important obligations. These obligations included compensation for death or injury (to'ato'a), reward for killing an enemy (fo'oa) or for providing defence from enemies (tarasina). It is also possible to 'buy' (folia) land in exchange for a quantity of shell money. Although this was not a commerical transaction, many people regard it as a new development influenced by the cash economy and there is no doubt that it has become more common as a way of dealing with increasing local migration since the colonial period. In all these cases the givers of the land retain a claim to it, especially if the recipients cease to use it, and on this basis the leaders of major clans may claim some kind of symbolic leadership over wide areas of land which were given to others by their ancestors, or settled with their consent.

As a result of migrations and gifts of land, most people belong to clans which genealogists identify as '(place) A to (place) B' or 'A to B to C', named not only for their land of origin but also for other places settled by their ancestors in later generations. But the local community identified as the 'group of people' (nwa'i to'a) of an area is likely to include not only those claiming to be leaders for the land but also people of other clans, living where they are 'born of women' or are leaders for small pieces of land, while their own true land is elsewhere. As a comparison with the clan organisation of Gwauna'ongi in the central bush, the complexity of actual communities can be illustrated by an area on the east coast known as Latea.

In the 1980s there were about 230 people living in Latea, including two clans originally deriving from Gwauna'ongi who arrived about ten or fifteen generations ago and each claim leadership for the land as the original or earliest surviving settlers. Two other clans which trace separate origins from the ancient shrine of Siale each came to Latea as descendants of women of one of these leading clans and later married women from the other leading clan as well. One derives from a group of brothers who moved in from the neighbouring coastal land of Fairū during the mid 19th century, and the other from a man escaping a feud in the central bush in the early 20th century. In the past the Latea clans formed four interrelated ritual congregations with their own priests, sending pigs up to ancient shrines in the central bush as well as sacrificing to their own and each other's local clan ancestors. But they are also related to the other clans of the district and thus have rights in neighbouring lands too. Hence, for instance the clan which arrived from Fairū now claims leadership of that land through descent from women of a leading clan which has no male heirs. The two leading clans of Latea have long been a minority of the Latea people, now three or four out of more than thirty households.

But these observations depend on where the boundaries of the land are drawn, for some of what was once accepted as Latea is disputed by claims that it belongs to several other lands. Although these disputes are recent, stimulated by competition for cash earnings, they derive from much older ambiguities in the relationships between these clans and their land. This itself reflects the essential flexibility of a traditional system of inheritance, which served not so much to allocate land according to boundaries, but rather to regulate a continuous process of adjustment between the needs of local groups and the availability of land. Besides their own clan lands everyone inherits a choice of lands where they can make their living, but inheritance may be invoked to legitimate their choices rather than to determine where they should live.

As Maenu'u points out, in their traditional relationship with the land, Kwara'ae regarded "man as a scarce resource" (1981:9,18), while the land disputes which divide Kwara'ae communities today reflect the values of the intruding capitalist economy, in which the scarce resource becomes goods and the land itself. In the past Kwara'ae valued land and its products not as commodities but as the basis of relationships, and with this understanding of the relationship between the people and their land, we can go on to look in more detail at the traditional social order governing their relationships with one another.

A 'TRADITION OF RULES'

Kwara'ae see this social order as a way of life governed by rules, *taki*, or 'law' as they prefer to translate it. Looking behind these rules to the relationships which gave them their force, we find a system of authority based on material support and violence, developing into formal exchanges of wealth and persons. As it was originally conceived and lived, their dead ancestors played a full and active part in this social order as ghosts, but to explain the role of the ghosts it is simplest to begin by analysing relationships among the living.

Like their claim to the land, the Kwara'ae 'tradition of rules' (*falafala ana taki*) is said to have been established by their first ancestor when he settled Malaita, and passed down by his descendants ever since. The concept of 'law' (*taki*) and the principles underlying it give important insights into how Kwara'ae perceive social roles and relationships among both the living and the dead, and how they responded to Christianity. In recent generations, as Kwara'ae cultural identity has become a political issue in relation to the culture of colonialism, some have attempted to codify this 'tradition of rules' in writing (as described in Chapters 7 and 8, eg. Ganifiri n.d., Rofate'e 1979, Tisa 1979). Although compiled to reaffirm tradition within a Christian society, these documents provide an appropriate introduction to the way Kwara'ae conceive traditional norms and values. One theme which emerges is the principle of *ābu*, which is a variant of the Oceanic word *tabu* or *tapu*, in Kwara'ae as in most of the languages and dialects of Malaita. The role of this concept in Kwara'ae culture needs to be examined in some detail, although its meaning will only be realised through an account of Kwara'ae society as a whole.[1]

The fact that 'tabu' has been adopted into English language and anthropological jargon does not necessarily help to explain its meaning in Kwara'ae, but it does provide an appropriate English translation for *ābu*, and 'tabu' will be used here with this Kwara'ae meaning. In Malaita the concept has been explained to many Europeans over the years and pondered by a number of anthropologists, but most writers have taken tabu to mean that something is forbidden, usually with spiritual sanctions, and for this reason they habitually translate it as 'sacred' (eg. Ivens 1930:237, Hogbin 1939:103, 116, Ross 1973:236,311). The significance of tabu in Malaitan traditional religion has been examined in more depth by Maranda & Maranda (1970) & by Keesing (1982a), who show how it expresses an opposition between the spiritual powers of men and the reproductive powers of women, but still without providing an adequate explanation of the concept itself.

In Kwara'ae too, tabu governed relationships between ghosts and men by opposing them to relationships with women, as we shall see. But men, women and ghosts belonged to a single social system and tabu has this religious significance in Kwara'ae because it is a governing principle of all relationships in their society. Ultimately tabu appears to be a way of dealing with power, of controlling not just the spiritual and reproductive powers of men and women but also the political power to which these powers contributed. Kwara'ae writings show tabu to be, in European terms, as much a legal as a religious concept, far wider in scope than anthropological studies have recognised. Its significance in Kwara'ae religion, in relationships between people and spiritual beings, can best be introduced by examining the relationships between people with which Kwara'ae writings on 'law' are primarily concerned.

Adriel Rofate'e of Gwauna'ongi, an acknowledged expert on the subject, lists some of the applications of tabu (Pijin *tambu*) as follows in his *Custom Book of Kwara'ae Taki, Halahala* (1979):

(1) First law in Siale [ie. in the origin of Kwara'ae] is man is not an animal, man is tambu.
(2) Malaita has many different ways of making things as holy.
(3) To make devil [ie. *akalo* or ghost] as your God, holy God.
(4) To make all properties in that house must [be] holy.
(5) Woman is tambu for anyone to walk over her legs or swear at her.
(6) Young girl is also tambu for anyone to swear at her or touch her body.
(7) Village is holy and all the properties in the village are also holy.
(8) Food that people can eat is also holy.
(9) A house that people put their food in is also holy.

By "holy", Rofate'e means *ābu*. As a second-generation Christian writing in English, he uses the translation accepted in Malaita and endorsed by early missionary linguists such as Norman Deck (1933–4). When *ābu* refers to things associated with spiritual beings, whether God or ghosts, 'holy' or 'sacred' is a not inappropriate translation, but Kwara'ae have a rather different understanding of what is meant by these Christian concepts to that of Europeans, including missionaries and anthropologists.[2]

TABU IN CONTEXT

Rofate'e's list summarises the main categories under which Kwara'ae have attempted to classify the rules of tabu, but these can be no more than examples, for it is not too much to say that, in Kwara'ae terms, everything which has a positive social value may be treated as 'holy' and accordingly subject to the prohibitions of 'law'. In many respects this interpretation of 'holy' has very little to do with whether something is associated with spiritual beings and sacred in European terms. But neither is tabu simply a way of saying that something has a social value. The underlying premise which Rofate'e and others only hint at in their writings, is that a thing is 'holy' only in particular contexts and circumstances, for tabu is a characterisic not of things in themselves but of the relationships between them. Hence point (5), "Woman is tambu *for anyone* [ie. any man] to walk over her legs". This is another reason why, as Keesing points out for Kwaio, "a gloss such as 'sacred' would be misleading", but in Kwara'ae it is not really sufficient to say that tabu can sometimes be glossed as "off limits" (Keesing 1982a:31,65). If a gloss were required, a better one might be 'sacrosanct', in the common usage which may or may not take literally the meaning of 'religious' in the Oxford dictionary definition "secured by religious sanction against outrage, inviolable". For whether or not things tabu are 'sacred', it is in this sense that they are prohibited.

To be more precise, in Kwara'ae something is tabu in a context where it has to be protected from specific prohibited acts which might *fa'alia* or 'spoil it' (to use the Kwara'ae translation). Things may be 'spoiled' by real or symbolic acts, by word as well as by deed. Where there is no question of one thing 'spoiling' another, the relationship between them is *mola*, meaning free of restrictions, neutral or, as Kwara'ae variously translate it, 'clear', 'open' or 'allowed', in that the actions concerned are permitted. *Mola* is the opposite or absence of tabu and hence is relative or contextual in exactly the same way, and even more difficult to translate.

The point to be stressed is that tabu actually marks the positive values which are to be protected even when it describes the forbidden acts by which they are 'spoiled', which are not tabu but, in one way or another, *ta'a*, 'bad'. This distinction is crucial to the role of tabu in social relationships, but it is not always immediately clear in Kwara'ae speech. Tabu does have negative implications, as children learn when their parents tell them "*ābu!*", to mean "don't" or "stop doing it", but this instruction refers to something they might spoil or damage. People may also say of a forbidden act, "it is tabu" (*nia ābu*), but they also explain that it is actually the thing which may be spoiled which is tabu, not the act of spoiling it. Of course, since protection of positive values entails prohibition of negative ones the two meanings are complementary, for the prohibitions specify the contexts in which things are tabu.[3]

'MAKE MAN TABU'

The meaning and significance of tabu is revealed in the circumstances under which certain things are marked for protection rather than being *mola* or 'open', and Kwara'ae writings on 'law' illustrate this by identifying things which it is particularly important not to 'spoil'. To treat something as tabu is *fa'aābua*, 'make it tabu', and the most general and fundamental principle, from which all the rules of tabu can be seen to follow, is *'fa'aābua ngwae'*, 'treat persons as tabu' (lit. 'make-tabu man'). In other words, you should show respect for persons, which is what Rofate'e means by "First law in Siale is man is not an animal, man is tambu". All breaches of the rules of tabu are offences against persons, either directly or by infringing their rights in other persons or property, and ultimately it is persons who are 'spoiled' as a result.

The rules of tabu set the basic standards of social behaviour. Hence a person's body is tabu in that physical contact or comment on it is regulated by rules of respect and propriety, which should safeguard the person from physical and verbal abuse, attack or injury. Besides persons, the property reserved for their disposal is tabu to others in the sense of private, insofar as stealing or damaging it 'spoils' and offends the owner. Their food is tabu to be stolen or spoiled and their houses are tabu to those who do not reside there to protect the household from theft, damage and misbehaviour. People should not enter a house without permission or when the owner is away, and when inside they should sit in the proper places and behave respectfully to their hosts according to various rules of etiquette. Neither should things be spoiled by 'swearing' (*taofi, kwala*), which breaks the rules by proclaiming indecent or offensive acts which would spoil a person if they were to be carried out.

Kwara'ae Christians often represent their traditional 'laws' as 'Ten Commandments' (*akwala taki*) which they compare to those of the Bible, but the morality is also distinctively Malaitan and characteristic of a tribal society of politically autonomous local groups. *Fa'aābua ngwae* enjoins respect for other people's rights, but these rights, and the corresponding obligations on the part of others, vary according to the social status of both parties and the relationship between them. It is this which defines whether an act is offensive and whether this actually constrains the offender, which is one sense in which tabu is a relative value, dependent on context. Insofar as rights and relationships are predicted by social structure, so are the rules of tabu. In this respect tabu is a way of defining social roles, in particular relationships of authority and power.

A basic distinction made by the rules of tabu is betwen the social roles of men and women, which ensure the seniority and dominance of men. On one level these roles are defined in terms of sexual propriety. It is permitted (*mola*) for a husband and wife to have sexual relations with one another, but all other sexual activity is forbidden as 'adultery/fornication' (*'usu'a*) and in this respect men and women are tabu to one another. This is one sense in which their bodies and homes are tabu; people should not be touched in certain ways by the opposite sex or be subjected to sexual allusion or innuendo, which includes symbolic acts such as a man sitting on a woman's bed or stepping over her legs. For the same reason men and women are tabu to one another when there is a possibility of illicit sexual acts, which usually means if they are alone together. But it is the woman rather than the man who is usually said to be tabu to illicit sex, for it is she and her menfolk who are most spoiled as a result. For a single girl it spoils her chances of

PLATE 5   *The 'kitchen' area of a dwelling house, open to visitors, with a*
private sleeping room at the back. The woman is cracking ngali
nuts with a stone hammer and anvil, near the fire with its rack of
firewood above (Photo by Ben Burt, 1984)

marrying well and bringing her family a good bridewealth. For a married woman it infringes her husband's right to sexual fidelity and stable family life for which he gave such bridewealth. In earlier times lovers risked being killed by the woman's menfolk. So it is that the rules of tabu assert the rights in their women which are basic to the superior status of men in Kwara'ae society.

In the same way tabu defines the rights and obligations which structure relationships of power and authority between men. Treating persons as tabu (*fa'aābua ngwae*) entails recognising their proper status and authority, including obedience to the wishes of parents and senior relatives and the teachings of the elders. Besides age, an important qualification for authority is seniority of birth, which helps firstborn sons and their descendants claim leading roles within their families and clans. But in Kwara'ae relationships of power and authority between men are in many respects negotiable, rather than being prescribed by biological distinctions as they are between men and women. In the past men made their submission to authority more or less by consent and their leaders lacked the power to impose obedience as the colonial government was able to do. To understand power in Kwara'ae traditional society, the relationships which gave the rules of tabu their force, it is necessary first to consider how men were induced to acknowledge and support authority.

The political system which the Kwara'ae 'tradition of rules' was designed to uphold and legitimate was based upon the triple foundation of spiritual power, wealth and violence. This is symbolised by what Kwara'ae and other Malaitans sometimes describe as three types of leaders: priests, 'important men' and warriors. It might be more appropriate to think in terms of three areas of political activity in which all men participated and a few found opportunities for leadership, but the relationship between these activities will become clearer as we build up a picture of the political system as a whole. First, continuing to exclude the role of the ghosts for the time being, we can consider the parts played by wealth and then by violence, which together formed the currency of exchange in relationships of power among the living.

EXCHANGING GOODS

In Kwara'ae people participate as full and valued members of their communities by giving and receiving goods and services. Compared to class-based societies, they did so in the past on more or less equal terms, since every family had direct access to the means of subsistence production, with little inducement for some to raise the material living standards of others by releasing them from the necessity to work for themselves. The exchange value of goods in the traditional economy lay less in their acquisition and accumulation than in the relationships created by the exchanges.

The idiom which dominates most economic exchanges in Kwara'ae community life is 'mutual help' (*kwai'afi'anga*). The crucial values of kindness and caring for others are shown particularly through giving and sharing food and hence are often referred to as 'eating well' (*fangale'a*), as distinct from meanness or 'eating badly' (*fangata'a*). An example of this is the woman carrying home food from the garden, who would always have some taro set aside to give to any relatives she met on the path, since it would be shameful to have a load of food and not to share it. As one man explains "If we go to market and get fish, we don't feel good if we are eating fish and our brother's children don't have any". Sharing of food goes on regularly between households in a village, and if they kill a pig for a feast, portions will be sent to neighbouring villages too. Women play the leading role here, and a family's reputation depends on the wife's generosity with food, hospitality and assistance with work, to her husband's clan and other relatives and visitors. Gifts also pass regularly between relatives living apart, nowadays with travellers to the Solomon Islands capital Honiara carrying bags of sweet potatoes and returning with manufactured goods and bags of rice from those earning money abroad to their families at home. Nowadays hospitality makes it possible for people to live at the expense of relatives for weeks at a time in urban areas where the hosts have a regular cash income and their guests do not.

In considering the ways goods are exchanged it is useful to bear in mind the distinction made by Sahlins between the expectations which people have of this kind of support, freely given by close relatives on the basis of 'generalised reciprocity' which does not specify the expected return, and the tendency to 'balanced reciprocity' in more distant relationships, when goods and services are given on the explicit understanding that they will be exchanged for something else at an appropriate time (Sahlins 1972:193–204). Kwara'ae do not help one another simply from disinterested 'generosity' (*alafe'anga*) so much as from 'reciprocity' (*kwaima'anga*), as a moral obligation with the expectation of some eventual return ('generalised reciprocity' in Sahlins' terms). However, they translate both concepts rather more expressively as 'love', which makes the point that kindness and self-interest may be hard to distinguish. Of course such 'love' may actually be the rhetoric which disguises self interest to ensure that people fulfill one another's expectation (see Weiner 1976:221–223). But, from another perspective, it also indicates that Kwara'ae expect amicable relationships to be based on material giving, helping and sharing rather than on the fruitless declarations of goodwill which often pass for 'love' among Europeans. This Kwara'ae understanding of 'love' is endorsed by the Christian teachings which most of them follow today (see I John 3:18) but it derives from traditional values which in the past formed the very basis of the people's economic and political security.

Where people have less reason to 'love' one another, more 'balanced' exchanges may be made. At markets, bush and saltwater peoples originally 'bartered' (*usia*) vegetables in direct exchange for fish, even under conditions of tension and occasional hostility between their communities. Other direct exchanges enabled people to convert food or labour into goods of more lasting value, including the kinds of wealth required for more important exchanges, and in particular shell money. Food, freely given to relatives and neighbours, could also be used to feed pigs as a medium-term store of wealth, and both pigs and food in large quantities, such as gardens of crops or hundreds of coconuts, fish or bamboos of ngali nuts for feasts, could be commissioned and 'bought' (*folia*) in standard values of shell money. In the past it was also quite usual to 'buy' many goods and services in direct exchange for shell money, almost as Kwara'ae nowadays 'buy' goods in a store, 'buy' cash for food in the market, or 'buy' labour for wages.

Shell money (*mani*, a Kwara'ae word, despite its similarity to the English) requires a brief explanation. Kwara'ae seldom make shell money beads themselves but obtain them by exchange with neighbouring peoples who do, and their value is a measure both of the labour required to produce them and of the scarcity of the red shell used for the most valuable beads. Larger types of beads, used throughout the northern districts of Malaita, are mostly made by the saltwater peoples of Langalanga and to a lesser extent of Lau, who exchange them with the bush people for food, or nowadays cash. In East Kwara'ae these are more or less interchangeable with the smaller types of beads made and used in Kwaio and 'Are'are to the south. Shell beads are usually strung in standard denominations, valued according to the length and number of strings and the kind and quality of the beads. Porpoise teeth, also strung and supplied by saltwater people, have recognised exchange values as well. In the past porpoise teeth and short lengths of certain types of beads were exchanged for goods and services of small value, but cash now serves this purpose instead. The most common shell money denomination used in Kwara'ae today is the high value northern unit, *tafuli'ae*; 'ten-legs' of fathom length strings of red with white and black beads. The equivalent denomination for the southern beads is *bani'au*; six strings of usually about six armlengths of small coneshell beads enhanced with red beads. Kwara'ae refer to either denomination as a 'red money', but they also use both the northern and southern types of shell money in various smaller denominations. All denominations have long had more or less standard cash values, which for *tafuli'ae* or *bani'au* in the 1980s might be $100 or $120, depending on the quality. In the past beads and teeth were also made up into costume ornaments such as bandoliers, belts, headbands and armbands, which also had recognised exchange values (see Burt 1990).

While a family may produce all the vegetable food they need in a season and build up a herd of pigs after a few years, gaining shell money requires a long-term investment, not only in hard work but also in 'mutual help'. When, as so often, shell money is needed in large quantities or at short notice, people can seldom afford to 'buy' all they need for other goods and they depend instead on the relatives and neighbours who have received their help in the past and may expect it in the future. But when they have to ask someone outside their immediate family for a 'red money' or a pig, this is likely to be 'given on account' (*kwate fāfia*) with a definite obligation to return it when the giver needs such help himself. So it is that informal gifts open the way for formal loans which enable people to meet the larger and even more formal exchange obligations necessary for security and good standing in their community. They achieve this by accumulating not wealth but credit, which enables people to put their hands on wealth when they need it. A family may have one or two 'red money' wrapped in barkcloth and hidden in the dwelling house, but there is less point in hoarding shell money than in using it to help those who will one day give help in return or, equally important, recognise that they are under an obligation to do so.

MARRIAGE AND EXCHANGING WOMEN

These obligations played an essential part in the authority structure of Kwara'ae communities, and this is nowhere clearer than in marriage exchanges. In Kwara'ae society, marriage is the foundation of moral relationships and the concern of all the relatives who have an interest in the new relationships which the union will create in present and future generations. A traditional marriage is an exchange between families, in which the husband's side 'buy the girl' (*folia kini*) by exchanging a bridewealth gift of shell money for her sexual and economic services and for the children she will bear for his clan. The bridewealth may have to be returned if she gives cause for divorce because she is barren, unfaithful or otherwise incompatible with her husband. In the past bridewealth would be the largest gift most men ever had to be responsible for, but its presentation is only a brief focus for a continuing series of exchanges through which wealth is accumulated and redistributed from generation to generation, to the advantage of senior men.

Some Christian churches now limit bridewealth to the comparatively small sum of five 'red money' (*tafuli'ae* or *bani'au*) or ten for elopement or pregnancy. Otherwise, depending on the prestige and influence of the families, it might include up to fifty or even one hundred separate contributions of shell money of various denominations, and nowadays cash. Marriage was, and usually still is, one of the times when a young man depends most on the support of his relatives. His close 'fathers' and 'brothers' usually provide most of the bridewealth, but much of it must be loaned (*kwate fāfia*), or returned from loan, by more distant relatives.

The principal bridewealth gift is the 'hanging up' of the shell money (*daura'ia*), which the wife's family come to collect in a formal presentation ceremony. When the quantity of bridewealth is negotiable the husband's relatives make an extravagant show of presenting as much as they can while resisting demands for more. There may be a heated argument before the wife's father accepts the shell money and takes it away to distribute among her relatives. In a traditional marriage the wife's side are then obliged to give in return cooked pigs of equivalent value as a marriage feast (*tolonga*) for the husband's side,

PLATE 6   *A bridewealth distribution. Ru'ulanga is handing out the shell money he has just collected for his daughter's marriage. This bridewealth was negotiated in the traditional way between traditionist and Anglican Christian families, and amounted to ten large 'red money' (tafuli'ae and bani'au) ten smaller shell monies, two strings of porpoise teeth, and $114 cash.*
(Photo by Ben Burt, 1984)

at which they also distribute meat and perform songs and epic chants (*kana*) in exchange for further gifts of shell money. The competitiveness of these exchanges helps to resolve the inherent tension between the two families, who are necessarily not closely related and have competing interests in the woman. The gifts show respect and dispel hostility, as they become in-laws who will continue to exchange gifts over the years and eventually, as blood relatives of the children of the marriage, find themselves on the same side in bridewealth exchanges in future generations.

Bridewealth acts as the material symbol of the relationships linking families and clans together into communities, not only as in-laws but also as contributors to each other's bridewealth. The contributions and redistributions remain 'alive' (*mauri*) until they are returned, preferably as bridewealth for other marriages in the future (to become 'dead', *mae*). Such debts may be inherited by the next generation, and since it is older, economically independent married men who have most shell money to lend, it is likely to be returned as contributions to the marriages of their sons or other close relatives rather than themselves. Men, and women to a lesser extent, are involved in a whole series of these loans and exchanges throughout their adult lives, and a man is committed more deeply when he marries. As time goes on his efforts to return his own bridewealth and contribute to others will be helped by shell money received for his daughters and the daughters of women whom he or his family may have given bridewealth for long before.

The scale of these marriage exchanges is illustrated by a written account kept by Samuel Sosoke of Sasadili, a senior man who received 38 contributions to his own marriage in the 1950s, including 13 large 'red money', 23 smaller shell money units and 2 pigs. By the 1980s all these gifts were 'dead', but his list of contributions of shell money, pigs and cash to the marriages of others had reached 70, of which about 30 were still 'alive'. Such a man may be judged successful in having given more help than he has received. In the past the network of obligations so formed would have maintained the authority of senior men through a constant imbalance between generations and between those who were more or less successful in managing their resources. The seniors help their junior relatives with bridewealth in recognition of the support they have received in work or occasional gifts. Among other things, this particular kind of 'mutual help' has for more than a century enabled senior men to claim a share of the Western goods and services which their younger relatives obtain usually from migrant work overseas. These may be given in various forms from cash and useful manufactured goods to free taxi rides around town.

The political implications of this process are reflected in the church-imposed bridewealth limit of five 'red money'. When Michael Kwa'ioloa married in the 1970s, his eldest brother helped him to raise this amount merely by selling a pig and using what they had recently received from the marriages of female relatives. Kwa'ioloa was relieved not to be burdened by loans, but at the same time some of his 'fathers' were annoyed at not being asked to contribute. As we shall see in later chapters, the obligations created by higher bridewealth could be regarded as detracting from the authority of the church, but five 'red money' is still enough to maintain the network of exchanges. Because he helps with cash another older brother who has three daughters, Kwa'ioloa may expect to receive shell money from their bridewealth which will later help towards the marriages of his own sons.

EXCHANGING WEALTH FOR PRESTIGE

Controlling the flow of goods and services which bound people together in such networks of mutual obligation was one means to leadership in Kwara'ae society. Someone who was particularly successful in involving himself in the affairs of his relatives might be recognised as the 'important man' (*ngwae 'inoto'a, ngwae lalifu*) of his clan and their local community. Such leaders were a Kwara'ae variant of the stereotyped Melanesian 'big man', with the important qualification, emphasised by Ross for Baegu, that they held their authority as much by co-operating as by competing with others and by supporting rather than manipulating their followers (Ross 1978a:11,18). The Kwara'ae ideal is that men gain influence in their communities by helping others meet their own needs and obligations.

One of the most important ways this influence was shown was in organising feasts, held to celebrate a variety of important events. The size of a feast obviously reflected the importance of the occasion, but this itself was a measure of the prosperity and influence of the organisers. Providing food for a feast required a great deal of planning and hard work, some of which the feastgivers may have had to pay others for with shell money. Gardens had to be made, pigs fed, coconuts and ngali nuts gathered, fish might be commissioned from the saltwater people and shelters built to house the guests, before the food was eventually prepared and cooked. A successful feast raised the name of the men who organised it and contributed the largest portions, giving them authority as the leaders responsible for achievements which enhance the standing of their local clan and community. The greatest feasts, as the largest co-operative enterprises of Kwara'ae society, spread an organiser's name abroad, until maybe he was recognised far beyond his own community as a 'famous man' (*ngwae talo'a*). These included sacrificial festivals and marriage feasts, but feasts were also held to celebrate occasions such as the opening of a new men's house, or today a new church or road. Until at least the 1960s great *siufa* feasts of vegetable puddings were still held in East Kwara'ae, more or less for the sake of feasting, using thousands of taros, coconuts and bamboos of ngali nuts, pounded in bowls too large for even the strongest man to shake up. The competition involved is shown most clearly in a type of exchange feasting (*daudau*) remembered from the distant past when groups would take turns to 'grab' large presentations of food from one another.

Both feasting and bridewealth have declined in scale in recent generations, and with them the influence of traditional 'important men', so the scope of their authority is now difficult to establish. Fifty years ago Hogbin described 'important men' in To'abaita as the leaders of small districts of no more than "200 followers" (1939:62). However, Keesing's rendering of the autobiography of the Kwaio leader and feastgiver 'Elota implies a rather more fluid sphere of influence, and a more likely model for Kwara'ae (Keesing 1978b).

MAKING AND BREAKING THE 'LAW'

Having considered the basis of authority in mutual support and dependence, we can look in more detail at the way it was manifest in the 'law'. In accepting the assistance and leadership of senior relatives and 'important men', Kwara'ae acknowledge their authority not only to deal in 'law', but also to make it by proclaiming 'laws' of their own. From this perspective the concept of 'law' serves to legitimate and regulate the political authority from which it derives its power.

PLATE 7   *Preparing for a feast, organised by Jemuel Misialo of Sulaifau at Afio in West Kwara'ae in 1983. Outside a large shelter built for the stone ovens and guests, pigs are being singed and butchered for baking. (Photo by Ben Burt, 1983)*

In a society where land and goods are valued for the relationships they can create rather than as commodities, a particularly important symbol of a man's status and authority is his ability to 'set rules' (*alua taki*) prohibiting such things to those who might otherwise feel free to share the use of them. He may, for instance, bar the path to a piece of land to stop others from gardening, stand branches upright on a reef to ban fishing, tie leaves around a tree to keep people from taking the fruit, or put up a written notice to safeguard his coconut plantation. The purpose is to 'forbid' (*lu'ia*) or 'prevent' (*fonea*) the thing concerned, with the implication that it is tabu to those from whom he wishes to protect it. Such 'rules' assert the rights of ordinary people, as 'leaders' for their land, trees and other resources, but beyond this they may also establish the prerogatives and privileges of those who claim to be political leaders. Stories of the past tell how men would reserve particular things by 'dedicating' them as tabu (*alafu 'ania*) and threatening to kill anyone who interfered with them. A famous warrior claims a tree from which he wants to make a shield, a senior man reserves a pool for washing his hands after eating people, and others again declare their daughters tabu for men to court or marry. Some even made their own persons tabu in unusual ways, like Bilitigao, the first ancestor of Kwara'ae, who is famous for having red hair which he kept wrapped and tabu for anyone to see. Such prohibitions appear to be as much assertions of status and authority as marks of concern for the thing prohibited. It is as if authority, based as it is on help and support given to other people, was being tested and demonstrated by resisting their normal expectations and demands, including the obligation to give and share.

But beyond this, the prohibitions of tabu actually create authority and power in the sense that people give others authority over them by submitting themselves to the observance of the rules. In conferring such authority on others collectively, they give it a coercive power which can be used against them individually. They can free themselves from authority only at the risk of losing protection and support and facing retribution which forces them into obedience or destroys them. As we shall see, these processes, revealed in the way tabu governs relationships among the living, also explain their relationships with ghosts and the crucial role of tabu in the operation of spiritual power. But the power which lies behind tabu is actually manifest less in the making of rules than in the consequences of breaking them. This challenges people to reassert themselves through whatever power they can exert, and it is the way Kwara'ae deal with breaches of tabu that reveals its role in mediating power on both a political and spiritual level.

Breaches of tabu are often referred to as *maladalafa*, meaning to act in a random and undisciplined or unruly (*dalafa*) way, like someone who is irresponsible or immature and hence insignificant and unworthy to be treated as tabu by others. The expression, used to describe all kinds of offensive behaviour, reflects the importance Kwara'ae attach to formal rules and conventions. Although difficult to convey in English, it can be glossed as to disregard, disrespect or dishonour. In effect *maladalafa* means behaving as if something were *mola* or permitted when it should actually be tabu, and it 'spoils' a person by treating him as if he were worthless. Instead of 'making him tabu' (*fa'aābua*), as he has the right to expect, behaving as if he were *mola* is actually to 'make him mola' (*fa'amolā*). A person's rights and status, which have meaning only in their acknowledgement as tabu by others, are denied and degraded by the act which 'disregards him' (*maladalafā*), resulting in an actual threat to personal worth and influence which is felt quite intensely as shame or loss of face. The response, especially for a man, is an attempt to reassert himself by retaliating, with anger and possibly with violence.

Resolution of the resulting conflict requires that the offended person be 'made good' (*fa'ale'ā*, in full, *fa'aogale'ā*, 'make him feel better'). This is done by reaffirming his status as tabu by *fa'aābua*, 'making him tabu (again)', meaning to restore respect in order to 'satisfy his mind' (*fa'atolia liana*). A person who feels he has been wronged is likely to demand a payment of shell money or other goods as *fa'aābu'a* (noun), and if both parties wish to preserve the peace they and their relatives will negotiate a suitable payment to end the matter. The purpose is to restore goodwill and remove the bitterness which might lead to further trouble, for Kwara'ae remember serious grievances for generations. For this reason the noun *fa'aābu'a* is best translated as 'restitution'.[4]

The amount of restitution is negotiated according to the seriousness of the offence, which itself is likely to depend upon the strength of the parties and the relationship between them. Within a local community, where people have to live with one another from day to day, they are more likely to settle their disagreements quickly and peacefully, mediated if necessary by the senior men whose authority they both recognise, with either or both of them giving restitution to the other to make peace. But, as Akin points out from research in Kwaio, although close relatives need to settle matters quickly and virtual strangers have no reason not to, distant relatives and acquaintances may well have political interests and reputations to advance and earlier grievances to pursue at one another's expense (Akin 1984). Under these circumstances disputes become the concern of groups of relatives, who feel a collective responsibility for one another, and receive collective blame. Today the possibility of conflict between such groups is ultimately contained by the authority of government courts and police, but people still often prefer to deal with serious offences themselves, negotiating much as their ancestors did generations ago, under the ultimate threat of violence.

This is illustrated by a case in the 1980s of an unmarried girl who was made pregnant by her sister's husband. Her menfolk tried to kill the man but he fled and hid in the bush, until a 'brother' arranged to pay them restitution for the fornication. This he negotiated while the man hid in his house and his enemies vented their anger by shouting threats and insults from outside. The restitution agreed, equivalent to a bridewealth of five 'red money', included one 'red money' bought for cash and two returned from bridewealth loans, which the giver should have saved for his own son's bridewealth if it had not been for the threat to his 'brother'. The real danger that such offences may lead to killing, even as in this case, in a well-ordered Christian Kwara'ae suburb of Honiara, emphasises the continuing importance of the shell money exchange network in Kwara'ae society. It is likely to be the younger men who most need shell money for restitution because of irresponsible behaviour and, as with bridewealth, it is their senior relatives who have to help them out. In the same way that shell money joins families in amicable relationships at marriage, so it restores relationships through restitution, and for this reason it is regarded as a symbol of peace.

EXCHANGING DEATH

But the threat of violence and death is more than just a matter of retaliation to 'pay back' or 'return' (*du'ua*) the offence, for taking someone else's life is the most forceful way anyone can assert the right to be 'made tabu' and reaffirm his status and self-esteem, to make himself 'feel good'. So it was that Bilitigao, the first ancestor, killed his own small grandson for seeing his tabu red hair, setting a precedent for many such dreadful deeds in later generations, which ceased only when the British took control of Kwara'ae in the 1920s. Until then, men who felt that the offence or their own status demanded a death might refuse to be satisfied by anything less, and if the offender or his relatives could not be killed the victim could be someone totally unconnected with the offence instead. Nakisi of Mānadari, one of the last men living to have done this himself, recalled how he went down to the coast and killed two saltwater women because his aunt had sworn at him. Rather than breaking tabu, from his point of view this was exactly the opposite; *fa'aābu'a*, a way of restoring himself as tabu.

From another perspective, disregarding the rules of tabu (*maladalafa*) could lead to the rules being, in effect, suspended altogether as people killed one another in a feud (*mae*, literally 'death'). Feuds are also regarded as exchanges, for a person is killed to 'return the death' (*du'ua maelana*) of a previous victim. But exchanges of death, rather than representing a breakdown in the exchanges of goods which linked people in mutual support, contributed to these exchanges when shell money was given as compensation (*to'ato'a*) to 'return a death', or as a 'blood-gift' (*toli'abu*) for wounding. Even today, when killers are imprisoned for murder under Solomon Islands law, compensation may be paid to prevent further killing. When Jim Kwa'i killed a man from Kwaio in a brawl in 1990, again in a suburb of Honiara, the massive compensation of 57 'red money' and $2,000 negotiated by community leaders and Members of Parliament reflected the danger of a feud between Kwara'ae and Kwaio. By comparison, the death in childbirth of the unfortunate girl made pregnant by her brother-in-law, for which he was also held responsible, resulted in the culprit's father' paying only five 'red money' death compensation (as distinct from the restitution for the fornication).

In the past it was also a common practice for those seeking a death to promise a 'reward' (*fo'oa*) to anyone who would kill for them. These rewards could also be of considerable value, requiring the same kind of effort to assemble as a major feast and including up to twenty pigs in cases early this century, with quantities of shell money and food. All this awaited the man who could kill the offender or one of his relatives. The reward was presented at a public ceremony, displayed with the shell money hanging from a platform and the trussed pigs and piles of vegetables below. The killer would dance up to the platform, gesturing with a bow and arrows and making short gasping cries, and the giver of the reward would drape the shell money over him. The killer and his men would then carry off the pigs and food to be eaten in a feast at which the shell money was distributed among their relatives.

Until the colonial government finally managed to stop killing, or at least to arrest those who still insisted on doing it, lives were constantly at risk from men seeking restitution or rewards. All men had to be prepared to fight on occasion, and whenever they left home they carried weapons such as clubs, spears, bows and arrows, guns, axes or knives, ready to defend themselves and their women and children or to take part in the brawls which could occur at large social gatherings. The old stories tell of raids which wiped out whole villages, but most killings within living memory seem to have been of one or two victims killed by stealth. Those who took the lead in feuds as particularly successful fighters and killers earned the reputation of 'warrior' (*ramo*). These were the men who probably collected most of the rewards offered in other people's feuds, which they distributed among their relatives to take their own part in exchanges of wealth. Warriors are remembered as dangerous and often impetuous men, but some of them were also regarded as guardians of morality who threatened and killed to uphold the 'law' and gain restitution for breaches of tabu. These warriors are now often compared to policemen, although the British refused to acknowledge this when they suppressed them with the aid of their own colonial police.

The chronic feuding of the past effectively backed up authority based on wealth. Fear of attack encouraged people to keep on good terms with their close relatives, particularly their local clan. Those who offended against such relatives could find themselves virtually defenceless, without either the help they needed to fight and demand restitution for themselves or the loans of shell money they needed to give restitution to others. Those who caused too much trouble within their own communities or brought them into dangerous conflicts with others might be cast out to fend for themselves, or even given up to be killed by some other group. This was the ultimate sanction for the political authority conferred by wealth.

In this society exchanges of goods and exchanges of death represented conflicting values which can be seen as the creative and destructive aspects of the Kwara'ae male personality, much as Keesing describes the roles of feast-givers and warriors in Kwaio (1985:247–8). But at the same time it is clear that wealth and violence complemented one another in maintaining the traditional political system. Wealth created and violence enforced the authority of the 'law' and of the senior men and 'important men' who were largely responsible for restoring tabu by negotiating and providing restitution for others. But Kwara'ae elders insist that in the past the real leaders of their communities were neither the men of wealth nor of violence, but the priests who mediated the spiritual power of their ancestral ghosts. Kwara'ae conferred this power on the dead through 'law' and tabu in the same terms that they created the political authority of the living. Having looked at political relationships among the living, we can go on to consider the spiritual dimension of power essential to the Kwara'ae understanding of their traditional social order.

PLATE 8   *Inside an old-style men's house. Aisah Osifera built his house at*
                 Fi'ika'o as a demonstration of Kwara'ae traditional culture,
                 decorated in the style of a shrine house and tabu to women. To the
                 left a raised door leads to the tabu inner room where he keeps relics
                 like the first ancestor's staff. (Photo by Ben Burt, 1979)

CHAPTER THREE

People and Ghosts, Religion and Politics

The way Kwara'ae conceive of their political relationships goes a long way to explain their relationships with the ghosts of their ancestors. It is no doubt a peculiarly Western approach to explain the spiritual in terms of the human, and people like Kwara'ae with a religious world-view are more inclined to seek spiritual explanations for human behaviour. But wherever the explanation begins, as far as Kwara'ae are concerned humans and ghosts were members of a single society, and the human and spiritual dimensions of their world cannot be understood except in relation to one another.

We will consider next how the kinds of relationships which conferred authority among the living also gave ghosts power both for and over their living dependants. We cannot assume that concepts derived from European religion will be adequate to explain these relationships and in particular the distinction of sacred from profane, which writers have often used to explain the concept of tabu, seems quite inappropriate. By recognising tabu as a principle of relationships between people, we can see how Kwara'ae conferred authority and power on ghosts through the observance of 'law', as they did with their human leaders. This enabled ghosts to give spiritual backing to a social hierarchy which was structured by a conceptual opposition between the spiritual values of men and the reproductive values of women. Tabu is also a key to the ritual procedures by which the power of ghosts was controlled and directed, through exchanges which also involved the ghosts in relationships of exchange among the living. In brief, relationships with ghosts were based on the same principles which created power and authority among their living descendants. This comparison may seem to reduce Kwara'ae religion to an analogue of human relationships, but more to the point it demonstrates the essential spirituality of their traditional cutlure.

SPIRITS

For Kwara'ae, the idea that humans and other beings may take spiritual as well as physical forms gives reason or purpose to events and circumstances which cannot be accounted for simply by human actions. This said, the relationship between the physical and spiritual aspects of a person is not always clearly comprehended and may be a matter of some debate. It seems generally agreed that there are at least three basic components to a living person; the 'body'

51

(*nonina*), the 'breath' (*mangona*) which animates the body and leaves it at death, and the 'spirit', which is how Kwara'ae Christians usually translate *anona* or *anoanona*. This 'spirit' is associated with the 'shade' (*nununa*), a shadow, reflection or image of a person, sometimes compared with a picture or photograph. The precise distinction between 'spirit' and 'shade' may be a matter of opinion, but in general 'shade' would probably be regarded as a non-material image of a person. 'Spirit' or 'shade' may act independently of the body, as when someone sees a person who is not actually there, or they may be drawn away from the body, causing sickness and death.

When people die they continue to have a spiritual existence, again in several forms. It is said that when traditionists die they go to the small island of Anogwa'u ('Empty-land', or Ramos Island) between Malaita and Isabel. Stories tell how visitors to Anogwa'u have heard them speaking and seen smoke from their gardens when there is actually nothing there, or have seen canoes complete with outboard motors which mysteriously disappear. But such matters seem to be of rather academic interest, since the living have few dealings with these distant beings. As one traditionist priest remarked, it is Christians who know most about where the dead go. Far more important are *akalo*, the beings which govern the everyday lives of the traditionists and not infrequently interfere in the lives of Christians too. At its most general, *akalo* may mean any being who can affect people's lives in unseen or mysterious ways as well as inanimate objects through which they may act. Some *akalo* are living creatures, such as certain sharks which protected saltwater people at sea and killed their enemies. Some bush clans had similar support from snakes, crocodiles, eagles and other creatures, and objects and substances with magical powers were also regarded as *akalo*. Then there are 'wild *akalo*' (*akalo kwasi*) of undetermined origin which haunt the bush, including a fearsome being like a man cut in half down the middle (*dodore*) and mischievous creatures like small hairy people. But most of the *akalo* which people had dealings with derived from particular dead persons, and it was these more than any others who dominated human affairs under the traditional religion. For this reason it seems appropriate, if not always completely accurate, to translate *akalo* as 'ghost', following a convention originally established by Codrington (1891:123), and *anoanona* as 'spirit' (in inverted commas).

How 'dead' ghosts actually derive from 'living' spirits again appears to be a matter of rather academic speculation. For example, the son of a senior traditionist priest explained that the 'spirit' both goes to Anogwa'u and becomes a ghost, only to agree after discussion with a knowledgeable second-generation Christian that it must be the 'breath' which goes to Anogwa'u because only 'breath' could speak as the dead there are said to do. Some say that wild ghosts (*akalo kwasi*) also come from the 'spirits' of dead persons, or that they may be ancestral ghosts abandoned by their Christian descendants. People may elaborate such theories to reconcile traditional concepts with the Christian concern for an afterlife, but in general the nature of ghosts is of less interest than how they behaved towards the living, and this could be a matter of life and death.

At one level the cultural reality of this behaviour is confirmed in the personal experiences which many Kwara'ae have of remarkable events or 'miracles' (*fa'anada*) which reveal spiritual intervention. Ghosts, usually identified as wild ghosts, may be encountered in the forest in a variety of forms. One which haunts the streams around the Bulia river in East Kwara'ae once caused a girl to fall down unconscious by appearing as a woman in traditional costume, and stunned a man by flying into his chest in the form of a small bird. Such experiences can be dangerous, even frightening people to death, and they are likely to occur at dusk or at night, when ghosts are most active, especially in places associated with traditional religious activities.

But personal encounters were also a means for ghosts to develop constructive relationhips with people. Even as Christians, people often dream of dead relatives who may offer them special powers or warnings of unforseen events, giving instructions and making demands in return for the benefits of their support and protection. Sometimes such messages came from living creatures behaving in unusual ways, and snakes in particular were regarded as ghosts or as their messengers when they came into someone's house. Some people also had revelations in which they 'saw' ghosts while they were awake or asleep, as distinct from merely dreaming of them. A person might become a medium for a ghost who would speak to other people through his mouth, causing him to tremble violently and giving a 'vision' (*mato*). A ghost might also possess or inspire (*ta'elia*) a man to give him remarkable strength in need. Those who have had this experience describe a glowing sensation or a feeling of lightness, strength and fearlessness. Such states could be induced through praying (*fo'o*) and symbolic acts involving mental efforts of concentration and intense emotion.

More often though, spiritual intervention is deduced as an explanation for events which are assumed to have significance for ghosts because they have such importance for the people who deal with them. These events are the answers to people's prayers or curses, the rewards for fulfilling their obligations to ghosts or the punishment for failing in them. Sickness in particular was often taken to be a sign that a ghost had something to communicate, and a priest would be asked to deal with it. If the ghost concerned had not already been identified by deduction or revelation, the priest would divine by taking a cordyline leaf and pulling on it as he recited genealogies, until the leaf broke at the name of the ancestor who was causing the sickness and hence making a demand.

Kwara'ae religion was concerned above all with maintaining good relationships with such ghosts, whose actions they saw in all the important events affecting their lives. From them they sought cures for sickness, delivery from danger and misfortune and assistance in enterprises from making new gardens to organising feasts or feuds. The ghosts who took most interest in the living were their dead relatives, especially senior men, who continued to watch over their living children and grandchildren (including those of their brothers and sisters) in death as they had in life. In particular, people expected support and protection from their ancestors in the male line, as members of the clan which they relied on most of all for human support and leadership of land. As generations passed, some of these ghosts continued to be remembered as important distant ancestors of major clans, no doubt reflecting their status in life and the numbers and success of their descendants.

'POWER' AND 'TRUTH'

But before going on to look at these relationships it is important to clarify how Kwara'ae understand the action of ghosts and the property which is so conveniently described in English as 'power'. The abilities of ghosts can be referred to in general terms as *ngasingasi'anga* (a noun form of *ngasi*, meaning 'hard' or 'strong' in the sense of firm and solid), which describes physical strength or force but can also mean political power and authority.[1] Under the traditional religion, the strength or power represented by the abilities and achievements of the living depended upon that of the dead. It was the 'strength' of ghosts which ensured people's health and prosperity, the growth of their gardens and pigs, kept the peace and ensured victory when the peace was broken, guided people's plans and endeavours and made some of them wealthy and successful. Ultimately the ghosts held power of life and death over their people.

But Kwara'ae seem less concerned with this power as a thing in itself than as a feature of their relationships with ghosts, perhaps as an analogue of social control over persons rather than of mechanical control over things. This helps to explain why they refer to the action of ghosts less in terms of their having 'power' (*ngasingasi'anga*) than of their being *mamana*. *Mamana* is the Kwara'ae variant of the Oceanic term *mana*, but the Kwara'ae use of this word throws serious doubt on the way many writers, mission scholars and anthropologists, Solomon Islanders and Europeans, uncritically follow Codrington (1891:192) in treating *mana* as a concept of spiritual power (eg. Tippet 1967, Whiteman 1983, Fugui 1989:78, White 1991:38). As Keesing has argued, this translation seems to derive from a Western tendency to "metaphorically substantivize power" which has contributed to a history of linguistic confusion (1984:150). Kwara'ae translate *mamana* as 'true', which is quite appropriate since it entails not only reality and veracity but also 'true' in the archaic English sense of effective and faithful. For Kwara'ae traditionists, ghosts are 'true' in that they can and will actually do what is expected of them.

This is not to say that Kwara'ae may not also "metaphorically substantivize power" (as *ngasingasi'anga*). Some describe experiencing the power of ghosts or of God as like electricity flowing into them (echoing Handy's familiar metaphor; see Keesing 1984:150). How their ancestors would have described the experience is another matter, but it is clear that Kwara'ae can and do use a concept of 'power' to describe the efficacy of both human and spiritual agencies. *Mamana* should perhaps be regarded as an idiom for describing the action of this power which represents it less in terms of the goals and objectives which it serves (as emphasised by Keesing 1984) than of the relationships through which it is brought into effect. Kwara'ae may say that something is *mamana* because it 'works' (and actually use this translation, as Keesing does), but when someone in need asks a ghost "be true to me" (*'oe mamana fuaku*) this is a request not simply to act effectively but also to be faithful and diligent, fulfilling obligations and roles. What is more such expectations are mutual, and in order that a ghost be 'true' to you it is also necessary to be 'true' to the ghost, to believe in him (*mamana fuana*), to have faith and be faithful to him, and to trust in him (*fīto'ona*). As Michael Kwa'ioloa explains this mental and emotional commitment, "If I believe in him, he is true for me" (*nau ku fa'amamanā* [lit. 'I make him true'], *nia mamana fuaku*). This relativistic approach is a recurring theme in Kwara'ae religion and underlies the processes by which they themselves conferred power on ghosts.

Being 'true' to ghost also requires diligence in obeying their instructions and accepting their demands. 'Truth' in this sense can be seen as fulfilment of the ideal that humans and ghosts help and support one another according to the basic moral values shown in dealings between relatives and neighbours, which Kwara'ae translate as 'love' (*kwaima'anga, alafe'anga*). People and ghosts are said to 'love' one another as parents and children or grandparents and grandchildren do, implying relationships of respect and authority based on mutual support and protection. In the Christian language which Kwara'ae use today, 'truth' and 'love' lay at the heart of their relationships with ghosts, obliging the living to obey a set of rules imposed by the ghosts and to exchange gifts and services with them. More specifically, as Kwara'ae explain it, this means 'living righteously' (*tualana ke 'olo'olo'a*) and offering sacrifices to 'worship' ghosts (*fo'osia akalo*).

MAKING GHOSTS TABU

The 'righteous living' which concerned the ghosts was largely a matter of observing tabu. Like men, ghosts require to be treated as tabu to a degree appropriate to their status, and this can be seen as the basis of their authority and power over their dependants. In fact the concept of tabu could be said to be central to Kwara'ae religion for the same reason that it was central to authority and power among the living.

Kwara'ae writings on 'law' instruct people to 'make ghosts tabu' (*fa'aābua akalo*, the meaning of Rofate'e's third 'law' given in the last chapter) and this has similar implications to 'treat a person as tabu' (*fa'aābua ngwae*). It requires respecting their rights and status by observing certain rules of behaviour (*taki*) to avoid 'spoiling' (*fa'alia*) and offending them. In accordance with the senior status and authority of ghosts, these rules were even more stringent than those which governed relationships among the living, although, as we shall see, they also protected living men because of their association with the ghosts. While alive, the ghosts had observed these rules themselves and passed them down from generation to generation as the foundation of the traditional social and political order. Through these rules the ghosts maintained a hierarchical social structure which gave ghosts authority over their priests, priests over their kinsmen and men over their women, each category being in various ways tabu to the ones below.

Ghosts were tabu in particular in that their positive values had to be protected from being 'spoiled' by the negative values of women. This required that dealings with ghosts be formally regulated and usually confined strictly to suitably qualified adult men. The inherent qualities of women posed a constant threat to this relationship, and they were not allowed to have certain kinds of contact with ghosts or with the men who dealt with them. The rules were based on the premise that everything associated with ghosts must be kept clean and pure (*sikasika, faulu*), and the effect of women upon ghosts was to make them *sua*. Since the aversion of ghosts to women focussed on their faeces and urine and on menstrual blood and childbirth, *sua* may be translated as 'polluted' or 'defiled' (as distinct from 'dirty', *bili, bulibuli*) and a woman could 'spoil' a ghost or a man because she would 'defile him' (*fa'asuā, fa'aōlā*) or 'feminise him' (*fa'akinia*). Defilement occurred by a kind of contagion or infection which flowed downwards, and relations between persons were structured so that ghosts and men were above women and should never be below them. This applied in all aspects of everyday life and governed the cultural arrangement of the Kwara'ae landscape.

Within a traditional village the worlds of men and women met in the dwelling house (*luma*), the focus of family life, regarded as the women's house. To protect men the side uphill from the central fire would be tabu for women to sit in while the side below would be open (*mola*) to both men and women. But men and boys would usually sleep and spend much of their time in a men's house (*fera*) which was tabu to women to prevent defilement and situated uphill, or at least not downhill, from the dwelling house. A man who had constant dealings with ghosts as a priest would have a back room or a separate 'tabu house' (*feraābu*) where he kept ritual objects and relics of the dead. This would be tabu not only to women but also to men who were not pure enough to deal with the ghosts. Away from the villages, usually on ridges where women would not pass above them, were even more restricted 'tabu houses' (*feraābu*), not always including actual buildings, which were the burial places and shrines of more ancient ghosts. Men might enter these areas for ritual purposes but the inner sanctuary of an important shrine would be so tabu that even the priest could enter only under very strict precautions. At the opposite extreme, downhill and outside the village, was the women's latrine and the menstrual house (*bisi*) where women remained during their periods. It was permitted (*mola*) for women to enter these places, but defiling (*sua*) for men. A pregnant woman would build her own childbirth house (*bisi kale*) further removed downhill, where she gave birth alone and remained with the baby for twenty or thirty days afterwards, too defiling to have contact even with other women, until she moved back in stages via the menstrual house to the living house and normal domestic life.

These rules of 'women's tabu' (*ābu'a kini*) aimed to ensure that defilement would be transmitted neither by people nor by objects or substances associated with them. This meant that men and women had to avoid one another's personal

PLATE 9   *A traditional village in 'Ere'ere, home of the priest Timi Ko'oliu.*
Beyond his wife's dwelling house with its pig fences, Ko'oliu's own
tabu house is just visible on higher ground to the left.
(Photo by Ben Burt, 1984)

possessions, that the furnishings and the fire, the food, water and everything else belonging to menstrual house, dwelling house, men's house and shrine had to be kept separate. This protected, at one extreme, senior men, priests and ghosts from, at the other, women especially when menstruating or giving birth. Maefatafata, daughter of Ramo'itolo the last priest of Latea, recalls how as a child in the 1930s she learnt not to step over her father's legs or even to touch his food, among a whole range of everyday precautions which required restitution to be paid if she broke them. It was the women who bore the main responsibility for observing these rules, which now seem very arduous to Maefatafata by comparison with life as a Christian. The rare exceptions were 'women priests' (*fataābu kini*), often the wives of male priests, who cared for certain important 'women ghosts' (*akalo kini*) and for this reason were guarded by similar rules of tabu to their male counterparts.[2]

RESTITUTION AND SACRIFICE

When ghosts were offended by breaches of these rules, it was their dependants, being in their power, who were likely to suffer the consequences. But a ghost's reactions to being 'spoiled' could be as indiscriminate as a man's, and any or all of a group of relatives might meet with misfortune, particularly the children, most vulnerable to sickness. In the same way that people looked for support and protection first and foremost to their own clan ancestors, so they expected to find these ghosts to be the cause of their sickness or misfortunes. Hence, when a priest tried to divine which ghost was responsible, he would begin by checking the names of the person's ancestors in the male line, and only if he received no confirmation would he try those of the mother's clan, and if necessary then the clan of the father's mother.

Offences against ghosts required that they be 'made good' (*fa'ale'ā*) by some form of restitution (*fa'aābu'a*) and for defilement it was necessary to 'cleanse' (*fa'asikasikā*) or 'renew' (*fa'afaolua*) the person or ghosts. The most serious offences would require a killing, of the offender or anyone else who was available, to forestall deaths caused by the ghosts by means of what was, in effect, a sacrifice to them. This seems to have been a common cause of killing in Kwara'ae in the past, a measure of the supreme right of ghosts to be made tabu. But such drastic measures were more usually avoided by making offerings to the ghosts, as restitution payments were given to resolve conflicts among the living. This was part of the system of sacrificial exchanges through which ghosts were induced to support and protect their dependants, and the procedures were much the same for requesting assistance or for making good an offence. For small requests, especially from the recent dead, an offering of roasted taro might be sufficient, and small denominations of shell money (*animani*) might be given as restitution for minor breaches of tabu. But for support in major projects such as a feud or a festival, and to 'make good' for serious offences, especially when sickness had resulted, it was necessary to 'bake pig' (*kōgwata*).

These offerings and accompanying prayers would normally be made by the priest responsible for the ghost concerned. A pig would be carried to the shrine where he would kill it by throttling with a vine around the snout, and cook it using the special fireplace and ovenstones which formed a focus of the shrine. While singeing and scraping the pig's bristles to prepare it for cooking, the priest would invoke (*fikia*) the ghost and explain for whom the sacrifice was being made by reciting the genealogies which linked them together. The sacrifice was a communal meal which the priest and other men shared with the ghosts, who enjoyed the smell of the burning bristles and, as some say, ate the spirit of the pig. But the meal was tabu and could not be eaten by women and children.

The Christian preacher Jonathon Didi'imae of 'Ere'ere recalls how, more than fifty years ago, his father taught him the importance of marrying a hardworking girl who was willing to raise pigs; "If you don't have any pigs you'll die, ... because our life comes only from pigs ... cooking them for the ghosts." As Didi'imae explains, a ghost might actually demand through dreams or possession, "Bring a pig for me and no-one will die, not your brother, not your wife, not your child". Indeed, affliction is sometimes described as if it resulted from the greed of the ghosts rather than from the misdeeds of their dependants. Through these offerings, ghosts were involved in the exchange networks of the living. Although some pigs were reared for sacrifice to particular ghosts and kept tabu, sacrifice also consumed large numbers of ordinary pigs, which people might have to borrow or buy for shell money. A run of misfortune could impoverish a family and leave them heavily indebted to their relatives.

TABU AND POWER

The demands of ghosts could become a burden and their power a threat, or so it came to seem once people were offered the alternative of Christianity. But it was the people themselves who conferred this power upon them. This was not simply because depending on ghosts for support and protection made people vulnerable to them but also because of the way they elevated the ghosts to positions of authority by making them tabu. Kwara'ae recognise that it was their submission to the rules of tabu which gave the ghosts power both for them and over them: a power which was by the same token destroyed when people changed their allegiance to the Christian God. To understand Kwara'ae relationships with ghosts and the implications of conversion to Christianity, we need to consider in some detail the way tabu mediated spiritual power.

The role of tabu in relationships with ghosts is clearly shown in the way

men came to ritual maturity. Until young men began to have dealings with
ghosts themselves, benefiting from personal revelations or partaking of sacrificial
meals, it was possible (*mola*) for them to mix with women without fear of
defilement. They could even visit girls in the menstrual area, risking retaliation
for breaking the tabu on chastity, but without offending the ghosts. But in so
doing they also deprived themselves of spiritual support and protection, and were
accordingly regarded as irresponsible, unruly and worthless (*dalafa*). When a
man did realise the need for spiritual support, probably by the time he took on
the responsibilities of marriage and family life, it was necessary for him to keep
himself tabu to women. Henceforth he could eat sacrificial meals with other adult
men, which in some clans would begin with a special sacrifice to 'make him tabu'
(*fa'aābua*), but he also became vulnerable to defilement. Kwara'ae Christians
also recognise this relationship, being free from the authority of ghosts unless and
until they are tempted to accept the support and protection which ghosts may
offer in dreams, which obliges them to follow the rules making ghosts tabu or
suffer the consequences. Those who are most tabu are correspondingly most
vulnerable to defilement. In 1984, when Timi Ko'oliu, last priest of the ancient
shrine of Masu'u'a (Anomula), went to the women's latrine to aid his wife who
was suddenly taken ill, the ghosts immediately struck him dead, apparently with
a heart attack.

This relationship between tabu and the power of ghosts is confirmed in the
way people explain the ghosts' reactions to defilement or other offences against
them. Some tend to regard the resulting misfortune as inflicted by the offended
ghosts themselves, for they are generally understood to have the power to kill
their dependants. One explanation for sickness is a ghost stealing away a person's
'spirit' or shade. But it is also said that if ghosts were displeased their protection
was merely removed from those in their care, leaving them open to affliction,
whether by people or hostile ghosts, much as a person's living relatives might
abandon someone who offended against them. This theory may help to resolve
the contradiction which some recognise between a relative being kind and
supportive in life but a cause of suffering as a ghost, for the implication is that his
power had been rendered ineffective. But the two interpretations are actually
complementary and reflect the effects of breaking tabu upon the living. When the
rules making ghosts tabu were broken, this treated them as if they were ordinary
or open (*mola*), for instance to contact with women, and they retaliated in anger
to reassert their status and authority which had been denied and degraded as a
result. In effect they must obtain restitution (*fa'aābu'a*) or lose the power they
had both for their dependants and over them. On one level this can be seen as a
human failure to be 'true' (*mamana*) in honouring a contract, which leads ghosts
to do the same. On another, it reflects the fact that ghosts have power only insofar

as others respect their authority and 'make them true' by believing in them
(*fa'amamanā*).

These interpretations of reactions by ghosts had important implications for
the way that Kwara'ae attempted to direct and control their power, or to
neutralise or destroy it altogether. They achieved this by manipulating tabu,
making things tabu when it was necessary to empower them and making them
ordinary or mundane (*mola*) when this power was to be removed. This sensitivity
of ghosts to defilement was both their strength and their weakness: the rationale
for tabu which conferred power upon them and the means by which they could
be made mundane and their power neutralised. In this context the power of
ghosts and the defilement of women can be seen as opposing but complementary
forces in Kwara'ae cosmology.

MALE AND FEMALE POWERS

These powers have to be understood in the light of the roles and values
associated with men and women in Kwara'ae culture. Most ghosts, being male,
conferred and supported masculine values. They ensured the benefits of men's
hard work and the rewards of stable and peaceful living, but they were also held
responsible for male aggression and violence. When Kwara'ae Christians describe
ghosts as making their dependants troublesome and violent they are not simply
maligning the traditional religion, but reflecting on the role of ghosts in a society
of feuding local groups, in which both men and ghosts so often demanded
bloodshed in restitution for breaches of tabu. Relationships with ghosts, like
those with men of authority and power, were ambivalent, creative and destructive; a source of support and protection tinged with the danger of retribution for
offences against their rights and status. For Kwara'ae, ghosts are 'like a spear
point at both ends', or as we might say in English, 'a two-edged sword'.

In contrast, women are regarded as peaceful and nurturing, raising
children and pigs and uniting the men of different clans through marriage as
in-laws and relatives. Women represent the stability of community life, as
opposed to the strength and violence of men. The important 'women ghosts'
with their 'women priests' played a similar role, promoting peace and calm,
prosperity and the growth of gardens and pigs (although they were as dangerous
as any others if defiled or disobeyed). Kwara'ae attempted deliberately to balance
these male and female qualities against one another in their relationships with
ghosts, so that while the power of ghosts was invoked by men, it was contained
by women. Women were supposed to have a pacifying or quietening effect on
ghosts, as on men, and this is one implication of defiling (*fa'asuā*) or 'feminising'
them (*fa'akinia*).

PLATE 10   *Women's costume as required by the religion of the ghosts, who*
                restrict the use of European clothes to avoid defilement. Le'akini of
                'Ere'ere wears the red-dyed cane belt of a single girl and her
                married sister Musuba'eko wears a belt of black fibre and white
                beads with a blue cloth apron. (Photo by Ben Burt, 1979)

Of course there is always a certain ambivalence between neutralising power and provoking it to retaliate, as the dangerous consequences of defilement show. In fact, since defilement makes ghosts react against the dependants in their power who are responsible for keeping them tabu, it could be used deliberately to harm them. Perhaps the most drastic way to do this was to defile a shrine, as enemies sometimes attempted during feuds, and women have been known to do as desperate guestures of defiance against their own relatives. A warrior, depending as he did on the power of a fierce warrior ghost, could be weakened or killed for instance by passing a woman's clothing over his head. More commonly people defiled others by swearing, for describing a defiling act not only insulted someone but also threatened his relationship with the ghosts, as would the act itself. Such offences were likely to provoke demands for restitution. In the 1950s, when some ignorant Christian boys made a foolish joke to the Latea priest Ramo'itolo about eating shit with his betelnut, it cost them one 'red money', but a few generations ago the consequences might be much more serious. Ramosala of Mānadari recalls how his father Totori once shot a woman dead as restitution because she swore defilement on his young 'brothers', and afterwards settled the matter by exchanging shell money with her family.

But under the correct circumstances women could act, often under the direction of men, to subdue the power of ghosts for the benefit of their dependants. At a simple level for instance, if a woman, particularly a woman priest, was to touch the arm of a man who was uncontrollably possessed by a warrior ghost, this would 'cool' and quieten him by making the ghost leave him, apparently without ill effect. Women ghosts could act in similar ways, as in one shrine where two women's skulls were buried on top of the tooth relic of a dangerous ghost dog to 'feminize' it and stop it attacking and killing people. Such controlled use of women's influence formed an essential part of certain rituals which activated the power of ghosts and hence were potentially dangerous to the human participants.

Sacrificial rituals invoked ghosts to be active or 'alive' (*mauri*), making them and their priests and the other men involved even more tabu than usual and subject to stricter rules with correspondingly serious consequences if they were broken. To return to normal life afterwards it was necessary carefully to make what was tabu open and unrestricted (*mola*) once again through special 'clearing' procedures (*mola'a*). On the principle that the act of making someone mundane or *mola* removes the power which being treated as tabu confers upon him, restoring everyday behaviour and relationships obliged the ghosts to retire from active involvement with their dependants. Acting as if things were *mola* was not only the consequence of removing tabu but also the means by which this was achieved. The crucial requirement was, as it were, to remove tabu without breaking it. This was achieved in stages, generally by the priest ceremonially performing forbidden acts such as eating the first morsel of sacrificial meat and other tabu foods to clear the way for others to do the same.

Making everyday life normal again meant returning men to the company of their womenfolk, whom they had set themselves apart from and excluded while they were keeping company with the ghosts. In effect the 'making clear' (*fa'amola'a*) after a sacrificial ritual allowed women to reassert their influence in community life while the ghosts retired to the background. This is particularly obvious in the concluding stages of the festivals in which a clan celebrated its strength and unity by offering major sacrifices of pigs to its ancestors, as we shall see. In such rituals men can be said to have used the qualities of women to control ghosts by shifting the boundaries between what was tabu and what was *mola*.

INTERPRETING TABU

In its effects upon the power of ghosts, defilement can also be seen as a kind of power, and in this sense women are also 'strong' (*ngasi*) like men and ghosts. But theirs is the power to quieten, to weaken or to kill, and for ghosts and men it is very much a negative quality from which they have to be protected by the 'tabu of women'. In Kwara'ae this relationship between male and female powers reflects cosmological structures like those described by Keesing for Kwaio and by Elli and Pierre Maranda for Lau, in which tabu mediates a symbolic opposition between the values of spiritual power and of childbirth. As in Lau, men's responsibilities for the dead ancestors could be said to balance or even compensate for women's responsibilities for reproducing the living (Elli Maranda 1974:178), representing an opposition between the 'actual', (natural reproductive) power of women and the 'ideological' (cultural and political) power of men (Pierre Maranda pers. comm. 1987). This in turn can be seen as part of a more general cosmological distinction between nature and culture, as outlined by Keesing (1982a:71–2). Further research in Kwara'ae might reveal the kinds of symbolic equivalances with Keesing illustrates for Kwaio between menstruation and sacrifice, childbirth and funerals or festivals (1982a:68), or the elaborate symbolism surrounding "the skull and the womb" which the Marandas describe for Lau (Maranda & Maranda 1970).

But there are problems in the way these authors describe the defiling qualities of women as tabu to men; "abu for containment of female powers" (Keesing 1982a:66) or "negatively" tabu (Maranda & Maranda 1970:840), and equivalent in this respect to the qualities of ghosts and men which make them tabu to women. In discussing this point, Kwara'ae state quite emphatically that something which is defiling (*sua*) is not tabu but 'bad' (*ta'a*), and it is evident that describing such negative qualities as tabu distorts the whole significance of the concept. The problem is probably one of semantic interpretation. Like Lau and Kwaio, Kwara'ae may say, for instance, that 'a menstrual house is tabu for a man to go inside' (*bisi nia ābu fuana ngwae nia leka 'i saena*) when actually implying that it is the man and his action which is tabu because the menstrual house would defile him. This, Kwara'ae explain, is the 'true' meaning of tabu underlying the ambiguities of common modes of speech. This is not to question the symbolic oppositions between male and female powers, nor to imply that female values are regarded as negative in any absolute sense. They are not negative to women, for menstruation is only potentially defiling, in the same sense that sexual activity is potentially adulterous, or eating is potentialy stealing. Only in the wrong context do actions cease to be acceptable and become offensive. But the fact that tabu always represents positive values does have implications for the way it mediates power.

In counterposing male and female values, Kwara'ae religion asserted that men's spiritual role as mediators with the ghosts was not only opposed to the reproductive role of women, but was also important enough to take precedence over it. Men recognised the power of women to stabilise and regulate their own power, but they attempted to control this by giving it a negative value in relation to the ghosts and themselves. In effect Kwara'ae men used the power of ghosts to control women and the power of women to control ghosts. In this male-dominated society the positive value of tabu marked the rights, prerogatives and authority of men, particularly senior men and leaders, and of the ghosts from whom their power derived, in opposition to the women whose submission they required. Women were tabu primarily in contexts where men's interests in them were at stake, and defiling when they threatened male claims to power. So men controlled women's reproductive powers, as they controlled their sexual and domestic roles, by means of tabu. But as Keesing points out, "By mystifying women's reproductive powers, Malaita men have exposed themselves to danger" (1982a:222). In more general terms, the price of being made tabu is the risk you take of being treated as if you were not or, to put it another way, the creation of power also creates the possibility of subversion. This goes to the heart of Kwara'ae ideas of tabu, in relationships among the living as well as with ghosts. Claims to status and authority in terms of tabu have to be backed up, by force if necessary, and making claims which others disregard may be more damaging in terms of humiliation and loss of respect than not making them in the first place.

It is the way Malaitans have used tabu to govern their relationships with ghosts that has encouraged anthropologists, in spite of their own reservations, to translate the concept as 'sacred' (see eg. Hogbin 1939:116, Maranda & Maranda 1970:846, Elli Maranda 1974:182, Keesing 1982a:70). But the way that Kwara'ae make things tabu (*fa'aābua*) shows that tabu can have very little to do with religion and that when they translate it as 'holy' they do not have the European concept of 'sacredness' in mind. Tabu sets ghosts apart not because they are sacred as distinct from profane but because, in a world view which unites the spiritual and human domains, they are *more* tabu than the living. Where the concept of tabu is associated first and foremost with ghosts, this is a measure of the range and strictness of the rules which they required their living dependants to observe in return for their support and protection; a cause and consequence of their key position in Kwara'ae society. The relationship between male and female powers plays such a large part in any discussion of tabu in Kwara'ae and other parts of Malaita not because it is central to the concept of tabu, as the Marandas and Keesing imply, but because tabu is central to relationships of power which rely so heavily on this male-female opposition. For tabu is ultimately about the control of power; a way of socialising the 'strength' (*ngasingasi'anga*) of both spiritual and human beings and controlling it by the rules (*taki*) which should govern relationships in society.

RELIGION AS POLITICS

Today all but a few Kwara'ae have ceased to treat their ancestral ghosts as tabu and their womenfolk as defiling, finding a more reliable and less demanding source of support and protection in Christianity. In many ways their conversion has been a 'clearing' process (*fa'amola'a*), leading to the abolition of rules of tabu and neutralising the authority of traditional leaders in the process. But to appreciate how and why this occurred, we need to look in more detail at how the power of the ghosts supported, and was supported by, the political authority of their dependants. For the ritual system through which Kwara'ae institutionalised their relationships with the ghosts was an essential part of the political system through which they organised relationships of power among the living, and attempted to resist the colonial order in a struggle which was at once political and religious.

Kwara'ae say that their true leaders in the past were their 'tabu-speakers' (*fataābu*) or priests, and even as Christians they sometimes describe clan leaders or 'chiefs' as '*fataābu*'. Of course it is clear that the priesthood was not the only source of authority. We have already seen how 'important men' (*ngwae 'inoto'a*) supported and organised their relatives in exchanging wealth and feasting, gaining authority which was backed by violence and feuding led by 'warriors' (*ramo*). But priests controlled the institutionalised ritual system which channelled the power of the ghosts in the interests of senior men in general. Insofar as their personal authority depended upon these political and religious relationships, these senior men may be thought of as a kind of political 'establishment' with vested interests in maintaining this system.

This establishment was fragmented by the values of self-determination and egalitarianism which divided local clans and communities, to the extent that

Europeans often found difficulty in identifying who the political leaders were. When a British government officer stationed in West Kwara'ae in 1910 was "Visited by about 180 people, more or less, all chiefs", he commented wryly that "The District appears to be inhabited solely by chiefs" (Diary 16 Jul. 1910). Within his own family and local clan every senior man does indeed have some claim to be regarded as a 'chief' (*gwaunga'i ngwae* or 'head-man', Pijin *tsif*), by which Kwara'ae today usually mean simply 'traditional leader'. Now that government and churches have brought local communities under more central-ised systems of authority, most 'chiefs' are indeed little more than representatives of local clans. In the past there was probably a constant tension between each man's desire to be his own 'chief' and his dependence on political leaders who did have real authority in their local communities. There was a corresponding interest in alternative sources of spiritual power, which the establishment seems to have contained variously by tolerating, suppressing or assimilating into the institution-alised ritual system dominated by ancestral ghosts.

Priests held their authority through the clan system which dominated people's relationships with one another and with the ghosts of their ancestors. A priest was normally the senior descendant of the ancestral ghosts he dealt with, ideally from the line of firstborn sons, trained by his father to assist him while he was alive and succeed him after he died. But he would actually be chosen by a ghost, through dreams or signs such as sickness, which meant that the first-born might be passed over or that the ancestors of a clan with no available men might choose a priest descended from them through a woman. Even Filo'isi, famous as the last senior priest of the great shrine of Siale, was a only sister's son of his predecessor Augwata. But a priest could not simply appoint himself, nor easily avoid the priesthood without risking death, at least in the days before the ghosts' authority could be avoided by joining a Christian church.

The priest's congregation and sphere of influence centred on his local clan group of fathers, brothers and sons and their families. As we have seen, these groups were quite small, probably seldom more than ten closely related men and their families, more often perhaps five or six or even less.[3] In 1984 the remaining thirty or so adult traditionists of 'Ere'ere had four priests between them, one of whom acted only for himself. Even if the priest was not also the most senior by descent and hence technically leader for their land, he would be the main authority on the genealogies demonstrating this leadership, which he had to recite during sacrifices to the ancestors concerned. Historical accounts and present opinion (including Maenu'u 1981:13) both confirm that priests acted as land leaders and representatives of their local clans. In the 1960s Ramo'itolo of Latea gave a memorable demonstration of this role in several land disputes with neighbours of other clans.

PLATE 11   *Priests of 'Ere'ere, the last traditionists in East Kwara'ae; Nguta,*
               Maerora and the priest for the ancient shrine of Masu'u'a
               (Anomula), Timi Ko'oliu of Sasadili. (Photo by Ben Burt, 1979)

But the priest's essential duty and the source of his authority was to
mediate with the ghosts, invoking their support and protection and making good
offences against them. This could be a heavy and arduous responsibility, not
merely for his people's livelihood but for their very lives, and it was supported by
power over life and death, for he could also hold back the blessing of the ghosts
or even invoke them to kill by cursing. A priest's authority and his acceptability
to the ghosts depended upon his being made tabu; too tabu to live a normal
domestic life with his wife and family or even to share food and water with men
who were not strict in separating themselves from women. In fulfilling his
responsibilities, he acted as the moral guardian of his people, ensuring that they
treated the ghosts and each other as tabu and led lives which were 'righteous'
(*'olo'olo'a*) and 'clean' (*sikasika*). Sickness and calamity could result not only
from offences against the ghosts themselves, but also from conflict among their
dependants, such as quarrels or killings, sexual improprieties, incest and im-
proper marriages. As the Christian preacher Didi'imae puts it, a priest was "like
a big pastor" (Pijin *titsa*). He was expected to demonstrate in his own life the

values which distinguished an 'important man', living quietly and humbly, staying at home and prospering by working hard on his gardens, raising pigs and acquiring shell money with which to help others. Indeed some say that priests were always 'important men', even though 'important men' were not always priests.

As 'important men', priests contributed to exchanges of wealth and feasting through the sacrificial system, receiving on behalf of the ghosts both pigs and shell money offerings used to buy pigs, which were shared with other adult men in sacrificial meals and festivals. Sacrifices to ancestors also brought together their dependants within the local clan and beyond. When people were asked for pigs by ancestors from whom they were 'born of women', the sacrifice reaffirmed relationships with uncles and cousins in other clans, and claims to their clan lands. When they sent pigs 'up' to the ancient ancestors of their own clan at the shrines they derived from generations ago, they joined a wider congregation of local clans under the leadership of a priest of the senior line. The priests in charge of the ancient shrines of dispersed clans, like Faureba in Gwauna'ongi as already described, had special opportunities for leadership through the hierarchical descent system.

FESTIVALS

Priesthood had its greatest scope for leadership in the 'festivals' (*maoma*, from *mao*, 'dance') which united the living and dead members of a clan in peace and friendship with relatives and neighbours in the wider community. These were normally sacrificial feasts held by all the men of a clan for all the ghosts whose relics they kept in their local shrine, on the occasion of the refurbishment of the shrine. But festivals were also very much for the benefit of the living, including those 'born of women' of the ghosts and other relatives and neighbours who came to eat and to be entertained and, of course, for the clan who demonstrated their own generosity by distributing great quantities of pigs and food while securing the goodwill of their ancestors.

As the great occasions of traditional community life, the organisation and procedures of festivals are worth describing in some detail. They show how the clan-based ritual system could unite large numbers of people in co-operative action and demonstrate methods for dealing with the power of ghosts which influenced the Kwara'ae approach to the new sources of spiritual power promised by Christianity. Festival procedures probably varied somewhat according to the ritual conventions and the size and strength of the clan concerned. The following account generalises from the recollections of several men of different clans.

The timing of a festival would depend on the pig-rearing cycle and on the decay of the shrine house thatch, which might last four or five years. But the time was actually decided by a ghost in the shrine, who saw that enough large pigs were ready and demanded a festival, perhaps by making someone sick. The priest would have to check how many pigs his clan congregation could provide, maybe up to ten or so, and organise each household to plant extra gardens of taro, timing the festival for the harvest. The contributors would normally be his close 'brothers' and 'sons', although in some clans it was not unknown for men 'born of women' to contribute too.[4] About a month before the gardens were ready, the priest would make a particularly tabu 'restricted' (*ete'a*) pig sacrifice to tell the ghost that the festival was going ahead. This began a 'tabu period' (*fa'i ābu'a*) while the men worked to refurbish the shrine, clearing vegetation, repairing stone walls and preparing materials to rebuild the house. During this period the festival congregation were forbidden to eat certain foods, particularly pigs, coconuts and fish, and they were not allowed to go to market, attend feasts, weddings or funerals, or be visited by people taking part in such ceremonies. Everyone had to stay quietly at home, isolated from outsiders and possible trouble, and the men were more than usually tabu for contact with women.

Eventually all the men went up to the shrine for several days to rebuild the house, which for an important shrine might be decorated with plaited walls and carved and painted boards and posts. The most tabu and critical stage was when the priest ceremonially took the skulls and relics of the ghosts out of the old house and installed them in the new or restored house. The men then shared a meal of taro-coconut pudding (*lakeno*) and fish, which made these foods clear (*mola*) to be eaten at the festival by men, though probably not yet by women. Then began a period of preparation leading up to the festival itself ten days hence. During this time there were two or three other essential 'restricted' pig sacrifices to ancient 'big ghosts' whose relics remained in places from which the clan derived. These included shrines they had left generations ago, in the charge of priests of senior branches of their dispersed major clan. These pigs, previously dedicated to the ghosts concerned, were so tabu that the first could be eaten only by the priests and the others could be shared only by the men giving the festival.

On the ninth day, firewood, bamboos and leaf were gathered for cooking, taro harvested, pigs caught and trussed, and everything was carried up to the shrine. If guests arrived at this stage, there might be a night of entertainment with food such as taro-coconut pudding and fish for the men and the singing of epic chants. Next morning, to begin the festival proper the priest sacrificed the first pig to the senior ghost in a tabu inner part of the shrine, reciting the list of ancestors for whom the festival was held and praying for support as he singed and scraped the hair from the pig's head. This made it clear (*mola*) for the other men to enter the shrine and butcher their own pigs under the direction of the priest, who scraped the head of each pig before it was scraped all over and gutted. The pigs were then cooked, small cuts and offal in bamboos or over the fire and the main carcasses in stone ovens, usually left overnight. When the meat in the bamboos was ready the priest ate a morsel from the first pig of each family group, ate betelnut and told the ghosts that he was 'making it clear' (*fa'amolā*) for everyone to eat the meat; men, that is, since women and children were still excluded.

The next day panpipe dances were performed at the danceground near the shrine for the entertainment of the ghosts as well as the guests. This was a time for ostentatious display, when people dressed in their best costume ornaments. The festival-givers might dress up a man who had been kept secluded and tabu, or display trophies such as a rare bird, or quantities of shell money. Then, returning to the shrine, the ovens would be opened and the meat, with taro and pudding, would be portioned out among the groups of guests and presented to their priests. Attention would be given to returning meat received at previous festivals and to rewarding the dancers. Then the guests would return home with their food, the hosts cleaned up the shrine and the priest closed it with prayers.

PLATE 12   *One of the dances performed at festivals for the ghosts. Riomea, dressed in shell-bead armbands and shell-disk necklace, leads a* sango *panpipe dance with hornbill batons and leg rattles. (Photo by Ben Burt, 1979)*

This 'main festival' (*maoma doe*) was a 'men's festival' (*maoma ngwane*), when women could come to watch and eat certain foods, but not partake of the meat, which was tabu to them, like other sacrifices. It was followed about ten days later by a 'women's festival' (*maoma kini*) for the women, children and men who were too undisciplined (*dalafa*) to eat sacrificial pigs. For some local clans this was a small feast with only two or three pigs, but for others it may have been as big as the men's festival, held over two days with epic chants at night or panpipe dances in the morning. The ritual procedures of the women's festival seem to have varied too, but its essential purpose was a 'clearing' (*fa'amola'a*) to end the tabu period of the festival. The pigs would be killed and cooked at a special hearth in an outer part of the shrine, and although this work was led by the priest, his wife or a senior woman also took an important part. Things became clear (*mola*) in stages. Before the pigs were killed they were splashed with coconut water to 'cool' them. To allow the women to eat the meat, the first morsel was eaten by the senior woman. One way of making the food clear was for the women of the clan, after bathing and decorating themselves, to line up while the priest splashed them with coconut water and fed them with morsels of meat and other food. At some stage the priest might also bake taro as a 'peacemaking' offering (*fa'asafi'a*) to lift all remaining restrictions on visiting or attending other ceremonies.

When the women's festival was over, the festival group could return to normal everyday life. The participation of women had made the ghosts retire and leave their dependants in peace, through a process of 'peacemaking' or 'cooling' (*fa'asafi'a, fa'agwari'a*). The use of coconut water in these procedures was part of a recurring ritual association of coconuts with women's powers, which explains why they were banned during early stages of the festival. Coconuts, from which 'milk' is made for cooking, seem to be a symbolic female equivalent to the skulls of the ghosts.[5] As we shall see, such symbolism was also used by Kwara'ae visionaries attempting to create 'churches' which drew on traditional as well as Christian ritual.

These festivals demonstrate the cardinal values of Kwara'ae political and religious life. A successful festival celebrated men's control over their spiritual and human relationships as they evoked the solidarity of their local clan, living and dead, while proclaiming their membership of more ancient clans and wider congregations through the preliminary sacrifices, and showing their generosity to relatives, in-laws and neighbours who came to be fed and entertained. The men achieved this through ritual procedures which conferred and invoked the power of ghosts by imposing rules of tabu which controlled the powers of women, and then gradually removed tabu as they used the power of the women to quieten or suppress the power of the ghosts. Priests directed these procedures and stood at the centre of all the relationships involved, between the clan and their relatives, men and women, living and dead.

The scale of a festival reflected the prosperity and power of the clan and its ancestral ghosts. In recent times, with congregations depleted by conversion to Christianity, they have been quite modest affairs. In 'Ere'ere in the 1970s three or four priests and their sons combined to sacrifice about ten pigs for their festivals, no more than one per man. A few generations ago things were very different, and old men today are still proud to recall festivals in their youth with a hundred or even a hundred and fifty pigs. Such was the case with Siale, widely regarded as the most ancient shrine in Kwara'ae. Among the many clans which trace their origins to the first ancestors who settled there from overseas, a group of four or five clans, widely dispersed from the lands near Siale for which they are named, joined to celebrate festivals at the shrine. Their priests each had particular ritual tasks under the leadership of the senior priest responsible for the Siale shrine itself. For the festivals a broad 'road' was cleared from the shrine entrance, leading through the danceground into a walled enclosure containing the houses and sacrificial hearths of important ghosts and the remains of a stone 'tower' destroyed by the gale which dispersed the first settlers. Each clan had its own thatch shelter around the danceground and, according to Osifera of 'Aimomoko, whose 'fathers' conducted the last of these festivals, Siale became "like a town". The most tabu stage of the festival, while the ghosts were being rehoused, was proclaimed with shell trumpets and everyone in the villages around had to stay indoors until the 'all clear' was sounded. People came from all over Kwara'ae just to see the sights, including the miraculous water supply, ducted in banana stems, which would flow back to its source if not treated as tabu. Osifera was overawed by all the important men with their pearlshell pendants, spears and clubs; "It was really something in those days."

Siale is by no means the only shrine where festivals on this scale were once held. It is difficult today to reconstruct the ritual organisation of Kwara'ae as a whole, but in the past such major festivals at ancient shrines would have reflected the strength and solidarity of groups of local clans, forming important political factions. The senior priest who could organise such a festival would have been an influential leader, which is how the last priest of Siale, Filo'isi of 'Aimomoko, is remembered today.

PRIESTS, WARRIORS AND 'IMPORTANT MEN'

In mediating the power of ghosts, priests could not only become feastgivers and 'important men', but also exercise some control over the armed force which was the ultimate human sanction for political and spiritual authority. The power of 'warriors' (*ramo*) came from ancestral ghosts too, particularly from 'warrior ghosts' (*akalo ni mae, akalo ana ramo'a*). These are the heroes of Kwara'ae folklore, ghosts like A'oramo, a ferocious warrior of about fourteen generations ago whose exploits are widely known from old stories and who gave fighting powers for his clan of Gwauna'ongi. Priests played an important part in mediating this power. Men planning to kill would first sacrifice a pig to a warrior ghost for support and protection, making them so tabu that they had to avoid women completely until, after the deed was done, they would sacrifice another pig in thanks to become 'clear' (*mola*) again. Warriors are also said to have been trained from childhood and put under the protection of a warrior ghost through a pig sacrifice by the priest. This made them particularly tabu to women, as priests were, and they were strongest while they remained unmarried and celibate. Some, like A'oramo, even became 'cannibals' (*fafanga*, lit. 'eater'), ferocious enough to eat human flesh raw, but they were regarded as dangerous exceptions.

Certain trained warriors (*ramo to'ofu*) were authorised by their community to enforce tabu, leading organised raids and assassinating appropriate victims to uphold the 'law', obtain restitution or collect rewards. For some clans this role is said to have been inherited, in a different line of descent to the senior priest. But unlike priests, official warriors were not essential to community life. Most men had to be prepared to fight on occasion and the title 'warrior' was probably applied loosely to any man who gained a reputation as a successful fighter. Priests often gave men special powers to fight, sometimes by implanting objects in their hands or limbs to make them strong or by giving them magical objects or substances to wear or carry. All men could join in eating someone their group had killed, although they would cook them, unlike the 'cannibals', and the meal was tabu to women and surrounded by restrictions, rather like a pig sacrifice.

Quite how important warriors were as political leaders is difficult to say. The Kwara'ae view today is that they had little authority, for despite the wealth they obtained by collecting rewards, killing prevented them from gaining the popularity and prestige of an 'important man'. But the authority of priests depended partly on the violent deeds of warriors to enforce the rules of tabu, as warriors depended on priests and ghosts to empower and authorise their deeds. In fact the roles of priest and warrior seem to have complemented each other as aspects of the Kwara'ae male personality, representing the creative and destructive powers which were also manifest in the nature of ghosts.

But Kwara'ae share with other Malaitans the ideal of a tripartite leadership in which the roles of priest and warrior are complemented by wealthy feastgivers or 'important men' of the Melanesian 'big man' type, representing three interdependent spheres of political activity. Political power depended on the economic obligations to senior men which bound communities together but it was backed by the sanction of violence and supported by the spiritual power of ghosts. The leadership of priests, warriors and 'important men' has been documented by various writers for most other language areas of Malaita from Kwaio northwards (Ivens 1930, Hogbin 1939, Russell 1950, Ross 1973, 1978a, all cited in Keesing 1985).[6] These descriptions often have a tendency to see the titles of leaders as definitions of roles or even formal offices, reflecting perhaps a Western expectation that leadership be specialised and institutionalised. This may explain why Kwara'ae appear to differ from other peoples of North Malaita, who are said to distinguish the role of priest from the hereditary 'important men' or 'chiefs' who acted as clan heads or feastgivers (Ivens 1930:84, Hogbin 1939:64, Russell 1950:5, Ross 1978a:12–13). In Kwara'ae priests are said to have been all these things too. But although priests could be said to hold formal office, 'important man' (*ngwae 'inoto'a, ngwae lalifu*) was more a descriptive title, as 'warrior' probably was in many cases too. Although Kwara'ae also speak of a supreme leader or 'lord' (*aofia*), this appears to have been an ideal of what leadership might achieve rather than an actual leader, at least in recent times.[7] As such it has become a symbol of recent attempts to build

PLATE 13   *Singing the deeds of ancient warriors. Le'ahuri of Sasadili, son of the priest Timi Ko'oliu, sings an epic chant about the famous warrior ghost A'oramo, accompanied by 'Arumae and the rhythm of sticks on bamboo lime bottles. (Photo by Ben Burt, 1984)*

a united political organisation under 'paramount chiefs', as it would earlier have inspired the ambitions of men like Filo'isi, priest of Siale, who described himself as 'Queen' of Malaita, like the supreme leader of the British (NIV Dec. 1943:5).

In describing priests as the true 'important men' of the past, Kwara'ae are voicing the ideal, which many hold as Christians, that society should be governed by spiritual rather than by secular authority, making the point that the two were inseparable in Kwara'ae traditional society. There may well be good reason to follow the Kwara'ae usage and call their priests 'chiefs', both to acknowledge "prevailing conceptions of chiefly leadership", as White's study of Isabel recommends (1991:11), and to recognise that they were engaged in what Sahlins calls "chiefly redistribution" through the sacrificial system. As this implies, "... kinship-rank reciprocity is laid down by office and political grouping", as distinct from being simply the personal creation of a Melanesian 'big man' who builds his own following around him (Sahlins 1972:209).

CONTAINING SPIRITUAL POWER

In mediating relationships with ghosts, priests stood at the centre of the threefold system of spiritual, military and economic power, upholding the rights and perogatives of the political establishment of senior men or, to put it another way, maintaining the social order by upholding the 'law' of the ghosts. The ritual system can be seen as a way of channelling spiritual power to this end. When spiritual and political leadership are one and the same, unauthorised relationships with spirits may pose a serious challenge, especially if they lead to new cults. The Kwara'ae establishment recognised this danger in their first encounters with Christianity, but spiritual dissent was not new to Kwara'ae society and it has not disappeared under Christianity. To conclude this study of the traditional social order, we will consider how spiritual power was contained and managed by the ancestral ritual system.

The priests' control of this ritual system, particularly over the crucial ritual of pig sacrifice, was firmly institutionalised in the system itself, to the extent that when priests died their congregations often found it easier to join a Christian church than to continue in the traditional religion without them, as we shall see. Becoming a priest was not simply a matter of being appointed by a ghost, for it required also a command of ritual knowledge passed down 'father' to 'son' from previous priests. This included the genealogies of the ancestral ghosts, and particularly the formulae to invoke them (*talana fiki'a*) in prayer and sacrifice. Appeals to ghosts without this authorisation might require restitution to prevent their retaliation for breach of tabu. But Kwara'ae generally treat important knowledge as valuable property and reveal it only when they wish to help someone, to the extent that they avoid giving other people's children the moral instruction they give their own. Priestly knowledge was guarded with particular care, as it usually still is even by Christians who have no intention of using it.

The priestly relationship with ghosts, guarded by both spiritual and human authorisation, was regularly recreated with the deaths of important people, and funeral rituals channelled the powers of new ghosts into the existing ritual system. It was priests and senior men rather than women and children who received the most elaborate funerals and became the most important and powerful ghosts. The death of a senior man might be acknowledged by a pig sacrifice and his family would go into a period of formal mourning during which they were tabu, not bathing, going to social gatherings or eating certain foods such as taro, pig or betelnut, as a sign of grief. The mourning period, only a few days for a person of little importance, might last a month or more for a priest or senior man. It ended with a 'clearing' (*mola'a*) feast and with gifts of shell money from the family to mourners to appease their grief.

The family of the dead would pay men to dispose of the body, which would usually be placed in a raised bamboo coffin in some special place in the forest. As it decayed, some of the remains would be taken as relics, usually including the skull and collar bones, but sometimes also the longbones, teeth, eyebrows or hair. These would be wrapped in a parcel of sago leaf and kept by the priest in his tabu men's house, sometimes with personal possessions of the dead, especially a man's bow. The rest of the bones would be discarded in the burial heap (*tafurae*) in the shrine. The relics were installed in the shrine house, maybe years later, when the dead person showed his power by making someone sick and demanding sacrifices. Then a 'tabu meal' (*fanga abu'a*), maybe with one or two pigs, would be held to 'raise' (*ereerea*) the person as a ghost (in the sense that a child or a garden is 'raised'). Through such formalities the dead were incorporated into the institutionalised ritual system under the care of the priests who invoked them as ghosts through their relics. Although ghosts by their nature could not be tied to particular objects or places, they were understood to have a special presence in these objects. Hence men would take relics to establish ghosts in a new place when they moved their own homes and they might seek to obtain relics, or even steal them, to gain access to a ghost.

However, the egalitarian tendency which encouraged each man to be his own 'chief' could also make him in a sense his own priest. Ghosts often approached their descendants in dreams and other revelations, and pieces of bone or teeth might even find their way miraculously into someone's possession as a sign that a ghost had decided to form a relationship with him. Such personal revelations seem to have been particularly important for fighting powers, and warrior ghosts might even approach men to demand sacrifices and make them kill. Young men would receive powers for fighting and for stealing pigs for secret feasts, often from someone recently dead whom they were close to in life, including today Christian ancestors who have never been ritually 'raised' as ghosts. There are certain standard procedures associated with this kind of power, including keeping a magical talisman and the usual tabu on contact with women. Ghosts of the recent dead might be of little importance in themselves, but they could also intercede with more ancient and powerful ghosts.

Men who have experienced the power conferred by warrior ghosts say it made them troublesome and aggressive. This power was inherently dangerous and open to abuse, as shown in the extreme by the legendary 'cannibals' who would kill for the sake of eating human flesh. In this respect fighting power was often at odds with the interests of leaders whose influence depended on peace and prosperity. Although priests may have had some control over the official warriors authorised to serve their communities, there may not always have been much to choose between them and the men whose fights and thefts caused the trouble which warriors were expected to deal with.

But although such personal relationships with ghosts may have enabled young men to bypass the ritual system in their search for spiritual power, most probably resisted authority only until they began to gain it themselves as they married, matured and developed a vested interest in the political system. This pattern can be seen in the youth of Clement Maletege O'ogau of Manadodo, born about 1920, who received pig-stealing powers when the tooth of a ghost came to him while sleeping one night at a shrine. The ghost told him to make a stone shrine for the tooth and to sacrifice taro and the first pig he stole with his help. O'ogau also received great strength from pebbles implanted in his arms and legs by a priest. Over the years he says these powers enabled him to steal 190 pigs and to perform feats of strength and endurance which have become renowned throughout the district. But despite a rebellious youth, O'ogau later succeeded his father as a priest and later in life, as a Christian, he became a respected community leader and Local Court Justice.

MAGIC AND SORCERY

Under these circumstances, personal relationships with ghosts posed little real threat to the priestly control of spiritual power. Nor did many of the other minor sources of power in common use, which often depended on the properties of objects and substances used as charms and medicines. In particular, the bark and leaves of certain trees were used for various purposes, including remedies for illness but also for instance, love magic or protection from sorcery. Some people still make a speciality of accumulating and practicing herbal remedies, but the knowledge is inherited and carefully guarded, for it is said that if shared it loses its power. Although such charms and treatments may conveniently be called 'magic', this does not imply a very significant distinction from other religious activities, for people invoked ghosts to make their magic work, and it is often referred to as a kind of 'ghost' (*akalo*).

These personal powers co-existed with the priestly ritual system, as many of them do with the Christian churches when used as 'traditional medicine', blessed by God instead of by ghosts. But there were other powers which would have been subversive of the status quo, particularly methods of causing sickness and death by unseen secret means, which may be referred to as 'sorcery' (*kelema*, a term loosely applied to several techniques; Pijin *poison*). It is difficult to be certain about the role of such powers in the traditional social order. In some Melanesian societies similar powers were once regarded as legitimate means of social control, wielded on behalf of established political authority and only becoming subversive when used without this authority as political relationships changed under colonial rule (see Zelenietz 1981, Tonkinson 1981, Barker 1990d). In Kwara'ae, where priests could use the power of the ghosts to kill, it seems more likely that sorcery represented an alternative source of power used, as old stories tell, without authority or justification and secretly in the hope of avoiding retaliation. Of course, like all killings, opinions about justification depend on who has killed whom, but it was when someone acted on their own account without the backing of their community that they were most at risk of being killed in return. This was no doubt the kind of situation when sorcery was used, or at least suspected. Sorcery was probably regarded as an abuse of spiritual power, as much outside the ancestral ritual system as it is now outside the church.

The basic techniques of sorcery are common knowledge, as becomes apparent when accusations are made. One method is to invoke a ghost over an object which is thrown at the victim, who later dies. Others include placing a 'ghost' on a stick laid across a path to attack a passer by with sickness, or using leaves and bark to kill, as they are used to cure, and invoking a ghost to make them effective. Such substances may be added to a person's food or drink, or their discarded food may be put into contact with these things, or fed to a poisonous snake, itself a kind of 'ghost'. Attacks like these remain an ever-present danger and an explanation for sickness, particularly when other explanations fail, such as affliction by ghosts or diagnosis by a doctor. People feel especially at risk among strangers, and they credit peoples of other languages with special sorcery powers which Kwara'ae may obtain from them. But sorcery is also blamed on people closer to home, including relatives and neighbours said to be acting from envy or from simple and almost involuntary malice. Users of certain kinds of sorcery are said to practise it first on someone in their own family and their power grows and takes them over so that they are driven to kill by the ghost concerned. Besides accusations by the victim, who may be visited by the spirit of his killer before he dies, sorcerers may be identified through dreams, omens and divination, and by gloating or appearing happy at a death.

People try to deal with sorcery like other kinds of killing. In 1982 a boy dying of a mysterious illness accused a man who had admired the new house he was building of sorcerising him, apparently from envy, and when the accused was confronted by a group of 'chiefs' he confessed and paid compensation (*to'ato'a*) of ten 'red money'. In the past he might have been killed. The following year a married woman in a Kwai saltwater community who appeared from a series of dreams and omens to have killed one of her in-laws was expelled and left to find her own way home to her family in Lau.

But not all cases are so straightforward, especially when sorcery, or accusations of it, are used to further political disputes. A case in 'Ere'ere in 1979 illustrates the point, when a traditionist claimed that his adopted child had died from sorcery placed on a branch cut by another man to bar a piece of land. The accused, a Christian, had evidence that the child was killed by an ancestral ghost for a breach of tabu. A meeting of 'chiefs' judiciously agreed that the Christian's actions had inadvertantly enabled the ghost to kill the child and they made him give a nominal compensation payment. But this was only the latest incident in a series of quarrels between the men and their families. The accusers remained dissatisfied and soon afterwards a group of armed raiders from Kwaio robbed the Christian's village; then the police intervened and stopped what might have developed into a bloody feud.

DEALING WITH NEW CULTS

If sorcery could be dealt with like other types of killing, other challenges to the priestly control of spiritual power may have been less easy to dispose of. When unauthorised personal relationships with ghosts, ancestors or others, proved useful and 'true' for other people as well, cults could arise which competed for the congregations of the ancestral ghosts. This actually happened in Kwara'ae when the traditional ritual system was thrown into crisis during the colonial period. In earlier times the priestly establishment seems to have met such challenges by incorporating new sources of power into the existing ritual system under the authority of the ancestral ghosts.

This could explain why living creatures such as sharks, snakes, crocodiles and eagles which were regarded as 'ghosts' (not such a good translation for *akalo* in this case) were so often associated with ancestors, as their incarnations, agents or messengers or as 'ghosts' first adopted by them. As such, relationships with these creatures were inherited by clans and mediated by the same priests who dealt with their ancestral ghosts. It is as if the ancestral ritual system had absorbed useful sources of power which originated outside it. Of course this is impossible to prove, but the way Kwara'ae dealt with new sources of power can be illustrated by an interesting story about the ancient shrine of Siale, related by Johnson Rara of the Siale clan of 'Aenakwata.

A priest of Lobo, near Fiu in West Kwara'ae once dreamed where to find a 'ghost' in the Ta'ilalo river near 'Aoke. This was a stone in the shape of a bonito fish which had swum up from the sea, and it gave peace and prosperity, enabling people to make great feasts. Later the people of Lobo were all killed for inadvertantly causing a gale which destroyed their neighbours' villages, and Kwanagwailo, a man from Siale whose mother was from Lobo, took the stone from their deserted shrine. He wanted to stop his 'brothers' from constantly fighting, so he put it in the shrine at Siale to subdue the other ghosts, and the men who objected moved away and continued to sacrifice to these ghosts elsewhere. From then on the stone kept all the other ghosts at Siale quiet and maintained peace, and people came from all around to sacrifice to make their gardens grow well. The ghost who had this power, Ko'obili'adoe, was also introduced from elsewhere as the father of Kwanagwailo's wife, who herself brought to Siale the miraculous water supply used at the festivals there. Until the Siale shrine was finally abandoned the 'stone of fame' (*fau ni talo'a*) as it was known, was kept in a part of the shrine house adjoining that of the presiding ghost Ko'ongwaro and it made the festivals at Siale peaceful and successful.

All this happened about fourteen generations ago, but in explaining rituals performed at Siale within living memory it also shows how Kwara'ae understood their ritual organisation to operate by incorporating new ghosts with new powers. In the past new cults or sects were probably continually developing, as among Kwara'ae Christians at present, and Rara himself recognised in the story of the stone of fame the same motives which eventually led Kwara'ae to escape from their ghosts by adopting Christianity.

But Christianity proved too powerful to be absorbed into the traditional ritual system in this way. As part of the political transformation of colonialism, this new cult of the 'European ghost' (*akalo ara'ikwao*) finally broke the power of the Kwara'ae ghosts and their priests, despite attempts first to suppress it and then to adapt and incorporate its perceived benefits and powers into an indigenous ritual system. The struggle between Christianity and the ghosts began at the end of the nineteenth century and is still not concluded to this day. Indeed, it may never be finally resolved for it goes on within Christianity itself, continuing in new form the ancient conflict between those who claim to mediate spiritual relationships and those who seek to resist their authority. The colonisation of Solomon Islands gave this conflict a new dimension and a new urgency within the struggle for political and spiritual control of Kwara'ae, in which the victory of Christianity has been the disintegration of the traditional social order of the ancestral ghosts.

MAP 3   *Kwara'ae, showing some of the places mentioned in this book.*

CONTINUE MAP 2 (RIGHT SIDE OF DOUBLE PAGE SPREAD)

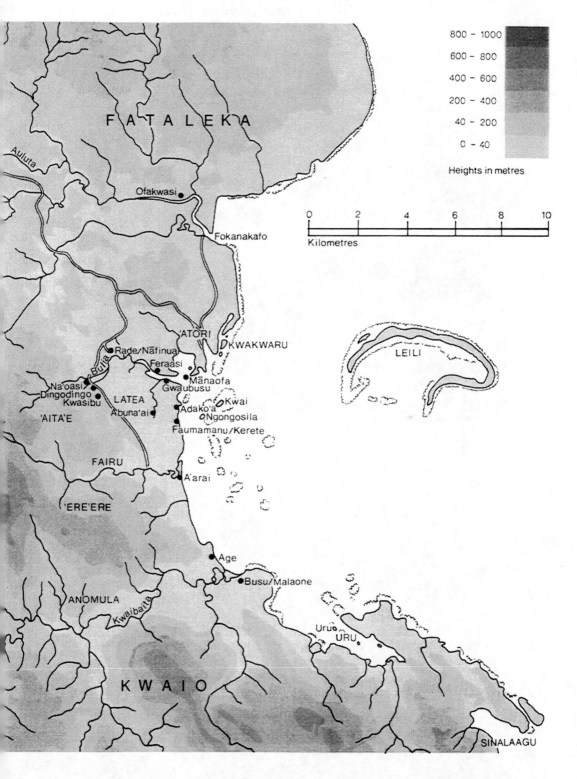

PLATE 14   *The east coast of Kwara'ae viewed from the island of Ngongosila, one of the saltwater communities who first encountered the Europeans. (Photo by Ben Burt, 1979)*

CHAPTER FOUR

Going Overseas (1870s to 1890s)

Although Kwara'ae history goes back twenty or thiry gener-
ations, by their own reckoning, their present understanding of their ancient way
of life has been shaped by four or five generations of increasingly rapid social
change. It is now a hundred and twenty years since Kwara'ae first began to be
drawn into the economic and political systems of the world beyond the Solomons
and during that time they have been continually adjusting to new pressures and
opportunities while maintaining a continuity with their past.

When the expanding empires of Europe first began to reach out to the
Pacific islands, Malaitans had no way of knowing what this meant for their own
way of life. Their first encounters with Europeans were traumatic, but they soon
learnt enough to safeguard their own interests. For the first thirty or forty years
Kwara'ae, like other Malaitans, gained what they wanted from the colonial
system as migrant labourers on overseas plantations without sacrificing their
political independence at home. Nonetheless they became dependent on the
colonial economy and opened themselves to the powerful challenges of European
culture and religion. In the process, foundations were laid for the eventual
subjugation of Kwara'ae and the other peoples of Malaita and Solomon Islands
by the political and economic power of the British, and by the spiritual power of
Christianity.

Until the 19th century, Kwara'ae geographical horizons extended no
further than the neighbouring islands. The saltwater people travelled by sea
around the coasts of Malaita and had relatives in distant parts of the island and
beyond. Some visited and received visitors from Gela, Guadalcanal and Makira.
They may even have suffered occasional headhunting raids from Western
Solomons (Zelenietz 1979:95), and in Kwai they still remember ancient feuds
with the people of Bogotu on Isabel. The Kwara'ae bush people would have
known of these places too, even if few of them ever ventured into a canoe, and
they understood that their first ancestors had come from a distant land via Gao on
Isabel and Guadalcanal, which can be seen from the Kwara'ae hills on a clear day.
But Malaita was the focus of their world, and even here it was unsafe to travel far
beyond the homes of relatives within Kwara'ae and the neighbouring language
groups of Kwaio and Fataleka.

Then ships began to appear off the coasts. As Kwara'ae recall, their
ancestors were unsure at first just what these strange objects might be; they called

them *baekobaeko*, as if they were predatory creatures like sharks or crocodiles, or *gwa'i mae'a*, meaning an epidemic of deadly sickness (similar to the interpretation of other Malaitans; see de Coppet 1977:23). When the ships came closer they were surprised to see strange people on the decks whom they came to know as 'whitemen' (*ara'ikwao*).

THE FIRST SHIPS

The first European ships to visit Solomon Islands belonged to the Spanish expedition of Mendaña, which called at 'Are'are in South Malaita in 1586, but of these and later explorers who passed by Malaita no memory remains in Kwara'ae. From the 1820s a few whaling ships visited the coasts of North Malaita, but their regular ports of call were at Makira, Sikiana and the Western Solomons (Bennett 1987:24–33). It was in these places that Solomon Islanders first began to trade with Europeans, exchanging provisions and sometimes working on the ships to obtain manufactured goods. By the 1840s, especially in the Western Solomons, they were also supplying turtleshell, pearlshell and *beche-de-mer* to a few European traders who were settling amongst them. But during the first fifty years of regular European presence in the Solomons, while other islanders were beginning to be drawn into the colonial economy of the Pacific, Malaitans remained uninvolved. A few ships were wrecked and crewmen captured or stranded around the Malaita coasts and in 1866 the Anglican Melanesian Mission ship *Southern Cross* made its first contact with Malaitans at Sa'a in the south (Corris 1973:7–15, Hilliard 1978:15,48). But in Kwai the earliest European visits which can be dated with any certainty were in the 1870s. Until then, although people must have seen ships and heard rumours of European activities elsewhere, the main impact of any ships that actually reached their shores may well have been the epidemics of foreign diseases for which they came to be remembered and named.

Many stories are still told in Kwai and other parts of Malaita of contacts and especially of conflicts with European visitors after this time, but it is not always easy to relate them to European chronology. While people may be able to place the characters of their stories a certain number of generations ago, they do not necessarily use generations to mark historical phases, such as the period when Malaitan culture was formed or when the first ships arrived. Hence the story of an early ship may even be assigned to the time before Malaitans had canoes, when they travelled on rafts propelled by sharks. When such stories can be compared with contemporary European writings they sometimes appear to confuse separate incidents or to exaggerate the achievements of local people, and the names of visiting ships, if they were ever known, have long been forgotten. All this is hardly surprising for stories which have been passed down via at least three or four people over a period of a hundred years. But the European version of events also has to be treated with caution, and second-hand accounts in particular are often contradicted by first hand reports. The most accurate accounts are no doubt those recorded from eyewitnesses in British naval and other official reports, but of course they cannot give the Malaitan perspective on the events. This has to be deduced mostly from Malaitans' own present day accounts, taken in the context of their history and culture in more recent and better documented times.

The earliest ships which Kwara'ae remember today confirmed any misgivings they already had about Europeans. According to Nakisi of Mānadari, probably the oldest Kwara'ae man alive in 1984, the 'first ship' came to the west coast and captured some Langalanga men, one of whom was called Idufau. Their people thought they had been killed and offered a reward to anyone who could recover their bones, but three years later they came back in another ship with boxes of marvellous new trade goods and this time others were willing to go away with the ship. According to a Langalanga story of what was probably the same event, the first ship dropped weights into the canoe of six Langalanga men who were fishing off Alite, pulled them from the water and took them to Fiji (Cooper 1970:37).

It was probably shortly afterwards that a similar thing happened at Kwai. It is said that a saltwater man called Misuta from Kwakwaru on the north coast of Kwai Harbour and others were fishing for bonito in a canoe near Leili Island when a ship appeared. Out of curiosity at the strange sight they went close enough for the crew to chase them in a boat, capture them and carry them off. Their people sacrificed pigs, asking the ghosts to reveal what had happened to them, and decided they must be dead. Then eventually the ship brought Misuta back. As Andrew Gwa'italafa tells the story:

> When Misuta landed back at Kwakwaru, my word, people were very very surprised. Then Misuta began to talk about the white man, ... and our people saw him with his wealth and all the things he came back with. So the story spread up into the bush, via the market, of how Misuta had come back wearing a jacket and trousers and talking in a different language and things like that, wearing big boots and everything.

When the next ship arrived, so the story goes, Misuta went to meet it and it had no difficulty gaining volunteers to travel overseas.

THE BEGINNING OF THE LABOUR TRADE

The story of Misuta accurately conveys how, in the early 1870s, Kwara'ae first became involved as labour migrants in the European colonial economy, as they have continued to be ever since. It was at this time that labour recruiters supplying the plantations of Fiji and Queenland began to extend their search for workers from Vanuatu to Solomon Islands. The early history of this 'labour trade' in the Solomons, popularly known as 'blackbirding', has been painstakingly compiled by historians such as Corris (1973), Scarr (1973) and Moore (1982, 1985) from documentary sources and oral history. Their research provides the broader historical background to local events in Kwai.

Recruiting ships began to visit the Solomons in 1870 and the first men were taken from Malaita in 1871. The 'first ships' remembered in Kwara'ae today were among the three or four which kidnapped men around the coasts of Malaita in that year. They included the *Isabella* from Queensland, which called at Langalanga and was no doubt the source of the stories told there (Moore 1985:36,38), and the *Ellen* from Fiji (Corris 1973:26). But the only ship which can be definitely identified as calling at Kwai in 1871 was the schooner *Nukulau* from Fiji. Its voyage was later investigated by the British Consul in Fiji as part of one of the most notorious scandals of the Pacific labour trade (Great Britain 1873), and many years later some of its captives from Kwai told their own story to a Fijian government clerk (Brewster 1937:230–236) and to Woodford, the first Resident Commissioner of Solomon Islands (Woodford 1901).

The *Nukulau* left Fiji in June 1871 on its second voyage to the Solomons, having previously kidnapped men in the central Solomons. This time it captured men at Malau (Three Sisters) and then sailed up the east coast of Malaita, taking more at Sa'a in South Malaita and at Aio and Sinalaagu in Kwaio. From Sinalaagu it came on to Leili Island, where thirty men in three canoes approached the ship. Two canoes came close and the ship's crew threw down pieces of iron, wrecking the canoes and killing one man. The rest swam to the third canoe but as it was taking them to shore the ship's crew shot and killed three of them, then the ship ran the canoe down and the crew pulled twenty-five of them out of the water into the ship's boats and tied them up. The people of Ngongosila Island still recall that the captives included Amasia of Ngongosila and Lau'a of Uru (but not Misuta of Kwakwaru). As the *Nukulau* sailed on it captured more men by similar methods at Dai Island, at Isabel and in the Western Solomons, before returning to Fiji in August with eighty-nine captive Solomon Islanders on board. To escape the attentions of the British Consul on Levuka, the captives were landed on Viti Levu where some were sent to plantations on the Rewa River.

But sixty were sold to a planter on Taviniu Island for £10 each and in December they were put on board the schooner *Peri* to be shipped there. These included Amasia, Lau'a and others, if not all, of the men from Kwai. They were still unaware of the reasons for their captivity and suspected that they were going to be eaten by the Europeans. Once at sea again and growing desperate at their ill treatment, they killed the crew of the *Peri* and threw them overboard. Then, unable to control the ship, they drifted helplessly and as food ran out the Kwai men began to eat the remaining prisoners. After five weeks, when all but fourteen of them had been eaten or had died from starvation, the *Peri* was found off the coast of Queensland by a British warship. Eventually the survivors were taken back to Fiji where they remained until Amasia and Lau'a managed to return to their homes thirty years later (Great Britain 1873:105–108, 115, 213–220, Beattie 1906:44, SCL Aug. 1900:19,20, Brewster 1937:230–236).[1]

By 1871 one seaman working in the trade estimated there to be

> ... about forty sail of vessels in the Pacific Ocean labour trade, kidnapping and blackbirding for the various plantations of Fiji, Taiti [sic], Queensland, Tana [in Vanuatu], and Noumea, New Caledonia. (Great Britain 1873:134)

Most of the Malaitans captured in 1871 would have gone to Fiji, although at least six arrived in Queensland aboard the *Isabella* (Great Britain 1873:123, Moore 1985:200). In the years that followed some Solomon Islanders went also to Samoa and New Caledonia, but most went to Fiji and Queensland. Like the men captured at Langalanga and Kwai, most of the early recruits from Malaita were saltwater people. But although they were taken by force during the first few years, people in Kwai agree that once some of them had returned home safely, rich in exotic European goods, others were eager to follow them to the land of the whitemen. By the 1880s men from the bush were recruiting too. Malaita and Guadalcanal were becoming the main source of migrant labour in the Solomons, since people there had less opportunity than on other islands for alternative forms of trade. Queensland had become their most popular destination because the wages and conditions were better and more of the recruits eventually returned home (Corris 1973:29–34, 38–41, Moore 1982:63).

As the trade developed and the recruiters became familiar with the Malaita coasts, they began to call regularly at certain 'passages'; points where the coasts were most accessible both to the ships and to large numbers of local people. In the early years of the trade the passage at Kwai was generally known to Europeans as Kwakwaru, after the district of the dominant saltwater group of the time who lived around the coast to the north of the saltwater islands of Kwai and Ngongosila. Ships would call here on their way between Sinalaagu and Uru in Kwaio and Atā and Lau Lagoon to the north.

With the recruiting ships came the warships of the British Royal Navy, attempting to regulate the trade. It was the conflicts caused by the labour trade which first encouraged the British colonial authorities to extend their influence to the Solomons, both to protect the interests of British subjects and to deal with their offences against the islanders. The kidnapping of labourers had already become a scandal in Vanuatu and by the time it began in Solomon Islands the colonial authorities in Queensland and Fiji were beginning to take steps to end the more obvious offences. Between 1870 and 1874 regulations were introduced and

Government Agents appointed to supervise recruiting on the ships (Corris 1973:27–29). Some Agents were more effective than others, but British authority beyond the colonial territories themselves depended ultimately on the navy, whose control over European activities was limited by legal as well as practical constraints. But in any case, the development of voluntary recruiting soon made kidnapping unnecessary and before long the islanders had also learnt enough about the trade to protect themselves. Soon the recruiters were on the defensive as the islanders began to attack them and their ships for vengeance and plunder. In return the navy was authorised to retaliate by attacking islanders and since those responsible could seldom be caught this usually involved shelling or burning villages (Belshaw 1950:50–51). The navy thus became identified with other European interests in opposition to the islanders, but its power was insufficient to give the recruiters very much protection around Malaita. Patrols were infrequent, incapable of penetrating into the bush and poorly informed about the geography of the islands.

PLATE 15   *The navy and the labour trade. The British man-of-war* H.M.S. Rosario *overhauls the recruiting schooner* Meg Merilies, *bound from Vanuatu to Fiji in 1871. This ship continued in the labour trade for many years, and its boat's crew was attacked at Kwai in 1881. (Engraving from Markham 1873: 84)*

FIGHTING AND TRADING

So it was that while Malaitans were travelling abroad to work for Europeans, they also found themselves in a military confrontation with them at home which lasted more than forty years, until the British eventually gained political control over their island. Of all the islands of the Solomons, Malaita proved the most dangerous to Europeans. Attacks on labour recruiters became a regular occurrence, and some of the most successful were in and around Kwai.

The story of one such attack is told by Andrew So'ai of Kwai Island, a descendant of the men involved. A few days after one ship had recruited some people from Leili Island and moved on, another came up the coast from Uru to Kwakwaru. Here it lured aboard some Kwakwaru and Kwai Island men with offers of trade goods, seized them, bound them and shut them in the forecastle. Sending a boat to the shore, the recruiters tried to capture Farobo of 'Aita'e, the old father-in-law of the previous captives, but in the struggle Farobo and two white men were shot. Some of the captives in the ship, with the help of their ghosts, got free and began to cut a hole in the side of the ship, which took on water and sailed for safety to Leili, where it sank. The captives broke out, overpowered the white men and escaped to the island with four of them. Despite protests from a man called Amasia, they killed and ate the white men and fed their heads as a sacrifice to the shark-ghost who had saved them.

On another occasion a ship is said to have been attacked and burned at the mouth of the inlet to the Bulia river. According to Timi Ko'oliu of Sasadili, whose 'grandfathers' took part in the attack, they were led by Diko of 'Atori, an important saltwater warrior leader influential in the Kwakwaru area. Ko'oliu recalls the common story that when the European crew were eaten their skin tasted of the soap they washed with. Yet another ship is said to have been sunk by bush men of Anomula at Talaiwalo reef south of Ngongosila. There seem to be no documentary sources which corroborate these stories, but there is good reason to believe that a number of ships may have been attacked or destroyed in the Solomons without being accounted for by Europeans at the time.[2]

The first Malaitan ship attack of which there are detailed records was in 1880. In September that year the schooner *Borealis*, recruiting from Fiji, came up from South Malaita and anchored near Uru Island. While the captain was away with the boats seeking recruits on the mainland, a large number of local men who had come on board to trade took the crew by surprise and killed five of them in a pre-planned attack. According to Keesing's Kwaio informants, the attackers were led by Maeasuaa of Uru Island. They looted the ship and fought off the returning boats, which made for North Malaita and returned two days later with three other recruiting ships. The recruiters recovered the *Borealis*, attacked Uru

Island and some mainland villages nearby and returned to Fiji with four prisoners (Western Pacific 1880, Great Britain 1881:525, Keesing 1986).

1880 was a bad year for Europeans in the Solomons, and in December the British warship *HMS Emerald* was sent from Sydney to investigate five attacks on ships crews in various islands. From Gela, where six crewmen of the warship *HMS Sandfly* had been killed in October, the *Emerald* sailed for Malaita and arrived at Kwakwaru. There Captain Maxwell met a number of local men, some of whom "were returned Queensland labourers and spoke English", and was told:

> ... that after the other schooners had left, the master of a Queensland labour vessel lying at this anchorage, a man called Taylor, had assembled a force of Quah-quahroo [ie. Kwakwaru or Kwai] men in addition to his own crew, and had attacked the island, driven the natives off, and had burnt the village, cut down all the cocoa-nut trees, and ruined it; that the natives of the island had been obliged to desert it and were scattered about the mainland. (Great Britain 1881:525)

On visiting Uru himself, Maxwell found that "the whole place was a scene of desolation" and decided that "there was absolutely nothing left for me to do".[3]

The lack of precautions taken by the *Borealis* could imply that the recruiters had heard of no previous attacks on ships around Malaita. But the captain should hardly have been surprised since he had already kidnapped men in the northwest of Malaita as captain of the *Ellen* in 1871 (Great Britain 1873:130, Western Pacific 1880:4, Moore 1982:60). Even if this was not the first attack on a ship in this area, it was probably Malaitans' first experience of European retaliation. And although the *Emerald* took no action against them, rumours of how it had burned and shelled villages on Gela in retaliation for the *Sandfly* attack would have provided the saltwater people of Kwai and Uru with further evidence, if it were needed, of their vulnerability to European military power. As Maxwell admitted, "I regret that my whole voyage in these islands has been one of apparently ruthless destruction" (Great Britain 1881:432).

However, the villages that suffered were all on or near the coasts. The people of Kwai would have realised, as Maxwell himself discovered, that it was virtually impossible for Europeans to penetrate any distance into the bush. His comments from the Western Solomons applied equally to Malaita and described the problems which Europeans were to face in the Solomons for many years to come.

> No one who has not tried it can have any idea of the labour of marching through the bush and reaching the villages situated even a short distance from the beach in these islands; the bush is so dense that it is most difficult to find one's way, and even the paths, when struck, are so obscure, and lead through marshes, over rocks and hills, and down into gullies in a way that takes all a white man's powers to travel along them. The heat is excessive and makes the work for men carrying

> rifles, ammunition, water bottles &c., most trying. As for hunting natives in the
> bush, it is wholly impossible: one cannot see more than a few yards round one,
> sometimes not a few feet ... (Great Britain 1881:531)

Such experiences proved to be one of Malaita's most effective defences against colonial domination, which only began to fail thirty or forty years later when local people were themselves induced to guide Europeans into the bush. So the devastation of Uru in 1880 was hardly likely to intimidate the bush men of East Kwara'ae. More suprisingly perhaps, it seems to have had little effect on the saltwater people either.

The next year, in May 1881, the Government Agent of the *Meg Merilies* reported an attack on one of the ship's boats by "the people of Eri-Eri ['Ere'ere] and Alasi [on the Kwaio coast north of Uru]". This is the earliest European record of some of the fiercest opponents of colonialism in the East Kwara'ae bush, for the people of 'Ere'ere have resisted Europeans and their works ever since, including Christianity, government and, latterly, anthropology. Captain Jones of the *Meg Merilies* had taken the boat, without the precaution of a second one in support, "to a river opposite Nongasila Island", probably the A'arai river which flows down from 'Ere'ere. Here four men agreed to recruit, but as the boat was leaving others called it back to shore for one more recruit and then "attacked the crew with tomahawks and spears", spearing Jones and wounding a Melanesian crewman. The crew fired on them, killing and wounding several, and the boat escaped. A similar attack had apparently been attempted there on the boats of the *Au Revoir* only the day before (Great Britain 1883:53–54).

But of all the attacks at Kwai which were documented at the time, the most successful was carried out by saltwater people less than a year and a half after the burning of Uru Island. This was the sinking of the brig *Janet Stewart* while at anchor off Leili Island in February 1882. Jack Mae of Ngongosila tells a story of this attack, which he says was was organised by Mae'ela of Ngongosila in retaliation for previous kidnappings by recruiters (although others give the credit to Maetalau of Leili). Mae'ela took a group of men first to Leili, where they enlisted others, and they went on board the ship with the plan that two men would mark out each white man. When the word was given they killed them all and smashed and looted the ship. It sank near Leili, where its remains could still be seen in Mae's time. The ship's boat had gone to Uru seeking recruits and when it returned they killed them too. The attackers did not know what to do with much of what they found on the ship, mistaking biscuits for pieces of wood and rice for white sand. This last incident seems rather improbable after ten years of labour migration and no doubt belongs to an earlier event, understandably confused in oral history a century old. But people today enjoy recounting the naivety of their ancestors, including the even less probable story of how they once tried to eat the boots of one of their white victims.

But there were survivors from this attack whose own accounts are a useful reminder of how stories can change when they are retold over several generations. Captain Thomas was away with two of the ship's boats following news of would-be recruits when the men came on board the *Janet Stewart*, maybe two or three hundred of them, offering to trade recruits and food. They took the crew by surprise and killed everyone they could find, including the Government Agent, four other white men and maybe also thirty-five recruits from South Malaita. When the attackers saw the boats returning from what had apparently been a false errand, they withdrew to an island. The captain found the ship on fire with mutilated bodies all over the decks and one crewman who had hidden and survived to tell the tale. They escaped in the boats and left the *Janet Stewart* to burn and sink (Great Britain 1882, Rannie 1912:70–71, Wawn 1893:244, Corris 1973:33).[4]

Once again the British navy came to investigate and in June the same year a warship arrived off Leili. On landing at Ngongosila Captain Dale found that everyone had already left, taking their valuables but leaving evidence of goods looted from the *Janet Stewart*. Unable to contact anyone on the mainland either, he "very reluctantly" destroyed the houses and some of the coconut palms on Ngongosila (Great Britain 1882). After this the saltwater people of Kwai seem to have decided that attacking Europeans was not worth the trouble it caused them. There were several more attacks on recruiters at Kwai during the next thirty years, but henceforth the attackers seem to have been bush men, who could retreat to safety in their forested hills.

Attacks on Europeans were probably carried out on much the same terms that Malaitans feuded among themselves. Although they took the opportunity to plunder the ships and evidently planned attacks for this purpose, they were also seeking to pay back the deaths, real or suspected, of men who had not returned from the plantations. As the stories from Kwai tell, the first attacks were probably in retaliation for kidnapping, but however men were recruited and whoever had caused their deaths, Europeans were held responsible as a group, as a group of Malaitans would have been. Hence from time to time rewards were offered for the deaths of Europeans; in 1895 eight thousand porpoise teeth were said to be on offer at Kwai (Corris 1973:42). The mobility of the saltwater people meant that these rewards could be collected anywhere along the coast and men from various places would co-operate in planning attacks on the ships. In 1888 the Government Agent of the *Ariel* was killed at Mānaoba in North Malaita to collect a reward offered as far away as Sinalaagu in Kwaio (Cromar 1935:264–266, 292–293). As a result sensible recruiters were constantly on their guard. Since most Malaitans were beyond the reach of naval patrols, the British authorities expected recruiters to protect themselves and criticised ships such as the *Borealis*, the *Meg Merilies* and the *Janet Stewart* for inviting attack by neglecting standard precautions. These included restricting the number of islanders allowed on board ship, posting armed guards during trading and covering a boat on the beach with a second boat offshore (Great Britain 1882, 1883:455,466).

But for all the hostility and resentment it caused, both recruiters and Malaitans came to depend on the trade. As Malaita became the main supplier of labour of all the islands in the Solomons its men gained a high reputation as strong and efficient workers, and some of the goods they received in return soon became necessities. By the 1880s recruiting on more or less amicable terms according to agreed procedures was more usual than either kidnapping recruits or attacking recruiters. Certain saltwater men became more or less reliable agents or intermediaries for the recruiters, most notably the famous Lau leader Kwaisulia. A man from Kwai Island called Taibo (or Taibu) worked regularly for the recruiter Cromer in the 1880s, travelling up and down the coast (Cromar 1935 Ch12). Douglas Rannie, Government Agent on the *Flora*, wrote a detailed account of a visit to Kwai in 1886 which shows how recruiting was conducted

PLATE 16   *Labour recruiting from a ship's boat. Although this photograph on the West coast of Malaita was taken in 1917, the scene is just as described during the previous twenty or thirty years (compare drawings by the 19th century recruiter William Wawn: Wawn 1893 frontispiece and page 11) (Photo by Martin Johnson, from the Martin and Osa Johnson Safari Museum, Chanute, Kansas)*

under armed truce when both parties had more to gain from trade than violence. The people of Fokanakafo on the border with Fataleka sent news of the ship up into the bush:

> Taking our English-speaking visitors with us the next day we went with the boats as arranged to the Quakwaroo River, [possibly the Bulia creek just south of Kwakwaru] and were met by a large crowd of natives — men, women, and children — and received a friendly welcome. ... All the men were armed with bows and arrows, spears, clubs, and the ubiquitous long-handled tomahawk. ... After a long confab half a dozen young fellows recruited; and in return for doing so each received a half-case of tobacco, an axe, a tomahawk, and a twelve-inch knife, together with a miscellaneous lot of pipes, beads, paint, jews' harps, matches, a sun-glass, as well as a small hand-mirror, all of which they handed over to their friends. (Rannie 1912:180–181)

The presence of women and children was an assurance of peaceful intent, but this was a time as troublesome as any on Malaita. A reward for the deaths of Europeans was on offer at Mānakwai south along the coast and the *Flora* was anchored where "The charred and blackened ribs of the *Janet Stewart* lying there in sight were silent proof of the need for constant vigilance". Only two days before, the Government Agent and some of the crew of the *Young Dick* had been killed by Kwaio at Sinalaagu just along the coast, and the following day Rannie himself had been fired upon while visiting the same place. The day after his visit to Kwakwaru thirty Kwaio men arrived to recruit, wishing to leave Malaita for fear of naval retaliation for their part in the attack on the *Young Dick* (Great Britain 1887, Rannie 1912:178–182, Keesing 1986, Woodford 1890:16).

The bush men of Kwai continued to attack recruiters during the 1890s, but the saltwater people, apparently unwilling to risk further retaliation, now began to co-operate with the Europeans and pursue their own grudges against the bush people instead. In August 1891 the boats of the *Sybil*, guided by Taibu of Kwai Island, were ambushed and fired upon by an estimated seventy guns when invited to recruit up the 'Bussu River', evidently the Kwaibaita which forms the Kwara'ae-Kwaio border. Four of the crew were wounded, European and Melanesian, but they shot three of their attackers. The man held responsible was Gala, a Kwaio bush man who was apparently seeking to return the death of a relative in Queensland. Two months later in October the warship *HMS Royalist* called on tour and, with guidance from Taibu, Captain Davies fired some shells at Gala's village in the hills above the Kwaibaita (Great Britain 1891:10,12,37).

A few years later, undeterred by this shelling only few miles down the coast, a group of Kwara'ae tried a similar ambush, apparently still trying to return the same death which had led to Gala's attack in 1891. Rumours of their plans were passed by saltwater people to recruiters and thence to the British authorities. The *Royalist* arrived to investigate in August 1894, only to receive news from 'Gooreah' of Kwai Island that the people of 'Aita'e had attacked the boats of the *Para* about six weeks before (Great Britain 1894:7,17–18). Samuel Alasa'a, a child at the time, recalls that his 'fathers' Sinamu of 'Aita'e and La'ugere from Latea attacked the boats as they came to recruit up the inlet of the Bulia river, firing at them but missing. Commander Goodrich of the *Royalist* found the saltwater people unwilling to guide his men to 'Aita'e, about two hours journey inland, so he fired thirty shells into the bush under the enthusiastic direction of the Kwai Island people. According to Alasa'a they were actually firing at smoke from gardens and no-one was hurt (but Goodrich's report does not confirm Alasa'a's story that he later apologised to Sinamu and La'ugere for the damage).

According to Goodrich,

> The bush tribes living at the back of this part of Malaita are undoubtably the most troublesome in the whole group [ie. Solomon Islands], but recruits are plentiful, so labour ships will go there; in this particular case I think the show of force should have some real effect, as no man-of-war had been to Kwai for many years; indeed, the natives could not tell me how many. (Great Britain 1894:7)

But he was underestimating the warriors of East Kwara'ae, as a knowledge of the *Royalist's* last visit might have told him, and it was almost another thirty years before they finally acknowledged British authority.

CHANGES AT HOME

Malaitans' occasional hostility to Europeans does not necessarily imply opposition to the labour trade itself, which continued to be as valuable to them as it was to the recruiters. Malaitans had various reasons for wishing to recruit. Some were fugitives or exiles fleeing trouble at home for whom a period abroad or permanent emigration offered an alternative to refuge in other potentially hostile districts. One of the best known Queensland labourers of East Kwara'ae, Fiuloa of Ubasi, had caused so much trouble for his family by stealing and other misdeeds that his 'brothers' were threatening to give him to some other clan to kill. Instead they gave him to a ship in exchange for two pigs and he spent ten or twenty years in Queensland. But most men probably recruited from a positive desire to work abroad, as they and their communities became dependent on the goods obtained for their labour. Almost all recruits were men, mostly young, and a period in Queensland or Fiji seems also to have become a chance for adventure before they settled down to the responsibilities of family life (Corris 1973: 46,47,53). But apart from the interests of the recruits themselves, the effect upon their home communities must also have been considerable. Unfortunately the limitations of 19th century records and the anecdotal nature of Kwara'ae oral history makes an assessment of the changes which occurred largely a matter of deduction or sometimes speculation.

We can be fairly sure that the labourers' earnings, mostly brought home in goods rather than cash which had a limited exchange value at home, were used like traditional wealth to establish their position in their communities rather than to enhance their own material standard of living. As with cash today, trade goods could be exchanged directly for traditional wealth according to recognised equivalences of value. But as a rule most goods probably became gifts to senior relatives, who were thus induced to support labour migration and to accept the labourers back into the community on their return (Corris 1973:113–114). Indeed, 'fathers' usually expected substantial gifts to allow their 'sons' to recruit in the first place (Corris 1973:55); "they paid for them with tobacco, axes and knives" as Timi Ko'oliu recalls, just as Rannie described. Recruiters understood such gifts to be essential if they were not to be accused of stealing the recruits (Great Britain 1883:449). By giving away most of their earnings, returned labourers built up the credit needed to gain help with bridewealth, restitution and other essential payments and expenses in the future. Trade goods thus substituted for the gifts and services they would have provided to their seniors if they had remained at home, and were accordingly later returned as goods of traditional value such as shell money and pigs as and when these things were required.

This much can reasonably be deduced from the practices followed today, when young men still pay bridewealth mainly in shell money rather than in the cash or manufactured goods which they use to help relatives on return from wage labour overseas. In the 19th century the fact that the labour trade gave young men access to new sources of wealth which were beyond the control of their seniors must have challenged the authority of the senior men and caused a certain amount of political disruption. No doubt elders compared the self-assertion of the young with the old days when their authority would have been respected as it should. However, the fact that such complaints can still be made today after more than a century of labour migration implies that the political system was actually adapted with some success to maintain the authority of senior men. It was not until the 20th century that the power of the priests, warriors and other political leaders was seriously challenged.

The various luxury goods which Rannie described on his visit to Kwakwaru were no doubt in great demand, especially tobacco, and they were typical of the trade at that time. But the goods which had most impact on the Malaitan way of life were steel tools and guns. By the time of Rannie's account, guns had been prohibited as trade goods for the Fiji and Queensland trade, but until 1884 they were both the most acceptable presents during recruiting and the prized possessions of returning labourers. After that time labourers still managed to smuggle guns and ammunition into Malaita under false bottoms in their boxes (Corris 1973:37,111,112). Some recruiters also continued to supply them and Mahaffy, a government officer visiting Malaita in 1902, was "positive that almost all Labour Ships offend" (Mahaffy 1902), although this was hotly denied by the Queensland immigration authorities (Immigration Agent 1903).

The importance of these weapons was also debated. Mahaffy (1902) warned of "An irresponsible savage armed with an excellent Winchester, which he well knows how to keep and how to use, numbered as he is in Mala[ita] by the thousand ...", while the immigration officer, repeating a common and probably prejudiced European opinion, retorted that "... an islander does not know how to keep a rifle" and "... does not know how to shoot straight with it" (Immigration Agent 1903). It has generally been assumed that guns increased the level of killing among Malaitans and changed the pattern of feuding (Ivens 1930:192, Keesing & Corris 1980:116–117), although to judge from stories of earlier times Kwara'ae were quite capable of killing people in large numbers with traditional weapons. Nonetheless, Malaitans prized their guns and the British authorities regarded them as a serious threat and took considerable trouble to stop both guns and ammunition being imported, with only limited success. The confiscation of guns later became an important feature of their programme to establish political control of Malaita and guns were so abundant that on one day in 1928 1,077 were handed in at the government station in West Kwara'ae (SCL 1928:62–63).

Nor is there direct evidence for the effects of steel axes and knives in Malaita during the 19th century, although their impact can be deduced. Studies from New Guinea indicate that steel tools may reduce the time needed to clear forest to a half or even a quarter of that taken with stone tools, depending on various circumstances (see Golson n.d.:53 for a review of these studies). In Kwara'ae the greater efficiency of steel tools is still recognised in the convention that land rights were established by clearing virgin forest using stone adzes as distinct from steel. This efficiency may have compensated for the loss of men's labour to the plantations, since steel axes are primarily men's tools, used for clearing gardens and house building. For much women's work such as planting, harvesting and preparing food the usual tools were and still are digging sticks and shell knives.[5] Steel tools would have enabled people to increase overall agricultural production, as old people still recalled up to the 1930s (Deck/Hogbin 1934–5). Any food surplus may well have increased the scale of feasting and ceremonial payments, enhancing the political influence of priests and other 'important men'. This may also have encouraged greater production of shell money, and could account for the Kwara'ae belief that it is a new medium for bridewealth, which was formerly given in utilitarian objects (Deck/Hogbin 1934–5:243).

The other important benefit of the labour trade was the new crops which the labourers brought back with them, making agriculture more diverse and reliable. Of these, sweet potatoes eventually became the main staple of Malaita. Samuel Alasa'a recalls his 'fathers' returning from Queensland and Fiji bringing food plants such as sweet potatoes, 'red tapioca' the 'short banana' and the 'big red chicken'. As he explains, the new foods saved people from relying on a famine diet of wild yams and sago pith when the taro crops failed.

MALAITANS ABROAD

These economic and political developments were only the most immediate effects of a deeper change in the relationship between Malaitans and the wider world. The personal experiences of the labourers themselves in Fiji and especially in Queensland had long term implications for Malaitan political and religious development. Since the end of the long-distance labour trade in the early 20th century, few people have had similar opportunities to observe European society or to mix so freely with Melanesians from beyond the Solomons.

Of the two places, Fiji was the easiest to adapt to since the Solomon Islanders spent much of their time among the indigenous Fijians. So many learnt to speak Fijian that at one time it was even considered as a possible official language for the Solomons under the British Protectorate (Ivens 1930:44). Like Amasia and Lau'a, the survivors of the *Peri*, some of the labourers also married Fijian women. Those who returned brought with them Fijian practices such as kava drinking, which continued until at least the 1930s in West Kwara'ae (SCL 1926:139), outrigger canoes, since largely fallen from use, and the new food-plants which are still grown. In fact many men seem to have made a point of living like Fijians when they returned to Malaita.

Queensland was less familiar. Ramonia of Ubasi told his grandson Andrew Gwa'italafa of his surprise at seeing the railways, the steam engines and the great sugar mills. Coming from Malaita at a time when European culture was represented by little more than visiting ships and their crews, the labourers' experiences of the bustling towns they visited on their days off must have been quite traumatic. In Queensland, more than in Fiji, the labourers had to become accustomed to the English language. Ramonia described how he learnt to use tools from a European overseer who gestured and made him repeat English words as he worked. But the 'English' in which the labourers became most proficient was a pidgin which originated in inter-island Pacific trade in the mid 19th century. This developed, with much Malaitan influence, into the language of the Queensland plantations and eventually into the Pijin which is now the lingua franca of Solomon Islands (Keesing 1988).

PLATE 17   *Solomon Islanders at Suva in Fiji in the late 19th century, outside
what is probably their church, decorated like a Kwara'ae shrine
house. (Photo from the Museum of Mankind, London)*

The experiences of the labourers have been described by Corris (1973 Ch. 5). Solomon Islanders in Fiji worked at first on cotton plantations and then later on the sugar cane plantations which replaced them in the late 1870s. When Indian labourers took over most of this work in the early 1890s Melanesians went to coconut plantations and other jobs. In Queensland most Solomon Islanders worked from the first on sugar cane plantations and in the sugar mills, which included some very large mechanised estates from the 1880s. For most men in both countries the work was heavy physical labour during most of the daylight hours for at least five a half days per week. Food and accommodation were seldom of a standard which Europeans would have tolerated and medical facilities were insufficient to prevent high rates of sickness and death. Conditions in Fiji were particularly unpleasant in the early years, with death rates of more than sixty per cent on one exceptionally bad plantation. However, pressure from Queensland government authorities and some company managers led to improvements in both countries during the 1880s and by the 1890s conditions were not intolerable as far as the labourers were concerned, especially when they worked on small farms rather than the large plantations. Their standards for comparison would have been the lives they had left behind them in the islands, and some at least returned home in better physical shape than they left (Corris 1973 Ch. 5, 115).

If the labourers took their material conditions more or less for granted as Corris implies, they were less tolerant of the way their employers, overseers and Europeans in general behaved towards them personally. The Europeans in Australia and the Pacific at this time, mainly of British origin, belonged to an empire which had been built on the exploitation of non-European labour and they shared the ideology of racial and cultural superiority which legitimated this system. Many justified the labour trade and its abuses as a means of 'civilising' the Melanesian workers. This argument was used on occasion to justify kidnapping or even to advocate the kind of slavery which had been abolished in the United States only five years before recruiting in Solomon Islands began (Great Britain 1872:30–31). Indeed, some planters in Fiji had actually migrated from the southern United States (Brewster 1937:218). The European attitudes of the trans-Atlantic slave trade and the arguments surrounding it were still very much alive in the Pacific in the early years of Solomon Islands labour migration. Many regarded Melanesians as little more than a source of labour to be exploited for their own gain, as 'niggers' to be treated with dehumanising contempt and often cynical brutality. Their racism is vividly illustrated in the stories, and the opinions, of popular writers who visited the Solomons in the early 20th century, particularly Jack London (eg. 1917). But even to those who opposed the inhumanities of the labour trade and devoted their time to the assistance of the labourers, Melanesians were still 'savages' who required the paternalistic guidance of Europeans to improve their inferior condition. Even Europeans who came to know and like Melanesians personally commonly referred to them as 'boys' rather than according them the dignity of 'men'.

Solomon Islanders, and Malaitans in particular, showed little inclination to acknowledge European claims to superiority, as they demonstrated by their reactions against them at home. But if recruiters learnt to treat Malaitans with a certain respect in their own island, plantation owners and their European overseers often resorted to verbal and even physical abuse (Corris 1973:83). Tension between Melanesians and Europeans sometimes erupted into serious violence, as in the notorious Mackay race-course riot of 1883 when Europeans attacked and killed Melanesians indiscriminately (Rannie 1912:67–68). In dealing with such conflicts the European authorities gave the more severe punishments to the Melanesians (Corris 1973:90–91, Moore 1985:160). The experience of European racism continued to rankle Malaitans until at least the mid-20th century, when it became a major complaint of the 1940s Māsing Rul movement.

During the 19th century such experiences undoubtably hardened Malaitan attitudes towards Europeans on Malaita itself. But beyond the immediate resentments it caused, Malaitan experiences of the labour trade would also have made them aware of the long term threat which Europeans posed to their political autonomy at home. Mixing with Australian Aboriginals and Fijians who had been dispossessed of their own lands made them realise the expansionist ambitions of Europeans, and long after the British had taken control of Malaita itself Kwara'ae were citing these cases in their fight to regain independence through Māsing Rul. European military power, as demonstrated from time to time by the patrolling warships of the Pacific fleet, may not have seemed an immediate threat to the bush people safe in their hills but the returned labourers at least would have been aware of the wealth and power which lay behind it in the Europeans' own land. Bearing all this in mind, attacks on European ships should probably be regarded not only as attempts to gain vengeance and plunder but also as the first stages of political resistance to colonial domination, anticipating opposition to the British presence on Malaita itself in the early 20th century.

CHRISTIANITY: MISSIONS TO THE PLANTATIONS

But although Malaitan military strength was undiminished and indeed enhanced by the labour trade, the subversion of their political autonomy was proceeding in more subtle ways. While European businessmen were putting Solomon Islanders to work building the plantation economies of Fiji and Queensland and the British colonial authorities were trying to safeguard this trade in the Solomons, others were working to transform Solomon Island culture through their religion. Although most Europeans had little understanding of Melanesian culture, it was clear to them that it conflicted with their understanding of Christianity and for many of them this made it objectionable. Those who took this problem seriously enough to join or support Christian missions did not always share the interests of the plantation sector, but they had their own interest in the colonial system of which they were a product. Even if missionaries were "not ... conscious advance agents of British imperial expansion", as Hilliard concludes (1974:94), their work benefitted from Melanesian submission to European authority, and they were ideologically committed to the growth of colonial power. The conversion of Solomon Islanders to Christianity played an important part in establishing British political control over their islands, and for Malaitans this process began on the plantations.

By the time the first Malaitans reached Fiji and Queensland, missionaries of the Anglican Melanesian Mission were already beginning to have some successes in the islands around Malaita, and their history has been researched in depth by Hilliard (1978). Anglicans came to regard the labour trade as a neccessary evil in the social and economic development of the Solomons but, underestimating the opportunities it offered to challenge the islanders' committment to their own religion, the Melanesian Mission concentrated its evangelical work in the islands. Their practice was to take islanders away to their base on Norfolk Island for training so that they might return to teach Christianity in their home districts, with the support of extended annual visits by European missionaries. In this way a number of Christian communities were established in the Solomons from the 1870s onwards, most successfully on Gela and Isabel. But on Malaita Christianity was still fiercely resisted. A few Christians established at Sa'a in the south, making little progress after many years of effort, were dispersed in the 1880s (Hilliard 1978:81–95). It was not until the 1890s that Anglican converts managed to establish the first lasting Christian communities on Malaita.

In the meantime Christians in Fiji, including the Anglican clergy among the resident Europeans as well as Wesleyan (Methodist) missionaries and their Fijian converts, were having rather more success with the Malaitans there (Hilliard 1978:103–106). Among the Anglican converts were a number of men who later returned to establish the church in West Kwara'ae (SCL Jan. 1899:5). Others included at least two of the survivors of the *Peri*, 'Alfred' Amasia and 'Isaac' Lau'a, who joined the Westleyan church. They married Fijian women and lived among the Fijians, so it was quite likely the Fijians who converted them (SCL Aug. 1900:19–20, Brewster 1937:234, 236, Woodford 1901).

In Queensland the Melanesian Mission also decided at first to leave missionary work to local Christians, but the Anglicans among them accomplished very little (Hilliard 1978:105–106). The London Missionary Society, also active in Melanesia, declined to work on the Queensland plantations because of its opposition to the labour trade (Hilliard 1969:41). For the first ten years or so Solomon Islanders in Queensland met little European opposition to the religious practices which they had brought with them. Then in the 1880s mission organisations supported by the Anglican and Presbyterian churches began holding classes to instruct plantation workers in Christianity, which proved very popular (Corris 1973:93–94). But most successful of all was the Queensland Kanaka Mission. In later years, as the South Sea Evangelical Mission, it eventually gained more converts on Malaita itself than any other mission and was particularly successful in Kwai.

The Queensland Kanaka Mission (QKM) developed from the work of Florence Young, whose brothers owned the Fairymead plantation near Bundaberg. As her autobiography (1925) describes, she began teaching the labourers there in 1882, later assisted by her sister-in-law. They gained such an enthusiastic following that by 1886 most of the men on the plantation were attending Christian classes during their free time in the evenings and on Sundays, and seventeen had been baptised. This encouraged Florence Young and her supporters to extend the work to other plantations and in 1886 they organised themselves as the Queensland Kanaka Mission for this purpose. They raised funds, gained the agreement of other plantation owners and employed their first

PLATE 18   *Solomon Islanders in Queensland, harvesting sugar cane on a 19th century plantation. (Sugar Industries Board photo, from the Mitchell library, State Library of New South Wales).*

paid evangelist. By 1900 the QKM had grown to a staff of twelve who, with the assistance of some of their Melanesian converts, were covering all the plantation districts of Queensland by 1902, except Mackay which was left to the Presbyterians (Young 1925:39–42, 127–128). By 1907 Florence Young was able to list the achievements of the QKM as follows:

> Eleven Mission centres covering the whole of the sugar districts in Queensland.
> A staff of nineteen European missionaries who devoted all their time and energies
> to the work under frequently trying and difficult circumstances.
> A weekly average attendance of from six to seven thousand at the Bible classes.
> Two thousand four hundred and eighty-four men and women converted and
> baptized in the Name of the Lord Jesus.
> Over one hundred native teachers (unpaid) taking regular classes under the
> missionaries' supervision. (Young 1925:181).

From 1890 onwards probably seventy-five per cent of Melanesians in Queensland gained some experience of Christianity, and for Malaitans in particular this was usually through the QKM (Corris 1973:96).

The QKM, and the South Sea Evangelical Mission which it later became, was organised as a non-denominational mission, attached to no particular church and dependent on a wide network of committed Christians in Australia and other European countries for voluntary work and donations (Hilliard 1969:42–43). Its purpose was above all evangelical: "salvation before education or civilization" as Florence Young put it (1925:39). Its members preached a fundamentalist Christianity heavily influenced at first by the Plymouth Brethren background of the Young family and by the Presbyterians (from which the mission came to be known as *Sikos* or 'Scotch').

CHRISTIANITY: THE MALAITAN RESPONSE

The reactions of Malaitan plantation labourers to the teachings of the QKM are only partly explained in the accounts left by the missionaries, who showed little understanding of the cultural backgrounds of Melanesians or of their circumstances as migrant workers in a foreign land. Melanesians were heathen to be converted and souls to be saved, and the success or failure of this purpose was seen in terms of the cosmic struggle between God and Satan. But the Malaitans had brought their own religion with them and continued to rely upon the power of their ghosts. Like the missionaries, they soon concluded that God and the ghosts were adversaries in a struggle for their allegiance.

Although they were unable to sacrifice to their ghosts, the Malaitan labourers took what precautions they could to ensure protection from them while they were abroad. As in more recent times, their priests, whose responsibilities prevented them from recruiting themselves, would have sacrificed to the ghosts for the protection of the labourers while they were away and to give thanks and return them to normal life when they arrived safely home. In the meantime the labourers took the power of their ghosts with them in the form of ritual objects and substances, as Justus Ganifiri heard from his father Fiuloa, who was converted to Christianity in Queensland:

> They carried with them some magic to help them, to keep them well, to keep them safe ... to defend them during the time they were working. This magic was really very powerful magic. Sometimes they had to fight with Europeans there and they trusted in these things.

The famous warrior Kamekame of 'Atori is said today to have performed remarkable feats in Queensland through the power of his warrior ghost, stopping a moving train with his bare hands, wrestling bulls and killing Europeans in brawls.[6]

Depending as they did on their ghosts, many Malaitans evidently regarded the missionaries with suspicion. Accustomed as they were to safeguard sources of spiritual power from the defiling influence of women, they would have found the prominent role of women in the QKM curious and probably disconcerting or threatening. By 1900 not only its leader, Florence Young, but half of the mission staff were women (Young 1925:128). According to Ganifiri. "They said that this thing which a woman was teaching, it was a defiled thing, it was going to spoil a man's power". This was apparently suspected to be a deliberate conspiracy by Europeans to weaken or subdue them: ". . .this woman has come to try to spoil our ghosts". The fact that the missionaries were so eager to impart knowledge which they proclaimed to be immensely valuable probably reinforced their suspicions, for this openness would have seemed in curious contrast to the secrecy with which ritual and other useful knowledge was guarded in Malaita. So it was that 'school', as Christianity became known after the mission classes, was seen by Malaitans as a threat to the power of their ghosts, as it later came to be regarded on Malaita. Ganifiri writes of his father's experiences:

> There was a missionary there, who started to preach the Gospel to them. They did not like to listen to him because their superstition was that if any man listened to his preaching, and looked at the picture of the crucifixion, his devil [ie. ghost], on whom he trusted might leave him and he might not have any good health in a strange land. (NIV Jun. 1956: 5)

Such thoughts were no doubt in the minds of two Malaitans who told a QKM missionary "we fright along school, suppose we come along school we get sick and die" (Young 1925:131).

Malaitans were of course correct in supposing that the missionaries wanted to destroy the power of the ghosts, whom they called 'devils' and identified with Satan. The missionaries may not have understood how threatening their efforts seemed, but in their own ways both parties recognised the political implications of conversion to the new religion. As far as Florence Young was concerned:

> Testimony as to the effect of the teaching ... came from employers and towns-people, in the Press and from the Bench. It was found that the Boys attending the classes became quiet, well-behaved and peaceable. (Young 1925:45)

This was precisely the objection made by a man who was probably speaking for many Malaitans when he said "Me no want-'im school. Suppose me come along school, by-and-by me no savee fight. Me go home along Island, man he kill-'im me" (Young 1925:47). While the missionaries saw this pacification as evidence of the power of God's love, Malaitans probably regarded it as a consequence of destroying or suppressing the influence of the ghosts by defiling (*fa'asuā*) or pacifying (*fa'asafia*) them. In any case, by accepting Christianity Malaitans implicitly rejected their ghosts and made an act of submission not only to God but to the Europeans, who found that the converts became steadier and more compliant workers (Young 1925:45). This was no doubt one reason why some men continued to resist Christianity and, considering the strength with which Malaitans resisted European domination at home, the achievements of the QKM were quite remarkable.

Part of the explanation may be sought in the political relationship with Europeans. Many Malaitans probably began to attend the mission classes in the hope that they could turn the knowledge of Europeans, and perhaps the power of their religion, to their own advantage in their resistance to European domination. Certainly the possession of such knowledge gave many Malaitans an increased confidence in their dealings with Europeans, which the Europeans recognised and resented as insubordination, as Florence Young reveals:

> If a Boy had attended a mission school in the Islands, and had received a smattering of education, even if he made no profession of faith in Christ, he would be labelled a "mission boy". Yet having experienced no change of heart, his familiarity with white men sometimes only led to a certain "cheekiness" of behaviour or self-conceit which was objectionable. Where the boys had been truly converted, it was of course a different matter. (Young 1925:44).

THE CONVERTS

But there is no doubt that many Malaitans, including a number of men from Kwai, were 'truly converted' to the satisfaction of Florence Young and the QKM. As strangers under foreign authority in a strange land they were far more susceptible to new ideas than they had been at home. Besides being freed from the religious and political authority of their home communities, many probably also felt remote from the reassuring protection of the ghosts which it ensured. Some may even have lost this protection when they departed overseas on bad terms with their families and priests. Those who signed on for second or third terms of work or intended to remain abroad indefinitely were presumably more prepared to consider new religious alternatives better suited to the land they were living in and some had perhaps reconciled themselves to life in a society dominated by Europeans who preached, or at least professed, Christianity. Membership of a mission congregation may have given them a reassuring sense of identity and conferred some prestige among their peers and Europeans, especially if they became recognised 'teachers' for the mission (Corris 1973:95). On the other hand, some men probably regarded Christianity only as a temporary source of protection while away from home, and several of those who led the resistance to Christianity in East Kwara'ae in later years had attended mission classes in Queensland. Others, including some of those who resisted most strongly at first, made a deep and lasting commitment to their new religion which they mantained in the face of considerable danger and privation when they eventually returned to Malaita.

One such man was Fiuloa, who took the Christian names Jimmy and Philip. According to his son Ganifiri, Fiuloa was a "hard case" who resisted the missionaries for a long time because he had his own 'magic' to protect him. Then he was quite suddenly inspired to 'take the Lord for his Saviour' and later became a leading evangelist (NIV Jun. 1956:5). But even those committed to Christianity like Fiuloa did not necessarily accept it on the terms intended by their European teachers. Instead they laid the foundations for what was to become a Malaitan form of Christianity which drew also on the insights and values of their traditional religion. The Queensland converts were not the first Christians to bring their new religion home to Malaita, but it was largly through their efforts that Christianity was eventually established as a viable alternative to the ghosts in Kwai and other districts of the island.

But the conversion of Malaita to Christianity only began after more than thirty years of long distance labour migration had laid the foundations for the colonisation of the island by the British. During this time, despite frequent armed confrontations, Malaitans were finding it increasingly difficult to keep their distance from the Europeans whose trade they had come to depend on. By the 1890s the saltwater people of Kwai had been forced to recognise the superior military power of the Europeans. As European commercial interest in the resources of the Solomons continued to grow it was only a matter of time before they made a determined effort to subjugate the Malaita bush too. When that time came the Christians played a crucial part as they fought their own battles for spiritual and political authority over the people of Malaita.

PLATE 19   *The Anglican church at Fiu in West Kwara'ae in 1906. Like other Kwara'ae churches in the past, it is decorated in the style of a traditional shrine house (compare with Plate 8, page 50), but the painted crosses and European clothes alike stand as symbols of the new religion.*
(Photo by J. W. Beattie, from the Museum of Mankind, London)

CHAPTER FIVE

God and Government Arrive
(1900s to 1910s)

Of the Malaitans who became Christians in Fiji and Queensland, some were so inspired by the evangelical message of the missionaries that they were determined to practise and preach their new religion on their return home. This proved a difficult and dangerous ambition, but a few of them persisted and in Kwara'ae some lived to see the eventual transformation of their society into a new Christian order which extended throughout Malaita and beyond. The first twenty years of this century saw the onset of these radical changes, as both Christian missions and colonial government began to establish their authority in Malaita. From this time the history of Kwai can be traced in increasing detail through the reports and correspondence of the Europeans involved, as well as from the personal recollections of old people still living in the 1980s.

Christians only gained a foothold in Kwai as the period of long distance labour migration drew to a close in the early years of the 20th century. By this time the saltwater people of Kwai were being forced to acknowledge the authority of colonial government, but for many years the communities of the Kwara'ae bush continued to resist Europeans and their religion almost as fiercely as they had for the previous thirty years. For the first ten years or so the warriors of East Kwara'ae were a real and constant threat to their Christian neighbours, but as government extended its power into the bush during the 1910s the Christians also began to establish themselves on the coast. Although local Christians and European government were each pursuing their own separate interests, for the first twenty or thirty years of the century they often made common cause in opposing what we have called the Kwara'ae traditional 'establishment'. Above all they shared a concern to suppress the killing which threatened both government authority and Christian security. For Kwara'ae this was a spiritual as well as a political struggle and as the establishment lost its influence people began to lose faith in their ghosts and seek new sources of spiritual power. By 1920 those who upheld the social order of the ghosts were themselves on the defensive against a new order supported by the power of God and government.

THE FIRST CHRISTIANS COME HOME

Even the Christians could hardly have imagined this outcome when they first began to return to Malaita in the last years of the 19th century. As they landed at their various home passages around the coasts they found themselves cut off at first both from their European teachers and from one another and, whatever their first intentions, most more or less abandoned Christianity. The first notable exception was Peter Abu'ofa, a QKM convert who came home to Malu'u in To'abaita in 1894 and persisted in practising and preaching Christianity there in the face of severe persecution (Hilliard 1974:45). He became a hero of the Christian movement whose story is still told in Kwai and other parts of Malaita. The first missionary support for Abu'ofa and others like him came from the Melanesian Mission, which began to visit them in the 1890s on tours in its ship the *Southern Cross* (Hilliard 1978:177). As the only mission then operating in Malaita, it did its best to encourage Christians of whatever denomination wherever they were to be found. Four missionaries associated with the QKM also went to help Abu'ofa in 1900 and 1902, but disease soon killed two and forced the other two to return home (Hilliard 1974:45–46).

The first successful Christian settlement in Kwara'ae was at Fiu in the West, where about fifteen Anglican converts led by Arthur Ako established themselves on their return from Fiji in 1898. Fiji seems to have made a deep impression on these men: they "dressed in Fijian style", grew Fijian crops, held prayers in Fijian as well as local languages and English, and they also played cricket. They were probably joined by Christian returns from other parts of Malaita as well as local people and by 1900 about one hundred people were associated with their church at Fiu, of whom thirty were baptized. This community continued to thrive despite harrassment from anti-Christian neighbours, who killed Ako himself in 1904 (SCL Jan. 1900:5, Mar. 1902:6, 1905:86, Awdry 1902:150, Hilliard 1978:177). Fiu remained the principle Anglican centre for the area and it was from here that Anglican Christianity was later taken up by many other communities in West Kwara'ae and eventually by some in East Kwara'ae.

The first Christians who returned to Kwai had less success. The earliest attempt to introduce Christianity in this area was made by Alfred Amasia, a survivor of the *Peri* tragedy who had been kidnapped at Leili by the *Nukulau* in 1871. Amasia returned from Fiji in 1898 or '99 with his Fijian wife Lewa and their son Inia and they settled on Ngongosila Island, where visiting Anglican missionaries met them in 1900 "established in a good Fijian house" (SCL Aug. 1900:19–20). Amasia was taught Christianity by Wesleyans, probably Fijians, from whom he learnt to display a notice in Fijian forbidding kava and tobacco

(Brewster 1937:236). But the people of Ngongosila were not impressed and objected to his overbearing efforts to convert them; "Poor Amasia seemed to have had a rough experience of it since his landing, for the people had boycotted him and he had been short of food. His wife, too, had been ailing ...", and she died not long afterwards (SCL Aug. 1900:19–20, Woodford 1901). The missionaries managed to take a boy away for training, but they had to pay for him much as if he had been a labour recruit (SCL Mar. 1901:11).

Then in 1901, as Amasia himself later reported, some other Christians returned from Fiji to join him; "Joseph Quienouri, Waisaki, and his Fijian wife, Bauleni [Pauline]." The Ngongosila people objected to this and in October 1901, when Pauline made the mistake of walking over and hence defiling the shrine of the Gwa'ilao clan, she was shot dead in restitution, with the authority of the Ngongosila leader Sana. A Gwa'ilao priest later died from the defilement. The killer, Giroro, husband of a Gwa'ilao woman, gave credit for the deed to their son Afu and they were rewarded with a piece of land. The Ngongosila people warned Amasia that "... if any more people want the lotu [Christianity] we shall kill them" (Woodford 1901). After this Waisaki moved to Sinalaagu in Kwaio and Amasia also gave up on Ngongosila and went off with Inia to Ngorefou in Lau. There Amasia became the leader of another group of Fiji and Queensland Christians who were attempting to settle in the face of harassment by local people and by the powerful Lau saltwater leader Kwaisulia, whose protection and authority they refused to accept. In 1902 Amasia was shot dead by two young men from Uru in return for killing their 'father' at Kwai before he was taken to Fiji thirty years previously (SCL 1939:185–186, Kwaisulia 1902, Ivens 1927:50).[1]

Isaac Lau'a, another survivor of the *Peri* who had been captured with Amasia in 1871, also returned from Fiji at about the same time to bring Christianity to his home at Uru in Kwaio, south across the bay from Ngongosila. At first he was no more successful than Amasia and also fled to Ngorefou after his wife was killed. By 1905 he had returned to Uru and gained some converts there with the support of the Anglican missionaries (Beattie 1906:44, SCL 1906:44).[2] But the Anglican presence at Uru lasted only a few years and it was at Lau that this church first became established on the east coast of Malaita, with Inia as one of its leading evangelists. In September 1902, shortly after Amasia's death, the Melanesian Mission's first resident missionary on Malaita, A. I. Hopkins, was stationed at Ngorefou (SCL 1939:174). Because of their association with the visiting missionaries, Amasia and Inia are remembered today as the first Anglicans on Ngongosila, but it was many years before this church gained any long-term converts there or elsewhere in Kwai.

'GOVERNMENT' COMES THE SOLOMONS

The experiences of these early Christians, which forced them to band together in isolated coastal communities often far from home, were typical of the difficulties and dangers which beset Christians on Malaita for many years to come. Their survival depended to an important extent on moral and logistic support from the missionaries, backed by protection from the British colonial authorities with whom the missionaries were sometimes able to intercede on their behalf. The British claimed formal responsibility for Malaita in 1893 when they declared a Protectorate over Solomon Islands, and in 1897 the first Resident Commissioner, C. M. Woodford, was established at Tulagi on Gela, within sight of the Malaita hills. This was the beginning of what Malaitans came to know as 'government' (*gafamanu*), a term describing the officers as well as the institution which eventually brought Malaita under British colonial control.

Woodford's power still depended largey on the British naval patrols which had long been attacking islanders in retaliation for offences against British interests. Since the Pacific Fleet was based in Sydney and acted in consultation with the Western Pacific High Commission in Fiji, its response to trouble in the Solomons was slow and unreliable. But Woodford also had a party of Fijian police, later replaced by Solomon Islanders, and a schooner to travel the islands, and he could draw on the armed support of the increasing number of European traders who were now beginning to settle in parts of the Solomons (although not in Malaita) (Belshaw 1950:51, Hopkins 1928:235). Much of his work was concerned with supervising European traffic and labour recruiting, but he was also able to keep in far closer touch with events on islands such as Malaita and to take action, either himself or by directing visiting warships. Whether or not Malaitans appreciated the implications of British attempts to 'pacify' them, they soon learnt that government was prepared to retaliate for attacks not only on Europeans, as warships had done in the past, but also on local people, especially Christians. It was Christians who were most inclined to seek government support and best able to do so, either directly or through the missionaries, and some even wrote letters to Woodford. So it was that 'Billy Zinamamu', one of Ako's people at Fiu, reported "... one Fiji Womon Been Kill this time abut to Week go ..." and asked "... you send one Man War Suhot [shoot] that palc [place]". The place was Ngongosila and the letter was probably delivered to Woodford by Amasia when he went to Tulagi in November 1901 to report the killing of Pauline (Zinamamu 1901, Woodford 1901, see also Corris 1973:137).

This plea was heard and government support for the Christians was demonstrated to the people of Kwai in September 1902, when Woodford's Resident Magistrate Mahaffy came to Malaita with the warship *HMS Sparrow* to deal with several reported killings around the coasts. Calling first at Malu'u, they shelled and burnt the offshore island of Oru when the people refused to give up two killers for arrest. Going on to Lau, they compelled Kwaisulia, the most powerful saltwater leader on the east coast of Malaita, to deliver to them Suemai and Waita, the killers of Amasia, who were later sentenced to seven years imprisonment (Woodford 1903). When the ship arrived at Kwai the saltwater people fled from Kwai and Ngongosila Islands to Kwakwaru on the mainland, no doubt warned what to expect by others further up the coast. They would have been well aware of the threat posed by the *Sparrow*, not least Sana (also known as 'Gerea' or 'Gooreah'), who had authorised the killing of Pauline, for he himself had encouraged the *Royalist* to bombard the bush people of 'Aita'e in 1894 (Waisaki 1902). But despite a threat that both islands would be destroyed, they refused to hand over Afu for killing Pauline and,

> The message having produced no effect the place was bombarded and everything upon it systematically destroyed by a landing party ... Between forty and fifty pigs were killed and several fine nets destroyed. (Mahaffy 1902)

The next call was for Gala of Busu across the Kwara'ae border in Kwaio, the same man whose village the *Royalist* had tried to shell in 1891 for the attack on the *Sybil*'s boats. This time Gala was implicated with 'Jacky Qui' (Kwai) in arranging the killing of a European recruiter on the *Roderick Dhu* near Uru, to collect a reward on offer in East Fataleka. Unable to reach either man, Mahaffy gave a warning to the saltwater people of Uru instead and went on to Sinalaagu. There he offered encouragement to Waisaki and other Christians before the *Sparrow* had to return and leave Malaita (Mahaffy 1902).

This expedition seems to have had an important effect on the saltwater people of Kwai. They had learnt the dangers of attacking Europeans when their islands were burnt by the British navy twenty years before, but after the 1902 attack they also refrained from attacking Christians. Henceforth Christians from the bush began to take refuge on Ngongosila Island from their opponents on the mainland, who were as little deterred by the navy as Gala had been. As Mahaffy reported:

> With the force at the disposal of the Government it would be mere suicide to attempt an armed expedition into the bush on Mala and until the supply of arms has ceased there will always be outrage all along this coast. (Mahaffy 1902)

The first serious government attempt to penetrate into the Malaita bush was in 1907, in retaliation for an attack on the recruiting ship *Minolta* at Bina in Langalanga. A party from the warship *HMS Cambrian* went several miles inland and destroyed four Kwaio bush villages, but even then they were unable to kill or capture anyone (SCL 1908:366, C. K. London 1910:148,159, Keesing & Corris 1980:12–13). Anglican missionaries probably echoed the views of local

Christians when they considered that Woodford was helping to promote peace on Malaita but that he was not doing enough (SCL Jan, 1900:5, Jan. 1906:6).

THE QUEENSLAND LABOURERS RETURN

However, the strength of the Christians continued to increase with the arrival of more and more returned labourers in the early years of this century. Christianity actually gained a foothold in East Kwara'ae, as in most districts of Malaita, only after the Queensland labour trade was stopped by the Common-wealth Restricted Immigration Act of 1901. From 1904, as a result of this racist policy to make Australia 'white', most of the Melanesians in Queensland were deported and by 1908 perhaps as many as 3,000 Malaitans had returned home, including many Christians.[3] The return of so many men in so short a time caused considerable disruption to life on Malaita and led to an increase in violent conflict. This was only partly suppressed by the presence of the warships *Torch* and *Cambrian* which patrolled around Malaita to threaten retaliation for attacks on the returns (SCL 1908:243, Corris 1973:136).

An important reason for this conflict was that the returns included men who had committed themselves to the way of life and religion of Queensland after many years residence and had intended to remain there, as well as others who appreciated the threat which Christianity posed to the traditional way of life which they wanted to resume. The Anglican missionary Hopkins tried to "roughly classify them into the actively Christian, the actively heathen, and the large neutral class who follow the line of least resistance". Hopkins blamed the conflict on the 'actively heathen' and his vivid characterisation of these men reveals a political reaction against Europeans and their culture from which he himself evidently suffered:

> He is self-important, vicious, a despiser of the white man and of the old native rule too and keen to stir up strife and to "pooh-pooh" the fears of his bush friends of the white man's power. He landed yesterday in polished boots, starched shirt and collar, tie, etc.; to-morrow he is running about naked, or very nearly so, shell in hair, gun in hand on some bush feud which his return has perhaps started.
> (SCL 1908:242).

Christians, on the other hand, were "... quiet-faced smiling men in shirts and trousers, with close cut hair and no ornaments ...". But as Hopkins admitted, their rejection of the traditional way of life itself provoked conflict, especially with self-assertive men like Alfred Amasia (SCL 1939:185). The smiles which greeted Hopkins and other missionaries and the clothes which impressed them, like the agressive manner and ornaments of their traditionist opponents, were symbols of alignment in the wider conflict between Malaitan autonomy and British colonialism.

PLATE 20   *'Heathens' from the Kwara'ae bush, with a 'Snider' rifle, in*
1906. They have come down to see the Melanesian Mission ship on
its visit to a Christian village at Fote on the west coast.
(Photo by J. W. Beattie, from the Museum of Mankind, London)

Some of those wishing to avoid the dangers of returning to Malaita found an alternative in recruiting to Fiji, but while the Queensland labour trade was closing down, opportunities for wage labour were also developing almost as rapidly in the Solomons. From 1905 Levers Pacific Plantations and then several other large companies began to take over from the few small European planters and to develop large coconut plantations. This was assisted by Woodford's concern to develop the economy of the islands so as to finance the colonial administration, and large areas of land were taken out of local control in New Georgia, Russell Islands and Guadalcanal. Malaita was less suitable for plantations and its people less easy to dispossess but the plantation economy depended on their labour, as the economies of Fiji and Queensland had done. So Malaitans continued to work abroad but henceforth they went mainly to plantations on other islands in the Solomons, still employed under indenture at a minimum wage of £6 per year plus a recruiting payment of about the same amount. By 1907 1,200 islanders were working on plantations in the Solomons and this had risen to 2,284 by 1909 (Corris 1973:106–107, BSIP 1911:46–47). The increase in local employment and the continued availability of guns in Fiji led the colonial authorities to prohibit Solomon Islanders from recruiting to Fiji in 1910 (Corris 1973; 148). For many years plantation work was a common resort for the Christians who found life intolerable on Malaita, for in Kwai as elsewhere the Queensland labourers who decided to stay at home and live as Christians needed a remarkable dedication to their new religion to survive the years that followed.

THE SOUTH SEA EVANGELICAL MISSION GAINS A FOOTHOLD

For most Christians their religion was the particular version of Christianity which they had learnt from the QKM. Being unfamiliar with the ritual demonstrated by the Anglican missionaries and unimpressed by their less sophisticated island trainees who had never been to Queensland, they continued to place their hopes on the missionaries they had left behind in Queensland (Hilliard 1974:46, SCL 1908:367). The missionaries of the QKM were at first reluctant to extend their work overseas but, with their congregations disappearing home to the Solomons and sending back letters for help, they eventually decided to move their operations there. The early years of their work on Malaita are described by Florence Young (1925:Chs.8–10) and by the mission's journal *Not In Vain*, which has continued to report its progress to this day. Further unpublished information is contained in correspondence preserved in the archive of the mission (the SSEM).

In 1904 Florence Young led a group of QKM missionaries on their first visit to the Solomons and despite Woodford's warnings of the dangers of

Malaita, they sailed as far as Malu'u to visit Abu'ofa and his Christian community. There were now up to two hundred people attending Sunday classes there, including refugees from various other parts of Malaita. On their second tour in 1905 the missionaries contacted Christians at passages all round Malaita, including Kwai Island and Ngongosila where several Queensland Christians were now living. From Malu'u they took a group of men, including some from Kwai, to help build the QKM's new headquarters and training school at Onepusu on the southwest coast of Malaita, which was opened in 1906. Like Malu'u, Onepusu "... formed a temporary refuge for boys from Queensland who were afraid or unwilling to return at once to their own passages, and also an asylum for refugees from many parts of Malayta" (NIV 1907–8:9). It later became the training centre for future generations of local Christians.

In 1907, with the deportation of Melanesians from Queensland almost complete, the Queensland branch of the QKM closed down and the Solomon Islands branch became the South Sea Evangelical Mission (SSEM) (NIV 1971: 9). (Malaitans often continued to refer to it as *Sikos*, the 'Scotch' mission). By now the mission ship *Evangel* had contacted local Christians at about forty places on its tours around the coasts of Malaita and five permanent stations had been established for resident missionaries (NIV 1907–8, Young 1925:256). The SSEM missionaries were a dedicated band and included a number of Florence Young's relatives, notably the Deck family. In 1909 her brothers became involved by extending their Fairymead plantation business to Malaita, forming the Malayta Company which had close links with the mission. The company began the first coconut plantation on the island at Baunani in Dorio (Hilliard 1969:52–53).

The Christians who had gathered on Ngongosila Island were led by a local saltwater man, Enoch So'ai, but included a number of men who were having difficulty returning to their own people in the East Kwara'ae bush. As Samuel Alasa'a recalls, these were his 'fathers' from places around Fairū and 'Ere'ere; Peter Kabulanga, John Sela'au, John Ngwaki, Moses Gwangwa'ufilu, Jonathon Ngwalasi, Samuel Kelema and Joshua Fa'asalo. It was at Ngongosila that the SSEM missionaries decided to establish a station from which to work the east coast, in 1906. Their first resident missionary was a Mr. J. Watkinson, who bought land from Maifo of the senior Anibongi clan on a corner of the island known thereafter as Sinai ('Sydney'). He built a house there for the mission and from this base he began travelling by whaleboat up and down the coast to encourage and support men who were trying to establish Christian settlements on the mainland (Young 1925:171,256, K. Deck 1909, NIV 1914).

In East Kwara'ae the most important of these early settlements was founded in 1906 by John Sela'au of Fairū, with his brother Peter Kabulanga and Luke Neomea. After returning from Queensland, Sela'au and Kabulanga had gone to Onepusu and to Ngongosila before moving to Faumamanu, a bush-saltwater marketplace where Fairū reaches the coast opposite Ngongosila. With the agreement of their Fairū relatives they cleared the forest, built themselves a single house and named the place Kerete (Biblical 'Cherith') (NIV 1908:37, 1914). A few years later the Queensland convert Jimmy Fiuloa of Ubasi decided to return home. His son Ganifiri recalls how after arriving from Queensland in 1904 he had moved between Malu'u, Ngongosila and Onepusu, where he married Deborah Dingana'ota, a widow from Malu'u who had been converted by her relative, Abu'ofa. In 1909 they came back to east Kwara'ae with her two sons and settled at Feraasi on the inlet of the Bulia river, also within easy reach of Ngongosila. Fiuloa was fortunate in gaining permission to live here from Mauara of 'Atori, an important coastal leader who controlled the area and seems to have taken some interest in Christianity himself.

Christian settlements were known as 'schools', after the Bible classes which had been such an important feature of Christian activities since the QKM began

PLATE 21   *Bible classes at the Onepusu training school in the 1910s. Joan Deck is teaching the men and her sister-in-law Jessie, wife of Northcote Deck, teaches the women.*
(Photo from the SSEM archive)

its work in Queensland, and 'school' (Pijin *sukulu*) became a synonym for Christianity. The leaders of Christian communities, as the evangelists and instructors of their people, were called 'teachers' (Pijin *titsa*). From the first the 'school' villages were rigidly separated from their traditionist neighbours, from both choice and necessity. The conflict of political interests between those whose power and authority derived from the ghosts and those who had chosen to depend on the God of the Europeans was manifest in a fundamental incompatibility between Christian and traditional ritual practice, which had been evident since the days of the mission in Queensland. According to Northcote Deck, who joined the SSEM in 1908, it was Abu'ofa who, as a result of ostracism and harassment by his relatives and neighbours at Malu'u, "... had established the precedent of "separation", and had discovered that a spiritual as well as a natural garden *must be fenced*" (NIV Apr. 1928:6). This conclusion, confirmed also in the experiences of Christians in Kwai and elsewhere, was endorsed by Deck, who considered that strict adherence to Christian ideals required "... a clean break from the heathen and their customs and superstitions". The principle was elevated into "a changeless law of God", as it tends to be regarded by strict Christians to this day (NIV Apr. 1928:6).

For the people Kwai, such a 'law' of separation is conceptually equivalent to the 'heathen customs' against which it is directed, particularly the rules of tabu protecting men and the ghosts from defilement by women. The equally 'changeless law' of the ghosts, being essential to their power and authority and contrasting so strongly with what Deck called "the liberty of a Christian land" (ie Queensland), was a prime target of Christian iconoclasm (NIV Apr. 1928:7). When Christians refused to make amends for often wilful offences against the rules of the ghosts by giving restitution, traditionists felt they had no alternative but to kill them. Even in their segregated villages these breaches could not remain a private matter for the Christians themselves, for they subverted established structures of religious and political authority and were regarded as a source of defilement which also endangered the well-being of their traditionist relatives and neighbours.

Hence the Christian withdrawal into separate communities was more than just a result of their own doctrines; it was also forced upon them by the hostile reactions of the traditionists, who needed to 'fence' their own 'spiritual gardens' from the Christians. It was clear from the Christian compulsion to preach that they were not satisfied with merely following their new religion themselves, but were intent on expanding their congregations and spheres of influence, ultimately to create a new religious and social order throughout Malaita. In this their interests coincided with those of the Europeans, in conflict with the traditionists who were seeking to protect their own autonomy. Even in Queensland, Christianity was suspected of spoiling the protective powers of the ghosts which the labourers depended on (NIV Jun. 1956:5). On Malaita it threatened the whole traditional structure of religious and political power.

PERSECUTING THE CHRISTIANS

While the saltwater people were reluctant to attack the Christians on Ngongosila after the government reprisals of 1902, the bush people of East Kwara'ae were still prepared to confront this threat by harassing the 'school' village on the mainland. Even when Christians remained on good terms with their own relatives in the bush, they were isolated from their support and protection in the 'school' villages on the coast. Being on the coast had its advantages, for it gave Christians access to the ships of the missionaries, recruiters and government, for support, a means of escape and a way of maintaining contact with other Christians around Malaita. Some coastal sites also offered the opportunity to preach on neutral ground to the people who assembled for the regular markets between bush and saltwater communities. Sela'au established Kerete at Faumamanu with this in mind and preached passionately to the crowds of several hundred people who regularly gathered for market from Kwai Island, Ngongosila and the neighbouring bush districts (NIV 1907–8:37). But an equally compelling reason for living on the coast was that the Christians were unwelcome anywhere else. The accessibility of the coast made it an unpopular place to live because of the dangers of attack in feuds between the bush and the saltwater peoples. This made the 'school' villages particularly vulnerable to warriors seeking victims to kill for vengeance or restitution, as well as to concerted attacks on the 'schools' themselves.

Fiuloa's experiences, recalled by his son Ganifiri, illustrate the choices these Christians faced between risking death in their own 'school' villages and retreating to live either as traditionists with their relatives or as Christians on the mission stations or plantations. Shortly after Fiuloa settled at Feraasi, a man called Kasa'i decided to kill him to collect a reward put up nearby at Ote in vengeance for a killing by one of Fiuloa'a 'brothers'. Fortunately for Fiuloa, he was still on good terms with his 'brothers' and when they heard of this a large band of Ubasi men came down to rescue him. They found Fiuloa standing Kasa'i off with a gun they had given him and they gave Kasa'i a thorough beating. Then they took Fiuloa and his family back to Ubasi for their own safety, where he was eventually persuaded to take part in sacrifices to the ghosts. It was only when he fell serious ill and Northcote Deck took him in the *Evangel* to Onepusu to recover that he took up Christianity again. For several years he worked at the Malayta Company's plantation at Baunani, preaching to the labourers and to the local Dorio people.

The Christians at Kerete faced similar problems. At first they would go back to sleep on Ngongosila each night for safety, but Sela'au made a virtue of necessity, hoping to demonstrate the power of God by braving the threats against his life by the bush people (NIV 1907–8:37). Eventually Kerete began to attract a number of other Christians, including Queensland converts who had been living on Ngongosila and elsewhere as well as some new converts and probably other refugees from the bush. But they were attacked repeatedly by men of the bush on the grounds that 'school' was spoiling the power of the ghosts. Over the years a total of six or seven were killed and two of the founders narrowly escaped death, while others retreated to live with their relatives in the bush (NIV 1914). Among those who struggled on was Joshua Fa'asalo, who was once miraculously unharmed by a shot in the head and chased his attacker off. Others included Nathan Uga'iniu of Sakwalo and Benjamin Manibili of 'Ere'ere, who later became important 'teachers'. But John (Joe) Ngwaki, Moses Gwangwa'ufilu and Ngwalasi were drawn back to the ghosts in 'Ere'ere when their relatives offered sacrifices for them and they became among the fiercest opponents of Christianity.

For a time Kerete provided a centre from which local Christians and missionaries could attempt to preach to the bush people. Despite the dangers, Northcote Deck was able to use it as a base from which he travelled several miles inland. In 1909, after three failed attempts, he persuaded four of the Kerete Christians to guide him across Kwara'ae from Kerete to Bina, making him only the second European to cross Malaita.[4] They evaded pursuit by parties of would-be killers only by "the Lord's doing", as Deck put it (NIV 1910). But in Kwai as a whole the Christians were making little progress and at Feraasi Fiuloa had given up for the time being. Further south a 'school' village at Busu in Kwaio failed when Jonathon Ngu fled for his life to Onepusu with the daughter of the warrior leader Gala (NIV 1913, Edge-Partington 1911c). Ngongosila offered Christians more security but there was inevitable tension with their neighbours on the densely populated island. The saltwater people seem to have felt that the presence of European missionaries gave them some protection from attack on occasians such as markets and the Ngongosila leader Maifo evidently approved their presence (NIV 1907–8:36, K. Deck 1909). But few people came to learn from them and by 1911 opposition from the island's leaders had prevented them gaining more than about seventeen converts out of an estimated population of three hundred (NIV 1915). One of the first to be baptised, in 1908, was a boy called Shadrach Amasia, who the missionaries prepared to become a leader of the saltwater Christians, and another lone student was young Timothy Anilafa who grew to be a prominent SSEM evangelist (NIV 1907–8:15).

Then in 1911, after a period of calm, the campaign of attrition reached a climax when the men of the bush made a final onslaught on Kerete and drove the

PLATE 22   *A view from the early Christian refuge of Ngongosila in the 1910s or '20s, looking towards the neighbouring island of Kwai and the Kwara'ae mainland in the distance.*
(Photo from the SSEM archive)

Christians out. As Alasa'a recalls, the crucial incident was when Angitafe of Fakula'e shot dead a Queensland Christian, Samuel Kelema. Northcote Deck reported that a man called "... Barnabas had been shot dead while working in the field, the gardens themselves had been raided by large numbers of bushmen, and a determined attempt had been made to massacre the whole school" (NIV 1914). Most of the remaining Christians fled for refuge back to Ngongosila. Later the same year, in June 1911, the SSEM suffered another serious setback in the area when the missionary then stationed on Ngongosila, Frederick Daniels, was shot dead on a visit to a new 'school' village south across the bay at 'Ailamalama near Uru, in Kwaio. The killers were seeking to cleanse themselves of a curse, but they chose Daniels as a victim because he and the mission were defiling their ghosts (Keesing & Corris 1980:13, Young 1925:215, Fifi'i 1989:75).

'GOVERNMENT' COMES TO MALAITA

Christian prospects only began to improve after the government started taking effective measures to bring Malaita under administrative control. A government station was established on Malaita itself in 1909, but it was several years before the permanent government presence had much effect in Kwai. The station, at Rarasu in West Kwara'ae, was known as 'Aoke after the nearby offshore island (misspelled as Auki) and has been the administrative headquarters for Malaita ever since. The first District Officer for Malaita, as District Magistrate, was T. W. Edge-Partington. He had a whaleboat and twenty to thirty police (often known locally as 'soldiers') from other islands in the Solomons, later led by a European Police Officer, Campbell. This force could exert little influence beyond the districts adjacent to 'Aoke along the west coast and at first Edge-Partington had to devote much of his resources to building the station and to defending it against attacks from the bush. But as he established himself he began to arrest occasional killers, thieves and runaway labourers, to confiscate guns and mediate in local disputes and feuds and to sentence men to fines, floggings and imprisonment (Diaries 1910–13).

News of these activities would have reached Kwai, only a day's walk away, but events soon proved that most bush districts still had little to fear from the government. In 1910 Edge-Partington made two armed forays into the North Malaita bush to retaliate on the killers of Christians at Ngorefou and Fo'odo, but he was successfully repulsed by local men. Recruiters and missionaries remained in constant danger of attack and were advised to take their own precautions (Diaries 1910–13, Court Minutes 1910–12:3–8, Barnett 1911, Edge-Partington 1914). Edge-Partington was well aware of his limitations:

> ... to expect a man to go into the bush on this Island and fight with a few boys is simply madness. I know that maniacs like Deck walk across with a few boys but the bush people know that he is a maniac and that he has not come to fight and they expect me to bring a squad of soldiers when I come. (Edge-Partington 1910)

Sensitive to the contempt with which his efforts were viewed by the warriors of the bush, Edge-Partington complained bitterly of his small and inexperienced police force ("... a hopeless lot to attack a bunch of unfrightened bushmen", "... half grown creatures ... that cannot even walk up a decent hill", "... a crowd of rotters"). He was constantly at odds with his superiors over his lack of resources and their reluctance to approve attacks on villages or to execute Malaitans for killing one another (as distinct from killing Europeans) (Edge-Partingon 1910, 1911e). He more or less gave up trying to respond to incidents which he reported only as "numerous school boy murders up and down the coast" (Edge-Partington 1911b). For the time being the warriors of East Kwara'ae evidently felt quite safe from a District Officer who could reach them only on patrols which had to go all the way round North Malaita by whaleboat and seldom came closer than Lau Lagoon. His presence certainly did not prevent them from attacking Kerete, nor did it lead to government retaliation for the attack.

But when Daniels was killed at 'Ailamalama, Edge-Partington's superiors felt obliged to react, despite their wish to restrain his "martial ardour" and their impatience at the risks taken by missionaries (Edge-Partington 1911a). In November 1911, five months after the event, Edge-Partington arrived at Uru in the government ship *Belama*, with Hopkins of the Melanesian Mission in attendance, followed by the warship *HMS Torch*. A force of about fifty police, seamen and marines went by night some distance into the Kwaio bush to the killers' village, where they killed five people and wounded five others and then returned to loot and burn the saltwater village of Uru Island (Court Minutes 1910–12:14–16, SCL May 1912:74).

Although the effects of this raid were felt in Kwai, it did not deter an attack on a ship there only three days later. Timi Ko'oliu recalls many details of this incident which were not recorded in European reports. When a well-known labour recruiter, Captain Louis Appenborn, arrived at Ngongosila on the *Ruby*, Gwangalu of Kwarutasi near 'Ere'ere sent his 'sons' to attack the ship and loot the trade goods it carried. A group of about ten men led by Maena'ia came down and were taken on board the *Ruby* to sign on as labour recruits. After dark they attacked and killed the ship's mate, but although they wounded Appenborn he managed to shoot several of them and imprison five in the hold. Of those who escaped, Maeanasua swam to the mainland but Gwangalu's son Lusumani swam to Kwai Island and was killed there by a man called Sigili and others. The captives were taken to Tulagi where three of them were later hanged and two sent to prison in Fiji (Diaries 1910–13, SCL 1912:74, Bell 1917, Keesing & Corris 1980:15, Dickinson 1927:177–178).[5] This disaster was the last attack on a ship at Kwai, but the matter did not end there. Ko'oliu remembers Gwangalu putting up a reward of twenty pigs to avenge the death of Lusumani and this was collected by relatives of the dead man, Ko'oliu's 'fathers' from 'Ere'ere. They were led by the warrior Arumae Bakete, who put Sigili under a spell by giving him betelnut, lured him to the mainland for a fishing trip, and killed him on the beach while his companions waited in ambush. A reward for the death of a European in vengeance for the men captured by the *Ruby* was still said to be on offer in 'Ere'ere in 1917, although it was never collected (Bell 1917).

One immediate effect on the *Torch* raid was an upsurge of hostility against Christians in the area. The Melanesian Mission withdrew its 'teachers' from Uru and lost its influence there until the 1930s (SCL Apr. 1913:59–60). The people of Ngongosila, as relatives of the saltwater people of Uru Island, apparently shared their grievance at the attack and reacted against the SSEM. The missionaries had to abandon their base on Ngongosila and the SSEM did not station a missionary there again until 1923, confining its work in the area to visits on tours by ship around Malaita. In 1913 *Not In Vain* reported:

> Nongasila has changed much since last it was described. ... The island is particularly hard to work. The heathen are more united and bitter and opposed than ever. Most of the salt-water boys we got from there in years gone by have, after training at Baunani or One Pusu, either stayed on with us or else have gone home and then recruited away, to escape being pulled back by the heathen (NIV 1913).

CHRISTIAN FORTUNES BEGIN TO CHANGE

Although the saltwater people were now afraid to kill Christians, they nonetheless made the bush refugees from Kerete feel so unwelcome on Ngongosila that they considered taking ship with missionaries or labour recruiters to get away. However after six months, in 1912, they took the opportunity to move back to the mainland when Sinamu of 'Aita'e decided to go to 'school'. Sinamu, who had attacked the boats of the recruiting ship *Para* in 1894, was an old but still influential warrior leader living at Fale, some distance up into the bush. Alasa'a, adding to Northcote Deck's contemporary report, recalls how Sinamu's son died of sickness despite sacrificing all their pigs. This made Sinamu so disillusioned with his ghosts that he moved down to the coast and approached his Christian relatives Sela'au, Kabulanga and Neomea on Ngongosila for protection from them. Together they built a 'school' village on a small offshore island at Gwaubusu in the inlet of the Bulia river. Here, no longer living at the sufferance of resentful traditionist hosts and protected by Sinamu's reputation, the Christians were able once again to attract followers from the bush. In a year or two there were twenty-five or thirty people in 'school' at Gwaubusu (NIV Apr. 1914). At about the same time another of the Kerete Christians, Nathan Uga'iniu, began a 'school' at Faubala, on his own land of Sakwalo, which later became an important Christian centre for the East Kwara'ae bush.

Although the events of 1911 had reduced the Christians of Kwai to despair, the foundation of Gwaubusu marked a turning point in their fortunes. Traditionist resistance was still strong as converts were pressured to return or even abducted by their relatives, but they suffered none of the armed attacks which had driven them from Kerete. Edge-Partington reported that "News of the [*Torch*] expedition has gone all over Mala, and seems to have had a very good effect" (Edge-Partington 1911d). Since the raid had penetrated some distance into the Kwaio bush it probably gave the bush people of Kwara'ae cause for reflection and henceforth there were some men at least who thought twice before killing even in a legitimate cause.

Others continued to resist the Christians by armed force and to defy the government, and it was some years before government forces were able to venture into the East Kwara'ae bush. But in the meantime the growth of Christian communities around Gwaubusu showed that local opposition was beginning to falter. From this time people began to come to 'school' not only as individuals but as ritual congregations; local clans who abandoned their ghosts collectively in a manner which became increasingly common as time went on. As these groups had a certain degree of ritual autonomy, their defection was perhaps of less immediate concern to others; to some extent it was their own business how they treated their own ghosts. But this development had serious long term implications for the opponents of Christianity, for the 'schools' gained strength and confidence as communities of close relatives. It was probably from this time that evangelists began the henceforth common practice of desecrating the shrines of new converts and burying or destroying the bones and relics of their ghosts; something that would have been difficult to do if they were not abandoned by a whole congregation. Depending how far such desecration was taken, it created a rift with the ghosts which made a return to their worship difficult or impossible and became a ritual of initiation and committment to Christianity.

After a few years a strong Christian community began to develop on the Bulia inlet around Gwaubusu. In 1914 Fiuloa returned from Onepusu at the request of a group of his Ubasi 'brothers' who wanted to go to 'school' because their shrine had been desecrated by one of their 'daughters' in a quarrel with her father. When she had done the same thing a few years before they had killed a man as restitution to the ghosts, but this time they were reluctant to kill for fear of retaliation by the government. Fiuloa brought these people, about six families, down to Feraasi and once more started a 'school' village there. Some of the people from Gwaubusu also moved over to join them. In 1916 Fiuloa's true brothers and close 'brothers', about six men and their families, convinced by his demonstrations of the healing power of prayer, at last responded to his preaching and came to 'school', allowing him to desecrate their shrine. Rather than stay at Feraasi they preferred to be further into the bush and so bought land at Rade further up the Bulia from Mauara of 'Atori, the coastal leader who had previously allowed Fiuloa to settle at Feraasi. Another large group of Ubasi people also moved down to 'school' at Rade about this time after a shrine was desecrated by young girls and they too destroyed all their ritual paraphernalia. There were probably others besides and Fiuloa also went to start another 'school' village for some Ubasi people in the bush at Talakali. By 1918 there were about ninety people at Feraasi and Rade, most of whom were members of Fiuloa's Ubasi clan and their families. With Gwaubusu nearby under the leadership of Sela'au there were now more than one hundred and thirty people attending 'school' in the area (NIV 1918). Rade, known today as Nāfinua, eventually became the principal SSEM centre for East Kwara'ae.

The missionaries hoped to make Gwaubusu a base not only for the bush Christians but, having given up their base on Ngongosila for the time being, for saltwater converts also. At first they had little success. Those they delivered there from training school "... have been enticed back to their old surroundings at Nongasila on plea of danger, and have mostly recruited away, because the heathen surroundings were intolerable, on the island." (NIV Apr. 1914). Missionary efforts to secure the conversion of promising young men did not help to improve relations with their senior relatives. The young Shadrach Amasia was for many years torn between the mission and his traditionist relatives on Ngongosila and in 1913 he was virtually abducted by Northcote Deck to prevent his father from drawing him back into the traditional political and ritual system (NIV 1907–8:15, 1913). In 1914, when a number of Ngongosila people moved out to the then uninhabited island of Leili, Amasia and others attempted to establish a 'school' there but, facing the same obstruction, he eventually retreated to teach at Feraasi before recruiting away for plantation work in 1919 (NIV 1915, 1918).

GOVERNMENT CHALLENGES THE WARRIORS

While the coastal Christians were now fairly secure from violent attack, the continuing feuding among the bush people made it difficult for them to take their message inland. Until the bush warriors were actually confronted by government forces there were still some who insisted on their right to kill and were prepared to fight to defend the political autonomy which enabled them to do so. One of the strongholds of resistance to both Christianity and government was 'Ere'ere. Several 'Ere'ere men and their close relatives from neighbouring districts were among the Christians of Kerete and Benjamin Manibili became a prominent Christian 'teacher'. But when the former Queensland Christian Moses Gwangwa'ufilu tried to preach to his people in 'Ere'ere they soon forced him to give up, and a later attempt by Samson Taba'ai to establish a 'school' village there in about 1912 was defeated by 1915 when he was shot dead and his companions driven away (NIV 1915). The anti-Christian and anti-government faction came to include Gwangwa'ufilu and Nunute'e of the leading Sasadili clan and their cousins John Ngwaki of Kwarutasi, also a former Queensland Christian, Iro'ima, and Arumae Bakete ('Bucket') of Kwarugwagalu'ai, who led them all in killing Sigili. They formed a tough and dangerous gang of fighters, and several of them had the reputation of warriors (*ramo*). Ngwaki became the principal warrior leader of 'Ere'ere, strong in the power of their warrior ghost and a violent opponent of Christianity. Jonathon Didi'imae remembers him as hot-tempered, quarrelsome and aggressive, armed with a spear and always ready to fight: "He was our warrior; everybody trusted in him because he could beat them all."

But when at last the government did confront the warriors of East Kwara'ae on their own ground they were unable to mount a concerted resistance. Their power was based on a system of feuding which itself made united opposition to the government difficult, dividing local communities in enmity under their own autonomous leaders. The Christians were probably not the only ones who welcomed the prospect of an end to killing, or were willing at least to seek support against their enemies by reporting the attacks they suffered to the government.

The man who finally brought Kwara'ae and most of Malaita under government control was William Bell, who was appointed District Officer in 1915. Bell's career has been described in detail by Keesing and Corris (1980). Unlike his predescessors, Bell extended his operations beyond the coastal areas far into the central bush. He is remembered as a hard and violent man who recruited and trained an equally tough police force of Malaitans, chosen for their strength. Bell forced the warrior leaders to recognise his authority by carrying out arrests and raids with increasing effectiveness. Crucial to his programme was the certification

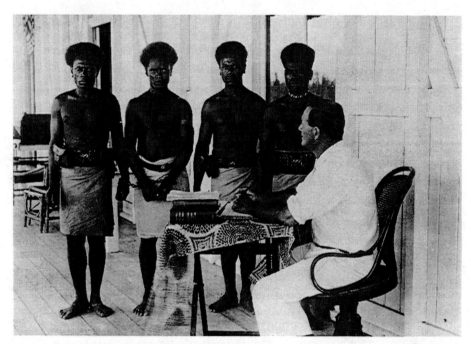

PLATE 23   *William Bell enforcing government law in 1917. As District Magistrate, he holds court over a killer under police guard at the government station at 'Aoke.*
(Photo by Martin Johnson, from the Martin and Osa Johnson Safari Museum, Chanute, Kansas)

and gradual confiscation of guns, begun by Edge-Partington with only limited success (Keesing & Corris 1980:68,77). Persuading men to give up their guns depended on the assurance of police protection, which Bell seems to have achieved by threatening local leaders from a position of superior firepower on his tours through the bush. By 1917 he was securing large deposits of shell money as "recognisances for good behaviour" from warrior leaders in various districts of North Malaita (Bell 1918a). In 1916 he patrolled from coast to coast across the Fataleka and Baegu districts and in September 1917 he led the first government patrol across Kwara'ae from 'Aoke station to Rade. On their return through 'Ere'ere, where Bell suspected that a reward was still on offer to avenge the *Ruby* incident, he was treated with polite hospitality and no-one dared attack his twenty-strong party (Bell 1917).

Bell's achievements were evident as early as 1918, when the SSEM missionaries noted them with great satisfaction. Following a tour of the east coast of Malaita, a general increase there in the numbers coming to 'school' was reported in *Not In Vain* as:

> ... the great movement among the heathen, over wide areas of Malaita, that has indirectly been the result of Government action. ... The result is remarkable. In all directions we hear of and meet large numbers of bushmen, or even whole tribes, who are preparing to move down to the coast and join the Christians.

> Numbers of these would long ago have come to school, but have been deterred by the fear of being killed in the Christian villages, where the muskets are few, and the people, humanly speaking, have been defenceless. (NIV 1918)

THE GHOSTS BEGIN TO FAIL

The increasing security of the Christian villages under Bell's administration was an important consideration for people intending to go to 'school', but it hardly explains why they wished to do so. Malaitan Christians seventy years ago gave their reasons for abandoning their ghosts in the same terms that Kwara'ae do today:

> ... being angry with the akalos, because, in spite of constant sacrifices of pigs, etc., they fall sick or their relations die. Others again say they are tired of the endless labour of raising large numbers of pigs to provide for these offerings to the akalos. (NIV 1918).

To the disappointment of the missionaries, who offered salvation through repentance, it was these dissatisfactions which Malaitan evangelists emphasised in their preaching:

> "We do not have to 'buy' our God like that. His Son has paid for us, once for all, at Calvary. Now we do not have to be making sacrifices of pigs, but He keeps

us strong and well. Your way is the way of hard work and no good. God's way is better.'' So, the emphasis is put on present benefits rather than on eternal rest and peace ... (NIV 1920:7).

The Christian alternative, once demonstrated as a viable way of life by the survival of its 'school' enclaves, must indeed have tempted many to free themselves from the traditional ritual system and the political establishment which it upheld. Christianity offered an end to the obligations of sacrifice, most irksome to those such as women and junior men who had less to gain from the economics of the ritual system, and removed the danger of defilement by women and the sometimes onerous rules of tabu which were intended to avert it. A desire for education and 'eternal life', which Hogbin gives as reasons for conversion in To'abaita, may also have drawn Kwara'ae to Christianity (1939:180–182), or perhaps a desire for widened horizons, social and economic improvements, European knowledge and power, which are said to have attracted converts in other parts of Melanesia and the Pacific (see eg. Hughes 1978:204, Trompf 1991:155). But it would probably be a mistake to explain Kwara'ae conversion mainly in terms of the attractions of the new religion. The ghosts had given their protection and power on the same terms since time immemorial and Kwara'ae had experienced European power, wealth and Christianity for forty years or more. What was changing was not simply that a new religion was available but that the growing power of government and the protection it gave to missionaries and local Christians was provoking a crisis of confidence in the old. Colonialism was creating an interest in Christianity by challenging the predictive power of the traditional ritual system or, in Kwara'ae terms, the actual spiritual powers of the ghosts. For many people the ghosts were failing to provide the support and protection they had always depended on.

Bell's particular achievement was in challenging the military power of the ghosts, upon which so much else depended. As time went on the ghosts were less able to confer victory or to guarantee political autonomy even in relations between local groups, let alone between Malaitans and Europeans. Some Kwara'ae themselves participated in this development for, as people recollect today, there were many who desired security from feuding and welcomed government efforts to suppress it. Christianity had a strong appeal to such people as an alternative religion of peace, ''... a way that was quiet, without fear, without being afraid of people being killed'', as Ganifiri puts it. Insofar as the ghosts assisted and even required killing in restitution for offences against themselves and their dependants and inspired the anger and courage of the warriors who carried it out, the desire for peace was a threat to their power and authority and to that of the political leaders they supported. Peace and brotherhood has been a central theme of the Christian message throughout Solomon Islands, where communities were traditionally divided by endemic feuding. But whereas traditional leaders in islands such as Isabel were able to to turn this to advantage and enhance their authority by promoting conversion (White 1991), in Kwara'ae peace was overwhelmingly subversive of the traditional political establishment, ideologically as well as politically.

Kwara'ae themselves tend to attribute the end of feuding and the consequent failure of the ghosts to Christianity rather than to the government, as Didi'imae explains:

> It was 'school', God, which spoiled the ghosts. ... Government put them in jail to prevent them from killing, wanting to stop them. But no; they went to jail or they were hung, but the ghosts worked strongly in us, always killing. Later on they brought the Gospel and we went to 'school' and that's because they said, as it says in the Bible, "Thou shalt not kill". But if you take up the ghosts, everyone is always killing.

The logic of Kwara'ae theology is indeed that Christianity should discourage killing, for Christian neglect of tabu and sacrifice undermined the power of the ghosts to enforce their authority in this way. But in this the government also played a crucial part. Even before Bell's time fear of the government had begun to inhibit some men from killing for restitution. As government retaliation became more effective it became increasingly difficult to carry out the killings so often required to cleanse men and ghosts of defilement, leaving people to suffer the anger of the ghosts or the withdrawal of their protective power. 'Going to school' became a common means of avoiding the sickness and death which might otherwise result and government protection also made this a way to escape the authority of the ghosts, their priests and the traditional establishment.

At the same time the failure or anger of the ghosts was having a serious effect on people's health and well-being, as periodic epidemics of alien diseases swept through Malaita. According to Ivens, epidemics of dysentery, influenza and colds began to occur after recruiting switched from Queensland to plantations in the Solomons (1930:45). Details of such afflictions are little recorded before the 1920s but it seems likely that mortality from epidemics has been a serious probelm for many years previously. Sickness challenged faith in the ghosts and led many people to convert over the years. Christians also suffered in these epidemics, sometimes perhaps more than others, due to their more crowded living conditions in the less healthy areas near the coasts, prone to malaria and other diseases (Hilliard 1978:26). Some reverted to their ghosts when deaths challenged their faith in God's healing power, but in the long term it was the ghosts who were most discredited by disease. Perhaps the provision of Western medicine by the missionaries had something to do with this. Medical treatment was a routine service provided by SSEM missionaries and 'teachers' (NIV 1907–8:34, 1918), especially by Northcote Deck, who was a doctor. *Not In Vain* is full of reports of people being cured of ailments, particularly chronic ulcers, for which traditional medicine had apparently provided no remedy, and sometimes traditionists (or relapsed Christians like Fiuloa) were taken to mission stations or 'school' for medical treatment and possible conversion. As with traditional cures, Kwara'ae associated the efficacy of such treatment with spiritual power dependent on ritual observances, which was consistent with the Christian emphasis on the healing power of prayer.

The SSEM missionaries were not averse to using other demonstrations of Western technology to impress potential converts too. From the earliest years Northcote Deck, a man of many talents, drew appreciative audiences with shows of lantern slides he had made as a preaching aid (NIV 1907–8:34). His brother Norman, who joined the mission in 1914, was fond of demonstrating how a magnet would distinguish a nail from a stick, as God would sort Christians from 'heathens' on the Day of Judgement. For some, if only the least sophisticated in Western ways, such incidents would have seemed not unlike the minor 'miracles' through which priests exhibited the power of their ghosts. Certainly the imagery of Deck's magnet played its part in the conversion of Christians like Didi'imae who recall it today.

When the Christian God had evidently broken the monopoly of spiritual power by offering an effective alternative, the sacrifices and observances of elaborate rules of tabu required by the ghosts came to seem a burden hardly justified by the increasing uncertainty of the benefits to be gained. So it was that the ghosts came to be regarded as a capricious, demanding and ultimately unreliable source of power, as they are described by Christians today. The Christians themselves compounded the effect through their own iconoclasm. Depending on their viewpoint, Kwara'ae give Christianity the credit or blame for undermining the powers of the ancestors by encouraging violation of their rules which neutralised (*fa'amolā*) or defiled (*fa'asuā*) the ghosts and their dependants rather than keeping them tabu (*fa'aābua*) so that they would continue to be 'true' and effective (*mamana*). The protection of the ghosts required that their dependants be 'true' to them in return and so Christianity spoiled (*fa'alia*) the ghosts by undermining the faith and the observance of the rules of tabu upon which their power and support depended. While Christians and missionaries demonstrated the viability of a new religion and way of life, government enabled them to do so by challenging the priests and warriors who mediated the power of the ghosts. But in Kwara'ae terms the political challenge was also a direct threat to the spiritual relationships which upheld the tradition social order.

The Kwara'ae view that Christianity spoiled the power of the ghosts actually has much in common with that of the SSEM missionaries, for whom the spread of Christianity was a victory in a contest of power between God and Satan, with whom they and Kwara'ae themselves identified the ghosts, as 'devils' (*defolo*) or 'satans' (*setan*). Ironically the missionaries' position seems to have blinded them to this point. Hence a comment in *Not In Vain* that "... only a few come [to 'school'] to escape the penalty of their sins" (NIV 1918). This is precisely what many converts were attempting to do, insofar as Kwara'ae understood the Biblical concept of 'sin' as equivalent to offences against ghosts, especially defilement (*fa'asua'anga*). It was when 'sins' against their ghosts appeared to be making the traditional religion untenable that they began to consider more effective alternatives.

'NEW LIFE': A LOCAL ALTERNATIVE

But not all these alternatives were under the auspices of the missions. During the 1910s a new cult developed, drawing on the power of spirits who were neither ancestral ghosts nor the Christian God, and providing a vivid illustration of how Kwara'ae perceived the relationship between the two religions. The new spirits seemed to offer an alternative to the ghosts at a time when many people were becoming dissatisfied with them but were yet unwilling to adopt the 'European ghost' (*akalo ara'ikwao*).

One centre of this new cult was at 'Atori on the coast north of Kwai Island, not far from the Christian communities on the Bulia inlet and Ngongosila. The 'Atori people had moved down from Gwauna'ongi in the central bush about six generations before, intermarrying with the saltwater people and becoming much like saltwater people themselves. Their leader was Mauara, an influential feastgiver who mediated between the bush and saltwater communities from his base at Mānaofa, an artificial island commanding the inlet to the Bulia river. Mauara must have been well aware of the alternative way of life offered by Christianity. Several of his relatives had been to Fiji and Queensland and in 1907 his young son Kōtiu had worked as a cook for the mission station at Ngongosila, quite likely sent to gain information (he was apparently not chosen for his dedication to the job) (NIV 1907–8;33). Later Mauara allowed Fiuloa and his 'brothers' to establish their 'school' villages on land under his control at Feraasi in 1909 and Rade in 1916. But instead of joining 'school' himself, Mauara began a new cult on the instruction of his father Diko (Ko'odiko'a). His grandson Kedeola (Kōtiu's son) remembers this cult and explained it with the help of his son Paul Oge.

Diko had been a warrior with a spectacular reputation, said today to have killed three thousand (sic) people as the leader of expeditions for vengeance and rewards from West Kwara'ae to Kwai island, besides being involved in wrecking a ship at Kwakwaru. In 1907 he was still regarded as an important leader (NIV 1908:33), but in his last years he retired to live on Ngongosila to avoid the many enemies he had made. Before he died Diko told Mauara that their various relatives should take his bones as relics and make offerings to him alone, as a mediator with all the other spirits of their ancestors. These spirits were known as *anoasa*, a saltwater term for the souls or 'spirits' of the dead which go to the afterworld, as distinct from ghosts (*akalo*).[6] This was to be the basis of a 'new life' (*mauri fa'alu*).

One man who probably took this 'new life' from Diko was Āsufe of 'Aisasale in the west-central bush, whose people were clan 'brothers' of the 'Atori people. In any case, Āsufe began his own cult at 'Aisasale at about the same time, as the Kwara'ae Headman Dausabea described in detail to Collin Allan in the 1940s (Allan 1974). According to Dausabea, Āsufe had revelations from a kind of spirit known as *bulu* and took the name Buluanoasa. *Bulu* is said to be a Kwara'ae equivalent of *anoasa*, so he may have incorporated the 'Atori spirits into his cult as well as into his name. First the *bulu* enabled Buluanoasa to divine the cause of another man's sickness as neglect of his ghosts, then it instructed Buluanoasa to discard his own ghosts, desecrate their shrines and adopt the *bulu* as his sole source of power and protection. In the process he gained a congregation, which may have included people from places like Ubasi. Fiuloa's brothers are said to have come to 'school' at Rade in 1916 only after the *bulu* they were worshipping as an alternative to Christianity had failed to protect them from sickness and trouble caused by the ghosts. With his associate Niusuri, Buluanoasa tried to impress his followers with miraculous demonstrations of power. Eventually the *bulu* began to promise the arrival of quantities of shell money, English money, guns and ammunition and the return of the dead, but when people followed the required procedures and built a house for the goods, nothing happened. Then the *bulu* told them to begin activities on the coast at Fou'o in 'Atori.

According to Kedeola, Buluanoasa, Niusuri and their followers came down to live at 'Atori with Mauara and his people in about 1917 and instructed them in the 'new life'. Together they built a large stone wharf at Naonausu, which still stood as late as the 1960s (where the motor road from 'Aoke now meets the East coast). The wharf was intended for use by the spirits of the dead (*anoasa*) when they came by canoe to visit the living from the afterworld island of Anogwa'u. It is said that *anoasa* could sometimes be seen travelling around, looking like real people but vanishing when you got close to them, and they appeared to the leaders of the cult. Whether they were expected to unload gifts for the living at the wharf is unclear, but they were a source of power for economic pursuits. When Mauara and his people went to catch fish or negotiate the purchase of food for a feast the *anoasa* would prepare the way for them to ensure success. They were also expected to assist with porpoise hunting, for teeth used as money. According to Dausabea, after three months building the wharf and making canoes a porpoise hunt was organised. Kedeola says that the porpoises were successfully lured to the shore but failed to land on the wharf as expected and so escaped.

This cult was more than a way of gaining wealth or bringing back the dead. At a time when Christianity was changing so many people's lives in the area, the 'new life' introduced some equally radical changes in people's relationships with spirits and with one another. These developments were not quite the same at 'Atori as at 'Aisasale, and they differed again at Gwa'idai, a place within 'Atori land where the people were of a different clan. But the cult as a whole had certain common features. First of all, new sources of spiritual power were expected to give protection from the old, the rejected ghosts of the ancestors. The *bulu*, as it was known at 'Aisasale, was supposed to block the power of the ghosts, and 'block' is one meaning of this word. This also seems to have been the purpose of the spirit of Diko at 'Atori and of a 'woman ghost' (*akalo kini*) which was involved in the cult at Gwa'idai. In each case the 'new life' nullified the power of ghosts by abolishing some of the rules of tabu which conferred this power and protected it from defilement by women. Hence when there was sickness at 'Aisasale, pigs were no longer sacrificed by priests and eaten by men but instead were killed by women and eaten by the whole family. In sacrifices at Gwa'idai it seems that scraping the pig's bristles was begun at the hindquarters instead of the snout. The 'new life', like Christianity, evidently required that things which had previously been tabu become permitted (*mola*), thus reversing roles and ritual practices. At 'Atori women still lived apart during menstruation and Mauara's house was tabu, but otherwise men and women lived and ate together as Christians did. Here, rather than sacrifice pigs, Diko was given offerings of taro, shell money and, in particular, coconuts.

The ritual use of coconuts demonstrates some of the ideas underlying the 'new life'. When coconuts were sacrificed at 'Atori they were broken in half and the water was spilt over the person to wash away the offences or 'sins' causing misfortune, once they had confessed to them. Silas Sangafanoa remembers seeing Buluanoasa at 'Aisasale line up his people each morning and break a coconut to wash them with the water. This was a ceremony of cleansing and renewal, symbolic of the 'new life', for 'new' (saltwater *fa'alu*, Kwara'ae *faolu*) also implies 'clean'. 'Cleansing' (*fa'afaolua, fa'asikasikā*) for offences against tabu was an important purpose of sacrifices to ghosts, but under the 'new life' this was done in a way which actually reversed the traditional ritual. Coconuts were often associated in traditional ritual with women and feminine influences. They could not be eaten during the period of a festival, when men and ghosts were especially tabu to women, and then later at the women's part of the festival (*maoma kini*) pigs were splashed with coconut water to make it clear (*mola*) for women to eat them, as part of the process of 'cooling' (*fa'agwari'a*) and removing tabu. The feminine associations of coconuts are clearly illustrated in the story of a woman, later worshipped as a 'woman ghost', who is said to have defiled all the sacrificial pigs of an enemy community by throwing a coconut filled with her urine down amongst them so that when the men ate the pigs at their festival they all died. Under the 'new life', coconut water seems to have been used to 'cool' or 'make clear' (*fa'amolā*) the very things which the ghosts required to be tabu, as part of a process of 'feminising' (*fa'akini'a*) which completely reversed the traditional rules governing spiritual power.

In this respect the 'new life' had much in common with Christianity, as Kwara'ae understood it. Beyond the obvious similarities in washing away sins and bringing back the dead, the 'new life' attempted a fundamental ritual and social transformation which illustrates how Kwara'ae at the time perceived Christianity as an inversion of the traditional order. Significantly the opponents of Christianity are said to have called it *akalo kini*, like the spirit worshipped by the Gwa'idai people, probably meaning a spirit or cult of women as well as a 'woman ghost'. This was no doubt partly a reflection of the prominent role of women missionaries in the SSEM, which would have had a deeper significance for Kwara'ae than it did for Europeans. In Kwara'ae, women ghosts and their women priests had the property of suppressing or pacifying male ones and promoting agricultural productivity. By involving women in religious ritual and allowing them to join and share with men, Christianity broke the rules of the ghosts, defiled them, blocked or destroyed their power and, in this process, pacified and quietened the men. This was the purpose of the 'new life' and Mauara in particular intended it to be a way of peace. He sent the dangerous 'Atori warrior Kamekame away to work in Western Solomons and concentrated his energies on feastgiving, in contrast to his warrior father Diko. The source of Kamekame's power was an ancient warrior ghost called Kwe'e who made men into wild and reckless fighters, but (for reasons which are not entirely clear) in Mauara's cult Kwe'e also changed his character and promoted friendship and harmony.

But although the new life of the Christians had evidently enabled them to survive and prosper, it did not work so well for the followers of the *bulu*. When the big porpoise hunt was organised at 'Atori (using coconut branches and nuts to bring the porpoises to shore), it failed. As Dausabea reported, after three days without catching anything the 'Aisasale people went home to the bush, disillusioned with the *bulu*. Back at 'Aisasale the cult collapsed, the *bulu* was denounced and people began to die of sickness. After a bizarre attempt to create a child from afterbirth (an extreme inversion of traditional values, in which afterbirth was particularly defiling) Buluanoasa and Niusuri also died and the survivors then joined the Anglican church (Allan 1974:186). Exactly when this occurred is unclear, for it was probably not until about 1934 that an Anglican 'school' was established at 'Aisasale itself (SCL 1938:174). Apart from this setback, the new life at 'Atori was rather more successful, as Mauara continued to be a prosperous and influential feastgiver for many years. His saltwater relatives came to make offerings and attend feasts for the *anoasa* spirits from Kwai Island, Ngongosila and Leili and from further afield in Fataleka and Lau. Some also came from the Kwara'ae bush to sacrifice coconuts to Diko, including two priests from Fakula'e who were later killed by their ghosts as a result.

The 'new life' cults were only the first of several attempts by Kwara'ae visionaries to resist the Christian missions by offering a different alternative source of spiritual power to the ghosts. They reflected the aspirations of those who wished to adapt to the changing times on their own terms, through a ritual system under their own control. But as the influence of government and the Christian faction continued to increase, more and more people found themselves obliged to consider Christianity itself as a means of resolving a growing crisis of confidence in the ghosts. However reluctant they may have been to join the Christian 'schools', most eventually found themselves with no alternative. During the first twenty years of this century the Christians had gained a firm foothold on the coast of Kwai. By the 1920s, as the government finally took political control of the East Kwara'ae bush, the ghosts were beginning to lose the struggle for the religious allegiance of the people of Kwai.

PLATE 24   *A Malaitan traditionist hears the Gospel, explained by an SSEM missionary with the aid of religious pictures.*
(*Photo from the SSEM archive*)

CHAPTER SIX

The Christian Transformation
(1920s to 1930s)

Although the growing influence of the government and of the Christian 'schools' had for some years been undermining confidence in the ghosts and the way of life they maintained, the military confrontation between them was not finally resolved until 1919. Following his tour across Kwara'ae in 1917, Bell remarked that "I regret to have to say that I do not think that such patrols will have any beneficial effect until a few inland arrests are made." (Bell 1917). By acting on this premise, he finally established the military supremacy of the government only one and a half years later. Soon the traditional system of religious and political authority was in a serious state of crisis in East Kwara'ae and by the early 1920s the movement of reaction against the ghosts was growing rapidly. The rejection of the ghosts was a piecemeal process, as individuals and local congregations faced their own particular crises of confidence in the traditional religion when their ghosts failed them or threatened to react against breaches of tabu. But by the time of the Second World War most people had joined the Christian 'schools' and transferred religious and political authority from the ghosts and their priests to the 'teachers' who mediated the power of God. In the process they helped transform Kwara'ae society by creating new social and cultural institutions appropriate to the new political realities of life under a colonial government.

SUBDUING THE WARRIORS

The Kwara'ae experience of the imposition of government adds significantly to Keesing and Corris' history of Bell's career (1980) and is worth recounting in some detail. For the people of the East Kwara'ae bush the crucial demonstration of government power was an incident in 1919 when Bell came to arrest Gului of Sakwalo at his village at Na'oasi in 'Aita'e, about half an hour's journey upstream from Rade. Samuel Alasa'a was one who remembered the event well and his account adds some important details to Bell's patrol reports.

In June 1918 Gului's wife had miscarried in the house, the kind of serious defilement for which the ghosts required a killing as cleansing and restitution. So Gului and another man from Na'oasi, Nafiramo, shot dead a woman called Maefa'ikwala nearby at Fauboso. Her husband Raraomea reported this to Bell, hoping perhaps that the government would take up the feud to return her death.

For some time fear of the Na'oasi people prevented anyone from guiding the government to them, but after some ten months, on 1st May 1919, Bell and his police came by ship to Gwaubusu, where Benjamin Manibili offered to take them to Na'oasi. They tried to take the village by surprise but Nafiramo fired at them and in the fight which followed four of the Na'oasi people were shot dead, including Nafiramo and another man of the same name, a young boy and a girl. Two were wounded, including Oganamae, their 'important man', and two policemen were shot in the leg. Gului himself escaped, after trying to shoot the police with Winchester cartridges which failed to fire (Bell 1918b, 1919a).

A few days later Bell tried to pursue Gului to Mausunga, home of Iro'ima (also known as Siau), one of the 'Ere'ere warriors whom he was also hoping to arrest for killing a man in vengeance for a previous death. Iro'ima escaped too but, as Alasa'a recalls, other men and women there resisted the police. There were struggles during which a girl threw Bell himself into a pool used by the pigs, and the police forced their way into a house where they abused the body of dead man waiting for burial and snatched a bag from his widow. (Bell omits these incidents in his report, could it be from embarrassment?).[1] They returned to the coast with three prisoners whom they later released, and avoided an ambush by the 'Ere'ere people only because Manibili led them by an unexpected route.

Although Bell's expedition failed in its purpose, it made as big an impact on East Kwara'ae as he could have hoped. For the people of Na'oasi the attack on their village was a particularly traumatic failure of their ghosts, who deserted them in the fight because the village had earlier been defiled by smoke from a burning menstrual house, as one of their descendants, Ngunu, recalls. Fearing further punishment from the ghosts for the shedding of blood in the village, the survivors fled to join an SSEM 'school' at Gwa'idalo in West Kwara'ae. The bodies of the dead were left to be buried by their relatives, Alasa'a and his 'fathers', who now saw for themselves the consequences of resisting the government.

If anyone still doubted Bell's power, it was confirmed by a similar incident not long afterwards at Lama, at the foot of Mount Alasa'a in the south-central Kwara'ae bush. Bell and his police came from 'Aoke, guided once again by Manibili, to arrest some men for a killing and when they resisted and attacked, the police shot two or three men dead. These were probably Maesala'a (or Dausabea), Siuasi (or Refo) and Kisita, who had already been arrested before but had escaped from jail at Tulagi (Bell 1919b).[2] Ironically, their deaths were accepted as vengeance for two previous killings by their relative Biliamae'a of Otefarakau and, as Moses Lebekwau of Fakula'e witnessed, a reward of six pigs put up by his victims' family was collected as a result. This was probably the last reward to be collected in Kwara'ae.

Despite some threatening talk which reached Bell's ears, even the warriors of 'Ere'ere were intimidated by these killings and reluctantly decided to give up killing people themselves. As Alasa'a explains.

> Our part of Kwara'ae saw it and were afraid: "Eh, if we kill a person perhaps Manibili will come with the government and shoot us." ... Afterwards there was no fighting in Kwara'ae. They were subdued because look, in these two places, Manibili went up and the police put them down. The 'Ere'ere men, whose names were high, went down.

When Bell returned to Kwai in October 1919, six months after the Na'oasi incident, he arrested Gului without any trouble as well as a killer called Otea of the central bush, who was probably a relative of the men killed at Lama and who had also previously promised to resist arrest. Iro'ima was left free only because he was dying in an epidemic (Bell 1919b, 1919c).

These government victories showed that some of the fiercest opponents of colonisation and their ghosts were no longer able to defend their independence, and they also confirmed the influence of the local Christian faction. Bell's informant and guide from Gwaubusu, Benjamin Manibili of 'Ere'ere, was one of

PLATE 25   *A group of armed men, arriving at a village to investigate one of Bell's early patrols into the Kwara'ae central bush, in 1917 (see Johnson 1944:18–19). (Photo by Martin Johnson, from the Martin and Osa Johnson Safari Museum, Chanute, Kansas)*

the Christians from Kerete and an active evangelist, and in assisting the government he evidently scored a victory of his own over the opponents of Christianity. At the same time, it may have seemed more than a coincidence that the ghosts were also failing to protect their dependents from other afflictions. The epidemic which killed Iro'ima in 1919 appears to have been one of several to strike Kwara'ae during this period. In 1920 *Not In Vain* reported that in Malaita as a whole "Influenza has been taking a heavy toll this year, coming in sporadic outbreaks" (NIV 1920:6) and there was a further outbreak in Kwai in 1923 (Norman Deck 1923b), with perhaps others besides.

REACTIONS TO CRISIS: THE BULU CULT

The events of 1919 and 1920, the culmination of many years of growing Christian and government strength, seem to have thrown the communities of the East Kwara'ae bush into a state of political and religious crisis. Northcote Deck reported their reactions in 1921:

> The constant defection of one family after another, ... to join the Christian schools, and their evident happiness and well-being as converts, has, for some years, been shaking the whole structure of heathen belief to its foundations. To-day, so great has become the alarm in the ranks of the heathen, that some desperate expedients are being resorted to by the praying men [ie. priests] and religious leaders in the interior.

> Thus in a number of tribes, the ancient akalos are being abandoned in prayer, as the old praying men have died off, and they are now depending on prayer merely to their dead fathers and grandfathers. ... Such tribes, too, are abandoning the old totems, such as the hawk and the dog [snake, shark, etc] and ... are no longer praying to them for fighting or protection. (NIV May 1921:4)

Although the SSEM missionaries might not have admitted it, joining the Christian 'schools' was itself a 'desperate expedient', but Deck was actually referring to the development of a new cult. Like the earlier 'new life' cult, this was also inspired by a *bulu* spirit, but it seems to have originated independently of the 'Atori and 'Aisasale cults. Some say that this *bulu* came from Langalanga or from an afterworld island called Agulusa'o or Fulifulisa'o.[3] According to Aisah Osifera of 'Aimomoko, it began when a rat spoke to a man called Lome, telling him its name, and he began to sacrifice to it. Lome began to preach and convince people that the rat was a "true God". As *bulu*, it was expected to block the power of the ghosts, protecting people from them and making sacrifices to them unnecessary, "like the mission".

The centre for this cult was at Alasa'a in the south-central Kwara'ae bush. Here, as Osifera remembers, its followers threw away the relics of their ghosts and devoted themselves to rituals modelled on church services in a building with the side walls converging on a tabu place at the back, opposite the door. Both men and women would pray and cry in a strange language, "like the mission", and make offerings of pieces of taro and sacrificial pork to the rat, which would run around inside making noises to convince people. Like the 'new life' *bulu*, which was still active at 'Atori if not at 'Aisasale, the rat *bulu* was evidently an attempt to reject the traditional ritual system and draw upon the proven power of Christian ritual without conceding the ritual and political authority of the Christian 'teachers' and missionaries. As Northcote Deck commented:

> It is significant that the new cults are called "schools", in imitation of the Christian "schools," and many of the old heathen "abus" or prohibitions have been abolished. Thus the Christians are offered free access to all the holy places from which the old akalo-worshipping heathen are excluded (completely reversing the old order of things). Thus they seek to counterfeit the liberty of the Gospel. (NIV May 1921:4).

As with the 'new life' cults, this reversal meant involving women in the mediation of spiritual power, allowing them to eat with men and join the 'services' for the *bulu*. As at Gwa'idai in 'Atori, the Alasa'a *bulu* was regarded as a 'woman ghost' (*akalo kini*). It may even have been identified with an ancestral 'woman ghost' or 'big woman' ('*afe doe*) cared for by women priests at Alasa'a, whose worship involved snakes, which are also mentioned by Deck as a feature of the new cults. At least one of the people who kept the *bulu* at Alasa'a was a woman, Nata, whose house was full of *bulu* rats, and it is also recalled that the followers of the *bulu* would wear cordylines around their necks to 'feminize' (*fa'akinia*) themselves and block the ghosts.

Among those who took up this *bulu* around 1920 were several families of the Siale clan of 'Aimomoko living at Okwala and two from Gwauna'ongi not far away, but they abandoned the cult after a short time when the *bulu* failed to prevent their ghosts from killing some of them. Despite these failures, the rat *bulu* was also taken up at various other places in East Kwara'ae, including Fauboso near Rade and Gwa'isata near the head of the A'arai river. To the west it had a centre in Langalanga where, according to Deck, "On one tiny island they have a number of holy rats, bought up in the bush, which they feed and worship." (NIV May 1921:4).

But the deaths continued, promoted perhaps by the influenza epidemic of 1923, which Norman Deck reported to have killed "many heathen in the bush" (Norman Deck 1923b). As the *bulu* failed to protect its dependants from what was apparently the anger of their ghosts, some abandoned the cult, but for some years other new followers joined. As late as 1928 a group of Ubasi people who had already abandoned their ghosts to join the SSEM changed their minds and took up the rat *bulu* instead (Norman Deck 1928b). Eventually the Alasa'a people began to die and the survivors fled to 'school' with the SSEM at

Fa'imaingwa'a in West Kwara'ae. Exactly when this happened is unclear, but in 1929 *Not In Vain* reported what may have been the end of the rat *bulu*, apparently in Langalanga at the home of a "man named Maligwasu, one of the originators of the [rat] Bulu cult ... started about ten years ago." After the death of one of his relatives his people "were terrified by spirit voices called Akalo-geni [women ghosts]" into accepting the intervention of an SSEM 'teacher' and going to 'school' (NIV 1929:4).

Today, sixty or seventy years later, it is not always clear exactly what the *bulu* was, so it is worth trying to clarify its meaning in this important episode in Kwara'ae history. Because of the failure of the *bulu* and the Christian attitude that it was no more than another 'devil', *bulu* today tends to be remembered as a 'false spirit'; the "foolish spirit sent by Satan", as Dausabea described the 'new life' *bulu* ('foolish', in Kwara'ae English, often being confused in sound and meaning with 'false'). Dausabea himself was highly sceptical about *bulu*, describing it as a forerunner of the 1940s Māsing Rul movement, which he opposed (Allan 1974:182).[4] This is similar to the perception of *bulu* (or *buru*) to the south in Kwaio, where it refers to a type of foreign spirit, maybe from Kwara'ae, which tempts individuals into adopting it instead of their own ancestors and then invariably lets them down (Keesing 1980:106–7, Akin pers. comm.). But this could well be a legacy of the failure of the *bulu* in Kwara'ae, and the term can hardly have had such connotations when people joined the cults. On examination, the term *bulu* seems to refer not to a particular type of spirit, effective or not, so much as to the function of 'blocking' or 'preventing' the power of the ghosts. This probably owed something to older practices, such as a kind of magic to neutralise or 'block' (*bulua, fa'abulua*) the power of enemies' ghosts and send them to sleep, by burning the leaf of a dark-coloured *bulu* plant (*bulu* also means 'dark brown' or 'black'). *Bulu* has similar implications elsewhere in North Malaita, referring to types of malevolent magic associated with women and women ghosts or used to immobilise enemies.[5] Of the Kwara'ae *bulu* spirits, including Diko, the *anoasa* and the rats, women ghosts seem to have been particularly appropriate to this purpose because they drew on well established ritual practices to subdue the power of ghosts by 'feminizing' to remove tabu. Of course the cults also drew on Christian ritual forms for the same purpose and maybe other sources of inspiration besides. The return of spirits of the dead may reflect both traditional Kwara'ae and Christian ideas, but in view of all the men from Kwai who worked in Fiji it could be significant that *bulu* is also a Fijian word referring to "the unseen world of the dead" (SCL 1910:593). Kwara'ae are fond of discovering new esoteric symbolic meanings when interpreting and reconciling tradition with new ideas from elsewhere, as they were evidently doing under the spiritual inspiration of the *bulu*.

Bulu may have been only one of several means by which Malaitans attempted to create what may be regarded as indigenous 'churches' during this time. At Fiu in West Kwara'ae, Anglican missionaries were disturbed to find kava drinking, originally introduced from Fiji, being practised in a Christian cult which lasted from at least the early 1920s to the 1930s, despite their repeated attempts to suppress it. Men drank kava ceremoniously in strict isolation from women, they invoked ghosts, attempted cures for the sick and had visions of angels (SCL 1924:134, 1926:139, 1933:104). The indigenous tradition of spiritually inspired ritual innovation from which such cults derived has continued to shape the development of Kwara'ae religion ever since, but as time went on the growing influence of the missions ensured that, even when this inspiration ran counter to their orthodoxy and institutions, it took on more conventionally Christian forms.

THE CHRISTIAN ADVANCE

Of those who sought an alternative to their ghosts during the 1920s, the followers of the *bulu* were apparently far outnumbered by those who went directly to the mission 'schools'. Such was the reaction to the influenza outbreak of 1920, for at Malu'u where it was most severe, and evidently elsewhere ...

> The epidemic has also been for the furtherance of the Gospel ... The mortality among the heathen has been heavier ... [than among Christians] with the result that larger numbers of them have been coming down to school than for years past. This ... is perhaps the most common cause of men joining the schools in all districts. (NIV 1920:6).

With the benefit of government protection against attack, the Christians were taking full advantage of the failures of both ghosts and *bulu* to spread their message. Missionary support for Christians in Kwai also improved when Norman Deck reopened the mission station on Ngongosila in 1923, using it as a base to tour the east coast and the Kwara'ae bush (Young 1925:256). During the 1920s the SSEM made rapid advances into the Kwara'ae bush, developing an effective pattern of evangelical work and laying the foundations for a local church organisation. Working initially from their bases in the 'school' villages near the coast, Christian 'teachers' made preaching tours of the bush districts or went to live and preach in traditionist communities, sometimes by invitation but often not. The most promising individual converts were taken for training to Onepusu so that they might return as 'teachers' to their own communities. Local groups which converted were drawn down to the coastal 'schools' or, as time went on, increasingly encouraged to establish their own 'schools' under such trained 'teachers' on their own land in the bush (NIV Apr. 1933:6–7). As converts

PLATE 26   *An SSEM congregation and their church, probably in East
Kwara'ae in the 1920s or '30s. (Photo from the SSEM archive)*

moved away into separate 'school' villages, old and new, local communities
broke up and re-formed under the ritual and political leadership of the 'teachers',
assisted and supervised on visits by the missionaries.

The progress of the Kwara'ae 'schools' was reported enthusiastically in *Not
In Vain*. By 1920 Rade had grown to about "eighty of the wildest bushmen",
and a new 'school' village had been founded at A'arai on the coast south of
Faumamanu (NIV May 1920). By 1922 there were six 'schools' in East
Kwara'ae, and by 1923 there were seven. (These were, in rough order of
decreasing size, Gwaubusu, Rade, Faubala, Dingodingo, Ngalikabara, Kerete
and A'arai). Along the coast there were other new 'schools' at Fokanakafo at the
mouth of the Auluta river in Fataleka and at Malaone (formerly Busu) in Kwaio
(NIV 1922:5, Norman Deck 1923a). Only one of these 'schools' was far into the
bush (at Faubala), but in 1923 *Not In Vain* noted that "the work is spreading fast
up into the mountains" in Kwara'ae, which was now "perhaps the brightest
district in the mission" (NIV Apr. 1923:6). In 1924 it was reported hopefully
that "... a chain of schools may soon be established on the road over the
mountains to the Government station at Auki, right across the island" (NIV
Oct. 1924:7). By 1927,

At the Nongosila end are about *seven hundred converts*, and a chain of villages stretches right across the island. Recently a band of [Langalanga] Lagoon teachers walked over to Nongosila, preaching to the heathen en route. On their way back they gathered in fourteen fresh converts, who are all under instruction now in Christian villages. ... in the mainland from Nongosila ... continually new little centres are opening up. (NIV Apr. 1927:5)

On Ngongosila itself progress was slower, partly due to the return of the influential Shadrach Amasia who had left the 'school' at Gwaubusu and renounced Christianity in 1922 for about five years after three of his children died (NIV Jul. 1922:5, Oct. 1922:4, Oct. 1927:4).

The history of these growing Christian communities is also the history of the distintegration of the Kwara'ae traditional ritual system and political establishment. This is actually many histories, the stories of scores of separate conversions in a long and gradual process which is still not quite complete in the 1990s. Local clans, families or individuals went to 'school' one by one, usually in response to purely local or personal crises in relationships with their ghosts or relatives. Without attempting a full account, the kinds of processes involved and some of the most significant developments will be illustrated here by the history of a few major clans, especially the people of Siale and Gwauna'ongi.

THE CONVERSION OF THE KWARA'AE BUSH

As previously described, Siale is a large and widely dispersed clan named for what is generally regarded as the most ancient shrine in Kwara'ae, founded by their first ancestor near the headwaters of the Auluta river in the central bush. Here four or five branches of the clan, 'Aimomoko, Fi'ikao/Fakula'e, 'Aenakwata, Tolinga and Kwarumalagiso, mostly living some distance from the ancestral lands for which they were named, joined to celebrate their major festivals. Many other clans deriving from Siale also sacrificed pigs there as a prelude to their own festivals. The shrine was probably the focus for important political alliances, and is still an evocative symbol of Kwara'ae tradition.

Several of the original Queensland Christians belonged to Siale clans, including Sela'au and Kabulanga of Fairū, whose ancestors came from Tolinga, and Fiuloa of the Ubasi clan, which derives from 'Aimomoko. When some Tolinga people from around Latea joined Sela'au at Gwaubusu after 1912, and especially when Fiuloa brought his Ubasi relatives down to the 'school' villages of Feraasi and Rade in 1914 and 1916, these were significant inroads into the great Siale congregation. But the conversion of Siale probably began in earnest with the crisis of 1919–20. It was at this time that the 'Aimomoko people living at Okwala, about four families, forsook their ghosts for the rat *bulu* at Alasa'a. They were led by Augwata, the senior priest responsible for the great shrine of Siale itself, and his defection must have dealt a serious blow to the traditional ritual system. Augwata was a man of some wordly experience who had worked in Samoa and when he moved to Alasa'a he named his village after the Samoan town of Apia. According to his daughter Betty Kalianaramo, Augwata was tired of the work of the priesthood and its restrictive rules of tabu, but when he broke these rules and ate with women the *bulu* failed to protect him and he was killed by his ghost. His wife and children then left to join the 'school' at Faubala, because she was a 'sister' of the 'teacher' there, the former Kerete Christian Nathan Uga'iniu of Sakwalo. Three of Augwata's 'Aimomoko 'brothers' also left Alasa'a but for the time being they returned to the ghosts.

But the ritual distintegration of Siale was under way. Augwata was succeeded as priest in charge of Siale by Filo'isi, also of the 'Aimomoko clan, but since Filo'isi was only Augwata's sister's son and not his 'son', some say that he never learnt the essential knowledge (*talana fiki'a*) to invoke the ghosts for the great festivals and sacrifices at Siale. The first people of the Fakula'e clan went to 'school' at about the same time, when five boys were taken by their mother to live at Gwaubusu after their father died from sorcery, because she was afraid they might meet the same fate. She chose Gwaubusu because her sister was married to Sinamu, the founder of the 'school' there. About 1923, Fiuloa began what was to become another important SSEM centre for the remaining Ubasi people at Fauketa on their own lands in the bush. Then more of the Fakula'e people abandoned their ghosts in about 1925, after two of their priests were killed by their ghosts because they had been sacrificing in the 'new life' cult at 'Atori. Their people, about five families, fled to Uga'iniu's 'school' at Faubala in Sakwalo. By the mid 1920s, although there were still many people following the traditional religion, the ritual organisation of Siale was rapidly falling apart.

The conversion of Gwauna'ongi, the large and ancient clan whose ritual organisation was described in Chapter 2, also began in about 1920 and was closely involved with the conversion of Siale. The two clans have a long history of alliance, and again the initiative came from the tireless evangelist, Fiuloa. Besides working with his own Ubasi people, Fiuloa also travelled to preach to his cousins of his mother's clan of 'Aiketa, a junior branch of the senior Gwauna'ongi clan of Faureba. At that time the 'Aiketa priest Galu was acting also for the shrine of Faureba, where the great collective festivals of Gwauna'ongi were held. Omani, who had been chosen by the founding ghost of Gwauna'ongi, 'Aitakalo, to succeed his father as senior priest at Faureba, was young, single and unwilling to take on the responsibilities involved. The story of their conversion is told by Omani's son, Adriel Rofate'e.

All the people of Gwauna'ongi were still relying upon their ghosts, including two brothers who had gone to join the *bulu* at Alasa'a but returned home when it let their father die. Fiuloa's preaching had no obvious effect until, about 1920 or '21, the priest Galu was unexpectedly killed in a fall, which precipitated a catastrophic rift with the ghosts. A young girl, angry at the ghosts' failure to save the life of her 'father', deliberately and openly defiled the sacrificial hearths in both the 'Aiketa and Faureba shrines. This was a desperate, potentially suicidal gesture, but one which had already been made by young Ubasi girls, as mentioned above. As it was, she fled into hiding and escaped her 'father's' attempts to cleanse the defilement by killing her. Probably the Na'oasi and Lama incidents were causing them doubts about actually doing so, or seeking restitution by killing someone else. In any case the Faureba and 'Aiketa people, as well as the men who had returned from the Alasa'a *bulu* and their clan, decided after deliberation to avoid catastrophic retribution from the ghosts by fleeing to 'school'. They confirmed the decision by eating all their sacrificial pigs, sharing them with the women and children, and two days after the incident everyone packed their belongings and walked down to join Fiuloa at Rade.

These converts, about nine families in all, comprised less than half of the total Gwuana'ongi congregation which used to contribute to the large festivals at Faureba, plus a fugitive from Latea who was married to a Faureba woman. Most of the remainder belonged to two other junior clans which had a certain ritual autonomy from Faureba and also celebrated their own small festivals at local shrines. They converted later in separate incidents but moved down to 'school' towards the west coast. Since that time some Gwauna'ongi families have moved at intervals to live with their clan 'brothers' and others on opposite sides of the island or in Gwauna'ongi itself, but most have remained in the districts where their parents and grandparents first went to 'school'. Their common descent and rights in their almost deserted ancestral land still provided the basis for co-operation and support, but they began to develop new ties with the local groups where they had come to live.

This story illustrates the way the new Christian communities formed and reformed as they adapted to the ritual requirements of their new religion. Even as Christians, initially under the instruction and ritual leadership of the 'teachers' at Rade, they retained a degree of autonomy. 'Joash' Omani, the prospective priest of Faureba, proved a keen Christian. He was sent to the training school at Onepusu and in 1922 Kathy Deck reported finding him "... lately baptized, ... the only teacher for a large and self-willed village" at Rade, but having problems ensuring church attendance (NIV Jul. 1922:5). Soon afterwards he bought a piece of land about half an hour's journey upstream from Rade, and the Gwauna'ongi Christians built their village there at Dingodingo, within reach of the other Christian communities but with their own 'school' on their own land. Here Omani married a daughter of the Latea fugitive and began to plan evangelical work of his own. With his wife and first child he moved back to Gwauna'ongi, built his house on Faureba land at Faisukui and began preaching to his neigbours in the bush.

Omani played an important part in the inland movement of Christianity and his village at Faisukui eventually grew into an important 'school' centre for the Kwara'ae bush. After some years of preaching to the people of Siale and Okwala he and his 'brother' Robin Rofa, a former warrior, had their first success in 1927. They cured a sick child by prayer and its father was so impressed that he, and later about four of his 'brothers', came to join the 'school' at Faisukui. These were the 'Aimomoko people who had joined the *bulu* cult at Alasa'a before returning to their ghosts under the leadership of Filo'isi as priest of Siale. Soon afterwards the other Gwauna'ongi Christians at Dingodingo moved back up to join them. Instead of becoming the senior priest of Gwauna'ongi as the ghost had once demanded, Omani was now the 'teacher' of a large and important 'school' centre where, in 1929, the first major meeting was held of one hundred SSEM 'teachers' from East and West Kwara'ae (NIV Jul. 1929:5).

CONSOLIDATING THE ADMINISTRATION

While the SSEM was extending its influence in this way during the 1920s, Bell was consolidating government authority and developing an effective system of administration, which further assisted the Christian cause. Feuding had more or less ceased and the police had a decisive military advantage as the confiscation of guns proceeded. In Kwai, Manibili's position as the local agent and intermediary for the government at 'Aoke was confirmed in 1922 when he was appointed as the first 'Headman' for what had now become the administrative 'sub-District' of Kwai (Native Affairs Book 1931–2:184). With permission from his Fairū relatives he founded the administrative base for Kwai at Faumamanu, once again making his own home at Kerete and building what was variously known as the 'court house', 'tax house' or 'council house' which Bell then used for government business on his tours around Malaita. Bell was laying foundations for a political system which now over-rode the authority of the traditional leaders. By 1925 Manibili had gained sufficient confidence and authority to be able to carry out arrests himself (Bell 1925a). He remained Headman until 1927, when he was replaced by Tommy Siru, also a strong Christian with experience in government service overseas (Native Affairs Book 1931–2). Although Bell still relied on the protection of his armed police, he no longer needed to use direct coercion to have most of his orders obeyed by the bush people of East Kwara'ae.

By 1923 Bell had enough information about the populations of the sub-Districts of Malaita and enough control over most of them to begin collecting an annual 'head tax' from all men. This put a strain on Bell's resources and he was personally opposed to it, but he managed to tax the whole of Malaita for the first time in 1923 and 1924 (Bell 1925a). The tax was set at five shillings, a quarter of that introduced elswhere in the Solomons, because of the shortage of money on Malaita and the difficulty in collecting it. Even finding this amount of money put considerable pressure on men to recruit for plantation work, as British policy for colonial economic development intended (Keesing & Corris 1980:74–80).

It was this tax which provoked the last incident of violent resistance to the government in Kwai. Jonathon Didi'imae describes how the 'Ere'ere warrior Ngwaki felt about the tax, voicing complaints which have been repeated in East Kwara'ae and other parts of Malaita ever since:

> Once the government came to tax, and he was very angry, he said "Alright, we'll kill the government so that he won't take tax from us. There isn't any copra here for us to get money and pay tax so we live here and we're poor and he's always coming to take money from us. It's just as if he's robbing us. The whiteman, we know that a man works for him and he pays him. But he comes and takes this money and he should give us money because he has come to our island. We'll kill him."

Ngwaki tried to put these ideas into action, as Didi'imae saw for himself. In October 1925 Ngwaki came down to Faumamanu with three of his brothers as Bell arrived to collect the tax. Bell was seated among his police as the drum signal was given for everyone to come forward with their money. Ngwaki handed in his brother Sulala's tax receipt instead of his own to provoke an argument and when Bell reacted he told him what he thought about the tax and struck him in the face, breaking his glasses and knocking him down. Sulala came to Ngwaki's aid, the police tried to arrest them and a brawl developed between the police and several of the 'Ere'ere men. Everyone else ran away for fear that the police would start shooting and Ngwaki and Sulala were arrested after a fierce struggle. They were charged with obstructing and assaulting the police, taken overland to 'Aoke and sent to prison at Tulagi (*Auki* Log 1925–7, Bell 1925b).[6]

This was a convincing final defeat for the warriors of East Kwara'ae. Ngwaki had been inspired by the warrior ghost of 'Ere'ere, but he was overcome and a large gathering of people from all over Kwai witnessed his failure. The attack was ill-planned and the crowd in general was unwilling to support it, or the result might have been different. Nor does Bell seem to have realised that Ngwaki had actually planned to kill him. But two years later, in October 1927, Bell and his white cadet and most of his police patrol were indeed killed in a very similar incident at Sinalaagu in Kwaio. The leader of the massacre, Basiana, was also protesting about the tax and he may well have learnt from Ngwaki's experience (see Keesing & Corris 1980).

PLATE 27   *Collecting the 'head tax'. This is how Bell would have appeared at Faumamanu, except that the police guard may be heavier since this photo of District Officer Garvey was taken at Uru in 1928, exactly one year after Bell was killed at nearby Sinalaagu. (Photo from Lady Patricia Garvey)*

Bell's death caused much grief and anxiety in Kwai among those, particularly Christians, who appreciated his achievement in bringing peace to the district, and people like Manibili who knew him personally (Joan Deck 1927). There were also fears of government retaliation and, as an Anglican missionary wrote, "Some 3,500 men went through to Auki in a period of four or five days from all over N. Mala, including swarms of bush people, to assert their loyalty and to show their sorrow" (SCL 1928:29). The government reaction probably made even the 'Ere'ere people feel relieved that Ngwaki had failed. About three weeks later the government mounted a major expedition into the Kwaio bush which killed about sixty people outright, took almost two hundred men to prison at Tulagi and led eventually to the deaths of two hundred people in all, by Kwaio reckoning (Keesing & Corris 1980:Ch. 11). The whole of Malaita was thoroughly subdued.

The Sinalaagu massacre, carried out with the support of Kwaio ghosts, was a stark reminder of the role of the traditional religion in Malaitan resistance to both government and Christianity. It is hardly surprising that traditionists in Kwara'ae felt threatened by the government retaliation in Kwaio, especially if they heard the rumours which reached Norman Deck that the government was considering the systematic destruction of shrines throughout Malaita to discourage further armed resistance (Norman Deck 1928a). In fact this never happened, but many Kwaio joined the missions to escape from government retaliation and from the consequences of police defiling their ghosts, and there was a similar reaction in Kwara'ae. In early 1928 the SSEM gained about a hundred new converts in East Kwara'ae (Norman Deck 1928c) and in the same year in West Kwara'ae people from the bush were reported to be coming to join the Anglican 'schools' as a result of the events in Kwaio. At the government station of 'Aoke about 1,077 guns were handed in on demand to the police in a single day (SCL 1928:62–63,144).

Ngwaki made his last gesture of now futile defiance against the forces that threatened the old order in 1933. This time his target was Nathan Uga'iniu, the evangelist from Faubala, whom Ngwaki had known at least since they lived at Kerete together after returning as Christians from Queensland. Didi'imae recalls the incident as a contest of power between God and the ghosts, when Ngwaki met Uga'iniu as he was preaching at a 'feast of fame' (talo'a) in Fakula'e. Uga'iniu said:

> "Jesus died for you Ngwaki, and he died for me". Ngwaki just grabbed a stone and threw it at the [religious] picture in Uga'iniu's hand ... and went and put it in the fire. Then everyone pulled him away; "Eh, if you burn it, the clouds will rain on us [spoiling the feast]". ... Then he just took hold of Uga'iniu and threw him on the fire too ... and took fire and burnt his mouth. "That's the mouth you're talking with. This 'school' thing, this thing I brought here, I'm not siding with that. It's the ghost of the whiteman". Then they came and pulled him away and pulled Uga'iniu away too. Everyone ran away from the feast; "Oh, Ngwaki has struck Uga'iniu ...." They just pulled at Uga'iniu and he said "Oh, it's alright; come and burn it again". Ngwaki was angry and wanted to kill him ... Well, when they had pulled him away, a light rain came.

The people at the feast evidently took the power of 'school' seriously and were not prepared to back Ngwaki, as some might have done ten or fifteen years before. Not long afterwards Ngwaki fell sick from sorcery after a visit to Fokanakafo in Fataleka and when he died of it in March 1934 this was said to be because of his attack on Uga'iniu. As Didi'imae commented, "That's why we say God is true".

THE CHRISTIAN TRIUMPH

The steady evangelical work of the SSEM, assisted by the shock of the government attack on the Kwaio bush in 1927, was given further impetus by a massive earthquake in 1931. This was the worst in living memory and so severe that, as the District Officer reported, "... it was not uncommon to hear pagans state that their "devils" had deserted them, and Christians assert that the Day of Judgement was at hand" (Annual Report 1931:7). About 140 people were reported to have joined SSEM 'schools' in East Kwara'ae that year as a result (Norman Deck 1931). These included a group of Mānadari people, near Siale in the central bush, who went to 'school' because they regarded the earthquake as a sign from God requested by a 'teacher' who had been preaching to them. A major influenza epidemic (introduced by the Melanesian Mission ship *Southern Cross*; Norman Deck 1931) which killed about 270 people in Kwara'ae later in the same year no doubt compounded the effect (Annual Report 1931:5). By 1933 the District Officer had formed the opinion that "The Kwara'ae bush natives are almost all members of the Missions" (Annual Report 1933) and from this period Kwara'ae was generally regarded by the government as the "most civilized district of Malaita" (Annual Report 1934:7).

By this time the SSEM was also making inroads among the saltwater people of Ngongosila and Kwai Islands, half of whom were Christians by 1931 (Norman Deck 1931). This owed something to the renewed efforts of Shadrach Amasia but also to the numbers of people from nearby mainland districts who had moved to 'school' with their relatives at the mission station on Ngongosila. These included some of Mauara's people from 'Atori, led by his 'son' Sardias Oge, who became a 'teacher' on Ngongosila in 1932. Mauara and his family continued to prosper under their 'new life' cult until he died after holding his last spectacular festival at Mānaoba, probably in the 1930s. Mauara's death was signalled by a lightning storm, evidence of his spiritual power, but from then on the cult he had led seems to have fallen into decline.

Until the 1930s all the Christians in Kwai had joined the SSEM, although there were strong Anglican communities of the Melanesian Mission in West Kwara'ae which were reaching into the central bush near Alasa'a during the 1920s (SCL 1926:139). But during the early 1930s the Anglicans also began to attract some converts in East Kwara'ae. In 1929 the priest of the 'Aenakwata clan of Siale was killed by lightning at their shrine because he had made an inadequate sacrifice, and before he died he told his five sons to go to 'school'. For some reason they decided against joining the SSEM and one of them, Ba'eakalo, with a Fakula'e man, Kuruiasi, went to Fau'au in West Kwara'ae to ask for an Anglican 'teacher'. They established an Anglican village at Lama in Fakula'e in about 1932. In about 1934 a visit by Solomon Islander Anglican lay preachers of the Melanesian Brotherhood secured more converts from the Siale clans of 'Aenakwata, Fi'ikao and Tolinga. By 1936 Lama included "46 catechumens, some of whom are already baptized" and the Anglican Church was firmly established in East Kwara'ae with other villages at Okwala and, towards the west, at 'Aisasale (site of Buluanoasa's *bulu* cult) (SCL 1936:90). Other Fakula'e

Christians founded an SSEM village on their own land at Taulalamua in the early 1930s and some of these also joined the Anglican 'school' at Lama, from which several other Anglican villages later developed during the 1940s and '50s. By 1934 the Melanesian Mission was also re-established on the east coast in nearby Kwaio at Uru and at Malaone on the Kwara'ae border, after an absence of more than twenty years (SCL 1934:21, 1936:90).

The only other mission which gained any following in East Kwara'ae before the Second World War was the Seventh Day Adventist Church (SDA). The SDA established a station at Uru in East Kwaio in 1924 and the SSEM missionaries watched them with suspicion, actively opposing both their doctrine and their methods. According to Norman Deck the SDA practice was to attract and obligate converts by offering presents and only later to introduce compulsory tithes and arduous rules against eating pig and other foods (Norman Deck 1927a, 1927b). But they seemed to have had little success in Kwai until, in the mid 1930s, an SDA evangelist from Choiseul in Western Solomons gained some converts of the Sasadili clan, who moved down from the hills above the Kwaibaita river to build a coastal village at Busu'ai near A'arai. According to Iniakalo, his 'fathers' joined the SDA because they wanted 'eternal life', education to gain employment and the benefits of the European lifestyle, while escaping from the demands of their ghosts.

Despite the inroads made by the SDA and the Anglicans and the resistance of a significant minority of traditionists, the SSEM was well established as the dominant religious faction in Kwai. In fact SSEM conversion and training had been so successful that Kwara'ae evangelists were now busy extending their work into other areas of Malaita and Guadalcanal. One of the mission's main problems was that the training school at Onepusu was not large enough to keep up with the demand for training and the need for more 'teachers' (NIV Jul. 1934:3, Jan. 1936:7, Norman Deck 1928d).

Considering the scale of the bush population which the resident missionaries were having to service in East Kwara'ae, the location of the mission station on Ngongosila was evidently becoming impractical. Sinai, the mission area of the island, was also becoming seriously overcrowded by the influx of people from the mainland who had attached themselves to the mission. In 1936 it was decided to rebuild the dilapidated mission house at Rade instead, and the resident missionaries, Mr. and Mrs. Neil, moved there (NIV Jan. 1936:7, Jul. 1936:2). It was from this time that Rade became known as Nāfinua. Leadership in the local church was now being assumed by Justus Jimmy Ganifiri, a son of Fiuloa, who had died in 1930. Ganifiri played an important part in the development of Nāfinua into the principal SSEM centre of the district and he later became a central figure in the mission as a whole. He was born about 1905, went to train at Onepusu in 1923 for seven years and then spent some time working for

European employers before returning home to work for the church. One of his first acts was to start an 'education school' at Nāfinua in 1938 for children and adults, which provided the first education for many of today's senior men and women of the district.

FILO'ISI AND THE LAST RESISTANCE OF SIALE

Such resistance as the traditionists were still able to offer to the continued advance of Christianity and government was led by the senior priest of Siale, Filo'isi of 'Aimomoko. Filo'isi regarded himself, and is still described today, as the ritual head of the whole of Kwara'ae and when he first took over the priesthood from Augwata in the early 1920s he did indeed hold a key position in the hierarchy of shrines on which the wider ritual organisation of Kwara'ae was based. He used to proclaim the ultimate derivation of all the clans of Kwara'ae and Malaita from Siale as the shrine established by the first man to discover Malaita, a claim repeated to this day by some leaders of Kwara'ae political movements.

Filo'isi met Norman Deck and heard him preach several times from 1925 onwards. Deck found him well acquainted with Christianity from six years of working in Queensland and recognised him as a major obstacle to the progress of the mission in the Kwara'ae bush (NIV Oct. 1925:7, Dec. 1943:3,5–6). Filo'isi's religious stand was part of his overall opposition to Europeans and colonialism. He voiced common objections to the rule of government law, to taxation and to dependence on money and his conversations with Norman Deck provide a good illustration of the debate over the merits of their different religions. By his own account, Deck

> ... contrasted the fruit of Satan's rule in Malaita, under the akalos, for before the missionaries and the Government came, how then the Akalos made men enemies, and made them steal, swear, fight and kill, and even eat one another. God on the contrary taught men to love one another, to stop quiet; God had sent the missionaries and the Government, and Malaita now was quiet.

Deck's analysis hardly told the full story, but as far as it went Filo'isi probably agreed with it. But he replied that the present times were bad, that men were just like women and "Me like 'im fight and kill 'im man. He good fella long me! Devil Devil he talk long me all same." Then, after some discussion, Filo'isi conceded,

> "Oh! me tired along Devil Devil this time, me work hard too much long devil, and too many people belong me lose, and my line he no plenty now; me lose 'im too much money long buy 'im pig pig for Devil, might me sling him this time."
> (NIV Oct. 1925:7).

Over the years, as the people of Siale and even his own immediate congregation of 'Aimomoko went to 'school', Filo'isi apparently began to consider the Christian alternative more and more seriously. He was persuaded to visit 'school' villages and the SSEM station at Nāfinua and to witness Norman Deck's magnet trick (NIV Dec. 1943:6). Although Filo'isi continued to sacrifice for those who still wished to do so, the last of the festivals which had been the pride of Siale was probably held in the early 1930s. But he continued to resist Christianity and by the early '40s he was working to hold meetings and build a house for re-establishing traditional 'law'. In 1940 he led a traditionist faction of twenty or thirty men in opposition to government plans to build a foot road across Kwara'ae from coast to coast. He maintained that a such a cleared way was the sole prerogative of the ghost at Siale, where a 'road' was made to lead into the shrine for the festivals. Underlying his objections was the fear that improved access to the central bush would open the area to Europeans, enabling them to take Kwara'ae land and assisting the government to exercise authority. The District Officer of the time did not take Filo'isi's objections very seriously, especially when he offered to waive them in return for a payment of £100 to appease the ghosts (Diary 1940, Tour Report 1940). The foot road went ahead, although more than twenty years later the first motor road across the island was prevented from passing through the central Kwara'ae bush by Filo'isi's 'son' Osifera for similar reasons.

When Filo'isi eventually went to 'school' with the SSEM at Kaole in West Kwara'ae in 1943 and abandoned his ghosts, it was for fear of their anger at an unacceptable marriage between one of his 'daughters' and her brother-in-law. That he was unable to prevent the marriage was no doubt a reflection of his declining authority, although it did have the predicted consequences of sickness for one of their relatives. After being cured from pneumonia by medicine and prayer, Filo'isi became so impressed with God's power that eventually he went to preach in Kwaio to some of those he had once sacrificed for (NIV Dec. 1943:6). But by 1948 he was noted by the government to have "little influence" (Tour Report 1948b). He died about 1954.

Filo'isi's conversion was a big occasion for his Christian relatives and neighbours and an important symbolic setback for the traditionists. It meant the abandonment of Siale, the removal of a major focus of inter-clan ritual organi-sation and the neutralisation of the dominant personality in the resistance to both mission and government. In Norman Deck's words,

> The whole of a large section of Kwara'ae is shaken to its foundations, but though quite a number of heathen, in fact two villages, have come in, the bulk of the heathen connected with him are still outside, hanging on to their subsidiary "fatabus." (NIV Dec. 1943:6)

But many of these people had already been reduced to ritually isolated minorities among their Christian relatives and neighbours and in the years that followed most of them also went to 'school' a few at a time.

THE CHRISTIAN TRANSFORMATION AND THE SSEM

By the time of the Second World War most of the people of Kwai had taken part in a massive social transformation. Radical changes in ritual organisation and community membership had accomplished an equally radical shift of political power from the now largely defunct traditional establishment of priests, wealthy men and warriors to new forms of leadership by 'teachers' and church elders. It is here that Hogbin's study (1939) seems most lacking, emphasising only the attractions and consequences of conversion to Christianity. In Kwara'ae, adopting the Christian way of life was also a movement to escape the discredited traditional past. This was achieved by joining a social order designed to accommodate or even complement the colonial authority of government and missions, rather than continuing a now futile opposition to it under the traditional order.

For many people this must have seemed like a final surrender to the European domination which they and their ancestors had been fighting for so long. Others probably regarded it as a positive response to the new opportunities presented by colonialism, including a means to end feuding under an ideology of Christian brotherhood and the rule of government law, as it had proved to be on other islands in the Solomons (see eg. White 1991, Zelenietz 1979). For some it also offered new routes to personal advancement through the church system instead of the traditional establishment. But whatever their personal gains or losses, there is little doubt that Kwara'ae regarded conversion as a radical transformation of the traditional order, and it did indeed involve a holistic social and cultural change.

However, as Sahlins predicts (1981:68) and White's study of conversion on Isabel confirms (1991:129), such transformations involve old cultural structures reproducing themselves in new form. In Kwara'ae, although conversion was accomplished by abandoning the rules making the ghosts tabu, the theology of the traditional order was itself employed to dissolve the structures of political power which supported it and to constitute the new Christian order in its place. For all its claims to be a new way of life, Kwara'ae Christianity was inevitably continuous with their traditional culture. This may be more evident to an outside observer than to the people involved, and it also goes deeper than the theological continuities observed by Hogbin (1939:191–204). Kwara'ae society continued to be based on a religious world-view in which human and spiritual beings belonged to the same social order, albeit a different order from that of the past, and relationships between them depended on the same basic theological premises. People still dealt with spiritual forces through local communities which acted as ritual congregations, as they always had done, and ritual activities remained an important focus of social life under new organisation and leadership. This leadership still drew much of its authority from the mediation of spiritual power, and 'teachers' held from God a similar authority to that which the priests held from their ghosts, with other senior men exercising their influence as 'church elders'.

But unlike the priests, 'teachers' were not necessarily the senior representatives of their own clans, nor did they always belong to the same clan as their congregations. Instead they held authority in a ritual system which cut across clans, often dividing major clans among different villages or even different denominations and bringing members of different clans together into the same village communities. This was partly a result of the history of conversion, which broke up so many clan-based communities and reassembled them under new ritual leadership as the opportunity arose. But Christian ritual organisation also required a change in settlement pattern for the bush people. Instead of living in small settlements based on local clans and scattered throughout the hills, many people were now concentrated in larger villages, often within easy reach of the

PLATE 28   *The congregation of the SSEM centre at Nafinua in their large*
iron-roofed church in the late 1930s or early '40s. Visiting
missionaries join a local church leader conducting a service from
the dais. (Photo from the SSEM archive)

coast. This was encouraged by the SSEM missionaries as a way of building the authority of the 'teachers' and ensuring church attendance, provided the villages did not become too crowded and unmanageable. One hundred people was regarded as the optimum size; larger villages were encouraged to split and smaller ones to attend Sunday services at the larger local centres under the influence of the senior 'teachers' (NIV Apr. 1923:6). But these new villages were still based on groups of relatives and no doubt local clans lived in their own sections of the village, as they do in large Christian villages today.

While breaking down the traditional clan-based ritual system, the SSEM created its own organisation on a far greater scale than anything which had existed in Malaita before. Protected by the government from the feuding which had fragmented Malaitan society in the past and guided by the missionaries with their resources and experience of church organisation, 'teachers' were able to develop ritual and political links between local communities and districts. Within Kwara'ae, Nāfinua and other major villages acted as centres where people from smaller villages in the neighbourhood assembled for major church services, especially on important occasions such as visits by the missionaries. The 'teachers' were able to assemble hundreds of people for such events, up to an estimated one thousand at one meeting at Nāfinua in 1939. The dispersal of evangelists from the main school centres like Nāfinua and the contacts made in training at Onepusu created a network extending throughout Kwara'ae and beyond, to other districts of Malaita. These relationships were maintained and strengthened through periodic conferences and prayer meetings which helped to promote a certain unity and co-ordination within the wider church (NIV Apr. 1933:7, Oct. 1939:3). From 1929 such meetings brought together 'teachers' from both sides of Kwara'ae and during the 1930s they were attended also by visitors from Kwaio and Fataleka (Norman Deck 1932a).

This organisation enabled the SSEM 'teachers' to develop and standardise a new set of rules governing human and spiritual relationships within their 'school' communities. In ensuring that the social and personal behaviour of their congregations was acceptable to God, the 'teachers' and elders created the social and ritual system in which they held their authority, which was equivalent in many respects to the system of rules that had ensured the support and protection of the ghosts. Initially, at least, they had some scope for interpretation of these rules from the Bible, with an emphasis on the Ten Commandments, for it was the policy of the SSEM missionaries to promote an indigenous Christianity in which 'teachers' were "... grounded in the word of God, and taught to apply it to their own lives and conditions" (NIV Apr. 1933:7, Hilliard 1974:51). Under the influence of Abu'ofa of Malu'u in particular, rules were devised and discussed among church leaders from different districts to formulate a more or less standard SSEM doctrine for Malaita as a whole.

But as long as the 'teachers' depended on the SSEM missionaries for training, guidance and logistic support, their opportunities to develop a local form of Christianity were limited by the doctrinal preferences of the missionaries. Attempts to introduce new ritual practices incompatible with this were condemned and suppressed. Hence for instance in the 1920s Norman Deck found he "had to deal with" a Fataleka man called Harry 'Ania who tried with some success to introduce new ritual rules to 'schools' in Kwai, banning women from taking part in prayer meetings on the grounds that they prevented the prayers from ascending to heaven (Norman Deck 1923b, 1924). This was probably only one of many concessions to traditional theology and ritual which local Christians tried to introduce without success. But apart from doctrinal matters, since the missionaries made little secret of their own contempt for Malaitan traditional culture their influence ensured that the standards of behaviour adopted as appropriate to Christianity reflected their own cultural prejudices. While the 'teachers' still lacked confidence in their own ritual knowledge, they were very amenable to what was described in *Not In Vain* as "the fiat of the Word of God, and when shown His mind revealed in that Word, accept it without question" (NIV 1918). In the same way that the missionaries could claim the authority to interpret the Bible to the 'teachers', so the 'teachers' held authority over their less educated congregations.

Although the rules of the SSEM proscribed certain practices as characteristically 'heathen', they also reaffirmed important traditional moral norms, restricting interaction between men and women to avoid illicit sexual activity and banning swearing, stealing and other causes of social conflict. Other customs, traditionally acceptable but proscribed ultimately because they were objectionable to the missionaries, included smoking, betel nut and local artforms such as costume ornaments, songs and dances. Clothing was insisted on as a crucial symbol of Christian identity. But of greatest significance were SSEM attempts to suppress practices which lay at the root of the traditional political system.

ECONOMIC AND POLITICAL REFORMS

Colin Allan, as District Commissioner of Malaita, commented on the SSEM attitude to traditional exchanges in a scathing report on the mission in 1951:

> By the giving of feasts the various individuals concerned achieve social prestige and secure for themselves positions of civil authority in the community. It is considered that when the teachers decided to forbid all feasting [except for church festivals] they were largely motivated by a desire to maintain their own position and power unthreatened by any traditional leaders . (Allan 1951)

There was doubtless some truth in Allan's conclusions, although in the cause of building the church this policy may have been rather less cynical than he implies. It may have originated in the Malu'u church, where Hogbin noted in the 1930s that the effect was indeed to destroy the influence of 'important men' (1939: 214). The same applied to attempts to abolish or strictly limit bridewealth, a source of controversy in Kwara'ae which is still unresolved to this day. Initially Abu'ofa tried to ban bridewealth altogether at Malu'u, but the bitter opposition this provoked led to a compromise limit of three *tafuli'ae* 'red money' units being set with the mediation of the missionaries and the approval of the District Officer. In the early 1920s the Kwara'ae SSEM 'schools' also adopted this limit under persuasion from Norman Deck. His argument was that the then normal bridewealth of thirty or forty *tafuli'ae* or more made it difficult for young men to marry by placing too heavy a burden of repayment upon them, degraded the women and encouraged "pride and covetousness" (Norman Deck 1932a, Deck & Hogbin 1934–5; 243, 369, 489). Predictably enough, the three 'red money' limit was later claimed to have weakened the authority of the senior men who provided the bridewealth and it also led to tensions with Anglicans and traditionists who did not observe it (Annual Reports 1934, 1940). With this restriction, and for similar reasons, came attempts to abolish the large wedding feasts which initiated competitive feasting and gift exchange between in-laws, but this was less easily agreed and was still under debate in church meetings in the 1930s (Norman Deck 1932b). In 1947, under the influence of the Māsing Rul movement, the Kwara'ae church raised the bridewealth limit to five 'red money', or ten in restitution for elopement, but some SSEM leaders continued to advocate marriage by 'free gift' in the European manner, in the face of widespread opposition.

Similar questions arose over the giving of restitution in settlement of disputes, which was also a source of influence for the senior men who acted as mediators and provided the goods. In ensuring the observance of Christian standards of behaviour to maintain harmony within their communities and in relations with God, church leaders took an important role in dispute settlement, as the priests of the ghosts had done before them. Accepting restitution was regarded as participating in the offence by deriving benefit from it, whereas the Christian way was to resolve conflict by confession, forgiveness and prayer, mediated by church leaders. Enforcement of Christian rules and mediation was sanctioned by ostracism or exclusion from church services and consequent withdrawal of God's protection. The missionary view was that "Cases of discipline are usually dealt with by the Church in a wise and Scriptural way, and the elders are taking more and more responsibility" (NIV Apr. 1933:8). Allan's comments reveal the frustration which the government felt with their independent authority: "... Before the war it was virtually the SSEM teachers who ran the village and dealt with sin like crime. They were quite merciless. They enjoyed their power ..." (Allan 1951). What Allan failed to recognise was that 'sin' really was 'like crime', insofar as it affected the well-being of the community as a whole in its relationship with God, just as breaches of tabu could endanger everyone's well-being under the ghosts. This was the basis for the authority of the 'teachers' and elders, as it had been for the traditional priests.

As the organisers of church activities, the influence of the 'teachers' pervaded every aspect of community life and they took on some of the roles of traditional 'important men' (*ngwae 'inoto'a*). It was they who organised the building of sometimes lavishly decorated churches, the feasts for church festivals and the entertainment of religious 'singing bands' which were the nearest Christian equivalent to traditional festivals and dances (NIV Apr. 1933:5). 'Teachers' also acquired some economic influence, although never to the extent allowed by the traditional exchange system which they were attempting to curtail. It was a matter of principle with the SSEM that teachers were not paid by the mission but were motivated by "... love to Christ and salvation of souls" (NIV Apr. 1933:6). The material assistance they did receive was of limited use within the traditional exchange system. In fact, Norman Deck was concerned that young 'teachers' might have difficulty marrying because the time spent on their work for the church prevented them from accumulating sufficient

PLATE 29   *An SSEM baptism in the sea, probably in the 1930s. Suitably qualified adults are examined and then baptised by a missionary, in a public ceremony by immersion in the Baptist manner. (Photo from the SSEM archive)*

bridewealth (Norman Deck 1932b). But such goods as were provided by the SSEM missionaries were dispensed by the 'teachers' and gave them opportunities for patronage, for instance in distributing Bibles and religious texts and clothing to new converts. Also important, the 'teachers' could offer their congregations medical assistance. Apart from the regular medical treatment they gave themselves, the SSEM missionaries from the earliest days also provided 'teachers' with homeopathic medicines to dispense to their congregations. While Europeans have sometimes considered the alcohol base of these medicines to be their main virtue, Kwara'ae themselves have faith in their efficacy and their provision was an important service by 'teachers' to their people.

The local congregations provided rather more material support. As priests had accepted offerings of shell money (*fo'osi*) to the ghosts and the government collected tax, the authority of the 'teachers' and elders was recognised in contributions made in cash and kind as church offerings (also called *fo'osi*) and 'tithes' (*tangafularu*). These they dispensed to help those in hardship, to support evangelists venturing into new districts, to clothe new converts and to assist the 'teachers' themselves. The education in basic literacy and numeracy which 'teachers' received also enabled them to gain better paid employment, and their pastoral work was frequently interrupted by periods of wage labour in other districts and islands.

MALAITANS AND EUROPEANS, MISSION AND GOVERNMENT

The new Christian order, modelled as it was on European modes of social organisation promoted by the missionaries, can be seen as an adaptation to the new political realities of the wider colonial order in Malaita. It was supported by Europeans in order to further the objectives of government as well as missions and implemented by Malaitans seeking to come to terms with these colonial forces by escaping the discredited and outmoded traditional order. As Guiart (1962) suggests for the Pacific in general, the apparently revolutionary changes were in a sense millenial in promising solutions to the problems of colonialism. But in the event, conversion proved less a solution than another step in the continuing struggle of resistance. Although both Malaitans and Europeans expressed satisfaction at the changes brought by Christianity, by the 1930s these seem actually to have represented a rather uneasy compromise in the continuing conflict between colonial domination and local resistance. The Christians of Kwai had long been diverted from this struggle by their conflicts with the traditionists, and on the European side the struggle was also obscured by a certain tension between the competing interests of missionaries and government. But the Christian

transformation did not ultimately resolve the underlying conflict between colonisers and colonised, as subsequent events showed.

One reason why the SSEM proved so much more successful on Malaita
than other missions was probably its "ideal of a self-propagating, self-
supporting, and self-governing Church", indigenous, independent of government and ultimately responsible only to the higher authority of God (NIV Apr.
1933:7, Hilliard 1969:59). In this it met some of the initial objections to
Christianity. Although Christians were in the early days allied with the government in opposition to those who were fighting to preserve the traditional order,
this did not necessarily mean they were satisfied with the colonial alternative. Like
the traditionists, Christians had an ideal of political autonomy founded on
spiritual power which was reflected in SSEM doctrine as it had been in different
ways in the struggle of the warriors and priests and in the *bulu* cults. The SSEM
position was described, with some indignation, by Allan:

> The teachers were taught that they must have complete authority and indepen-
> dence when they went to their different stations. ... They were taught that all life
> was devoted to God; that nothing but God mattered. ... So they considered that it
> was their duty and task to concern themselves and dictate in every aspect of village
> and district life (Allan 1951:7).

When Malaitans used Christian doctrine to justify their resistance to
government authority, the government reaction was to blame the missionaries.
This attitude went back to the days of Edge-Partington, whose irritation with
SSEM Christians once provoked the telling comment that:

> If the S.S.E. Mission taught their boys to have a little more respect for the
> government, instead of packing their heads full of trash which they do not
> understand, they would be doing some good (Edge-Partington 1912).

Allan went so far as to accuse the SSEM missionaries of refusing to acknowledge
the legitimacy of the government's role in the "constitutional and social development of the people" in its insistence on the primacy of local religious rules over
government social policy, and of bringing pressure to bear on government officers
in Malaita through the High Commissioner and the Colonial Office. He may
have been doing the missionaries an injustice if, as Hilliard states, "Convinced on
scriptural grounds of the necessity of an absolute distinction between Church and
State, the SSEM missionaries were not interested in applying political pressure
either locally or in the homelands" (1969:59). But for all this, as a District
Commissioner noted in 1948, previously, "... the Government was prepared to
leave most of the real administration of the district in the hands of the missions"
(Tour Report 1948b). Despite their disputes, mission and government were
heavily dependent on one another to secure their own separate objectives.
Government benefitted from Christian opposition to feuding and (Allan's

comments not withstanding) from missionary support for its own legitimacy. Government also depended on the missions to educate its growing body of Solomon Islands administrative staff and recognised the value of this work by exempting 'teachers' from the head tax until the 1930s (NIV Apr. 1933:5,6). During the '30s government tried to introduce its own curricular standards into the mission training schools as an alternative to setting up schools of its own (Norman Deck 1932a). Missionaries for their part depended above all on government law enforcement for protection from the kind of harrassment which had made the lives of Christians so difficult in the early years of the century and they recognised that colonial rule promoted Christian conversion.

In fact government officials and missionaries generally co-operated amicably enough despite their differences, and frequently to the detriment of local people. SSEM missionaries would report offences against government law, even turning in runaway plantation workers to the District Officer (Court Minutes

PLATE 30   *Norman Deck translating the Scriptures, through which so many*
                 Malaitans learned to read and write in their own languages. He is
                 working here with Clement Maelalo of Langalanga, at Onepusu in
                 the 1920s. (Photo from the SSEM archive)

1910–12, Bell 1916). The government recognised a responsibility to protect the missionaries even when they seemed to be bringing disaster on their own heads, as when Daniels was killed at 'Ailamalama. Edge-Partington's comment on that occasion makes the essential point: "Missionary or no Missionary Daniels was a white man" (Edge-Partington 1911a). The government tendency to blame the missionaries for its conflicts with local Christians reflects a paternalistic attitude towards Malaitans which the missionaries shared and which was actually an important part of the problem. Far from being pawns in a power game between mission and government, the Christians of Kwai and other parts of Malaita had their own dissatisfactions with both.

Allan was writing his report on the SSEM at a time when Malaitan claims for political and religious autonomy had led the SSEM 'teachers' and their people into direct confrontation with both government and missionaries through the anti-colonial Māsing Rul movement. Māsing Rul united the whole of Malaita following the Second World War, proving that the deepest divisions were not between Christians and traditionists or government and missionaries, but between Malaitans and Europeans. As Māsing Rul was explained to the missionary Gibbins, the difference was between rich and poor, oppressors and oppressed (NIV Dec. 1950:4). It was Christianity, and the SSEM churches in particular, which enabled the people of Kwai to organise themselves so effectively in this emerging conflict between a ritually organised Malaitan political system and a secular British administration.

PLATE 31   *The American military base at Point Cruz, Honiara. The wartime*
                buildings of permanent materials were on a scale never before seen
                in Solomon Islands, and helped inspire the Māsing Rul 'towns'.
                (Photo from Andrea Bannatyne)

CHAPTER SEVEN

Māsing Rul: the Maasina Rule Movement (1940s)

The Second World War was a time of trauma and excitement for Malaitans, who experienced at first hand the vast numbers, the wealth and the destructive power of the distant industrial countries which invaded the neighbouring islands of the Solomons to fight out some of the decisive campaigns of the war. For the people of Kwai, as for most Malaitans, the war came at a time when they were ready to reassess the changes they were making to their society and their relationship to the colonial forces which had made these changes necessary. Over the previous seventy years they had conceded first their economic and then their political autonomy and had revised their religious and political system to meet the new realities of the colonial order. But for all their efforts first to resist this order and then to participate in it by accepting Christianity and government, they still found themselves excluded from control of the colonial institutions which had come to dominate their lives. The war seemed to offer a chance to change all this. Inspired by traditional values of political autonomy founded on spiritual power and drawing upon their experience of colonial institutions and political organisation, they were encouraged to develop their own alternative to the now discredited colonial order. The result was the remarkable island-wide movement of Maasina Rule, known in Kwai as Māsing Rul. The effects of this movement have lasted far beyond its demise in the early 1950s, as a crucial phase in the political and religious development of Malaita and Solomon Islands.

Recent research has made Maasina Rule one of the best documented and most thoroughly discussed anti-colonial movements in the Pacific. Laracy (1971, 1983) and Keesing (1978a) in particular have clarified the history and ideology of the movement as a whole, drawing on the recollections of its participants as well as on documents left by them and their European opponents. Their insights provide the essential context for examining more detailed accounts, including some well-informed reports by the colonial administration (eg. Sandars 1946) and the autobiography of the East Kwaio Maasina Rule leader Jonathon Fifi'i (1989).[1] But Kwara'ae recollections indicate that, in an island far from homogeneous in culture and history, districts such as Kwai developed their own interpretations of what was actually a locally organised movement.

MALAITAN EXPERIENCE OF THE WAR

The history of the Second World War as it affected the Solomons has been summarised by Laracy (1988a, 1988b). To the islanders the causes and origins of the war must have been something of a mystery. Kwara'ae apparently saw the conflict in terms of their own experience of feuding for restitution and vengeance, and few could have comprehended the economic and territorial objectives of the world powers. Silas Sangafanoa, who was at Tulagi when the Japanese invaded, attributes the war to Japanese retaliation for the British mistreatment of a Japanese fishing boat crew who were arrested and imprisoned at Tulagi in 1940, with the result that one died and (incomprehensibly to Kwara'ae) was cremated.

This incident was just one local echo of a war which was already well under way in Europe and Southeast Asia, spreading to the Pacific after the Japanese attacked the British at Singapore and the Americans at Hawaii in December 1941. To Europeans in the Solomons it was then evident that the Japanese advance into Southeast Asia would extend to Melanesia. Only a week later, reports of Japanese movements in the Pacific were causing panic in the Solomon Islands capital at Tulagi as Europeans and Chinese sought to make their escape from the islands (Wilson 1942). By February 1942 most had been evacuated to Australia, leaving only a few government officers and others as a 'Defence Force' and as 'coastwatchers' against the Japanese advance. Many Malaitans were abandoned by their employers on plantations and had to be shipped home by the government. Government headquarters were moved from Tulagi to 'Aoke and then, as the Japanese came closer, to Fulisango in the West Kwara'ae bush. Many of the missionaries also left the Solomons, although five from the SSEM remained on Malaita, including two at Nāfinua in East Kwara'ae (NIV Dec. 1945:9). The islanders, who could appreciate the threat from European reactions if from no other cause, had nowhere else to go and awaited the invasion with trepidation.

The Japanese, moving into the Solomons from the northeast, reached Tulagi in May 1942 and began to establish themselves on Guadalcanal. They had extended their control no further when the Americans invaded Guadalcanal in August. On Malaita, a Japanese detachment which landed at 'Aoke and made its way northwards remained only a few months before being destroyed by the Americans in November 1942 (NIV Dec. 1945:10, The Big Death 1988:198, Fifi'i 1989:45–46). But although Malaita avoided further invasion, the six months of fierce and destructive battles which followed on Guadalcanal were close enough to cause great alarm before the Japanese were defeated. From the central Kwara'ae bush people could see searchlights in the night sky over Guadalcanal and hear the great guns and bombs exploding. Some were so frightened that they fled their villages to hide in the bush or dug holes to hide in in case of a Japanese invasion. Warplanes flew over Malaita and Kwara'ae were fascinated to see three Japanese airmen as they were taken by the police overland to 'Aoke after crash-landing near Atā (see also Fifi'i 1989:46–47). The nearest serious incidents to Kwai were when American planes bombed first Laulasi Island in Langalanga in August 1942, killing about twenty-five people, and then Uru in May 1944, killing one man (Laracy & White 1988:24,139,143, NIV Sept. 1944:4, Dec. 1945:10).

The people of Kwai became more involved in the war when the British government began recruiting a 'Labour Corps' to work for the American armed forces on Guadalcanal. Most of the 2,000 men who volunteered in 1943 were Malaitans. Some of them took a direct part in the fighting as scouts, but even the non-combatant labourers sometimes faced considerable dangers. Taeman Riki-mani of Suli'ua describes how on arrival at Tenaru on Guadalcanal, he and his companions were set to work at once digging foxholes for themselves and immediately had to shelter from Japanese air-raids, wondering what the British authorities had let them in for. They worked building airfields, laying steel matting for roads, stacking cargo and clearing storm-drains. On one occasion, leaving their air-raid shelter too soon, many were killed when their whole camp was bombed (see Fifi'i 1989 Ch.4 for the most detailed account of the Labour Corps episode).

Malaitans' experience of working for the Americans was probably as traumatic as that of their fathers and grandfathers who left their island for the first time to see the whiteman's world as labourers on the plantations of Queensland. Not only were the Labour Corps exposed to the fearsome military power of the industrial world. Equally important, after seventy years of harsh working conditions under racist European overseers and twenty or thirty years of paternalistic British political control, they began to glimpse the possibilities for a more profitable and equitable relationship with wealthy and powerful foreigners. The American servicemen treated islanders with the kind of respect and gener-osity which Europeans in the past had feared would bring their prestige into disrepute. They were critical of British colonial rule and supportive of the islanders, encouraging them to believe that they would have been better treated under America. Besides the white soldiers, there were others from origins with which the Malaitans could identify: Hawaiians who described their superior standard of living under America and American blacks (whom some Malaitans identified Biblically as 'Egyptians') who struck back when abused by the whites, as Solomon Islanders could seldom afford to do. (see Fifi'i 1989:54–56 for a revealing account of conversations with American soldiers).

The American soldiers were generous with 'their' military equipment and supplies, giving away goods in quantities never before possessed by Islanders. Othaniel 'Aifa'asia recalls how this reflected on British behaviour. Labour Corps wages, although paid out by the British, were believed (despite British denials:

PLATE 32   *Working for the Solomon Islands Labour Corps. The men are*
                 unloading cartons of beer at an American ration dump on
                 Guadalcanal in March 1944. (Photo from U. S. Signal Corps)

Holton 1945) to have been provided by the Americans. The labourers suspected that their wage of £1 per month, although high by local standards, was only a fraction of what the Americans were prepared to pay. Their suspicions that the British were denying them the full benefits of American generosity were confirmed when, at the end of their service, they were ordered to return the firearms the Americans had given them, and especially when restrictions were placed on the amount of army goods they were allowed to keep. Each man was limited to two blankets, one camp bed, one bag of rice, one case of corned beef, one case of biscuits and one uniform. Large quantities of goods were confiscated by the British Solomon Islands police and burnt before their eyes. This was at a time when, as District Officer Sandars reported from Malaita, "The natives are desperately short of clothing" (Sandars 1943). If the British authorities were concerned about the logistics of shipping these goods home, as Tom Russell recalls, this was lost on the Malaitans, who took it as confirmation that the British were trying to keep them in their place. Such incidents added to the longstanding complaints against the colonial political and economic system which were later voiced by Māsing Rul.

REACTIONS TO THE WAR AND THE ORIGINS OF MĀSING RUL

With the virtual collapse of the British administration during the war, the labourers were encouraged to explore the alternative prospect of continued American patronage. From early 1943 collections of money were being made to offer to the Americans in the hope of buying their support (Sandars 1946). By August that year rumours were circulating on Malaita that the Americans were intending to take over from the British. South of Kwai in East Kwaio there was talk of rejecting government law, which had been inoperative there since early 1942. District Officer Sandars had no hesitation in attributing such attitudes to "contact with the more irresponsible elements of the U.S. Forces" and he advocated a programme of government propaganda to "re-establish confidence" (Sandars 1943).

The effects of the war were not lost upon the SSEM missionaries either. A report by Griffiths in 1943 considered that

> Many of the natives will not be content to live the simple village life with which they were satisfied in the past. ... The wages and presents they have received, and the prices that have been given for native foods, fruits and curios will make them expect much more in the future. (NIV Dec. 1943:4).

Vance saw it as the Mission's task "To guide the natives with their new found knowledge and independence of thought into sound moral and spiritual channels" (NIV Dec. 1945:10). But it was too late for blandishments from either mission or government. As the Labour Corps began to return home the discontent became organised, resulting eventually in the rejection of both these sources of European authority.

Kwara'ae attribute the origin of Māsing Rul to Nori, a man from 'Are'are who became the nominal head of the movement for the whole of Malaita. After working in the Labour Corps, Nori is understood to have received inspiration or even instructions for Māsing Rul in a meeting with an American army officer. Gului of Sakwalo from East Kwara'ae was also present and was a local source of information on the incident. As the story goes, Nori received a letter from an American lieutenant giving him access to the foxhole where General MacArthur was staying at Luga. He was told to talk to MacArthur before returning to Malaita to make a committee for the island to expel the British government. Rikimani recalls the details:

> We had finished working with the Americans for one year, then we went back to Malaita. At that time this man Nori went to a big man from America at Henderson airfield. ... He said "What, Nori, have you people got a big man to look after you?" Nori said "Oh, we have only the British government ... to look after us. Only the British." It was then that the man from America said "Oh, this

man is from a different country. But your country in Solomon Islands; what, is there no man for you to put as a big man to look after you and look out for you?" Nori said "Oh no". He said "You should go home to make Māsing Rul so that you can put up a man to be a big man for you.[2]

On his return home from Guadalcanal, Nori joined the 'Native Council Movement' which was being organised in 'Are'are to press for economic and social development in accordance with traditional values. A movement of resistance to the government was developing independently in North Malaita, led by Lau saltwater people who established contact by sea with the activists in the south. By the end of 1944 rumours of these movements were circulating throughout the island, and by early 1945 Nori and the northern leaders were exchanging visits and ideas and involving men from other areas, including Kwai. Nori took over the leadership in 'Are'are with Timothy George and they began drawing up a programme of action and sending out instructions throughout Malaita. The first of these was a ban on labour recruiting in support of a claim for plantation wages of £12 per month, which became one of the movement's main acts of resistance to the government (Sandars 1946, Laracy 1983:17–18,21, 117–119,127–128, Annual Report 1947:5).

A reaction against the British was probably developing in East Kwara'ae at the same time. One Māsing Rul activist, Clement O'ogau of Manadodo, recalls how a series of so-called 'trak' meetings were being held in the adjacent district of Kwaio to discuss the state of relations with Europeans and the government. Attending from the Kwara'ae side of the Kwaibaita river, O'ogau remembers the meetings voicing complaints about poor plantation wages:

> "We make the paddock for them, then it bears fruit, they make copra, they take the money; they don't give us good money or good wages. So it means the white men are robbing us. ... We are like dogs. They make a dog go into the scrub to attack a wild pig; well, they eat the good parts of it and throw the bones away for the dog."

O'ogau and others began to organise similar meetings in Kwara'ae, touring around, carrying the word across to West Kwara'ae and Langalanga and explaining the goals of the growing movement:

> We want one big man to be important for us, so that we are under this man. So then, this man will ask us for tax and we'll give it. But if the white man asks, we won't give it. Because if we pay tax to him he'll take our money and won't build up anything in our island. He takes it to do his work and to build up his living. ... The big man we put up, he won't be against England or against the work of the government, but he'll work by our laws. ... He'll be between us and the government and the Europeans for employment, or if we need anything we'll ask this big man to ask them; good wages or a good way of life or good things like that.

These were the kind of complaints to which Māsing Rul was addressed. But despite the story that Nori received "Māsing Rul" from the Americans, it was apparently only as the South Malaita movement spread throughout the island that it took this name, originally Maasina Rul, the 'Rule of Brotherhood' in the language of 'Are'are (Laracy 1983:19). In this ideal of brotherhood Kwara'ae recognised their own tradition that all the peoples of Malaita are 'brothers' by descent from one common ancestor who came from overseas and settled at Siale. Nonetheless, they changed the name of the movement to 'Māsing Rul', the Malaitan pronunciation of the term by which the British came to know it, 'Marching Rule.'[3]

MĀSING RUL COMES TO KWAI

The programme which became Māsing Rul was brought to Kwai by Nori himself. His first visit was probably en route to meetings with the northern leaders in Lau early in 1945. He arrived by ship at Faumamanu, where local people were now accustomed to assemble for government business and taxation, and addressed a meeting which was carefully concealed from the government Headmen who came to investigate. While local activists began to organise the movement according to Nori's instructions, his message was repeated on later visits. As Sandars reported (now as District Commissioner), in June 1945 "The movement was spread by a "patrol" 300 strong which went from Small Malaita up through Ari Ari and Koio to Eastern Kwara'ae ... where it was spread through the S.S.E.M." By October Māsing Rul had been taken up throughout Malaita. When Nori visited East Kwara'ae on a tour of the northern districts in June 1946 he received an elaborate ceremonial reception from the leaders of a fully developed Māsing Rul organisation (Sandars 1946).

Men who attended Nori's public meetings remember him instructing them in a whole programme of activities. They were to make communal 'farms' of sweet potatoes, build new houses in 'towns' near the sea, move down from the bush and appoint 'duties' to guard the towns. Instead of paying taxes to government they were to raise money themselves by collecting American dollars and selling the produce of the 'farms', to present to the Americans apparently with the idea of buying their 'freedom'. The names of the movement's supporters were recorded and about ten local leaders who began to implement the programme were approved by Nori as 'Leader Chiefs'. It was they who toured the bush villages, holding meetings to explain Māsing Rul and starting the collections of money. From these meetings a local organisation was developed in line with the Māsing Rul programme for Malaita as a whole. The heads of local clans ('lines' in government jargon) became 'Line Chiefs' representing their own people in the movement and, of the activists who emerged as 'Leader Chiefs', the foremost leaders became 'Full Chiefs'. The titles of chiefs were not necessarily fixed or generally agreed. Rather, like the traditional role of 'important man', they reflected the political influence and support of individual leaders. Today, and no doubt at the time, men who took part in Māsing Rul are not always clear as to the titles or roles held by leaders, which seems to throw doubt on the model of a formal heirarchy of chiefs described by District Commissioner Davies (Annual Report 1947) and repeated by Laracy (1983:20). Besides the 'chiefs', many young men took the part of 'duties' to carry out the chiefs' instructions and there were 'clerks', 'treasurers' and other officials responsible for particular tasks. As the movement became co-ordinated throughout Malaita, Kwai became one of nine separate Māsing Rul districts of the island.

This organisation drew virtually the whole population under the authority of the chiefs, the main exceptions being the government Headmen and their families. Tommy Siru, the senior Headman of Kwai subdistrict, was already personally unpopular and distrusted by local people and remained an active agent of the government, providing information on Māsing Rul activities and later assisting in the arrest of its leaders. His assistant Dausabea only temporarily associated himself with Māsing Rul and another, Lebesau, also co-operated with government (Sandars 1946, Tour Report 1948, Forster 1948).

One of the first tasks undertaken was the Māsing Rul 'tax' or 'collection' to replace the head tax which the government had been unable to collect since the beginning of the war. This was a particularly important symbolic gesture of recognition of the authority of the chiefs to whom it was given, analogous to the 'offerings' (fo'osi) of shell money, food and cash given to traditionist priests and church leaders. It was also a gesture of 'independence' from the British, which was why, apart from the value involved, the head tax had always been resisted by those Kwara'ae who resented government control. British recognition of this made the tax an equally crucial issue for the government (Sandars 1946). Besides, as former District Officer Dick Horton points out, since the administration was entirely supported by revenue raised in the Protectorate, even the small amount it contributed was significant.

Government officers recognised the inadequacy of the services they provided to the islanders and could hardly afford to improve them, but exactly what the government spent its tax on was perhaps not the point. When Kwara'ae complained of seeing no benefit from it, they were thinking rather of the failure of the British to meet their general expectations of assistance, especially in contrast to the Americans. Hence one purpose of the Māsing Rul tax was understood from Nori's message to be the presentation of money to foreigners who were expected to come to Malaita to help them, and for most people this meant the Americans. Some interpreted this as buying their 'freedom' from the Americans, which is more or less what the leaders of the movement eventually attempted to do. The first collections, made while everyone was still living in the bush, varied from one pound to one American dollar or half-dollar per man. The money was held by the Line Chiefs and later passed to senior chiefs in the 'towns'. Here further collections were made, in some cases to raise large amounts, in others more or less continuously.

Raising money was also one purpose of the 'farms'. People continued to support themselves from their own gardens up in the bush, where preferred foods such as taro were grown. The easier to cultivate but less desirable sweet potatoes grown on the 'farms' were sold in the markets, as bush people had always sold or exchanged their surplus crops, and the money raised went to Māsing Rul funds. According to District Commissioner Davies;

> 1946 saw the building of these "farms" by communal labour, until by the end of the year large potato farms could be found all round the coast of Malaita. Once these gardens were ready, the construction of the new villages [ie 'towns'] was begun. The last three months of 1946, saw a decided increase in the tempo of developments and there was a frantic scramble to build their villages as fast as they could. ... By about March 1947, these villages were completed. (Annual Report 1947)

In East Kwara'ae the 'towns' may have been occupied by this time, but people still had not completely abandoned their homes and gardens in the bush and building work in the 'towns' was continuing. This was reported by Clark of the SSEM in June 1947, following a visit to the east coast of Malaita:

> In all these "towns" the people have only made kitchens in most instances, but when their gardens have been moved down to the coast they will build good Marching Rule model houses. (NIV Jun. 1947)

THE MĀSING RUL TOWNS

The basic purpose of the 'town' settlements was to assemble and organise the people so that they could work together more effectively and achieve the aims of the movement. According to Justus Ganifiri,

> We wanted to do something for money, and it's no good if people are scattered all around in villages all over the place in the bush. We wanted to learn how to live well. Good housing, a clear place, clear away the bush and things like that. Then if somebody got enough money and maybe he wanted to run a store, then he could do it where plenty of people were living. But if you live with one person in one village, there's nothing for you to do. You just work in the garden, then come back, sleep, work, come back, sleep, the pigs run all over the place and things. So that was the idea of the town.

But the 'towns' were also a response to rumours that, as Davies reported, "... a "colony" of foreigners was coming to invade Malaita and dispossess the people of their land". The 'towns' were regarded as a defence for coastal areas from the kind of takeover which had occurred on Guadalcanal during the war (Annual Report 1947). It was planned that if others such as the Americans came to fight for them, they would be assembled ready to help and the fighting could go on in the empty bush. Some people at least also expected the Americans to bring 'cargo' to the towns. But the fear of land alienation already had a long history in Kwara'ae, where it was recalled from the early days of plantation work how the Fijians and Queensland Aborigines had been dispossessed of their lands. In 1940 the fear of Europeans taking land was an important reason given by Kwara'ae traditionists for obstructing the government foot road across the island. During Māsing Rule the Fijian experience was cited as a warning (Laracy 1983:106) and that of the Aborigines was compared with the still resented government purchase of land for 'Aoke station.

Most of the 'town' settlements in East Kwara'ae were along the southern part of the coast, most of which has a long and accessible sandy beach. Furthest south, near the Kwaio border, a 'town' was built at Age near the promontory of Fau 'i Fote by people from both Kwara'ae and Kwaio. Moving north, there were settlements along much of the beach at A'arai and at Faumamanu and 'Adakoa. Further on, separated from 'Adakoa by extensive mangrove swamps, was Nāfinua, not actually on the coast but on the inlet of the Bulia river. Even further separated from the other 'towns' of the district was a settlement of Kwara'ae and neighbouring Fataleka people at Ofokwasi near Fokanakafo on the northern border of Kwara'ae. The saltwater islands of Kwai and Ngongosila were already concentrated settlements, until then the largest in the district, and the people here remained where they were. The size of five East Kwara'ae 'towns' (probably including 'Adakoa with Faumamanu) was estimated at "about 500 people in each" (NIV Jun. 1947:5).

The 'towns' comprised two rows of buildings lining a 'road' which, from 'Adakoa to A'arai, was the main footpath running along the coast. The houses were of standard shape and size, each with a kitchen beside it, the whole 'town' being carefully laid out, in some cases with a tape measure. This layout was inspired by the American army camps, but there were also men's houses (fera) besides various communal buildings such as churches and meeting houses for Māsing Rule activities. At Nāfinua a stone paved foot 'road' was built, about a quarter of a mile long, leading to a stone wharf on the Bulia river which still stands (reminiscent of the wharf built at 'Atori by followers of the bulu cult in about 1917).

The towns which people joined depended partly on where they were living in the bush but also on the clans and religious sects they belonged to, as well as on the influence of particular Māsing Rul leaders. Many of those at Faumamanu belonged to the clans of Siale, some being followers of the SSEM, but including also a number of Anglicans. Others included a group of SSEM people from Mānadari who were persuaded to move there by the Māsing Rul chief Kalu'ae when most of their clan followed Matangani to Nāfinua. The adjoining settlement at 'Adakoa included the people of Latea, the clan land on which it was built, some of whom were SSEM and some traditionists. Followers of different mission sects built their houses in separate sections corresponding to clusters of clans under their own Line Chiefs. This is clear in Clark's contemporary description of A'arai, probably the largest of the East Kwara'ae 'towns', which reached from the A'arai river all the way to the Namo'ere'ere river and was said to include "about 600 people".

> The SSEM has about a dozen houses at one end ... then a small gap before seven
> Seventh Day Adventist houses, then ten Melanesian Mission [Anglican] houses,
> and finally about forty or more SSEM buildings. (NIV Jun. 1947)

These people were from Suli'ua and from the Sasadili clan of 'Ere'ere, which included also the largest remaining group of traditionists in East Kwara'ae. The traditionists lived somewhat apart on the bush side of the 'town', separated from the Christians to protect themselves from defilement. The settlements from 'Adakoa to A'arai were probably less distinct as separate towns than was Nāfinua, and the spheres of influence of their senior chiefs seem to have been less clearly defined. Again many of these men were mission 'teachers' but not necessarily of the same sects as most of their Māsing Rul followers. Two of the first Leader Chiefs, probably recognised as Full Chiefs, Kalu'ae and Waeman Maetia, were Seventh Day Adventists, a minority sect of Sasadili-'Ere'ere people. The 'towns' at Ofokwasi and Age were probably aligned more closely with the Māsing Rul districts of Fataleka and East Kwaio respectively. Co-operation was closest between the 'towns' from Nāfinua to A'arai, including the saltwater islands of Kwai and Ngongosila. Even here the local chiefs probably had considerable autonomy and it is significant that each 'town' kept its own Māsing Rul funds.

Insofar as Māsing Rul had a political centre or headquarters in Kwai, this was Nāfinua. Nāfinua 'town', with less than fifty households, was by no means the largest of the Māsing Rul settlements but it was already the principal local centre for the SSEM. The core of the Nāfinua group were Ubasi people, many of whom had been living in SSEM villages on the Bulia since the second decade of the century. Association with the Nāfinua church also encouraged people from other clans to join the Māsing Rul town there, like the Gwauna'ongi people whom Fiuloa had brought to 'school' at Nāfinua in the 1920s. Others came from the clans of Mānadari, Kwalo, Ualakwai and Siale. Apart from a handful of Anglicans and one or two traditionists, all the people at Nāfinua belonged to the SSEM. Their Māsing Rul leaders were SSEM 'teachers', of whom the most important was now Justus Ganifiri, the son of Fiuloa who had moved the mission station to Nāfinua and founded its 'education school'.

'Teachers', as the pastors of the church, were already the ritual and political leaders of their local communities, mediating with God as the organisers of the ritual activities which dominated community life. Their authority, the education they received at the SSEM training school at Onepusu, their experience in organising religious conventions between districts and the contacts they developed in the process, were all put to the service of Māsing Rul throughout Malaita (see Laracy 1971). In East Kwara'ae one of the first to become involved was Nathan Matangani, who began organising Māsing Rul meetings and tax collections in the bush villages to develop the following which built the 'town' at Nāfinua. Regarded as a Full Chief, he travelled as spokesman for the Nāfinua group to meetings with chiefs of other areas. But when it came to appointing a Head Chief to represent Kwai in the Māsing Rul movement as a whole the choice was between Ganifiri and Stephen Sibolo, also recognised as Full Chiefs. Sibolo was a saltwater man from Ngongosila and a sergeant-major of police at 'Aoke. He remained an influential Māsing Rule leader, but in the event it was Ganifiri

PLATE 33   *Justus Jimmy Ganifiri of Ubasi, Māsing Rul Head Chief for East Kwara'ae, in 1977. (Photo from the SSEM archive)*

whom the people chose as Head Chief, at a public meeting held by Matangani. As Head Chief, Ganifiri became one of the nine chiefs who, with Nori, led Māsing Rule for Malaita as a whole. He had the prestige and influence to co-ordinate Māsing Rul activities throughout Kwai, but his power base was at Nāfinua and the other 'towns' developed their own organisation under their own chiefs.

The occupation of the 'towns' brought the Māsing Rul organisation into effect. At Nāfinua, decisions taken by Ganifiri, Matangani and one or two other senior chiefs in private meetings were communicated to the people by a Leader Chief, Taeman Timi, who instructed the duties to see that they were carried out. Taeman Timi and another Leader Chief, Krispas Biru, acted as treasurers for the Māsing Rul funds and records were kept by a clerk, Ben Banau. 'Duties' also acted as runners for the chiefs, convening meetings and carrying messages within and beyond the district and as police to keep order in the town. In this way the people were organised to perform the programme of communal labour required to develop the 'farms', 'towns' and other projects. At Faumamanu everyone had to work three days each week on the 'farm' and if they missed the work, after a warning, their names were written down and they were fined five shillings. The harvesting and sale of the sweet potatoes was recorded by a clerk. A further two days a week were spent on people's own taro gardens in the bush, from which harvested crops were taken to the town and stored in pits. Clark was impressed by the "regimentation":

> At Nafinua the bell rang. I saw men, women, girls and boys carting stones and
> making a road to the water place. [ie ending in the wharf built on the Bulia river].
> The bell rings for midday rest. Then bell and work again. (NIV Jun. 1947)

The government condemned the discipline of the 'towns' as oppressive, and the 'duties' who supervised it as "... the most dangerous element of the movement, and a constant threat to peace and good order" (Annual Report 1947). But although there was evidence for some coercion and intimidation in other areas of Malaita, life in the East Kwara'ae 'towns' is remembered as peaceful, with everyone quite happy with the arrangements. There was probably a good deal of excitement to be had, particularly for young people, in the novel life of such large communities, although this in itself led to certain tensions and disputes.

REAFFIRMING TRADITION

Although Māsing Rul was built upon European modes of organisation, this was put to the service of Malaitan values, as Kwara'ae and others began to reassess their ideas of tradition as an alternative to the values introduced by the colonial order. Under Māsing Rul, tradition (*falafala*), or *kastom* as it was referred to in Pijin (English 'custom'), became a symbol of Malaitan autonomy, of the right to determine their own way of life according to values derived from their own culture and history rather than that of their colonial masters. Exactly what these values should be is a matter of debate to this day, but even during Māsing Rul only the most conservative traditionists would have sought a return to pre-colonial society. For most Kwara'ae tradition was and is acceptable only within a Christian way of life, as recognised in the distinction drawn between 'Christian tradition' and the 'heathen tradition' of the pre-colonial past and non-Christian minority. Christian tradition is taken to be those values which can be supported by the Bible, as interpreted with variations by the various mission churches. By developing the many parallels between Christian and traditional theology and ritual, Kwara'ae Christians assert the indigenous foundations of their new religion. Such rationalisations may date back to the first converts on the Queensland plantations, but it was probably during Māsing Rul that this indigenous Christian theology first began to contribute to tradition or *kastom* as an anti-colonial ideology.

Central to this ideology is the story of the first ancestor of Kwara'ae, who is said to have instituted traditional values in the form of ten 'laws' analogous to the Biblical Ten Commandments, as already mentioned. This idea was promoted in particular by Filo'isi, the priest of Siale, who had learnt of Christianity in Queensland and had been working to re-establish traditional 'law' before eventually converting in 1943. Traditional 'law' and dispute settlement became a crucial issue in Māsing Rul. From its earliest days the colonial administration had claimed the right to deal with disputes between local people, particularly to maintain the peace when bloodshed was involved. Although government courts came to recognise offences against 'native custom', the application of penal sanctions such as fines, imprisonment and execution could not actually resolve disputes, as traditional practices of restitution (*fa'aabu'a*) were intended to do. Hence it was an objective of Māsing Rul to give control of the legal system to local leaders who could reconcile the parties through a proper consideration of tradition. As 'teachers' in the SSEM, many of the East Kwara'ae Māsing Rul leaders had long been involved in dispute settlement under the authority of their churches, a role somewhat resented by the government. The SSEM actually opposed restitution and encouraged settlement by forgiveness and prayer, but under Māsing Rul the chiefs dealt with disputes in their own court system according to traditional principles, which they attempted to codify as 'law'.

At both A'arai and Nāfinua 'custom houses', decorated in traditional style, were built for meetings where the work of discussing and compiling lists of 'laws' went on. Foremost in this work was Ganifiri, who wrote a detailed book of *The Law of Living in Kwara'ae, the Country of Siale* (Ganifiri n.d.) describing ten 'laws' or categories of correct social behaviour, each with numerous subdivisions. As a statement of traditional values, rather than a lawbook in the European sense, this book represents one of many attempts during Māsing Rul and since to institutionalise Kwara'ae culture in European terms. Māsing Rul 'courts' were held in the 'custom house' at Nāfinua, presided over by Ganifiri and Sibolo, dealing with all kinds of disputes from adultery to land cases. Offenders were summoned if necessary by 'duties', the parties and their witnesses stated their cases and either or both were ordered to give restitution or, if they had Christian objections, fines to the court instead. The courts seemed to operate to the satisfaction of all concerned and, despite its opposition, the government was initially unable to find any complaints against their decisions which could give grounds for legal action against them (Cameron 1947e, 1947f).

MĀSING RUL REACTIONS AGAINST THE BRITISH

While implementing a practical programme of community development and political reform, Māsing Rul also held out hopes for external support from foreign intervention, encouraged by the experience of seventy years of colonialism. The economic development for which Malaitans had been working since they first began recruiting to plantations to obtain manufactured goods had always depended on participation in an economic system controlled by Europeans. They had observed the wealth this system created in Queensland and Fiji as well as in the Solomons and were well aware of the contribution which their labour made to it. Māsing Rul was conceived as a revision of the relationship between Malaitans and the European controllers of development and wealth. Although it was intended as a programme of self-improvement by people working for themselves rather than for European exploiters, at the same time it also continued to seek power and wealth from European sources, under more favourable conditions than in the past. This involved a certain mysticism, insofar as people would have admitted limited experience and incomplete understanding of the forces involved. In Kwai some credence was undoubtably given to rumours of 'cargo', which today tend to be attributed to other areas of Malaita. But the expected benefits of foreign intervention seem to have been more in the nature of what might now be regarded as 'foreign aid'.

The question was how such aid was to be obtained. Some Māsing Rul leaders placed their faith primarily in renegotiating their relationship with the British, and this was a continuing theme in Māsing Rul representations to the government. Others had more radical and, as it proved, less realistic, aspirations to reject the British, maybe rebel against them, and seek help elsewhere. The relative emphasis on these two options varied at different stages of the movement, but appeal to the Americans was taken to be a basic feature of Nori's message from the first. As the confrontation between Māsing Rul and the government became more acute, and especially as the goals of the movement appeared to recede, this approach gained more and more support in Kwai and throughout North Malaita. There were recurrent rumours that the Americans were arriving to fulfill the aims of Māsing Rul, and people reacted against the British accordingly.

Ganifiri was one of those who opposed this tendency and eventually found himself left behind by the increasing militancy of the radicals. His own account gives some impression of the debate. At an early stage of the movement he attended meetings at Onepusu, the SSEM training school on the west coast of 'Are'are, power base of Nono'ohimae. While supporting the basic aim of self-determination, Ganifiri had misgivings about some of the more radical proposals which he heard there. It was being said that "If we do these meetings, America will give cargo to us", that everyone should join the Roman Catholic Church, already influentual in South Malaita where the movement had begun "... so that the Roman Catholic bishop or the Pope will give us the things we want", and that they should dispense with the British. Ganifiri's doubts were reinforced by a conversation at Onepusu with District Commissioner Sandars and he concluded that "many things in Māsing Rul ... were dangerous and did not appear to be in accordance with the Bible, as I saw it". When Nori and Nono'ohimae came to Kwai and addressed a meeting at A'arai, Ganifiri replied with his own modified proposals. He reaffirmed Māsing Rul demands but denied the possibilities of receiving American 'cargo' and spoke in favour of remaining under the British. But such policies did not ultimately convince most of the followers of Māsing Rul, whose resentment of the British became increasingly obvious to the government during 1946. As District Commissioner Davies observed at the time "... there is much to indicate that the reality of power lay with the local committees which surround the Head Chiefs rather than with the Head Chiefs themselves" (Annual Report, 1947). Many, including Ganifiri's people at Nāfinua, were beginning to prepare for some kind of military confrontation.

The military arm of Māsing Rul was the 'duties', also known as 'soldiers' or 'police' (RP or 'Royal Police'). As the Māsing Rul equivalent of the government Malaitan police or 'soldiers' who had imposed and maintained British authority for the last twenty years, they were an important symbol of Māsing Rul claims to self-government. They drilled with wooden rifles, a practice established by the SSEM training schools (Young 1925:180, Keesing 1978aII: 47) and formed guards of honour, like the government police, but for the Chiefs. But they drew inspiration also from the American army and, besides carrying wooden police truncheons, wore American khaki uniforms obtained through the Labour Corps.

The 'duties' were intended to act as guards for the 'towns', and as a fighting force if necessary. To this end, each 'town' had one or more 'sergeants' who drew upon their experience of the war to train an 'army' as a 'field force' or 'home guard' secretly in the bush. They dug foxholes, divided themselves into two sides and practised jungle warfare. There was some talk of an uprising against the British but the prospects for this were poor since they had only traditional weapons, although there was also talk of obtaining firearms from the Americans. The main purpose of the training was to prepare them to fight alongside the Americans or any other country which needed them, with a view to obtaining the benefits this had already brought them during the war. Who they were to fight against was not always clear, but some people at least understood it to be the British, whom the Amerians were expected to expel.

FROM NEGOTIATION TO CONFRONTATION

Although the more radical proposals of Māsing Rul were being voiced within the movement from the start, it was some time before this led to actual confrontation with the colonial government. As Keesing has described (1978aII: 49–53), the movement passed through several phases, beginning with the wartime experience and the subsequent formulation of its aims and organisation. Early Māsing Rul activities were so carefully concealed from the Headmen that the government only became aware of the movement late in 1945 (Annual Report 1947). After a period of sympathetic interest on the government's part, its relations with Māsing Rul steadily deteriorated as each party tried to counter the other's political initiatives, leading eventually to outright confrontation and repression. In the process the more cautious leaders like Ganifiri lost their influence to a new set of uncompromising militants, who dominated the later stages of the movement from 1949 to 1952.

For all their past grievances against the British, by the time of Māsing Rul Malaitans were dealing with a new school of colonial officers who now saw their purpose as the decolonisation of Solomon Islands through the British Government policy of Indirect Rule. Since the war they had already had some success in the Western Solomons and Guadalcanal in setting up Native Courts and Councils which were empowered to administer their own tax funds. But initial attempts to organise 'Councils of Elders' on Malaita from 1941, including a Council for Kwara'ae under Headman Siru, were interrupted by the war and frustrated by Māsing Rul opposition (Malaita District Journal 1940, Annual Report 1941). As Tom Russell recalls from his time as District Officer on Malaita, "Marching Rule made us impatient because this was simply deferring a process that was going to lead to self-government and independence".

At first the government regarded some Māsing Rul developments with favour as showing "a desire to co-operate with one another" and "a keen desire for self-improvement" which could be built upon by training for economic and political development under government leadership (Sandars 1946). But eventually, "... when about the middle of 1946 the existence of illegal training and drilling was discovered", the potential threat to government authority determined the government to break the power of the Māsing Rul chiefs (Annual Report 1947). This decision was reinforced when, on 26 December 1946 Māsing Rul chiefs from all over Malaita came to 'Aoke to put their demands to District Commissioner Sandars at a meeting of 5,600 men (Annual Report 1946). The chiefs' tone was conciliatory, saying that "the people belonging to Marching Rule wished to co-operate and take advantage of the benefits that were offered to them in the way of education, medical help and agricultural and other vocational training" (Annual Report 1947). This was Ganifiri's attitude when he spoke to ask for a chief for all Malaita. But although Sandars expressed approval of most of the chiefs' stated aims, he refused to concede the crucial point of their right to participate in courts dealing with 'native customary matters' (Annual Report 1946).[4]

This refusal strengthened the hand of the militants and the Māsing Rul policy of non-co-operation continued, all but bringing the work of the government to a standstill throughout Malaita. Not only were its efforts to re-establish an administration frustrated but government services were rejected and even treatment by the Medical Officer was refused at Nāfinua among other places (Annual Report 1947). In a mood of increasing militancy, early in 1947 rumours that the Americans had returned to Luga were spread by Nelson Kifo, the second most senior chief of West Kwara'ae. At a meeting at Nāfinua of Māsing Rul leaders from Kwaio, Kwara'ae and North Malaita, it was agreed to make another collection of dollars to send to the Americans to obtain rifles and ammunition with which to expel the British. $2,000 was later delivered to the residual American force on Guadalcanal. (Fifi'i, quoted by Keesing 1978aII:66). In March 1947, when the government managed to circumvent the Māsing Rul labour recruiting ban, the Head Chiefs threatened to call a general strike. This incident revealed to the government the deep involvement of Sibolo in Māsing Rul at Kwai and he was dismissed from his post as sergeant-major of police at 'Aoke (Annual Report 1947, Laracy 1983:25–26).

Recognising the growing opposition to the government in Kwai, Sandars tried to station Administrative Officer Cameron in the vacant SSEM mission house at Nāfinua, but this was blocked by members of the local church (Norman Deck n.d.). The position in Kwai was made clear to Cameron when he visited the area in June 1947. The people and their chiefs refused to operate a Native Court or set up a Native Council under the authority of the government, as provided for in recent government regulations according to the policy of Indirect Rule. Rejecting the unpopular Headman Siru, they demanded instead to form their own council to rule according to tradition under Ganifiri, as a leader appointed by the people rather than by government. For the most part Cameron found the people's attitude firm but conciliatory, but the growing militancy was revealed in incidents such as the insistence by the people of Kwai Island that he pay for drinking water and the overt hostility of Krispas Biru, a senior chief at Nāfinua. But to Cameron there still appeared to be some possibility of reasserting government authority by negotiation and as yet little cause to take legal action against the Māsing Rul courts (Cameron 1947a,b,d, Davies 1947b).

Matters came to a head at another meeting at 'Aoke between the Head Chiefs and Sandars on June 30. About 7,000 people came to hear the leaders of the northern districts, including Kwara'ae and East Kwaio, present Sandars with a demand for self-government which he recognised as "a declaration of independence". Their spokesman, Kifo from West Kwara'ae, declared that government councils and courts were to be rejected and henceforth disputes would be settled by *alaha'ou'ou*, nominally supreme leaders modelled on the traditional chiefs of South Malaita. The southern leaders were more cautious and from this time the movement as a whole became split as the northerners pursued their militant course, openly defiant of government law (Annual Report 1947). Henceforth the people of Kwai, like the other northern groups, considered that their independence from the government had been achieved, although they still received Cameron quite amicably when he visited the district again in July. Ganifiri reaffirmed the independence of the Māsing Rul courts and the authority of the chiefs, but Cameron nonetheless compared the East Kwara'ae movement quite favourably with northern districts such as Malu'u where the government was treated with open defiance and hostility. He attributed this to the moderating influence of leaders such as Ganifiri, Sibolo and Sardias Oge, the SSEM 'teacher' on Ngongosila. But even while he was there Kifo arrived to appoint Sibolo as *alaha'ou'ou* at a large meeting on July 29 (Cameron 1947f, Annual Report 1947).

GOVERNMENT REPRESSION

By this time the government had already made plans to arrest the militant Māsing Rul leaders of North Malaita, which it began to do on 31 August, using three ships and a force of 50 police. So many of the Malaitan police were, like Sibolo, involved in Māsing Rul themselves that the government had to rely on men from Western Solomons (Annual Report 1947). Then on 18 September, Cameron and a party of police came by ship to the east coast and arrested first Fifi'i, the Head Chief at Sinalaagu, then Ganifiri at Nāfinua and, the next day, Sibolo at Ngongosila. No resistance was offered by either the chiefs or their people (Cameron 1947g). By October 230 men had been arrested in the northern districts as well as all the Head Chiefs throughout Malaita, the chiefs being charged primarily with holding illegal courts. The population as a whole also received a warning in the form of a visit to Malaita by three British warships (Annual Report 1947). People in the areas affected were apparently rather subdued by all this at first, but soon became even more intransigent in the face of government efforts to re-establish the administration. Eventually, under new leadership, Kwai became one of the most militant areas of Malaita.

One of the government's attempts to restore administrative normality in Kwai was an instruction for local people to repair the tax house at Faumamanu. The response of the people of Faumamanu and A'arai was partly to demolish it. District Commissioner Davies responded to this challenge when he arrived by ship with Cameron and twenty-five Western Solomons police early in November 1947. He addressed a large crowd and threatened them with imprisonment when they refused to repair the house. "The next morning when the people were to assemble to work on the tax house, the fifty required were found on the beach with their belongings already packed", ready to go to prison (Davies 1947a). The police arrested them with fourteen others who had obstructed Headman Siru in bringing witnesses to court before the District Commissioner, as well as Kalu'ae, the senior chief at Faumamanu. One of the arrested men, David Kosionami, describes how they were shut in the hold of the ship, half suffocating and without food, the police throwing ashes over them and ignoring their complaints. When the ship reached Malu'u in North Malaita, ten prisoners were taken ashore and shown to the people there as a warning. They were sentenced to two months imprisonment and from 'Aoke some were sent to prison at Honiara on Guadalcanal, where they worked to build the new post-war capital of Solomon Islands, clearing land with their bare hands.

One consequence of the open confrontation with the government was a change in attitude to the missionaries of the SSEM. The first sign of this was when the SSEM superintendant, McBride, "received a cold and suspicious reception" on a tour of the east coast, including Kwai, in February 1946 (Norman Deck n.d.). But on a visit to Kwai in the first half of 1947 the missionaries were as well received as ever and reported brightly on the success of 'teachers" meetings and church services. At this stage their principal misgivings were over the removal of Christian influence from traditionist communities still living in the bush when the Christians moved to the 'towns', and the tendency for Māsing Rul chiefs to usurp the role of the SSEM 'teachers' in settling disputes according to traditional values and in contravention of SSEM policy. But, while bewailing the "menace" of ukulele and guitar playing by young men in the 'towns', Clark was able to thank God that the unity of Māsing Rul was "built upon the solid foundation of the Word of God" (NIV Jun. 1947:4–6).

While Māsing Rul was a problem only for the government, with which the SSEM had always had differences over the political autonomy of its churches, the missionaries seemed little concerned with the political implications of the movement. But when it began to affect their own work they soon sided with the government. By August 1947 they were beginning to regard Māsing Rul as a threat, impeding their work by preventing the recruitment of trainees and labourers, "... an independent movement, anti-government and anti-white ... establishing a rule of terrorism over the people" (NIV Dec. 1947:3). Tomlinson later described Nori as "indoctrinated by Communists", assumed that Māsing Rul Christians had been "hoodwinked" by Satan, and stated the missionaries' common opinion that "their disobediance to the Government is directly contrary to God's Word" (NIV Sept. 1949:11). In 1947 McBride even dismissed Ganifiri as a 'teacher' in the SSEM on the request of District Commissioner Sandars (Norman Deck n.d.). After the arrests people refused to tolerate this attitude any longer and began to run the church for themselves. By early 1948, on a visit to Nāfinua, the missionaries Clark, his wife and Norman Deck were boycotted by almost everyone. The few 'teachers' who would meet them refused to hear any criticism of Māsing Rul and raised an old demand that they be paid by the Mission for their pastoral work, which had always been against SSEM policy. Other people refused to speak to them, to accept medical aid or to hear them preach,

> ... BECAUSE they said we are paid for doing it and they were not going to be used as a means for our enrichment.

> ... when I walked into the church, they walked out. I took a service for about a dozen folk, our own staff and a few of the anti-Marching Rule people. (NIV March 1948:4–5)

In 1948, following the example of other districts of North Malaita, Māsing Rul followers in East Kwara'ae began to fortify their 'towns' with fences and towers; leaf-thatch buildings up to six stories high, in imitation of American army watchtowers. Sentries were posted at the top in the expectation of the arrival of help from overseas. It was apparently unclear who was coming or what would happen, except that new developments were at hand and that the towers were for defence and to accommodate the visitors in a forthcoming conflict, probably involving the Americans. In July 1948 the government began a concerted attempt to break Māsing Rul by force. Beginning with the most militant areas of North Malaita, ships with Western Solomons police started to visit the 'towns', ordering the demolition of the fences and towers on the grounds that they illegally restricted free movement and demanding census information in preparation for resuming taxation. As men almost universally refused to comply they were arrested and the fortifications destroyed.

As the headquarters for Kwai, Nāfinua was one of the early targets of this campaign. According to Taeman Timi, the government and police arrived in three ships, broke up the fence and towers, set fire to some buildings and took sixty-five men off to jail at 'Aoke. As before, they were harshly treated and made to work clearing bushes all day long with their bare hands. Nowhere in Malaita was resistance offered to these arrests. The men

> ... passively and peacefully disobeyed all orders and proceeded to gaol in a thoroughly orderly manner. The atmosphere was one of strained but controlled exhilaration — the patient suffering of the martyr for the cause. (Annual Report 1949–50)

In Kwai those who were prepared to fight the British were reminded that they had no rifles and that Nori had told them they could win freedom not by fighting but by going to prison. Questioned about their leaders in court, each man denied that anyone but himself was responsible for his actions and pleaded guilty to the charges. It was said that, if they were 'humble' and trusted in God, they would 'overcome' and at this stage the government action did little to weaken the people's resolve. When the Nāfinua men returned from jail they immediately set to work to restore the 'town' and 'farm'.

As the government campaign in North Malaita continued during 1949 the repeated mass arrests began to strain the government's resources. As Russell explains, this goes some way to explain the harsh treatment of the prisoners, working without tools and short of rations. The campaign also began to disrupt the people's lives but without actually breaking the passive resistance of Māsing Rul (Annual Report 1949–50). Hence it was almost a year before action was taken against the remaining Māsing Rul 'towns' in East Kwara'ae. Then, on 12 June 1949, District Commissioner Masterman on an overland patrol served written notices of the fence demolition and census. Early on the 21st he returned with police in four ships and arrested a total of sixty-six men at Faumamanu, 'Adakoa ('Gwaisaia') and A'arai and destroyed the towers and fences (Diary 1949). As the chiefs had time to prepare, the men to be arrested were selected beforehand, taking into consideration who would remain to care for families left behind. The next day, stopping at Malu'u, they were all sentenced to twelve weeks and sent to Honiara. The prisoners were treated like others before them: the police threw the food they had brought into the sea and gave them nothing to eat until they reached Honiara. Those left behind suffered too, for many women and children took refuge in the bush and as their old villages there had decayed away they had to live in the small temporary houses used when working their gardens.

THE RESISTANCE REFORMS

But far from distintegrating under government pressure, Māsing Rul in Kwara'ae had by this time developed a new focus of organisation, well concealed from the government. The arrest of the Head Chiefs and the persecution over the fences and tax made way for the emergence of a more militant leadership based

PLATE 34   *The British authorities on tour in 1949. Fataleka chiefs not
                 involved in Māsing Rul, at Fokanakafo just north of Kwai, meet
                 Resident Commissioner Gregory-Smith, accompanied by District
                 Commissioner Masterman, labour recruiter Ernie Palmer (in
                 shorts) and District Officer Tom Russell (in kilt).
                 (Photo from Tom Russell)*

in West Kwara'ae. In this Māsing Rul district the unity of the movement had
already begun to break up by 1947, as Head Chief Shadrach Joe lost his influence
when he proved unwilling to lead a direct confrontation with government (Tour
Report 1948). Among the more radical leaders to come forward were Kifo,
Sukulu of Su'u and Sau, a former police sergeant of Fokanakafo, where
Ofokwasi 'town' was situated. But foremost in the continuing struggle was Eriel
Sisili of Namongisu near Bina in southwest Kwara'ae. Sisili's activities are
documented in detail in the Annual Reports for Malaita District for 1949 to
1952, on which most of the following account is based. In 1948, while Shadrach
Joe went on to become a government Headman, Sisili began to organise a
movement known as the 'West Malaita Council of Property Owners' or
'Kwara'ae Council', among other names. This came to involve Māsing Rul
followers in many parts of Kwara'ae and in adjacent areas of Kwaio and Fataleka,
as well as developing links with other districts of the North Malaita movement.

In East Kwara'ae its principal leaders included a pro-Māsing Rul Headman, Takanakwao of Mānadari in the central bush and Krispas Biru, Ganifiri's militant deputy at Nāfinua.

Sisili's Council placed a heavy emphasis on the promise of American intervention and on reforms inspired by the United States constitution. Attempts were made to contact the Americans remaining on Guadalcanal and from mid 1949 rumours were circulated that they were about to return to expel the British and bring 'cargo'. The government regarded these rumours as deliberate fabrications, as Kwara'ae themselves tended to conclude, at least after they failed to materialise. It is even said that someone, perhaps Sukulu, left footprints on a beach in Amerian army boots and dropped cigarette ends, to make people think that the Americans had landed.

At one stage, probably in the second half of 1949, another attempt was made to buy American support. Some time after the Head Chiefs were arrested, the Māsing Rul funds at Nāfinua had been sent for safekeeping to Sisili at Namongisu by Biru and Banau, as treasurer and clerk, with the authority of the Māsing Rul committee. This in itself was an important acknowledgement of Sisili's leadership, made also by other Māsing Rul districts from Kwaio northwards. After Sisili had held the money for some time, Langalanga people who had been travelling back and forth to Guadalcanal brought news that an American had advised them to buy American support to free themselves from the British. So Sisili sent a big suitcase of money, so much that it took all day to count, to Guadalcanal in a Langalanga canoe with twenty-five men. According to Adriel Rofate'e, one of the Nāfinua 'duties' chosen for the task, they were escorted by two sharks invoked by the Langalanga men to protect them and when they reached Gela another two sharks took over. Landing at Koli Point on Guadalcanal, they were hidden and fed by local people and took the money to an American who was selling off surplus war equipment to the British. But he refused to take it, explaining that the Americans had come to expel the Japanese and that they should appeal to the British government. So they took the money back to Sisili, from whom it was eventually taken by the government on his arrest; over $1,000 according to the report.

Henceforth preparations were made to confront the government once again with a new set of demands. On their return to Kwai, Rofate'e and others began to organise meetings to explain the American's message and to press the government to release the Head Chiefs and send a 'big man' from England to negotiate with them for their freedom. By now other possibilities were beginning to recede. By November 1949 the hope of American intervention faded with the final ceremonious departure of their forces from Guadalcanal and the government had completed the removal of the towers throughout Malaita. Enthusiasm for life in the 'towns' was beginning to wane and when the men of Faumamanu and A'arai returned from prison they began to rebuild their villages in the bush. Furthermore, to force the tax and census issue the government began another programme of arrests in November of all the Māsing Rul leaders who still refused to co-operate. The Māsing Rul response changed and instead of offering themselves for arrest men began to run away and hide in the bush when the police arrived, leaving only the women and children in the 'towns'. This caused the government even more difficulties and was regarded as even more defiant. Henceforth the leaders of the Kwara'ae movement, like Sisili himself, remained out of reach of the government in the bush, and so did most of their followers.

On 22 November 1949 Sisili called a mass meeting of the Kwara'ae movement at 'Aoke to present their demands to District Commissioner Masterman in a letter, which was later well summarized by District Officer Allan:

> It traced the history of mankind [from Biblical evidence] and stated that the people wanted a better way of life and that they wished for representatives from their own numbers to work under the Government to bring this about. The letter summarized the four main points in terms of independence for Malaita, recognition of native customs, increased incomes, happiness for all. (Annual Report 1949–1950:14)[5]

Masterman was an officer of the old school, less compromising than some of his predecessors. His response was negative and another mass meeting, including men from other parts of Malaita, was called for 21 December. Here Sisili read out a manifesto demanding

> ... one man to speak for Malaita on all native affairs, Courts and Councils to be re-established, the nine chiefs to be released, and the division of the people into those that obeyed [ie. recognised] the law and those that did not. (Annual Report 1949–1950)

Tom Russell, present at this meeting as District Officer, remembers it as tense and volatile, the crowd armed with traditional weapons and a few guns responding with cries of agreement to Sisili's rousing speech until the government party thought they were going to attack. But Masterman stood his ground, refusing to make concessions until taxes had been paid, and the crowd eventually dispersed peacefully.

In growing frustration a third and final meeting was planned, at which it was apparently intended to make an armed attack on the government if the demands were refused. The South Malaita leaders, increasingly wary of the militancy of Sisili's movement, declined to back this move and the government responded to the rumours by intensifying its programme of arrests in the northern districts over the tax issue. There were renewed rumours of the return of the Americans with arms and cargo. Disturbed by the deteriorating relations between the government and the people, the new Resident Commissioner,

Gregory-Smith, began to negotiate with the imprisoned Head Chiefs. They were eventually released on 8 June 1950 on condition that they forsook Māsing Rul and tried to persuade their people to comply with taxation, following which a Council for Malaita was promised with half the members elected, under the District Commissioner and a Malaitan Vice-President.

Ganifiri for one was satisfied with the proposed reforms. While in prison at Honiara he had addressed a letter to the President of the United States through the Americans at Luga asking for confirmation of rumours that America was going to come and give freedom. He recalls the reply as "I and England are friends" and that they should "continue asking England and she will open the door to your asking and give you what you want". This apparently convinced him to negotiate seriously with the British. In a meeting at 'Aoke just before his release, with the High Commissioner, District Commissioner and Headman Dausabea, his requests for economic and political development were conceded (despite Dausabea's recommendation that Māsing Rul followers be shot!).

THE STRUGGLE FOR A COUNCIL AND THE FINAL COMPROMISE

In most parts of Malaita, the release of the Head Chiefs gradually encouraged compliance with the government's demands and administration began to return to normal. But in several areas of the north, and particularly in East Kwara'ae and parts of West Kwara'ae, the resistence led by Sisili's Council continued as before. When Ganifiri and Sibolo returned home and tried to convince their people to compromise they found themselves rejected, with no further influence over the movement. The government had effectively destroyed the moderate faction and was left to face the militants.

Sisili's Council continued to reject the government and to encourage hopes of American intervention, attempting once again to gain support from Americans still believed to be on Guadalcanal. By the end of 1950 Sisili was reformulating the aims of the movement and developing proposals for a 'Federal Council' based on a 'Declaration of Independence', "a facsimile of the famous American Declaration with the name of 'Malaita' in place of 'America'", as Allan described it (Annual Report 1949–1950). The name of the organisation was taken from the 'Federal Council of the Churches of Christ in America', an influential ecumenical movement of 'social gospelism' (Fulbright 1986:96). From documents later confiscated by the government, "The Federal Council was shown to receive its power from President Roosevelt, Winston Churchill, the Four Freedoms and the Atlantic Charter", interpreted according to the principles of fundamentalist Christianity (Annual Report 1949–1950; see Laracy 1983 section H for full documents). Sisili planned to confront the government with this formula at a mass meeting at 'Aoke in December 1950. However, by this time the government was making some progress in persuading people to pay the tax and Kwara'ae militancy was sufficiently weakened for the District Commissioner to ban the meeting and for the police to turn people away without resistance. Another mass meeting planned for January 1951 was also banned and Sisili's attempts to negotiate with the District Commissioner broke down over each party's insistence on meeting on its own ground.

Gaining confidence from Sisili's failure to mobilise his following, the government decided to crush him. On the night of 27 January a carefully planned police raid on Namongisu took Sisili by surprise and he was arrested and his documents and Māsing Rul funds taken. The police themselves were surprised by the local resistance; drums spread the news and they had to stand off three armed parties on their way back to the coast. Kwara'ae say that the police beat up Sisili's wife and that he told the people not to fight back, but this did not prevent his followers from threatening to attack 'Aoke.

In the following months the Federal Council continued its activities under Sisili's brother Maekiki, with instructions relayed from Sisili himself in jail at Honiara. In April notices were distributed for display throughout Malaita proclaiming the authority of the Federal Council and its intention to fight the government, although most were intercepted or removed by the Headmen. Some attempts were also made to build fortified settlements in the central Kwara'ae bush and to obstruct a government geological survey. The government's efforts to explain and organise a District Council for Malaita on the lines proposed the previous year were met with suspicions and counter-claims for the authority of the Federal Council and rumours continued to circulate that the Americans were returning to support it. In August Federal Council supporters were persuaded to attend a mass meeting at 'Aoke called by the government for leaders from all over Malaita, but once again their demands were rejected, this time by the Minister of State for the Colonies. In September, having been held on a number of interim charges, Sisili was finally sentenced to twelve years for 'treason felony' (later reduced to three) (Laracy 1983;162).

By early 1952 the Federal Council was proposing its own Council as an alternative to the government one and attempting to carry out government functions such as a census and demarcation of land. The government meanwhile decided to implement some of its own reforms to meet the longstanding Māsing Rul and Federal Council demands, establishing the District Council, Native Courts, a shipping service, education and economic development programmes, all backed by a written propaganda campaign. In the face of continued opposition from Takanakwao, Sau and Irofolia of the Federal Council, the District Council was convened in July on the basis of two elected and two appointed members for each subdistrict, of which almost three quarters were actually recruited. By September, the government having suspended its campaign against tax defaulters, Federal Council leaders finally met the District Commissioner and agreed to participate with the District Council in a new Malaita Council.

The Malaita Council involved a number of concessions on the part of the government. Its president was to be a Malaitan, under the authority of the High Commissioner and Protectorate law rather than the District Commissioner. It was to have a majority of elected members and be responsible for taxation. An amnesty was also given on unpaid back taxes. Followers of the Federal Council were in a majority on the Malaita Council, its first President, Salana Ga'a of Areo, was a leader of the movement, and he was succeeded for a time by Eriel Sisili himself. Even so, when the Malaita Council was first convened in January 1952, areas led in the Federal Council by Sau, Takanakwao and Irofiola (ie. Fokanakafo, central Kwara'ae and Fo'odo respectively), still had not chosen their representatives.

AN ASSESSMENT OF MĀSING RUL

As far as Kwara'ae were concerned, the formation of the Malaita Council signalled the end of Māsing Rul in its guise of the Federal Council. For some the Malaita Council became the successor to Māsing Rul, representing the 'independence' which they had been fighting for. For others it was still 'government', to be opposed by other means in the future. But the significance of Māsing Rul went beyond the constitutional reforms it achieved, which were in any case a compromise with existing British colonial policy. Māsing Rul represented a crucial phase in the process of Malaitan social and political development which began with the onset of the colonial period. Its antecedents can be traced back to the beginning of the 20th century or before and its consequences have been evident in Kwara'ae politics throughout the forty years since.

In discussing the local antecedents of Māsing Rul, Keesing and Laracy have drawn attention to various Malaitan 'politico-religious movements', including the Kwara'ae *bulu* cults which Headman Dausabea compared to Māsing Rul in discussions with Allan in 1951 (Allan 1974, Keesing 1978aI:257–258, Laracy 1983:32). The *bulu* cults did indeed foreshadow Māsing Rul as attempts to take control of the changes introduced by colonialism. But, as alternatives to the European-dominated mission 'schools', they were actually part of the wider movement to reject discredited traditional sources of spiritual power which also led to Christian conversion. Māsing Rul was a continuation of the social upheavals of the previous forty years, but it is probably not very useful to regard it, in Keesing's terms, as a 'politico-religious' movement with antecedants in particular religious cults. In seeking spiritual support for human endevour

Māsing Rul was doing no more than follow a basic principle of Kwara'ae and Malaitan culture, that the political is religious and the religious political.

Unlike the earlier movements which had sought solutions to colonial crises through new sources of spiritual support, Māsing Rul drew upon spiritual powers that were by now well tried and tested; on God through the churches they already belonged to or, for a minority, on the ghosts they had never ceased to worship. In the 'towns' each mission sect had its own church, built not as a first priority but after work was well underway on the 'farms' and houses (NIV Jun, 1947:6). Traditionists sacrificed pigs for the success of Māsing Rul; Christians prayed. As Taeman Timi, 'teacher' and Leader Chief at Nāfinua says, "We looked to God so that he would guide us, so we prayed like this: 'God, it's you who knows. ... You can give it for us. Not us alone; we want you to do it for us.' "

Nor is it sufficient to see Māsing Rul, in Worsley's terms, as part of "a trend from religious cult to political activity" in Melanesia (Worsley 1968:239). Māsing Rul may indeed be recognisable to Europeans as "a proto-nationalist political party" (1968:192) because it demonstrated an understanding of the workings of the colonial order which largely corresponds to the European view of the system. But this hardly does justice to the Malaitan vision of Māsing Rul as an alternative to the colonial order, the culmination of efforts since at least the beginning of the century to adapt their whole traditional social order to meet the new social realities of colonial domination. Rather than look for religious cults or political parties, it is more instructive to consider how Māsing Rul built upon Malaitan experience of colonialism. Its achievement was to restructure Malaitan society from a fragmented, tribal level of social organisation into an island-wide political system with a degree of co-ordination which had never before existed. In this endeavour Malaitans were inspired by the benefits which accrued to Europeans from their control of such systems, and they built upon their own experience of government, missions, business and, latterly, the American army.

A foundation was provided by the Christian churches, particularly the local organisation of the SSEM, developed largely by Malaitans under the guidance of European missionaries. Sandars observed how the Mission, with its regular 'teachers'' meetings and networks maintained by correspondence "... provided an almost ideal instrument for the dissemination of ideas" (1946). Forster reported that:

> The SSEM teachers hold monthly meetings of Church elders in Bali [ie. North Malaita] and Kwara'ae. These are MR [Marching Rule] meetings and this mission and all its works are MR. Services and schools are held for the dissemination of anti-Government propaganda. (Tour Report 1948)

From the missions Malaitans also learnt the symbolic as well as the practical value of writing. They attempted to legitimate traditional values in written records as well as to record Māsing Rul finances and co-operative activities and to communicate political decisions within the movement and to the government. From the government itself they had learnt the political advantages of and the institutional arrangements for centralised authority under 'chiefs' who could exercise control over large numbers of people; something early government officers had sought in vain to find before setting up their own system of Headmen. Māsing Rul was run by a loose hierarchy of officers: 'chiefs', 'duties', 'clerks' and 'treasurers', all in conscious imitation of the colonial system which it hoped to supplant. The Americans provided further inspiration, for 'towns' and 'farms' as well as for proposals for 'independence', including the constitutional demands of the Federal Council. The symbolic trappings of the American army also provided an appropriate alternative to British forms. By controlling the symbols as well as the substance of the colonial order and its American alternative, Māsing Rul sought to rebuild the self-esteem of Malaitans which had suffered so much under colonial domination (as Laracy observes 1983:34), as well as the political autonomy they had lost.

At the same time many Kwara'ae appreciated their dependence on foreign sources for the wealth, education, training and services which they sought to acquire through Māsing Rul. Their limited understanding of the economic and political forces involved as well as desperation in the face of Māsing Rul's failure to control them, goes some way to explain the rumours of 'cargo' and American intervention which came to the fore in the latter stages of the movement. The question of 'cargo' has been much discussed by authors concerned to counter the colonialist denigration of Māsing Rul as a 'cargo cult' (Keesing 1978aII:68, Laracy 1983:150). For Kwara'ae, expectations of 'cargo' were at the time not necessarily either religious or irrational. They were not associated with spiritual forces and they were precedented by the recent experiences of the war. In view of their failure to materialise, it is hardly surprising to find Kwara'ae today dismissing rumours of cargo and Americans as deliberate fabrications which damaged Māsing Rul by distracting from its real purpose, but this does not mean they were not accepted at the time. But it is also important to recognise how characterising Māsing Rul as a 'cult' concerned with 'cargo' helped the British to avoid some uncomfortable questions as to the causes and aims of the movement. It may even be, as Fulbright argues (1986:108–124), that the colonial authorities were themselves responsible for introducing the cargo rumours by voicing unjustified but self-fulfilling suspicions that Māsing Rul was a variant of the more cargo-orientated movements of New Guinea. Government efforts to deny the prospects of cargo would themselves have inclined people to believe in it.

But whatever the role played by rumours of Americans and cargo, it is unlikely that Māsing Rul could have fulfilled its more radical programmes in the long term without making the kind of compromises with the colonial system originally proposed by men like Ganifiri. In the absence of centralised political and economic structures which were firmly institutionalised in the local society, the organisation of Māsing Rul was sustained largely by the momentum of the movement, its developing programme of activities and its struggle against the government. As the government tended to assume, Māsing Rul leaders may well have taken this into account in the development of their programmes (Annual Report 1947), and some of the rumours of Americans and cargo may have been deliberately calculated to sustain enthusiasm for the movement.

The problem faced by Malaitans in Māsing Rul is one they have faced before and since, of how to turn a popular movement into new permanent social institutions. It is evidently easier for a colonised people to achieve this in collaboration with their colonisers than in opposition to them. This was the case with the Malaita Council, in contrast to Māsing Rul or the Federal Council, as it had been for the mission 'schools', in contrast to the *bulu* cults. But the failure of indigenous alternatives should not obscure the contributions which Malaitans made to the colonial institutions which were established in their place. Māsing Rul was a phase of intense activity, provoked by the crisis of the war, in the long and continuing process by which the people of Kwai and Malaita have made their own adaptations to the changes which the colonial order has pressed upon them. They tried with some success to direct these changes according to their own vision of their future. Many of the themes developed in Māsing Rul, of political autonomy under spiritual authority, of Western institutions incorporating traditional values and of economic development with overseas support, have continued to influence the history of Kwai ever since.

PLATE 35   *Some of the East Kwara'ae chiefs, with the author, at a meeting at Kwasibu in 1991. They include Cornelius Kwasite'e, Hon. Alfred Maetia M.P., Nelson Konabako, John Gamu, Adriel Rofate'e, Frank Ete Tu'aisalo.*

CHAPTER EIGHT

Towards 'Independence' (1950s to 1980s)

In the forty years since the great social experiment of Māsing Rul came to an end, many of its objectives have been fulfilled. During this time Kwara'ae have gained a measure of control over the institutions of government and church which now play such an important role in their lives, as part of the wider process of political decolonisation of the Solomons and other 'Third World' countries once subject to the governments of Europe. They have also gained some of the prosperity sought by Māsing Rul, largely as a result of increased demand for the natural resources of Solomon Islands in the growing world economy. To complete this history of the way Kwara'ae have reshaped their society during a century of colonialism, it is necessary to trace their route back towards 'independence', if such it is, under the new Solomon Islands state which has developed since the war. For although Kwara'ae have realised some of the ambitions of Māsing Rul, they still experience many of the contradictions of a society which is subject to state government and increasingly dependent on the capitalist economy but which has its foundations in a tribal culture of self-sufficiency and self-determination.

Although the formation of the Malaita Council signalled the end of militant opposition to the British, it did not resolve all the problems which Māsing Rul was trying to address, even in relation to the colonial government. The end of the Māsing Rul was also the beginning of a new phase in resistance to colonialism, as Kwara'ae continued to seek 'freedom' and 'independence' on their own terms. These terms reflect the political culture and religious world view of their own pre-colonial past, as well as the experience of new ideas and institutions introduced by their colonisers. In particular, many Kwara'ae have continued to reassess the traditional culture which was so seriously undermined by their conversion to Christianity, and tradition has come to represent the self-determination they lost with colonisation but somehow still hope to regain. Since the end of Māsing Rul Kwara'ae have taken part in a number of popular movements and reforms variously combining traditional and Christian values in negotiation with both government and missions. In doing so they have continued to draw strength from spiritual as well as human sources, seeking ritual as well as political solutions in a continuing struggle for self-determination. But increasingly the religious and the political seem to have developed through separate movements and institutions, a distinction more characteristic of European or colonial culture than of Kwara'ae culture which will emerge in the history which follows.

THE CONTINUING DECLINE OF THE GHOSTS

By the time of the war the focus of religious conflict in Kwara'ae was shifting away from the competition for allegiance between God and the ghosts, as followers of the traditional religion were reduced to a dwindling minority. The debate over the merits of the two religions continued in the same terms and the traditional religion continued to represent resistance to colonialism in support of the common goal of self-determination under spiritual authority. But this position became increasingly difficult to sustain as traditionist congregations declined to small family groups and the remaining priests found themselves responsible for more and more ghosts who had been abandoned by others, but with less and less human support. This eventually left some individuals unwilling to join their relatives in 'school' but unable to continue sacrificial activities either.

The saltwater people of Kwai were already overwhelmingly Christian by the time of the war, and by the end of Māsing Rul the remaining traditionists of the Anibongi clan on Ngongosila had also decided to go to 'school'. Finding difficulty in maintaining the ritual system of the ghosts as a minority among their Christian neighbours but resisting the SSEM to the last, in 1950 most of them joined the Anglican church. This was introduced not from Kwara'ae but by Anthony Saru from Walade in South Malaita (later a Solomon Islands national politician), who had come to live with his mother's people on Ngongosila. The Anibongi priest Mamali removed the relics of his ghosts to a small islet nearby. When he died ten years later and his son Jack Mae joined the Anglicans the ghosts were finally abandoned on Ngongosila after fifty years of resistance to Christianity.

The conversion of the saltwater people eventually led their coastal neighbours at 'Atori to follow. After the 'Atori feastgiver Mauara died his son Ketei took over leadership of the clan and the 'new life' cult and Ketei's clan 'brother' Sardias Oge, a 'teacher' on Ngongosila, persuaded him to let the Christians there make gardens on 'Atori land. Ketei's doubts were confirmed when the Christian women defiled the wharf of the *anoasa* spirits by ignoring menstruation rules and in about 1951 he and about ten other people at 'Atori died as a result. The rest later joined Oge on Ngongosila, so ending the 'new life' *bulu* cult.

In the East Kwara'ae bush most remaining traditionists were also reduced to small isolated groups. Such was the situation of Ramo'itolo, priest of one of the leading clans of Latea (as referred to in Chapter 2). Some members of Ramo'itolo's clan had been Christian since the 1920s in association with the

Gwauna'ongi people who moved to Dingodingo nearby. During the 1960s Ramo'itolo sent his two married sons to 'school' to protect them and their families from the consequences of his own ritual mistakes. But in 1966 when the priest of one of the other Latea clans, his son-in-law, died, Ramo'itolo took responsibility for this man's brothers and sons too. Ramo'itolo only had the resources to sacrifice on a small scale, with festivals of only three to five pigs and it seems that he took on more responsibilities than he could adequately fulfill. His death in 1969 was attributed to the anger of ghosts whom he had missed from his sacrifices. Most of his congregation then went to 'school' except for his oldest son who went to live with traditionist relatives in 'Ere'ere.

The 'Ere'ere people, ever fiercely independent and resistant to all things European, were the last to keep up a more or less complete programme of traditional ritual activity in East Kwara'ae. They maintained ritual links with a number of traditionists at Rageto and Otefarakau in the central Kwara'ae bush and with relatives among the predominantly traditionist people of the East Kwaio bush. Even in 'Ere'ere many people have, over the years, moved down to nearby 'school' villages or spent periods in 'school' when misfortune struck before returning to their ghosts. The senior priest of the 'Ere'ere group, Timi Ko'oliu, was in charge of the important and ancient shrine of Masu'ua (Anomula), but he also had to sacrifice to senior ghosts abandoned by their descendants elsewhere in Kwara'ae. When he was killed by the ghosts in 1984 for defiling himself while trying to rescue his sick wife from the latrine, his son did not succeed him and the most important remaining focus of traditional spiritual power in East Kwara'ae was lost.

'INDEPENDENCE' AND THE SSEM

For most Kwara'ae the ideal of self-determination under spiritual authority was now inspired by Christianity, and particularly by the SSEM ideology which had supported Māsing Rul. But although the formation of the Malaita Council realised some of the political objectives of Māsing Rul, the contradiction remained that the SSEM churches which had contributed so much to the strength and organisation of the movement were still formally under the authority of European missionaries. Malaitans had been able to take control of these churches during Māsing Rul only by boycotting the missionaries who opposed them. But as a result, despite their initial misgivings, the missionaries were obliged to recognise that Malaitans could and would manage their own churches, with or without their help. They were thus reminded of the stated objective of the SSEM "to bring into being churches which from the outset are self-governing, self-supporting and self-propagating" (NIV Jul. 1975:9). With the demise of the Federal Council the hostility which had greeted SSEM missionaries on previous tours around Malaita began to diminish. In 1951 they were able to preach at Nāfinua with Ganifiri's support and by 1952 they were once more holding large services and meetings with other East Kwara'ae church leaders formerly active in Māsing Rul (NIV Jun. 1951:8, Mar. 1952:3). Confrontation was replaced by constructive discussion in which the missionaries were represented by Rev. W. Gibbins, who was appointed by the SSEM in 1951 to reorganise the indigenous church.

The development of this church is described in the SSEM's own history in *Not In Vain* (Sept. 1974, Mar., Jul. 1975). Gibbins worked with Timothy Anilafa, a senior 'teacher' from Ngongosila who had remained loyal to the missionaries and government in opposition to Māsing Rul. They began to organise the SSEM local churches into a total of twenty district 'Associations' which were to form the basis for an independent church organisation for Solomon Islands as a whole. East Kwara'ae formed one such Association in 1953, with former Māsing Rul Head Chief Justus Ganifiri as President. Training was given in organisational practice, record keeping and accounting, which Malaitans had already found necessary during Māsing Rul.

In response to demands voiced in Māsing Rul, the SSEM also began to expand its secular educational services, opening a new school at Su'u in Dorio in 1950. Like the training school at Onepusu, Su'u concentrated at first on basic literacy for Bible study but as time went on it also increasingly prepared men to take over church administration and to benefit from the new employment opportunities developing after the war. By 1960 the SSEM had set up an education programme to train local school teachers and develop a system of village schools from which some pupils could progress into more advanced central and secondary schools. Another important development in Kwai was the building of a maternity centre and clinic at Nāfinua in 1959, organised by Ganifiri and funded by the SSEM. The centre was staffed by European nurses who trained Solomon Islands women (including Ganifiri's daughter), and it has continued to be the medical centre for Kwai ever since (NIV Dec. 1959:5, Mar. 1960:9).

Malaitans began to take over administrative and ritual duties in the SSEM formerly carried out by missionaries from about 1953. Eventually, in March 1964 at a conference at Abu near 'Aoke, a constitution was agreed and the new church was formally inaugurated as the South Sea Evangelical Church (SSEC) at a service attended by about 1,300 people (NIV June 1964:2). The South Sea Evangelical Mission (SSEM) became a separate support organisation, based in Sydney, through which European missionaries continued to play an essential role as advisors providing education and training. Missionaries were represented on the SSEC Executive and one was chosen as the first SSEC President, but henceforth Europeans contributed their support at the invitation of elected

PLATE 36   *Delegates representing 282 Solomon Islands local churches at the*
inaugural conference of the SSEC in 1964, assembled in front of
Abu church in West Kwara'ae. Rev. A. Hawley, the first
President, is seated in the centre, with his successor Ariel Bili of
Ngongosila immediately behind him.
(Photo from the SSEM archive)

Solomon Islander church leaders. Most of these were from Malaita, the main
stronghold of the SSEC, and many were from Kwai, including the first Solomon
Islander President, Ariel Bili of Ngongosila. In 1965 Justus Ganifiri became the
head of the whole SSEC organisation in Solomon Islands as General Superintendent, and his deputy and successor was Jesreel Filoa of Kwai Island.

The SSEC thus became the first autonomous mission church in Solomon
Islands. Although there were similar pressures for local control within the
Anglican church, with the foundation of an indigenous 'Church Association' in
1953, it was not until 1975 that the Europeans gave up their leadership through
the Melanesian Mission and the islanders took control of an independent 'Church
of Melanesia' (see Whiteman 1983:293–300).

Although the building of the SSEC satisfied some longstanding demands,
it took place against a background of political frustration and religious dissent
which continued to challenge the SSEM and led to a number of defections during
the 1950s. Ever since Māsing Rul, waves of Christian religious enthusiasm have
swept Malaita at intervals, sometimes leading to movements against government

and missions as well as to various new ritual developments and reforms. One such movement occurred in 1955, when England Kwaisulia from Lau led a group of evangelists on a tour from Malu'u to Radefasu in West Kwara'ae, holding a series of 'revival' meetings in SSEM villages. Kwaisulia, a grandson of the famous Lau leader of the same name, was brought up in the traditional religion and joined the SSEM after a brief attachment to the Anglicans. He was acknowledged to have spiritual 'gifts' and the prayer meetings on his tour were characterised by miraculous signs and ecstatic hysteria among the congregations, interpreted as visitations from the Holy Spirit (Maetoloa 1985:124).

'INDEPENDENCE' AND THE JEHOVAH'S WITNESSES

Kwaisulia's revival movement was followed shortly afterwards by a similar outburst of religious enthusiasm caused by the Jehovah's Witnesses, a church unrepresented among the many Christian sects in Solomon Islands up to that time. Malaitans may well have met American Jehovah's Witnesses while working in the Labour Corps during the war, but the church only began to arouse interest during the 1950s. It was first taken up and spread by Clement Fa'abasua, a West Kwara'ae man belonging to the SSEM. Fa'abasua is said to have found a copy of the Jehovah's Witness magazine *Watchtower* in the office of a European manager while working on Lever's plantation in Russell Islands in 1954, and he obtained doctrinal texts by sending off a coupon to their Australian office. Later, in 1956, according to another well known story, a Jehovah's Witness leaflet was found in Russell Islands floating at sea in a bottle by another Kwara'ae man, who gave it to Fa'abasua and they wrote away to America and received a magazine. Fa'abasua began to travel around preaching the Jehovah's Witness message and made contact with an American Jehovah's Witness named 'Batson' who was disposing of American wartime business in Honiara. They preached there together until they were arrested and imprisoned for a month on the grounds that Batson was doing missionary work without a permit. On his release, Fa'abasua continued to preach, first in Russell Islands where he was heard by other Kwara'ae workers, and then back home in Malaita, where he soon gained a large following both in Kwara'ae and in the north at Malu'u.

An important attraction of the Jehovah's Witnesses, at least initially, was in their American associations. As preached by Fa'abasua, this appeared to offer renewed possibilities for the 'freedom' and 'independence' expected from America during Māsing Rul, and an alternative to the Australian and British missions to which most Christians already belonged. Particularly appealing was the expectation that the Jehovah's Witnesses overseas would pay local 'teachers' and church leaders for the expenses of pastoral work, in contrast to the SSEM policy of collecting the money from the local congregations, which had become a focus of resentment during Māsing Rul. But the theology of the Jehovah's Witnesses had a more fundamental appeal, which helps to explain why the church has retained its following long after these initial expectations proved over-optimistic. The Jehovah's Witness renunciation of 'the government of the world' in favour of 'heavenly government' formed a particularly appropriate expression of the Kwara'ae claim to self-determination under indigenous leaders whose authority derived, ideally, from their mediation of spiritual power. But instead of confronting the government politically, as Māsing Rul had tried and failed to do, Fa'abasua's followers dissociated themselves from secular authority, acknowledging 'worldly government' but refusing to participate in it, according to the Jehovah's Witness interpretation of Biblical precepts (in this case *Romans* Ch. 13).

When Fa'abasua and the converts he had gained returned to Malaita their preaching was received with considerable enthusiasm. Large meetings, some lasting several days, were held by Fa'abasua at Maga in West Kwara'ae and at Taba'a in the central bush, and an American missionary arrived to address them. These were among perhaps twenty Kwara'ae villages which joined the Jehovah's Witnesses, mostly in 1956 and 1957. Most converts came from the SSEM, although some came from the Anglicans and Catholics in West Kwara'ae, and most converted as entire village congregations. In East Kwara'ae the movement was led by Elijah Sareto'ona of Tolinga, a prominent member of the SSEM and one of Fa'abasua's converts in Russell Islands, whose village at Abuna'ai in Latea became the local Jehovah's Witness headquarters. In the 1980s the East Kwara'ae district was said to have more than five hundred baptized adult 'kingdom publishers', most of whom were converts from the late '50s and their descendants. Many others probably considered joining the church in those early days, although the ardent 'witnessing' which its members still carry on seems to have gained fewer new converts since. Until the wave of conversions died down, the movement caused some concern to the government, which suspected in the talk of 'freedom' and American support a revival of anti-government feeling in the wake of Māsing Rul. But, as Worsley's theory of such movements predicts, although the Jehovah's Witnesses reject existing political systems they also renounce political explanations and solutions, representing instead a 'passivist' millenial reaction to political defeat (Worsley 1968:239–243).

THE REMNANT CHURCH

Another movement which developed at the same time, influenced by the Jehovah's Witnesses but arising from Kwaisulia's 'revival', was the Remnant Church, founded by Zebulon Sisimia. This has previously been documented not only by myself (Burt 1983), but subsequently also by Maetoloa (1985), on whom the following account also draws. Sisimia was an SSEM Christian living in the former Māsing Rul 'town' of Radefasu in West Kwara'ae, on the coast of Langalanga lagoon. During the demise of Māsing Rul and of the Federal Council, which had its centre in Sisili's base in the same area, Sisimia had begun to reformulate the aims of the movement by research into the Bible, much as Sisili seems to have done. Sisimia did this under the influence of the Seventh Day Adventist church, which he had experienced on Guadalcanal while working for the Labour Corps after the war. His efforts were opposed by the SSEM leaders of Radefasu but received their crucial impetus from Kwaisulia's visit in 1955. Meetings between Kwaisulia and Sisimia at that time culminated in both of them being violently possessed by the Holy Spirit, which instructed them to found a new indigenous 'Remnant Church' based on Sabbath observance.

Kwaisulia returned to Lau, where he attempted to institute the new church, although most of his followers there eventually returned to the SSEM. Sisimia's insistence on establishing the Remnant Church in Kwara'ae led to his expulsion from Radefasu and after a few years he moved up into the bush with a following which has mostly held to the church ever since. In formulating their doctrine, Sisimia was influenced by several ideological trends current in other

PLATE 37   *Zebulon Sismia, visionary founder of the Remnant Church.*
(Photo by Ben Burt, 1979)

Kwara'ae movements. Besides the doctrines of the SDA, he drew on those of Fa'abasua's Jehovah's Witnesses, to proclaim that true 'freedom' and 'independence' would only be achieved under 'God's government'. This Sisimia distinguished from all previous historical forms of worldly government and identified with the 'theocratic government' given by God to the Children of Israel. The Remnant Church is further identified with the Children of Israel by claiming descent from the Lost Tribes of Israel through the first ancestor of Kwara'ae and all Malaita, developing a theme already expounded by Kwara'ae political leaders such as Filo'isi. On this basis the church is held to represent the true tradition of Kwara'ae instituted by this ancestor, as a variant of the ideology of 'Christian tradition' being proclaimed by other Kwara'ae movements. It also incorporated important traditional concepts rejected by churches of other denominations, in particular the tabu on defilement by women.

The goal of the Remnant Church is 'spiritual freedom' under a church independent of the state, unlike existing churches. The church should be spread by tireless evangelism to embrace the whole of humanity, for the sake of salvation from the destruction of the world as predicted in the Book of Revelations. But the Remnant church took this doctrine a step further than the Jehovah's Witnesses. In acknowleging the authority only of 'God's government', it recognised only 'God's law', the Ten Commandments, and 'God's tax', church collections as made by the SSEM. From 1956 members of the Church began to refuse to pay taxes and in 1959 they refused to comply with the government census. From 1958 the government began sending them to prison for three month terms and in 1960 Sisimia was imprisoned as the ringleader, later escaping and hiding in the bush until 1963, by which time the tax strike was more or less over.

After the initial enthusiasm in the political and religious ferment of the late 1950s and early '60s, the Remnant Church ceased to make further headway, but it has maintained a following of about a hundred people in the central bush towards the southwest of Kwara'ae. Despite widespread scepticism, tending to outright opposition in Kwara'ae as a whole, its leaders have continued to contribute their own controversial message to Kwara'ae politics.

CONSTITUTIONAL DEVELOPMENTS AND LOCAL REACTIONS

The religious movements of the 1950s and '60s were part of a broader reaction to colonialism and to the government administration, which was also undergoing far reaching constitutional reforms during the same period. While seeking to assert autonomy through their churches, Kwara'ae were also trying to influence these constitutional reforms by developing their own alternative local political system based on traditional values. Again this had its beginnings in Māsing Rul, when Kwara'ae began their first organised attempts to re-establish a tradition rooted in the past but adapted to the colonial present and appropriate to the values of Christianity.

The constitutional reforms introduced by the colonial administration, in line with the British policy of 'Indirect Rule', were intended to prepare Solomon Islands for eventual decolonisation. When it was established in 1952, the Malaita Council was the first of a series of District Councils set up throughout Solomon Islands as the local government of what was eventually to be a representative system of state government. These Councils became responsible for the collection of tax, from which they funded their administrations and local government services, and they could pass "resolutions for the welfare and good government of the native inhabitants of the district" (Allan 1957:74). But in Malaita there was at first little government organisation at the local level of the 'subDistricts' such as Kwai. While other island Councils were developed from smaller local councils, the Kwara'ae and other 'councils of elders' which the government had tried to set up in Malaita before the war had been abandoned during Māsing Rul. The Headmen, who had proved so unpopular during Māsing Rul as agents of the colonial government, were now answerable to the Malaita Council, but they were gradually phased out and replaced by other officials. Siru, the senior Kwai Headman, was in any case ready to retire.

Henceforth government was represented locally mainly through a new system of 'Native' or 'Local Courts', of which there were fourteen throughout Malaita (Allan 1957:75). The people of Kwai agreed to have a 'Native Court' in 1953 and several of the senior men appointed as Local Court Justices were former Māsing Rul leaders, with Justus Ganifiri as Court President and Timan Takanak-wao, former Headman and Federal Council leader, as Vice-President (Native Affairs Book 1951–4:271). The Malaita Local Courts took on many of the judicial duties formerly carried out by colonial government officers and their Headmen, going some way to meet the important Māsing Rul demand that the people should hold their own courts. The courts were intended to "administer native law and custom" as well as certain colonial regulations and the resolutions of the Malaita Council. But they were still ultimately subject to the colonial legal system and the authority of the District Magistrate, a colonial official, and they could not deal with offences which involved more than a certain level of penalties (Allan 1957:75). In fact, they were similar to the courts which the government had planned to develop when it set up the local councils before the war.

Although the Malaita Council and its courts were eventually accepted as a government concession to Māsing Rul demands, and were almost a legitimation of Māsing Rul itself as far as the colonial administration was concerned, they were nonetheless a compromise which restored recognition of colonial authority. So despite these reforms and the efforts of the Malaita Council to disassociate itself from the colonial government during the 1950s, many Kwara'ae still felt that the new local government system did not adequately represent their interests and particularly their concern for tradition or 'custom' (*kastom*). To judge from the attitude of Colin Allan as a senior government official during the 1950s, the colonial government had little sympathy for the ideals of 'custom', which he regarded as obstructive and "backward", wasting the time of the District Councils (Allan 1960:162). By the late 1950s and '60s there was a growing feeling in many parts of Malaita that local people should themselves work for greater self-determination under tradition. But this time instead of an island-wide movement, people in Baegu and Baelelea, 'Are'are and Kwaio developed separate local organisations (see Keesing 1982c:362–363). In Kwara'ae there was a movement to reinstate tradition which eventually resulted in a system of 'chiefs' parallelling the local government system (as described in Burt 1982, which the present account supercedes).

REVIVING TRADITION: THE 1960s MOVEMENT

This tradition movement has had various leaders, working generally in co-operation but sometimes in rivalry with one another. In Kwai the main centre of activities developed at Kwasibu in Latea, an abandoned hilltop shrine overlooking Kwai harbour where the East Kwara'ae 'chiefs' continue to meet to this day. One of the main organisers here was Adriel Rofate'e of Gwauna'ongi, a major contributor to this book. Rofate'e is a son of the SSEM evangelist Joash Omani who first moved to the area when Fiuloa, father of Ganifiri, brought his family down to 'school' from their home in the central bush in about 1920. Rofate'e was born in 1928, took an active part in Māsing Rul as a young 'duty' at Nāfinua 'town', and carried out his own researches into traditional culture, partly from old Filo'isi, the last priest of Siale. Rofate'e was supported in his work by Ganifiri who had already made an important contribution to the promotion of tradition when he began recording Kwara'ae 'laws' and holding 'courts' as Head Chief during Māsing Rul. In 1962 they organised the building of a 'custom house' at Kwasibu and from 1963 they held regular meetings there of senior men and clan leaders from all over East Kwara'ae.

The purpose of these meetings was to discuss and codify 'traditional law' (*falafala ana taki*), deciding how far it was compatible with Christianity, and to record genealogies for all the clans of the district. The men who took part were regarded as the *fataābu* (priests) of their clans, although of course most were Christian. It was felt that the government Local Courts, even under local Court Justices, were not settling disputes according to correct interpretations of traditional rules. Such doubts about the government legal system were shared by some Court Justices who were themselves active in the tradition movement, including of course the Court President, Ganifiri, as well as the Vice-President Takanakwao. One growing cause of disputes leading to some serious court cases at this time was land rights, and genealogical knowledge was seen as the key to resolving such problems under a system of traditional authority. Most of the records of the Kwasibu meetings were written and kept by Rofate'e, who began to build the reputation he now holds as a loremaster and expert on matters of tradition. The work at Kwasibu continued until 1965, by which time Ganifiri was becoming preoccupied with work for the SSEC as he went on to become its General Superintendent. It was considered more or less complete when the 'custom house' was destroyed by a gale in 1965, and the meetings ceased.

While the Kwasibu meetings were going on, some of those taking part were also involved in more militant action in the name of tradition. Aisa Osifera of 'Aimomoko in particular was a strong opponent of colonialism who had gone to 'school' in the SSEM only when obliged by the conversion of his 'father' Filo'isi in 1943. Living at Faufanea in the central bush with little means to earn money, Osifera raised the old objection to government tax because, as he said, he received nothing in return for it. In 1962, while work was beginning at Kwasibu, he refused to pay his £1 tax to the Malaita Council and was taken to court. In 1963 he held a meeting at Faufanea to discuss the wider issues of tradition and persuade others to join his stand against tax. Among those who supported him was Sisimia, whose Remnant Church had already been refusing tax for some years. There were others who joined the tax strike for a while, but it collapsed by 1964 after about thirteen men were taken to court and imprisoned. But at the same time Osifera began a 'tax for tradition', collecting contributions of five shillings (the old government 'head tax' rate) from many supporters of the tradition movement in East Kwara'ae. This continued for many years, providing funds for tradition activities. It was compared to the *animani* offerings of shell money given to the ghosts and, like SSEM church offerings, the Māsing Rul 'tax' and the 'tax for God' of the Remnants, it represented an alternative to the authority of government.

The meeting at Faufanea reflected a more militant tendency within the tradition movement of the time, with some traditionists calling for the reinstatement of killing for sexual offences as in pre-colonial times. But such demands were opposed and contained by the Christian majority, more willing to support the kind of activities going on at Kwasibu. Osifera continued his own stand when he opposed the building of a motor road across Malaita through Siale land, just as his 'father' Filo'isi had done twenty years before and for the same reasons. In 1964 he assaulted and drove off a road survey party and although he was arrested and sentenced to six months imprisonment he succeeded in stopping the road.

ORGANISING TRADITION: THE KWARA'AE 'CHIEFS'

The Kwasibu meetings in particular helped Kwara'ae activists to develop a model of traditional political organisation based on the pre-Christian ritual and political system but adapted to act as a pressure group within the developing state political system. This model draws on the ancient story that all Kwara'ae are descended from the first ancestor who discovered Malaita and whose descendants dispersed generation after generation to settle the whole of Kwara'ae or even the whole of Malaita. As already described, this story is fundamental to Kwara'ae conceptions of tradition, explaining their identity in relation to their land, the ancestors who claimed it and the way of life they handed down from the past. It also provides a structure uniting the Kwara'ae people into a single group with an ethnic identity which probably never existed in pre-colonial times.

Kwara'ae clans are linked by common ancestry and ranked by seniority of birth into a few dispersed major clan groups. Rofate'e considered that theoretically it should be possible to trace these links back in time to create one great genealogical 'tree' for the whole of Kwara'ae, uniting them all as 'brothers' under their most senior clan leaders. On discussion it was agreed that the first and senior shrine must be Siale, since other clans showed they had 'come out' from Siale when they offered preliminary 'restricted' (ete'a) sacrifices to the ghosts of ancient ancestors there before holding their festivals. The problem, as Rofate'e has found, is that when the genealogies of different clans are compared they are full of disagreements at the crucial higher levels which decide how major clans are related. The same names occur of ghosts who once received sacrifices in particular shrines, but brothers in one genealogy may be fathers and sons or grandfathers and grandsons in another. How often such comparisons could have been made in the past, when clans were divided by constant feuding, is difficult to say. But since all genealogical variations raise questions as to the relative seniority of the ghosts, there was and is ample opportunity for their descendants to disagree over who should take the senior leading role in whatever political activities they are involved in. Hence their traditional ritual system has provided Kwara'ae leaders with a vehicle not only to organise for a common purpose but also to indulge some divisive personal and factional ambitions.

The Kwara'ae tradition movement was only one of many pressures upon the Solomon Islands government as the British began to prepare the islands for 'Independence'. During the 1950s and '60s Solomon Islanders were gradually brought into the Protectorate government 'Council', which included a majority of elected members by 1970. During the '70s, under the influence of its Solomon Islands members, the government brought in further reforms to decentralise the administrative system (Ifunaoa 1983:203, Wolfers 1983:157). From 1974 'Area Committees' were set up in Malaita to represent the interests and demands of local people to the Malaita Council. East Kwara'ae had one Area Committee appointed from influential senior men and West Kwara'ae was covered by several others. At the same time Kwara'ae leaders once again began to promote their own ideals of traditional authority and 'law'. Meetings were held by Osifera, now living at Fi'ika'o, and by Takanakwao at Magura, both in the central bush, and similar activities were going on in West Kwara'ae.

By the 1970s an important figure in West Kwara'ae was Arnon Ngwadili of the 'Ailako clan, a prominent SSEC 'teacher' living at Kilusakwalo. From his travels to Australia and Papua New Guinea for training in 1973–4, Ngwadili began to question the European cultural bias of SSEC rules and to favour the more positive approach to traditional culture which had long been taken by the Anglicans in Kwara'ae. He began to take a leading part in tradition activities in the West, joining others to compile 'laws' and genealogies and establish positions of traditional authority. With government approval they began to set up a system of 'chiefs' based on the Kwara'ae clan system and Ngwadili contacted the East Kwara'ae leaders to take part. In 1975 at a meeting at Osifera's village at Fi'ika'o in the central bush, the East Kwara'ae activists appointed several of their leaders as 'Paramount Chiefs' to represent some of the major clans and factions within their movement. These included Rofate'e for Gwauna'ongi, Osifera of 'Aimomoko and Jemuel Misialo of Sulaifau from West Kwara'ae for Siale, and Nakisi and Takanakwao for Mānadari. At the same time a number of other men were recognised as 'Tribal Chiefs' for various local clans. In February 1976 West and East joined in a great meeting at 'Aimela, the Malaita Council headquarters near 'Aoke, to celebrate the unity of the Kwara'ae people under tradition with feasting and dancing. Fifteen Paramount Chiefs in all were formally appointed, including those from the East and the others, including Ngwadili, from the more populous West Kwara'ae and Langalanga. About 180 Tribal Chiefs of minor clans were also recognised.

This system of chiefs paralleled the new developments in local government which many of the chiefs were also involved in but, lacking the authority of government, the roles of chiefs are not always so clearly defined. While a local clan may agree who is their senior 'leader' (fa'i na'ona'o) or Tribal Chief, the Paramount Chiefs of East Kwara'ae were appointed by meetings of activists, and they are leaders for the purposes of tradition rather than general leaders of the major clan groups they represent. The title may also be used by other senior men who can claim to be local community leaders, and there is not always agreement about which Paramount Chiefs should be the leaders of the movement. Working together often means putting claims to genealogical seniority to one side, but disagreements tend to result in disputes as to whether Siale or Mānadari or Gwauna'ongi or some other ancient shrine was more important in the traditional ritual system. In particular, East and West Kwara'ae tend to disagree as to

PLATE 38   *Leading figures at the great meeting of Kwara'ae chiefs at 'Aimela in 1976. In the front row (left to right) Naftalai Rigamanu of 'Ailako, Adriel Rofate'e of Gwauna'ongi, Selwyn Ngwadili of Toto, Aisah Osifera of 'Aimomoko, Arnon Ngwadili of 'Ailako; in the middle, Jemuel Misialo of Sulaifau; in the back row, Lafea of Langalanga, Busuakalo of Gwauna'ongi, Selwyn Kwaifi'i, Ingita of Otefarakau. (Photo by L. Laka, UNESCO, from the National Museum of Solomon Islands)*

whether Siale or 'Ailako should be the symbolic head of Kwara'ae tradition. But for all these difficulties, the 'custom chiefs', as they are often called, by organising for various purposes into 'committees' and other groupings, have managed to exert an important influence on the development of Kwara'ae politics, and win significant concessions from government.

The achievement of independence by the Solomon Islands state in 1978 was greeted with enthusiasm as the culmination of years of struggle against colonial domination, but it did not actually do a great deal to satisfy Kwara'ae demands for their own 'independence'. The Area Committees became 'Area Councils', Malaita District became a 'Province' and the Malaita Council became the 'Provincial Assembly' (Wolfers 1983:160). Henceforth Area Council members were elected and began to include younger, better educated men. Eventually provision was made for four Paramount Chiefs to be full members, and these were Rofate'e and Osifera for East Kwara'ae with Ngwadili and Misialo for the West.

As far as the government was concerned, the Area Council system was intended to develop closer links between rural communities and their Provincial administrations, giving local people more control over economic and political development and, in the process, also consolidating central state authority (Ifunaoa 1983:204, Wolfers 1983:157–158). Kwara'ae, however, have seen local government also as a means to greater local autonomy and even political separatism, for some of their leaders would prefer to leave Malaita Province altogether and form their own 'Province'. In 1982 a Kwara'ae delegation led by the West Kwara'ae Member of Parliament, Alan Taki, took this proposal to the Prime Minister in Honiara, joining demands by other Malaitan politicians that present Provincial administrations be reduced to co-ordinating groups of autonomous Area Councils.

The underlying constitutional issue that concerns the chiefs is the right of local people and their leaders to direct and adjust to the changes which are coming over Kwara'ae society at an ever increasing rate. The chiefs' organisation is a response to political and economic forces which threaten to undermine the traditional values on which the Kwara'ae way of life is based, leaving them, in Ngwadili's words, "like a coconut drifting aimlessly into the sea" (Ngwadili 1977). Two issues which have particularly concerned Kwara'ae ever since Māsing Rul are rights in land, the basis of their livelihood and identity, and the rules of 'law' which govern relationships between them. The Kwara'ae relationship to local and central government is central to these questions but the problems they are trying to address arise equally from the rapid economic development which has occurred since the war, which must also be taken into account in explaining the present significance of tradition in Kwara'ae.

ECONOMIC DEVELOPMENT

When the British began to rebuild the infrastructure of the Solomons after the destruction of the war, Malaitans played an essential part as the main source of migrant labour and in the process they began to move into new areas and occupations. During the 1960s, while the government was spending a large proportion of its funds on developing the new capital of Honiara, new employment opportunities began to draw Kwara'ae away from the overseas copra plantations which were still their main source of income up to that time. Men from East Kwara'ae moved to Honiara to build the town, learning new skills in construction and other expanding industries. They made their own houses and gardens on the outskirts of town, brought their wives and children over to join them and many of them stayed. Today there are large Kwara'ae 'urban villages' at Kobito, Matariu and other places in the hills behind Honiara, with a shifting population of migrant workers and visitors as well as many long-term residents. They work in a variety of jobs, learning an increasing range of Western skills in the commercial economy and government service. This has been assisted by improvements in education, actively supported by government. After the war grants were given for mission education work and by 1953 the first secondary school was eventually established at Aligegeo near 'Aoke (South Pacific 1955: 128).

Life in Honiara is certainly more agreeable than on the plantations which were the principal source of cash income in the past, but it has brought its own problems. While it is easier for wage earners to live with their families, it is also easier for visitors from home to stay for long periods, often without employment or income of their own, at the expense of their relatives. Young people in particular are exposed to more cosmopolitan and liberal values, Melanesian and European, freed from the constraints and authority of their home areas. Many young men cause a good deal of trouble when they come to enjoy the excitement of town life, spending their time as 'wanderers' (Pijin *liu*, from a Kwara'ae word meaning 'pass by') involved in fighting, drinking and stealing, often in conflict with men from other districts and islands. Despite the efforts of church leaders and chiefs in the Kwara'ae urban village communities to maintain the discipline and moral standards of Malaita, Honiara can offer an escape from authority and responsibility and represents many of the moral problems which concern the advocates of tradition. The underlying reason for this urban migration is that opportunities to earn money and benefit from the expanding Solomon Islands economy have not developed at the same pace in rural Malaita, especially in areas such as Kwai which for a long time lacked good communications with 'Aoke and Honiara.

The economic development which has occurred in East Kwara'ae, although improving living standards, has also caused new social problems. It was only in the 1950s, with the new policies which followed the war, that the government began to promote rural development in Malaita by encouraging cash cropping, supported by agricultural extension services and subsidies. The first major project was to introduce cocoa, which was gradually taken up from the mid-'50s and became quite popular until crop failure due to 'black pod' disease in the late '60s emphasised the unsuitability of the particular variety involved. It was not until the late '70s, with the introduction of new varieties, that cocoa became a successful cash crop. But by the late '60s government was also giving encouragement and subsidies to coconut planting for copra, a more conventional crop already familiar to Kwara'ae from plantation work, if not from cash cropping on their own account. Soon after, in the early '70s, a programme was begun to introduce cattle, also with government subsidy. Like cocoa and coconuts, cattle were also intended for export, but Kwara'ae often find them more useful for local consumption as an alternative to pigs (especially the Seventh Day Adventists). Although there were thirty or forty cattle projects in East Kwara'ae by the late '70s they have generally proved less suitable for Malaitan farming than the traditional pigs. Large areas of land have to be cleared for grass and may be degraded as a result, new husbandry techniques have to be learnt and, compared to pigs, cattle are difficult to transport and market.

In Kwara'ae these programmes have brought most prosperity to the West, which has access to the markets at 'Aoke and thence to Honiara, and is close to government services and served by some of the first roads in Malaita. Communications to East Kwara'ae remained difficult until the early 1970s, with travel either by foot across the bush or by sea around Malaita. Then, on request of East Kwara'ae Delegates to the Malaita Council, the motor road from 'Aoke to Tiuni in the central bush was extended eastwards to the coast at 'Atori by 1973. The road goes north through Fataleka, the more direct route across the Kwara'ae bush having been blocked by Osifera in 1964. Even so, many people in Kwai were now within two hours' truck journey of 'Aoke, dramatically improving their access both to markets and to the Provincial administration. Government services were further improved with the establishment of a local administrative centre on the road near 'Atori, including a police station and court house, and offices of the livestock and agricultural development authorities and malaria control. (The former administrative headquarters Faumamanu is inaccessible by road because of extensive mangrove swamps). In 1983 the road was extended north to Fokanakafo and south to A'arai, most of way along the East Kwara'ae coast.

The biggest single commercial project in East Kwara'ae was a sawmill at Gwarimudu on the road near 'Atori, set up in 1977 by a company called ATASI (Alliance Training Association of Solomon Islands), founded by New Zealand Baptists in association with the SSEC to promote economic development. The company shipped sawn timber to Honiara where it ran a timber yard, a food store and a hardware store, and it also became involved in transport operations for the SSEC. At 'Atori ATASI leased 47 acres of land for logging and made separate agreements to cut logs from other lands. There were logging and sawmill jobs for up to fifty or sixty men, trained by New Zealand managers, and some were even sent to New Zealand for further training. With wages, rents and timber royalties many families in the area were able to buy more manufactured goods, and a

PLATE 39   *Inside a general store at 'Aoke. Besides a wide range of*
                  manufactured goods and food, two tafuli'ae *shell monies made in*
                  nearby Langalanga are also on sale. (Photo by Ben Burt, 1991)

Chinese firm from 'Aoke open a store at 'Atori. People improved their houses
with cheap timber and some invested in small businesses such as running motor
trucks or small 'hawker license' stores.

   But despite the benefits it brought, the sawmill was beset by problems.
Disputes arose over the leasing of the land, the prices paid for logs, the level of
wages and work conditions and claims for mooring fees at 'Atori wharf. There
was also a general suspicion that, despite the company's links with the SSEC, it
was actually more interested in making money than in assisting local people. The
disputes actually threatened the continued operation of the sawmill but when it
eventually closed down in 1985 this was due to a row over irregularities in the
company's operations in Honiara and probably also financial problems. As a
result the largest single source of employment in Kwai disappeared and in the
next few years many of the families who had depended on this income moved for
work to Honiara.

THE COSTS OF DEVELOPMENT

The new prosperity which the growing cash economy has brought to Kwara'ae since the 1960s has introduced changes which will probably prove to be as far reaching as those caused by the spread of Christianity in the 1920s and '30s or by the beginning of labour migration in the 19th century. In the past, probably until the war, cash earnings and the goods they bought seem to have been largely absorbed into the rural economy as gifts and help given by migrant workers to their relatives at home in return for traditional goods and services, especially for shell money and pigs required for major ceremonial payments. The traditional economic system in any case tended to level out differences in wealth, which was valued primarily for the relationships it could create by being given or loaned to others. Although the Christian churches, especially the SSEM, seriously undermined traditional leadership by limiting feasting and bridewealth exchanges, wealth was probably still redistributed, partly through church activities, rather than being used for private consumption. Besides, cash earnings were low and so manufactured goods were in short supply.

By contrast, economic development since the war has led to marked differences in wealth. In the 1980s some communities in East Kwara'ae, especially those following the traditional religion, still lived almost entirely by subsistence gardening, possessing hardly any manufactured goods beyond basic steel tools and a few clothes and making minimum use of government or church services. But they have relatives living nearby in houses furnished or even built in European style, with manufactured cooking and eating utensils, smart clothes and various conveniences and luxuries such as kerosine lamps, radio-cassette players, books and sewing machines. Besides gardening, they may buy food such as rice, tinned meat and fish, tea, sugar, flour and biscuits. Their income may come from employment, cash cropping or other business ventures, but it usually depends on a good education which itself often results from the previous generation's involvement in the churches. Material success or the prospect of permanent employment, especially for those in Honiara, may free such people from some of their obligations to share their wealth and support their relatives. The practice of migrant workers giving all their earnings as goods to their fathers to share among the family has also declined as young men feel less dependent on the traditional exchange economy at home. In general people may feel they have more to gain by hoarding or consuming their new wealth than by using it to help others according to the best traditional values, and the result is jealousy and conflict within local communities.

Such tensions are increased by the inevitable competition for resources, especially land, which results from these kinds of rural economic development. This competition is partly due to a rapid growth of population, which has approximately doubled since the 1930s (see page 16), but also to the new possibilities for cash income from land in accessible areas within reach of the coasts and roads. Whereas people's need for land under subsistence gardening is finite and limited in area and duration, when there is money to be gained both can expand indefinitely. The traditional system of land rights gives every person a number of lands to use and every land a number of people to use it. But this system was developed for short term use of small areas and makes no provision for cash cropping of trees, cattle farming and logging, all of which prevent gardening for long periods. Any such project which provides one group with a cash income is at the same time likely to deny the opportunity to garden or earn money to someone else who also has an inherited right to make use of the land, even if they have no claim to 'leadership' for it. As a result, economic development has been accompanied, and inhibited, by bitter land disputes which have divided relatives and local communities. Since 1960, disputes over the leadership and boundaries of Latea land, as mentioned in Chapter 2, have led to three government court cases and a number of hearings by the 'chiefs', and there are several other lands in East Kwara'ae with a similar record. These disputes tend to focus upon who actually inherits the land, with long arguments over genealogies and traditional rights. They do little to resolve the underlying problem of how to create equitable rural development appropriate to Kwara'ae traditional values. (See Burt 1991 and Gegeo 1991 for discussion of these land and development issues).

The divisive effects of this economic development underly the concern of the Kwara'ae chiefs for the 'tradition of the law' which has played such a large part in the activities of the tradition movement since the 1960s. The solution they propose is to clarify the rules which should govern people's relationships with one another and the genealogies which decide their relationship to the land, so upholding a moral code and system of authority based on tradition. After the great 'Aimela meeting in 1976 the chiefs began to hold their own 'custom courts' to settle disputes as an alternative to the government Local Courts. These are more or less formal events, depending on the seriousness of the offence, which give each party and their witnesses the chance to state their case before a group of senior men as chiefs who discuss and decide what restitution or compensation should be given to make amends according to traditional rules. In 1979 the special problems of settling land disputes led the chiefs to set up a committee, the 'East Kwara'ae Customary Land Board', again trying to avoid disputes going before the government courts. These developments received government approval only on condition that the chiefs did not claim the authority to enforce their decisions or challenge those of the government courts. The effect is that the chiefs' courts, rather like traditional leaders, mediate disputes with the support of public opinion. People may prefer them to the government courts, where some

PLATE 40   *The Anglican Bishop of Malaita blesses the Kwara'ae chiefs, who have met to discuss issues of tradition at a feast organised by Paramount Chief Jemuel Misialo at Afio in 1983.*
(Photo by Ben Burt)

feel at a disadvantage due to lack of education, but these courts with their police backing are always available to dissatisfied parties, in effect as a means of appeal. Despite reminders from the Chief Magistrate and police, Kwara'ae chiefs sometimes found it hard to accept that their judgements had no formal recognition in government law and they continue to press for greater authority. Since 1985 a national law has prevented land disputes being taken to Local Courts until they had first been deal with by the chiefs, but their decisions are still subject to the authority of the Local Court.

While much attention and energy is devoted to disputes over the control of land, people are also beginning to realise that this is only a symptom of deeper problems resulting from economic development. As far as the land itself is concerned, cash earning projects such as coconut plantations and cattle fields are not only degrading the forest but also putting pressure on garden land, leading to shortening bush fallow periods and further degradation of the forest. This was aggravated by damage from Cyclone Namu which struck East Kwara'ae in

1986. Increased reliance on manufactured goods with the availability of cash also means that forest materials for local manufactures may be less highly regarded and less carefully conserved than in the past. With a rapidly expanding population, Kwara'ae could soon face serious environmental problems and an uncertain future.

Having traced the history which has brought Kwara'ae to this situation, as Christian peasants increasingly involved in the global capitalist economy and its ubiquitous Western culture, we can go on to look in more detail at the society and culture, and particularly the religion, with which they now face their future in this wider world. Kwara'ae see themselves becoming increasingly Westernised, with considerable misgivings, but from a Western point of view a deeper look at contemporary Kwara'ae society reveals more continuity with their past than at first meets the eye. A study of Kwara'ae society in the 1980s reveals that spiritual relationships are still central to the Kwara'ae world-view, and that they have created a Christian social order which reflects many of the insights and values of their traditional religion.

PLATE 41   *Children of Nao'asi, an SSEC village of Gwauna'ongi people in East Kwara'ae. (Photo by Ben Burt, 1984)*

CHAPTER NINE

The Christian Social Order

In earlier chapters, Kwara'ae traditional culture was explained as a system of relationships and rules founded upon the spiritual support of the ancestors who had created the social order and passed it down to their descendants. With this social order Kwara'ae faced the Europeans who arrived in Malaita more than a century ago, first to exploit its people and then to colonise their land. At first it served them well enough as they avenged their dead and defended their independence by attacking recruiters, defying government officials and intimidating local collaborators, particularly Christian converts. But as their warriors were inevitably subdued by the colonial government and their priests failed to ensure the well-being of their congregations, Kwara'ae gradually abandoned the ghosts who supported these leaders and renounced the way of life they had inherited from them. Presented by the missionaries with a religious solution to what Kwara'ae themselves saw as a religious problem, they turned instead to God for spiritual support and protection and so transformed their society to deal with the new realities of the colonial world.

The history which has shaped the Kwara'ae society of today from their 'tradition of the past' is above all the history of Christian conversion. When the missions persuaded people to abandon their ghosts they struck at the root of the whole system of spiritual and political authority which supported the traditional establishment of priests, 'important men' and warriors. These leaders were well aware of the threat and many did all they could to oppose it, but when their influence was simultaneously undermined by the colonial government the ghosts who supported them began to lose credibility. As the new 'school' communities grew and established themselves they began to develop their own political establishment of 'teachers' and church leaders whose authority also derived from spiritual support, but through the new ritual system of the mission churches. This long and often painful process which began at the turn of the century is still not quite completed ninety years later. But during this time, as their ghosts once helped Kwara'ae to resist colonialism by armed force, so Christianity helped them to deal with the British by coming to terms with the colonial order. As Christians they began to participate in the colonial system until eventually they were able to confront their rulers with their own alternative visions of the future through Māsing Rul and the movements which followed. These visions drew support from the spiritual power of Christianity, through a reinterpretation of traditional values which continues to inspire the struggle for self- determination.

With this understanding of Kwara'ae traditional society and the history of its colonial transformation, we can go on to look in more detail at the Christian social order they have created in its place. As it was under the authority of the ghosts, Kwara'ae today is still very much a religious society, in which the community organisation of relationships between people is also the ritual organisation of relationships with the spiritual beings they depend upon for support and protection. Although these underlying principles derive from the traditional order, the Christian society they now support is different in some important respects. New spiritual beings support a new ritual and political establishment through an institutional system modelled on European church organisation and adapted to life in a wider state-organised society. But the important point as far as Kwara'ae are concerned remains that this establishment continues to hold authority through the mediation of spiritual power. As it was in the past, this power is channelled and controlled through the ritual system, which is challenged, reformed and developed in the same terms, through spiritual authority and inspiration.

We will look at this new social order as it appeared in the 1980s in the South Sea Evangelical Church or SSEC, the largest church organisation in Kwai which, as the Mission, SSEM, has dominated the religious history of the district and indeed most of Malaita. The SSEC is one of those churches which Barr classes as "conservative evangelical groups and fundamentalist sects", characterised by a "Strong emphasis on 'revivalism', an authoritarian view of the Bible, an anti-hierarchical view of the church". This helps explain how it differs from the "mainline denominational churches", represented in Kwai by the Anglican Church of Melanesia (Barr 1983:109). However, the comparisons which concern us here are not with other Christian churches but with the traditional order which they have supplanted. The SSEC continues to build upon the social transformation achieved under the European-led SSEM to develop an indigenous Christianity which also has strong foundations in the religious experience and values of Kwara'ae traditional culture.

THE LOCAL CHURCH

In abandoning the ghosts, Kwara'ae abolished a social order in which they inherited the human relationships which sustained them, the land which was their home and livelihood, their way of life, culture and social identity, from the ancestors whose ghosts were also their source of spiritual support and protection. The ritual system which mediated the spiritual power of the ghosts was also the political system which conferred power and authority on the leaders who united communities as ritual congregations and divided them as feuding factions. The Christian transformation struck at the foundations of this system, not only by destroying the power of the ghosts which supported it but also by rejecting the very principle of descent in building the new ritual organisation of the church. As a result the relationships of descent which still link people to one another and to their land are no longer founded in the spiritual relationships which support and protect them, for although God is everyone's 'father', he is no-one's ancestor.

Under Christianity ritual congregations are based on villages rather than clans, for although they may be united by common descent this is a human preference, not a religious requirement. For example, a group of Gwauna'ongi people has formed the core of one such congregation since the late 1970s. In the 1980s, Adriel Rofate'e, 'Paramount Chief' in the 'custom chiefs' organisation, lived with three or four of his own and distant 'sons' and their families at Dingodingo (not far from the SSEC centre of Nāfinua) where his 'fathers' settled after they became Christians and left their home in the central bush in the 1920s. They shared the church of a nearby village of seven or eight households, mostly families from three other branches of the Gwauna'ongi clan, at Na'oasi (below the hill where Bell's police attacked a village of that name in 1919). But apart from the fact that the men of the two villages were clan 'fathers' and 'brothers', their common descent played no part in the organisation of their church. Although Rofate'e was 'Paramount Chief' for Gwauna'ongi as a descendant of the priests of the senior Faureba clan, this gave him no special position in the church, especially as the two senior men at Na'oasi were a former senior SSEC official, Ben Banau, and Ariel Arini, once an active evangelist. Other members of the Gwauna'ongi clan are widely dispersed, and from time to time families have moved between East Kwara'ae, West Kwara'ae and Honiara to live with other clan 'fathers' and 'brothers'. Besides, several families of other clans from two or three neighbouring villages, with their own churches for daily services, also attended the church at Na'oasi for services on Sundays and especially for the monthly 'Lord's Supper' (Holy Communion). Over the years some of these villages have joined and others have left the Na'oasi congregation, while yet others which are equally close as relatives and neighbours have become separated ritually by leaving the SSEC for the Jehovah's Witnesses or Holiness Fellowship Church.

Na'oasi represents a common pattern in which villages based on local clans organise themselves for ritual purposes as a 'local church'. Most of these villages are now hardly larger than traditionist ones, and probably much smaller than most Christian villages in the days before Māsing Rul, despite a great increase in population and household size. In 1986 there were only about 10 villages in East Kwara'ae with over 10 households, and the average size was 4.4 households (Solomon Islands 1986). Everyone in a village nearly always belongs to the same church denomination, usually for the same reason that they are living together, as relatives with a common religious history. Some may live together because they belong to the same denomination rather than the same clan, in the same way that the early Christian converts were brought together by their choice of religion, while others again may change denomination to that of the relatives they choose to live with. But groups of villages join in larger congregations less as relatives than as neighbours. These congregations may change from time to time, no doubt as much because of disputes and alliances as for strictly ritual reasons, and in recent years they seem to have become more local and fragmented. Until the late 1970s the Na'oasi congregation were among six villages or more who all joined for the 'Lord's Supper' at the major SSEC centre at Nāfinua.

CHURCH ORGANISATION

The church forms the focus for community life. A church building is often the finest in the village, maybe decorated with plaited bamboo walls or given an expensive iron roof and sometimes even glass windows, which very few people can afford for their own houses. Although it is a 'tabu house' (*feraābu*), unlike the 'tabu houses' which were the shrines of the ghosts, the church is part of the village and open for men, women and children to participate in its rituals. Ritual responsibilities and spiritual power are also far more widely distributed in the SSEC than under the traditional religion, or even in denominations like the Anglicans which rely upon a professional priesthood. The SSEC ideal is a 'priesthood of all believers', and both men and women are encouraged to take on ritual duties to develop their own personal relationship with God.

Although everyone attends church services more or less regularly from the time they are children, they begin to participate fully in the church by being 'born again', when they become responsible adults or perhaps much later if they were brought up in the traditional religion or otherwise resist Christian teachings. When a person has 'accepted Jesus' and demonstrated his change of heart (*liana*, lit. 'mind') to the satisfaction of senior members of the church, he may be given church duties to encourage responsibility, under supervision and instruction, such as Sunday School teaching for the children. He can also train to be baptised, which involves passing tests of religious knowledge and then being 'tabu bathed' (*siuābua*) by immersion in water in a public ceremony, after the Baptist manner. Once baptised a person becomes a full 'member' of the church, a 'Christian' in the strict SSEC sense of the word, qualified to take part in the most important ritual of the 'Lord's Supper' and in the running of the local church.

As 'members' of the church, most of the adult men and many of the women of a congregation of villages will belong to the 'church committee'. They form what is in many ways an assembly or council which deals with community affairs and they appoint or elect some of their number as church officials. Several will be 'deacons' who officiate at services, clean and maintain the church, keep good order in the village and the church, organise major church events and feasts and arrange hospitality for visitors on church business. The most senior and influential men will be 'elders', a man of good education will act as 'secretary' to keep records and accounts of the money contributed by the congregation and others take the tasks of Sunday School teachers and leaders of particular church activities.

The greatest responsibilities of all belong to the 'pastor', who is elected by the members of the local church to be the religious leader for the group of neigbouring villages. The pastor is the 'teacher' of former times who acts as religious instructor, advisor and confessor, helping to settle problems in people's relationships with one another and with God by mediating disputes and encouraging them to live clean and pure lives. He officiates at important services such as the Lord's Supper, represents the local church in the wider church organisation and may also act for the community in dealings with government officials. The work is arduous, time consuming and unpaid, often taking the pastor away from his family on overnight visits from one village to another or on preaching tours and meetings further afield, so suitable men are not always willing to become pastors or remain so for long. Pastors may be quite young men for whom it is a considerable honour, showing the respect of their community and its confidence in their maturity, religious experience and spiritual strength from God. Michael Kwa'ioloa recalls when he was first elected pastor in the 1970s:

> At that time I thought I was just a child, but when I took on pastoral work I was the father of the people. Because everyone relied on me. ... It was a great thing in my life, because I was quite a junior man in these things and I thought that no-one would listen to me, but the true power of Jesus spoke to the people in their hearts and they obeyed me.

The church committee meets in the church each Sunday to organise the programmes of services and other work which not only maintain the congregation's relationship with God but also govern the routines and communal activities of village life. Services follow a well established pattern of choruses and hymns, prayers and Bible readings, guided, though not prescribed, by orders of service derived from the SSEM and published by the SSEC (eg. SSEC 1977). Although Bibles and hymn books are usually in English, most of the service is conducted in the Kwara'ae language. A large proportion of the congregation are directly involved by having particular ritual duties assigned to them. A list of such duties for the Na'oasi 'Local Church Programme' included "Sunday Service, General Service, Hymn Conductor, Chorus, Long Prayer, Offering,

Children Talk, Closing Prayer, Church Cleaning." Some services develop to include preaching and other individual contributions such as singing performances and demonstrations of spiritual 'gifts'. The ritual programme is full and demanding, at least during periods of greatest religious enthusiasm. Basic services are held daily, morning and evening, while Sundays are largely devoted to extended services and church business, including a monthly service for the Lord's Supper. In addition, special 'fellowship' services may be held for particular purposes as required, beginning in the evening and going on till late at night. These may be for 'prayer' for a particular enterprise, for 'confession' to cleanse a person's sins, for 'testament' by someone who wants to preach, or for 'praise', which may involve ecstatic revival meetings going on all night. When a number of churches come together for 'conventions', services begin in the middle of the week and go on for four or five days until Sunday.

PLATE 42   *A singing band from Na'oasi and neighbouring villages. Choruses are sung to the accompaniment of wooden clappers as they march up and down in the light of a pressure lamp.*
(Photo by Ben Burt, 1984)

In addition to the programme of services, many people organise into other groups for particular ritual purposes. A 'women's band' to look after women's interests holds its own meetings and annual service. Groups of men may form special preaching bands (*lifurongo'a*) to tour other villages and districts. Popular 'singing bands' of both men and women practise regularly to entertain their own and other villages with night-time performances of religious choruses and marching in a distinctively Malaitan choral style.

THE SSEC AS A POLITICAL SYSTEM

The SSEC thus provides a system of local community organisation based, as under the traditional religion, on the spiritual relationships which unite its members as ritual congregations. But the local churches are in turn organised into a wider system of organisation on a scale and level of integration never achieved by the traditional sacrificial system even when it linked dispersed clans as the congregations of major shrines. Through the system of church Associations, committees and officers developed during the reforms of the 1950s and '60s, local SSEC congregations now participate in a ritual organisation which extends beyond Kwara'ae to the rest of Malaita and other islands in the Solomons, and ultimately around the world through the networks of international evangelism.

The SSEC local churches of East Kwara'ae all belong to a single District Association, in which they are represented by their pastors and an executive committee of elected officials. Some rituals such as baptisms are held by the District Association as a whole. The President, Secretary and two other delegates from each of the District Associations of Malaita meet for the Island Conference held each year, which also elects an executive committee and officers. Every two years these same delegates meet at the General Conference which includes all twenty District Associations of Solomons Islands. They elect the executive committee for the national Church, including the General Superintendant as head of the Church, the President as chairman, the Principal of the Onepusu Bible College and other officers, who together with the Presidents of the Island Conferences form the Council of the SSEC. A Ministry Committee organises training and sending students and missionaries overseas.[1]

Through this organisation a man who dedicates himself to serving God and his church can advance by election from officer and pastor of the local church through the District Association to the highest offices of the SSEC hierarchy. In the process he may receive training and improve his general education by attending Onepusu Bible College and may even be sent for several years training overseas, qualifying him for senior administrative as well as pastoral work. A few of the most senior church leaders have been ordained as Ministers (titled 'Reverend'), including Justus Ganifiri for East Kwara'ae District and Arnon

Ngwadili for West Kwara'ae. Officers and administrators are also ritual leaders, each being inducted and dedicated for this work at services conducted by officers above them in the heirarchy. So local church officers are inducted by their pastor, pastors by the District President, District President by a Minister and Ministers by the President and other senior officers of the SSEC as a whole.

The SSEC system of decision making by committee and leadership by election seems very appropriate to a society accustomed to collective responsibility and authority conferred by consent. It is a type of organisation now adopted also for local government and for bodies which Kwara'ae have created for themselves, such as the chiefs' organisation. But it is in sharp contrast to the way priests were chosen as senior descendants of the ghosts to stand at the centre of the traditional ritual and political system, in a role which Kwara'ae sometimes describe as equivalent to a Christian pastor. Although Christianity has maintained a social order based on spiritual power, the abolition of descent as a qualification for religious leadership has helped Kwara'ae to transcend the political limitations of the old clan-based ritual system.

The traditional social order was tribal and politically fragmented, each local community supported in conflict with the next by the spiritual power of their own ancestral ghosts. Under Christianity, where God is no-one's ancestor, the descent relationships which still divided people are in theory irrelevant to the spiritual relationships which sustain and unite them as members of a congregation. But since God is at the same time everyone's 'father', Christianity also proclaims all men and women as 'brothers' (*ngwaefuta*), an idiom for friendship and co-operation even more potent to Kwara'ae than to Europeans. Such brotherhood has provided the rationale for peaceful co-existence and co-operation between local communities as well as for the creation of political movements uniting the people of Kwara'ae and Malaita to confront the wider world. This is apparent in the ideology of Māsing Rul, which united the whole of Malaita under the 'Rule of Brotherhood' (*Maasina Rulu*), as it is in the Kwara'ae concern for their common descent from the first ancestor which has united them in their demands for self-determination ever since. This ideal probably goes back to the first Kwara'ae Christians, who may well have appreciated that the benefits of peace and order enjoyed by Europeans in Queensland and imposed by them in the Solomons required a new morality in which all men, not simply close relatives, could treat one another as 'brothers'.

As Barker puts it, Christianity in the Pacific "introduced its followers to an enlarged and vastly complicated world" in both a practical and an ideological sense, giving them a means of understanding the colonial order and an "enlarged social and spiritual community" (1990a:16). In providing Kwara'ae with the religious philosophy and spiritual support to re-order their fragmented society for participation in this new colonial order, it has served the kind of purpose which

Horton (1971) attributes to both Christianity and Islam in Africa. It brought about a shift towards a universalistic morality authorised by a supreme deity within a world view more "macrocosmic" than that of a people confined to the traditional "microcosms" of autonomous local communities. This 'macrocosmic' perspective would have become increasingly appropriate as Kwara'ae found themselves drawn into the wider economic and political relationships of the colonial system. The ritual organisation as well as the doctrine of Christianity helped them to organise themselves accordingly, from the early networks of SSEM 'schools' to Māsing Rul, the chiefs' organisation and the independent SSEC.

CHRISTIAN AND TRADITIONAL AUTHORITY

At the local level the SSEC provides an organisational structure for the local community through the local church committee which, being composed of most of the mature and responsible adults, is concerned with all kinds of village affairs. They may set a weekly work programme for the village, including some days for gardening and marketing, others for co-operative farming and work for the village and the church. They stage the feasts which celebrate important events in the church programme and others public occasions, often on Sundays after service, and sometimes elect a 'mission chief' to deal with non-ritual matters.

The most serious responsibility of the committee is to govern people's relationships with one another and with God. Church leaders have less opportunity to impose obedience than the traditional leaders of the past, whose authority was sanctioned by the protection they gave from killings for restitution and feuds, nor are they supported by the authority of government law. Their power depends upon the voluntary submission which underlies both human and spiritual authority in Kwara'ae society, in the sense that people give others power over them by becoming dependent on them. The members of the church depend on support and protection, both human and spiritual, which their fellows and leaders on the committee can suspend by putting them under 'discipline'. For a period of days or weeks a person may be put 'outside the church', which means that they have to sit at the back of the church during services, as if they had not been 'born again' or baptised, instead of participating as full members of the congregation. They may even be put under a discipline of 'silence', so that no-one will speak to them. If they are contrite and submit to these measures, mending their ways and attending service every day, they will later be formally accepted back into the church. If they refuse there is little more the church can do. But like a child who runs away from a beating, someone who defies church authority also deprives himself of support and protection from God and from his relatives and neighbours, if any further problems befall him. When eventually he or his family is struck by misfortune or sickness, he finds himself drawn back into the church.

This authority, spiritual and human, helps the church maintain harmony within the congregation. Disputes beyond the immediate family should normally be brought before the pastor or church committee, who will try to mediate, persuading the parties to settle their differences by confessing and forgiving the offence and become reconciled by praying together. This is one way in which the authority of the church upholds the rules which make members of the SSEC acceptable to God. But, as in traditional society, making rules means claiming authority, and the authority of the church may be contested. In particular, SSEC rules try to prohibit a range of traditional practices which many members of their congregations find it very difficult to give up, and in enforcing these rules the church is engaged in a continual struggle with other sources of authority.

Although SSEC and other Christians have replaced the traditional establishment of priests, 'important men' and warriors with a new establishment of pastors and church elders, many continue to advance their political ambitions by traditional means. These include helping relatives and neighbours in need, sharing traditional wealth and participating in bridewealth presentations, wedding feasts and restitution payments. If a man has a cash income he may give money and store-bought goods to senior relatives and if he is well educated he may also help them to deal with government and other agencies on matters such as taxation or development programmes. But although the traditional values involved in helping others, 'reciprocity' (*kwaima'anga*) and 'generosity' (*alafe'anga*) are enjoined by Christianity as 'love', church leaders in the SSEC and other fundamentalist denominations also warn against showing 'pride' through ceremonial payments and exchanges. This acknowledgement of the political influence conferred by generosity underlies church attempts to supress traditional presentations which go back to Peter Abu'ofa's ban on bridewealth at Malu'u at the beginning of the century. But such bans are not easy to uphold, especially when dealing with relatives and neighbours of other denominations who are not bound by them. SSEC leaders may have to go beyond preaching and persuasion and exercise their political influence within the local congregation by persuading the church committee to put under 'discipline' those who refuse to comply.

Bridewealth is still a source of controversy. Although Kwara'ae churches of most denominations have agreed the bridewealth limit of five 'red money', people disagree over whether larger payments should be made for 'stealing' the girl, and some still oppose bridewealth altogether. In the late 1960s, the saltwater church leader Lucius Noi managed to abolish bridewealth among the SSEC congregations of Kwai and Ngongosila. Ganifiri also preached against it in the bush and SSEC leaders like Ben Banau of Gwauna'ongi, secretary of the East Kwara'ae Church Association in the 1970s, sometimes managed to prevent bridewealth payments among their local congregations. But such efforts have not gone unchallenged and the result is constant debate and some uneasy compromises. Within a congregation such as Na'oasi, one man may give his daughters in 'free gift' marriage, but another who would prefer not to accept his daughter's bridewealth may give it instead to his brother, and others accept five 'red money' instead of ten when a girl is 'stolen' probably only from fear of being put under 'discipline'. The devout women of one family even refused meat brought home by their husbands from a wedding feast because the girl's father accepted seven 'red money' instead of five for his daughter's elopement. Similar arguments

PLATE 43   *Some Kwara'ae wedding photos. After a display of the standard five tafuli'ae shell money bridewealth and the church service with white bridal dress and bridesmaids, Nancy Lauta poses as a 'traditional' bride dressed in shell money, while her father-in-law, Marcus Bualimae of Tolinga, holds his gun to add to the effect. (Photos 1990, from Michael Kwa'ioloa)*

develop around other traditional presentations. One senior man, on being presented with a killed pig by his visiting in-law, was persuaded by the threat of 'discipline' to make a nominal return gift of another pig, instead of making a competitive show of generosity by giving a 'red money' in the traditional way.

Restitution and compensation payments cause similar problems. On one occasion in the 1970s, a father was compelled by church 'discipline' to return the $100 he had received from a man who made his daughter pregnant. In another case a $20 restitution payment for seducing a woman was ordered to be returned by the Vice-President of the East Kwara'ae SSEC Church Association, but when a senior 'chief' argued against this in the church committee the decision was reversed. But if others demand traditional payments it may not be easy to refuse. When a dispute goes beyond the local church congregation it may also be beyond the authority of the church to resolve, especially when it involves other people who do not follow the same rules as the SSEC. Although a local church may put its members under 'discipline' for accepting restitution, this can be less serious than the original grievance, and the consequences of refusing to pay restitution for offending others can be physical attack and even a killing. The examples of restitution and compensation in Honiara given in Chapter 2 both involved members of the SSEC. Likewise, those who refuse to accept bridewealth may still find themselves obliged to pay it, and even Ganifiri paid bridewealth for his son's marriage.

Whereas in the past the economic influence deriving from such presentations was appropriate to the spiritual leadership of the priest as an 'important man', for fundamentalist Christians it is more likely to be in opposition to control of spiritual power. Rather than depend on people's material obligations to one another, the SSEC provides an authority structure based on a European model, in which men are elected to official positions and progress up through the hierarchy by ability. Ironically, authority in the church may depend less on the Christian value of 'love', as Kwara'ae understand it, than traditional authority once did. Hence those now recognised as traditional leaders, whether as heads of clans, experts on tradition or men of traditional wealth, organise themselves as 'chiefs' quite separately from the church, although some of them may also be church officials. The church authorities may refer to the chiefs disputes over traditional matters such as land rights or restitution which they cannot resolve themselves, but many Kwara'ae prefer to see this as a sphere of activity separate from the spiritual concerns of their churches.

Through the strong and pervasive authority of SSEC local church organisation, Kwara'ae have tried to resist what Berger describes as the Christian "concentration of religious activities and symbols into *one* institutional sphere", which has contributed to the Western distinction between religious and secular activity (Berger 1967:128). This is probably a common concern among Melanesian Christians, recognised for instance by the people of Isabel in their attempts "to renew images of the "chief" by infusing them with the moral and spiritual power of the church" (White 1991:208). In Kwara'ae many tensions between the church and the kind of traditional activities dealt with by the chiefs remain unresolved, although other possibilities are shown by a few men such as Justus Ganifiri and Arnon Ngwadili who have managed to combine the authority of church and tradition in distinguished positions of religious and secular leadership.

CHRISTIAN LEADERSHIP AND RITUAL KNOWLEDGE

Being based on spiritual rather than human power, authority in the church depends upon a man demonstrating himself to be an acceptable mediator with God on behalf of the congregation. In practice this depends heavily on mastering the necessary ritual knowledge, and this is the means by which the church establishment channels and controls spiritual power, as did traditional priests. Of course ritual knowledge is not sufficient in itself. The SSEC, of all churches, also emphasises the importance of everyone's personal and direct experience of God, and this has probably been an important part of its appeal compared with other churches as well as with the traditional religion since the earliest times. The first 'teachers' were sustained in their difficult and often dangerous work by their strong personalities and conviction of spiritual support, and this appears to have impressed their converts and congregations. Such men demonstrated the power of God by miracles such as curing sickness through prayer, surviving attacks of violence or sorcery which sometimes led to the deaths of their opponents, or calling on signs from God to convince and convert sceptics. As Ganifiri recalls, "There was great power before, when it all started. This also made them believe, "Eh, maybe this is better [than the ghosts].""

But from the earliest days of the SSEM, ritual knowledge has been promoted as an important qualification for leadership in the church, particularly knowledge of the Bible. SSEC doctrine continues to hold this fundamentalist view of "... both Old and New Testaments as being the inspired Word of God and also as being the only true guide for faith and life" (SSEC 1977:48). Religious knowledge is supposed to be open to all, men and women, and the local organisation of the SSEC churches is intended to train the congregation to conduct ritual activities for themselves. But for all this, not everyone can gain the education necessary to achieve a deep understanding of the Scriptures, especially to the standards set by highly trained church leaders and missionaries. In former times some insisted on a certain level of literacy in the local language as a requirement for baptism and hence full membership of the church. The missionaries had always been rather suspicious of spiritual inspiration undirected by

orthodox ritual and were naturally on guard against Christian-inspired movements such as the *bulu* cults, which in their terms were mere counterfeits of
Christianity. So those who could not demonstrate a good grasp of ritual
knowledge were not supported as church leaders. Despite his remarkable
evangelical achievements, Ganifiri's father, the Queensland convert Fiuloa, was
passed over in favour of other 'teachers', for the missionaries regarded him as "a
very poor teacher, being unable to read, and is very superstitious. " (NIV 1918)

In practice the level of ritual knowledge required for senior positions in the
church was and remains more or less esoteric. Instruction was eagerly sought by
many converts from the earliest days of the Kwara'ae church but, until Ganifiri
started his 'education school' at Nāfinua in 1938, even the most basic education
was more or less restricted to the select few who passed through the training
school at Onepusu. This education was heavily centred on ritual knowledge for,
in Florence Young's words, "The Bible is our sole lesson-book and the only
education is given in reading, writing, singing, numbers and simple arithmatic"
(Young 1925:241). As more and more educated 'teachers' emerged over the
years, the spiritual inspiration of men like Fiuloa became even less sufficient in
itself to attain leadership in the church. In more recent times as the general level
of education has advanced, so has the standard of religious training, with
scholarships for a few to religious colleges overseas, in New Zealand, Australia,
South Korea and elsewhere. Senior SSEC leaders today are well educated and
well travelled men whose work for the church requires the kind of experience and
expertise which is very difficult to acquire without formal training.

SPIRITUAL INSPIRATION IN THE SSEC

But although all Christians require a certain level of ritual knowledge and
depend upon the deeper knowledge of their reigious leaders, the SSEC has
continued to develop the Kwara'ae gift for communicating directly with spirits
and mediating their power through dreams, visions and spirit possession.
Malaitan Christians have had such experiences, interpreted as 'evangelical
awakening' or 'spiritual revival', ever since the 19th century in Queensland
(Young 1925:161,173, Barr 1983:111) and spiritual inspiration played an
important part in the developement of mission Christianity, as well as in reactions
against it such as the *bulu* cults and the Remnant Church. But in the days of the
SSEM it was not the normal experience of ordinary members of the church. As
Philip Udua, brother of Ganifiri, explains,

> Just the leaders had power and they prayed for healing, because when they were
> ready to be teachers and leaders they prayed, anointing them, they were filled with
> the Holy Spirit and worked by the Holy Spirit.

More recently, spiritual inspiration has become a common experience among ordinary men and women and it may be as usual now for SSEC Christians to receive dreams and visions of God, Jesus Christ and other Christian spirits and symbolic images as it was for their ancestors to have such experiences from ghosts. Although this development forms part of the worldwide 'charismatic' or 'pentecostal' movement and Kwara'ae trace it back to the Pentecost, it also draws upon their traditional religious culture. People 'convict' by the Holy Spirit in the same way that their ancestors were possessed or inspired by ghosts, and the experience (Kwara'ae *ta'elia*) with its physical sensations of trembling and glowing is said to be similar in either case. This occurs particularly during enthusiastic church services, during which people may publicly confess and repent sins and backsliding and then receive counselling from the church leaders. Occasional 'revivals', like Kwaisulia's movement of 1955, continued during the 1960s, often stimulated by 'crusade' tours of foreign evangelists who addressed massive congregations at SSEC centres such as Onepusu, Su'u, Abu and Malu'u. *Not In Vain* reported a characteristic occasion on Ngongosila in 1964:

> Once again there was that working of the Holy Spirit: when the appeal was made people came from everywhere to the front [of the church] with a sincere desire to get right with God. ... Leaders told us afterwards that they had been moved to tears as they saw hardened back sliders ... returning to the Lord.
> (NIV Mar. 1964).

But the most dramatic and far reaching development of spiritual intervention in the SSEC came when Malaita was caught up in the worldwide 'charismatic' or 'revival' movement originating in Britain and North America during the 1960s. When it reached New Zealand, the Maori evangelist Muri Thompson and his preaching team were invited by the SSEC to visit Solomon Islands in 1970. Thompson began his 'crusade' in Honiara where for two weeks his prayer meetings were attended by large crowds every night, with many coming forward to confess their sins and receive counselling. From Honiara he came on to Onepusu for the SSEC annual conference in August. After a few days there Thompson's preaching was leading many of the assembled church leaders and missionaries also to make public confessions of sins and grievances, uniting them to gain the blessing and inspiration of the Holy Spirit (NIV 1970:3–5). Accompanied by some of the SSEM leaders, Thompson continued his tour northwards up the west coast of Malaita via Abu and Malu'u, where he had a similar effect. But the mood changed when he reached Kobiloko in Lau (incidentally the home of Kwaisulia, founder of the Remnant Church). According to Ganifiri, who witnessed these events himself, "the Holy Spirit started to work" and people began to have visions and to drive out 'evil spirits' (that is ghosts). They went on south to Uru where events reached a climax, as Ganifiri recalls:

> While we were praying and singing and hearing the word of the Bible, in the morning while Mr. Muri Thompson was preaching ... suddenly we heard something like thunder starting in the sky, making a big noise as if you were beating a drum. ... it came on and on directly above the church building ... and people started crying, started to fall down, started confessing their sins and started to speak in other languages. ... People standing outside ... saw something like a flame fall on to the church and after that a big wind blew.

Such miracles were repeated as the tour went on towards south Malaita, with people having visions of 'evil spirits', of Jesus on the cross, the opening of Heaven and other remarkable things. When Ganifiri returned to East Kwara'ae similar things happened as he addressed a church service at Nāfinua, with people crying, speaking in tongues and prophesying. In this way the 'revival', as it became known, spread throughout Malaita and beyond, and it has been followed by further revivals and waves of religious enthusiasm ever since.

Although the development of the SSEC as an autonomous church can be traced back at least to the time of Māsing Rul, it was the spiritual inspiration resulting from the 1970 revival which introduced some of the important ritual practices which now distinguish the church. Since then demonstrations of spiritual power have become well established within SSEC ritual, especially through spiritual 'gifts' which enable people to communicate messages and power from God. In the 1980s church services regularly included demonstrations of the 'gift of writing' in which someone is inspired to 'write' on the church blackboard in what seem to be foreign scripts. The precedent for this is said to be the writing on the wall in the Book of Daniel. The writing directs the congregation to appropriate Biblical texts, which are identified by another person who has the gift of 'interpretation'. At times of greatest religious enthusiasm, some people also demonstrate the gift of 'speaking in tongues', as in the Pentecost itself. Other gifts include 'revelation', which enables people to receive symbolic and prophetic dreams, or 'healing', through which they can cure sickness or injuries by praying or laying on of hands, or 'casting out devils'.

Onesmas Omani, first son of Rofate'e of Gwauna'ongi, is one of many to have received such 'gifts' from revival, enabling him to interpret 'writing' in church services. For instance, once while his family were all praying aloud over his sick child and trying to discover if they had caused the illness through their own misdeeds, the 'gift' of divination showed him the wild ghost which was responsible and they chased it away by prayer. Such spiritual 'gifts' are generally regarded as a sign that God is working through the church, bringing the blessing of his power into people's lives and uniting them in the work of the church. But

PLATE 44   *A Sunday service at Na'oasi. On this occasion members of the*
              'women's band' lead their special annual service. On the main
              blackboard is the theme of the children's Sunday School, and
              spiritually-inspired 'writing' by the old woman on the left.
              (Photo by Ben Burt, 1983)

they also demonstrate that ultimately the ritual knowledge of the church establishment and the missionaries is not essential for access to the power of God. As Taeman Timi explains:

> If anyone can't read or is not educated, but if he accepts Jesus Christ, Jesus Christ is in his life, well, he cuts through by Jesus. Jesus will give his Holy Spirit to live with him and the Holy Spirit will teach him ... to know how to live and be there to do his work.

SPIRITUAL DISSENT

The 1970 revival was supported by SSEC leaders who, like Ganifiri, recognised that the enthusiasm and spiritual gifts demonstrated by their congregations were revitalising the church. But spiritual inspiration may also act to challenge the authority of the church establishment. A man like Michael Kwa'ioloa may be inspired by his own spiritual experiences to train for office in the church, become a pastor and be elected to senior church committees, eventually to become a respected figure in his church and community. But some are also led by their visions and spiritual 'gifts' to question church authority. At one time Stephen Binalu, Rofate'e's second son, was devoting all his spare time to evangelical work as a fiery and passionate preacher, explaining that he preferred to remain outside the ministry of the church to act as a critic of its failings. For him church office represented vested interests in authority and he saw his own role as challenging the 'received tradition' of the church on the basis of his own direct inspiration from God. His preaching, in church and with preaching teams, was inspired by visions he had received and interpreted through Biblical research and he saw himself playing the part of the Biblical prophets, the voice crying in the wilderness. Men like this continue the evangelical work of the early Kwara'ae Christians, countering established authority with the power of spiritual inspiration in what is a Kwara'ae as well as a Christian tradition.

Of course there is always the risk that such dissent may provoke rifts within the church. Kwara'ae generally take a quite pragmatic attitude to church membership, changing it as they once exchanged the traditional religion for Christianity, according to the benefits they expect to receive. There have probably been more defections from the SSEC in Kwara'ae than in any other district of Malaita, resulting in the establishment of the Remnant Church and the Jehovah's Witnesses during the 1950s, and other churches since. The Remnant Church in particular shows the possibilities for people being led by visionary leaders into forming new sects. These defections have not been due solely to spiritual inspiration, for even the success of the 1970 revival did not remove all dissatisfactions with the SSEC and a few people continued experimenting with new church denominations for reasons which recall the hopes of overseas material aid once raised by Māsing Rul. Of course the significance of this distinction between spiritual and material motivations depends on how far material benefits are accepted as a legitimate purpose of spiritual support.

In 1974 Clement O'ogau, a local community leader, Court Justice and former Māsing Rul chief, introduced the Baptist church to his village at New Valley on the Kwaibaita river. He learnt of it from the war hero Jacob Vouza on Guadalcanal and his people decided to join so as to receive support from the Baptist church overseas, which came in the form of money to pay pastors and parcels of supplies such as books and clothes. Then in 1979 Nelson Fo'ogau from West Kwara'ae, a former Federal Council activist, introduced the 'Holiness Church' (OMS) which he had apparently learn about from a religious magazine. The ritual of this church is similar to the SSEC, but one of its attractions was that the 'mother church' in Australia was expected to give financial support to local churches in Malaita, paying for pastors' salaries, education and other things, in return for offerings contributed by the local churches. This was contrasted with collections made by the SSEC, which not only had to support itself but by this time was actually sending money abroad to support mission work in Papua New Guinea. When Fo'ogau came to preach in East Kwara'ae his message was taken

PLATE 45   *The Anglican priest for Kwai district, Father Nelson Safu of Fakula'e, in his church at Fa'iketo. His role in the church service illustrates the contrast in ritual organisation between the Anglicans and the SSEC. (Photo by Ben Burt, 1983)*

up by Zebulon Olitani, pastor for about six SSEC villages near Nāfinua. Two of these villages and some others joined Olitani in the Holiness Church, while the remainder of his congregation later became the Na'oasi local church. They worked hard to raise money but sceptics who remained in the SSEC say that they received little from the church in Australia in return.

Such experiments continue with varying degrees of success. In 1983 a few men in West Kwara'ae, including Jemuel Misialo, Paramount Chief among the Kwara'ae chiefs, joined the Apostolic Church. Again they heard of the church from an Australian religious magazine and they joined because, unlike the SSEC, it does not oppose important traditional practices such as bridewealth and restitution payments. Such dissent from established churches has not been confined to the SSEC. For a while in about 1980 a man named Ilala gained a following among Anglicans in East Kwara'ae after a vision from the angel Gabriel gave him healing powers and led to new interpretations of the Ten Commandments in line with traditional values.

TOWARDS AN INDIGENOUS CHRISTIANITY

Such rifts in the church are only one consequence of the way SSEC Christians participate in the development of their religion in line with the ideal of a 'priesthood of all believers'. Now more than ever, direct spiritual encounters confirm the doctrine of a personal relationship with Jesus, frequently renewed by spiritual revival. People's confidence in this relationship lends conviction and legitimacy to the otherwise difficult and contentious task of changing the received doctrine and ritual of the church. As Barr indicates in his review of Melanesian "ecstatic religious phenomena" (1983), such experiences can be seen as a way of reworking local religions, traditional and Christian, in the pursuit of spiritual power. This is recognised, and approved, by European missionary Christians such as Ray Overend, Australian Director of the SSEM, who also warns against an "imitative" Christianity based on Western forms but lacking spiritual vitality (1990:6). Even the Western-derived SSEC orders of service include the reminder that "... we must never forget that there must still be room for variation (change) under the guidance of the Holy Spirit of God" (SSEC 1977:5).

As the dominant church in Malaita, the SSEC has made a particularly important contribution to the development of an indigenous Christianity, distinctively Melanesian or perhaps even Malaitan. But in so doing it also participates in a much wider movement among formerly colonised peoples to create local forms of Christianity appropriate to their own cultural traditions and contemporary circumstances. Barr's brief review (1983) shows the SSEC revival to be one of many 'Holy Spirit movements' in the Melanesian region, "providing a model or prototype for other similar movements" which SSEC evangelists (some from Kwara'ae) have promoted in areas such as the New Guinea Highlands. Similar processes are at work in other parts of the world, notably among the myriad independent churches of Africa. Ranger considers that "the real nature of Central African Christianity was shaped as much by the 'converts' from below as by the missionaries from above" (1975:10), and Ojo describes how Nigerian Christians have, like Kwara'ae, drawn upon the worldwide charismatic movement in their efforts to adapt Christianity to their own society and culture (1988:189). Kwara'ae continue to respond to religious innovations originating in the West, from revival movements to new mission sects. Possibly, as Horton explains the situation in Africa, they are looking for the secrets of a personalised religious theory underlying the unacceptably impersonal material-ism which dominates the ubiquitous Western and colonial culture (Horton 1971:106). But if this is what they find, it is more likely to derive from their own local religious culture.

In his review of research into African religious movements, Fernandez (1978) points to the realisation by mission scholars that local religious world-views should be recognised as contributions to the development of Christianity, rather than be measured against Western Christianity as the universal form of the religion. In the terms which Horton describes African Christian movements, the SSEC is developing new forms of "explanation, prediction and control of space-time events" (1971:102–104). Whether Western Christianity really stands in contrast as 'other-worldly', as Horton supposes, may be doubted, especially for people like the SSEM missionaries. But one characteristic of African and Melanesian world-views which does distinguish them from some Western ones is that, as Fernandez warns, the ideas underlying them are "embedded in images, symbols and actions" (1978:222). This makes Horton's type of intellectualist explanations in terms of Western conceptual frameworks meaningless to the people involved and, as Overend recognises from a missionary point of view, the "sophisticated schematics" of Western theology may also prove irrelevant to them (1990:29).

In reworking their religion, Kwara'ae prefer to rely on spiritual rather than intellectual guidance, and in this sense the SSEC, for all its European-style church and ritual organisation, is very much an indigenous church. It was created and is now controlled by local people and is continually revitalised through the spiritual inspiration of its congregation. Overend's explanation of revival is that "Suddenly the spirit of God set free the beautiful spontaneity of the Melanesian heart and beautifully sanctified it" (1990:6). But Kwara'ae Christianity may owe even more to Melanesian culture than this Christian perspective acknowledges, for even in what is now an overwhelmingly Christian society there are strong continuities as well as conflicts between Christianity and tradition. A look at this ambivalent relationship will conclude this study of Kwara'ae religion, to consider how the culture of their contemporary Christianity has been shaped by the 'tradition of the past'.

PLATE 46   *Michael Kwa'ioloa, sometime SSEC pastor, with his father Samuel Alasa'a of Tolinga-Fairū, former traditionist priest and witness to the arrival of missionaries and government in Kwai. Alasa'a has dressed to demonstrate the traditional costume of his youth. (Photo by Ben Burt, 1984)*

CHAPTER TEN

Kwara'ae Christianity and Christian Tradition

Looking beyond the new Christian social order and ritual organisation of Kwara'ae, it remains to examine how Kwara'ae themselves understand the relationship between their Christianity and the traditional social order it has replaced. In particular we will consider why, in a society which is now almost entirely Christian, where followers of the traditional religion have become a marginal and politically insignificant minority, this relationship continues to be an important issue, full of troublesome contradictions which may have serious implications for the future development of a rapidly changing society.

The underlying reason for the continuing conflict and tension between Kwara'ae Christianity and tradition is that the two categories were historically constituted in opposition to one another as the ideologies of alternative social orders upheld by competing political factions. From the Kwara'ae point of view this tradition-Christianity opposition was central to the broader conflicts of colonialism. But its political implications changed and developed over time, as attempts were made to compromise or mediate the opposition and eventually to reconstitute and Christianise the concept of tradition itself. At the same time, Kwara'ae have also in a manner of speaking 'traditionised' Christianity, but in a way which perpetuates the Christian-tradition opposition within the Christian social order. It is in this sense that tradition, although no longer a political threat to Christianity, continues to be a focus of contradictions in Kwara'ae society.

CONSTITUTING AND RECONSTITUTING 'TRADITION'

In looking into these contradictions it is important to recognise the ambivalence of the Kwara'ae concept of 'tradition' itself, reflecting changing and conflicting attitudes towards traditional culture and the religion of the ghosts which came to symbolise it. Although 'tradition' (*falafala*) denotes the way of life and culture created and passed down by their ancestors from ancient times, the images which Kwara'ae hold of it inevitably reflect a long and continuing debate over the colonial transformation of their society.

Whatever 'tradition' meant to Kwara'ae in pre-colonial times, the concept would have gained a new political significance when they were presented with the alternative of Christianity under colonial rule. Before this time the contradictions inherent in Kwara'ae culture may well have led to reflection and debate on matters such as men's and women's roles, or conflicts between egalitarianism and hierarchy, but colonialism gave such contradictions new meaning within visions of new ways of life. In the process a new cultural self-consciousness would have emerged, distinguishing indigenous ways of life from the alternatives, with an awareness sharpened by political resistance to the European intention to change Kwara'ae society by political and religious reforms. Some evidently began to appreciate that their continued self-determination and political autonomy depended on recognising the way of life of their ancestors as a distinctive indigenous tradition and fighting to retain it. Others with less stake in the traditional social order were more willing to sacrifice it for the sake of the benefits of colonialism represented by Christianity. From the first the Christian enterprise was represented by European missionaries and accepted by Kwara'ae as a spiritual, political and cultural struggle against their existing way of life, as the converts began to introduce European-inspired social reforms in the name of their new religion. The traditional social order as a whole inevitably became identified with the ancestral religion as 'heathen', meaning non-Christian, which Christians did their best to give a negative value.

At first the Christian movement made common cause with the Europeans, represented by missionaries and government, while the traditional religion of the ghosts, by giving spiritual support to their opponents became, as it continues to be, a symbol of anti-colonial resistance. But pressed by colonial forces, this resistance soon began to compromise as it tried to take advantage of the new spiritual powers introduced by Christian ritual. The *bulu* cults were early attempts to create what might be called indigenous 'churches', under human and spiritual authority which was based on an understanding of the Christian message informed by Kwara'ae rather than European religion. Inevitably these cults were unable to compete in the long term with more orthodox churches supported by the organisation, resources and authority of the missions. If the *bulu* cults represented a compromise between tradition and colonialism, for many people joining the mission 'schools' was an admission of defeat.

But as the Christian communities gained in strength and self-sufficiency there was a gradual political realignment. Christians and traditionists were obliged to acknowledge that they had more in common with one another than with their European colonial masters, as they demonstrated through Māsing Rul. It was then that Christians realised the potential of their new religion by turning it against the Europeans and enlisting God's support for an anti-colonial movement. Like the *bulu* cults, Māsing Rul was an attempt to appropriate the power of colonialism and turn it to the cause of self-determination, but this time inspired by the institutions of government and army as well as the missions. Like the *bulu* cults, it adopted European forms from an understanding informed more by the Kwara'ae world view than that of the Europeans who had introduced them. But in seeing this as no more than a misunderstanding, Europeans themselves misunderstood the movement, which is better judged by its achievements. As the *bulu* drew upon traditional culture to create indigenous 'churches', so Māsing Rul used it with some success to introduce indigenous 'government'.

Māsing Rul was a crucial stage in a continuing movement throughout Malaita to reconstitute concepts of tradition as political ideology. This ideology has been distinguished analytically by the Pijin term *kastom* (from English 'custom') (Keesing 1982b), although for Kwara'ae themselves *kastom* is simply Pijin for *falafala*, 'tradition'. There is now a considerable literature on the politics of *kastom* or tradition in the Pacific (particularly contributions to Keesing & Tonkinson 1982 and Jolly & Thomas 1992), including studies of Kwaio and Kwara'ae on Malaita (Keesing 1982b, 1982c, 1989b, Burt 1982). Much of the discussion has focussed on "reinventing traditional culture" (Keesing & Tonkinson 1982) or "creating the past" (Keesing 1989b) as part of the phenomenon of "the invention of tradition" (see Hobsbawm & Ranger 1983).[1] These rather tactless expressions reflect a recognition of tradition "as a symbolic construction, a contemporary human product rather than a passively inherited legacy", the result of processes which, as Linnekin suggests, are better described as 'cultural construction' (1992:249).

In reconstituting a concept of tradition made self-conscious by resistance to colonialism into a political ideology, Malaitans have, as Keesing suggests, succumbed to a colonial hegemony of ideas which leads tradition to justify itself in colonial or Western terms (Keesing 1989b:22,28). This reflects both the necessity to fight Western institutional power by Western means and the intellectual and symbolic power which political dominance confers on Western culture. Such hegemony is evident in the Kwara'ae chiefs' campaign for tradition which has developed since the 1960s. This movement responded to growing prosperity and increasing local control of church and government, which was occurring in apparent fulfilment of the demands of Māsing Rul as the British prepared for political decolonisation. The chiefs, mostly Christians and including leading figures in both church and local government, sought to direct these reforms by reinterpreting and institutionalising their visions of traditional leadership, 'law' and land rights so as to have tradition incorporated into the developing institutions of the Solomon Islands state. By such means, as Keesing says, "the dominated reproduce the conceptual and institutional structures of their domination, even in struggling against it" (1989b:25). Perhaps they have little alternative.

As Keesing has pointed out, "*Kastom* is an apt and powerful symbol precisely because it can mean (almost) all things to all people", uniting Christians and traditionists, urban elites and rural villagers and even the diverse peoples of new nation states in reactions to colonialism which over-ride their conflicting

PLATE 47   *Celebrating 'tradition'. Dancers, dressed to look old-fashioned in*
             loincloths and ornaments, perform at the great meeting of
             Kwara'ae chiefs at 'Aimela in 1976. (Photo by L. Laka,
             UNESCO, from the National Museum of Solomon Islands)

sectional interests (1982b:297). What in local culture stands for tradition as a
symbol of indigenous values, and what in relationships with the wider world it
stands against, varies with historical circumstances. Tradition has been used to
justify Kwara'ae claims for political separatism under their own 'Province'. It has
been invoked by the Solomon Islands' governing elite to build a national identity
through what Keesing has called "the fetishization of culture" (1989b:31) by
celebrating occasions such as the tenth anniversary of state independence in 1988
with performances of traditional arts. It was used with equal conviction in 1989
by disaffected young Malaitans rioting in Honiara town centre in protest against
a public insult, who showed the strength of Malaita and its tradition by exacting
a $20,000 restitution payment from the Solomon Islands government.

CONSTITUTING CHRISTIANITY

Other Melanesian societies may also invoke tradition in contests with
government, or with commerce (see eg. Otto 1992, Foster 1992:286), but for

Kwara'ae it is the relationship of tradition to Christianity which seems most problematic and full of troublesome contradictions. Historically the cause of these contradictions is the way Kwara'ae Christianity was constituted in opposition to the traditional social order and religion, under the inspiration of the missionaries' Eurocentric convictions of cultural superiority. Some Melanesian societies seem to have managed more or less to transcend this colonial legacy, whether by coming to regard their new religion as encompassing the old (Kaplan 1990), as reaffirming the traditional moral order (Smith 1990), or by using the opposition to validate new Christian identities (White 1991). But many Kwara'ae seem more inclined to perpetuate the suspicion of traditional culture shown by fundamentalist missionaries of the SSEM. This is particularly striking in the longstanding segregation of Christians and traditionists into separate local communities, creating divisions which dominated Kwara'ae politics during the first thirty or forty years of this century. Keesing (1989a) observes this situation still continuing in Kwaio from the perspective of traditionists divided politically and ritually from their Christian neighbours, confirming that each threatens the other's ritual integrity within a shared religious world-view. Although few people in Kwara'ae still find themselves in this position today, the tradition-Christianity opposition continues at another level within Christian society. In converting to Christianity Kwara'ae have also reproduced in a new form some of the fundamental premises of the traditional religion, and as a transformation of the old order Christian society has also reproduced within itself the contradictions between them.

Again, we will concentrate here on the Christian society of the SSEC, as the dominant church in East Kwara'ae. But although there are important contrasts in ritual and doctrine between the SSEC and some other local denominations, as Ross' survey of Malaitan churches in Baegu has shown (1978b), for present purposes these are less important than the religious similarities between all Kwara'ae Christians. Whether they belong to the SSEC, whether they defected from it to join new churches such as the Jehovah's Witnesses, Baptists or Holiness Church, or whether they belong to the longer established Seventh Day Adventists, most people in East Kwara'ae belong to fundamentalist churches. And although this study refers less to the large minority of Anglicans, they also share the same underlying religious world-view and conceptual system, which derives as much from traditional religion as it does from European Christianity. When discussing their religion, people may refer for authority to the Bible or the doctrine of their church, but the insights which inform their own understandings of Christianity owe as much to the religion of the ghosts. Kwara'ae Christians have always had much in common with their Kwara'ae traditionist opponents which they did not share with their European missionary allies, and their

Christianity still reflects the perspectives of the original converts who tried to understand the new religion in terms of the old.

Despite the European missionaries' efforts to guide Kwara'ae into a Christianity based on the European cultural tradition, Kwara'ae have in many respects adopted the new religion according to a traditional understanding of the nature of people and spirits and of the relationships between them. As elsewhere in Solomon Islands (see Harwood 1982:232), there were sufficient coincidences between this perspective and that of the missionaries for the parties to work together to mutual satisfaction by responding to one another in standard formal ways, but each did not otherwise need to understand much about the other's culture. Hence few Kwara'ae except the most Western educated seem to have accepted European Christian cosmology in its own terms and it is not too much to say that the long and close partnership between Kwara'ae Christians and their European missionaries has been based on a very imperfect understanding of each other's religions. There is also a certain irony in the fact that SSEM missionaries actually encouraged European values as they sought to promote an indigenous Christianity, while at the same time Kwara'ae church leaders were creating an indigenous Christianity as they sought to introduce European values. In some respects Kwara'ae have incorporated their traditional religion into Christianity despite their intention to reject it.

ALTERNATIVE RELIGIONS AND SHARED COSMOLOGY

But the opposition between the traditional and Christian religions depends first of all on the fact that Kwara'ae themselves accept the reality of both, whatever they think of their merits. Even before they were prepared to accept Christianity they quickly understood it to be a spiritual force to be reckoned with, as traditionists who have spent their whole lives resisting it continue to do. Likewise, in accepting Christianity Kwara'ae have not denied the existence and power of the ghosts, and although Europeans in general tended to dismiss this as mere 'superstition', SSEM missionaries, past and present, are also convinced that real spiritual powers are at work through the traditional religion. Within Kwara'ae, where the two religions have co-existed now for at least ninety years, they have long since accommodated to one another socially and theologically, and even when people are divided by their religion they remain members of the same society.

The often close association between Christians and traditionists is well illustrated in the life of Michael Kwa'ioloa, whose experience of both religious communities, recorded in a lengthy autobiography, has contributed so much to this book. Kwa'ioloa was born in 1953, a son of the former traditionist priest Samuel Alasa'a of Tolinga and Arana, daughter of the 'Ere'ere warrior 'Arumae

Bakete. Alasa'a's children were brought up as Christians but as relatives and neighbours of Ramo'itolo the Latea priest and his family, and Kwa'ioloa's elder sister married Ramo'itolo's son. When he died she married the son of Timi Ko'oliu, the senior 'Ere'ere priest, and lived as a traditionist until she was killed by a woman ghost in 1982, for refusing to become her priest. Kwa'ioloa himself went to the SDA school on Guadalcanal, was 'born again' following the revival of 1970 and became first a pastor and later a member of senior church committees in the SSEC. But this did not prevent him supporting his traditionist relatives and in-laws in 'Ere'ere in 1977 by claiming restitution from the SDA when their hospital plane flew over and defiled their shrines[2]. The experiences of people like Kwa'ioloa and his family have long given Christians and traditionists a good understanding of each other's religions and contributed to a religious world-view broadly shared by both. What is at issue in the continuing debate between them is not so much alternative world-views as alternative social orders based on allegiance to alternative sources of spiritual support and protection.

In treating conversion to Christianity as a change of allegiance, the substitution of new spiritual relationships for old, Kwara'ae have inevitably brought the theology of the old religion into the new. This is probably common to Melanesian Christians in general, and for Solomon Islands it is attested by Whiteman's study of "indigenous Melanesian Christianity" on Isabel seventy years after the traditional religion was abandoned there (1983 Ch. 6). The question is how this Christianity should be described or interpreted. Whiteman and other mission scholars are understandably concerned to compare it with their own ideals of what 'indigenous Christianity' could be. Like Hogbin (1939 Ch. 8), who long ago pointed to certain continuities between the old and new religions on Malaita, and Ross (1978b) in his survey of the mission churches, they treat 'indigenous Christianity' as a variation on an essentially European cultural theme, rather than as the product of a Melanesian religious tradition. For present purposes it is more illuminating to change the emphasis and compare Kwara'ae Christianity with the spiritual relationships of their traditional religion.

It is not difficult to see Christian deities in terms familiar from the religion of ancestral ghosts, with God as the father whose power is mediated by his son Jesus Christ and who acts through the Holy Spirit as a 'tabu spirit' (*ano'i rū ābu*). Stephen Binalu, as a reflective and philosophical SSEC preacher, has tried to explain the mystery of the Trinity as God being the soul (*mangona* or 'breath'), Jesus the body (*nonina*) and the Holy Spirit the 'spirit' (*anoanona*) of one being, implying that the Trinity is also manifest in the three parts of a person recognised by traditional theology. As an alternative to God, ghosts are generally identified with Satan, who some think of as God's son, a former angel, although for older people *setan* is merely an alternative Pijin term to *devol* (*defolo*), meaning 'ghost'.

People often have their own theories on parallels between the two religions, but although they may differ on the details, God and Satan generally seem to behave in very similar ways.

As alternatives, the basic difference between the two religions is that while traditionists treat ghosts as tabu, Christians treat God as tabu, and each recognises that it is very difficult to do both. With Christian deities as with the ghosts, treating them as tabu by observing the rules of behaviour which they set is an acknowledgement of authority which confers upon them power both for and over their dependents. But the Kwara'ae understanding of Christianity, by taking as its cardinal rule 'thou shalt have no other God but me', has made it difficult if not impossible to accept the spiritual support and observe the necessary rules of both religions at the same time. This makes each religion a threat to the authority of the other, and Christians are thus obliged to free themselves from the ghosts. This is not as easy to achieve as most people would hope. As ancestors, ghosts continue to be present in the social relationships, the culture and the minds of Christians, even of the second or third generation, and they constantly present themselves as a spiritual alternative to God, which is quite unacceptable to Kwara'ae Christianity.

CHANGING SPIRITUAL ALLEGIANCE

In this sense ghosts continue to play an important part in the Christian theology which rejects their role as spiritual protectors of their descendants. At the same time they continue to behave as predicted by the traditional religion, and Christians accordingly try to escape, resist or subdue them by methods deriving from traditional ritual. In general terms, Kwara'ae conversion to Christianity has been a process of 'mola-making' or 'clearing' (fa'aābu'a), destroying the influence of ghosts by removing tabu and making them mundane or ordinary (mola). This is the effect of ignoring or breaking their rules, under God's protection and in accordance with his own rules.

In the early days especially, Kwara'ae saw this very much in terms of breaking and abolishing women's tabu and they identified Christianity as a 'woman ghost' or 'women's cult' in which men and spirits were no longer tabu to defilement by women. It is clear that the role of women in Christian life was expected to subdue or destroy the power of ghosts, as women's influences were used in a more limited and controlled way for the same purpose in traditional ritual. Hence the attempts to substitute new sources of power by abolishing women's tabu in the bulu cults of the 1910s and '20s. But although ghosts ceased to be tabu and were deprived of power when their congregations ceased to honour them, special precautions were necessary to prevent them from retaliating or causing further trouble. Like other rituals to deal with ghosts, these focussed on their shrines and relics. While some congregations simply abandoned their shrines to decay, others deliberately desecrated them, either throwing away bones and relics or helping 'teachers' to bury them and pray over them and the shrine, so 'spoiling' (*fa'alia*) the ghosts and freeing their dependants from their relationship with them. Riomea of Fakula'e describes how, after his family went to 'school' in the 1930s, they returned to their shrine and fumigated it by burning a Bible to chase away the ghosts, a standard procedure reminiscent of the effects of smoke from a menstrual house fire.

Few people are willing to live without spiritual support and protection and those who freed themselves from the ghosts did so to put themselves under the protection of God, if only to guard against the displeasure of rejected ghosts. This change of allegiance required them to follow a new set of rules making God and themselves tabu, authorised by the Bible rather than by the ghosts. Of course much of what Christians regard as immoral and anti-social, such as stealing, swearing, violence and illicit sexual activity, are also offences against traditional tabu. But Christian rules also guard against what Jesus referred to as a Christian's three enemies, Satan, the World and the Flesh, which represent the ghosts and many of the practices they permitted or encouraged. Christian rules are subject to various interpretations, as reflected in the doctrines of different Christian denominations. For the SSEC, forbidden 'heathen customs' include excessive bridewealth, restitution and other traditional presentations, as well as many traditional arts, smoking and betelnut. In general Kwara'ae interpretations of Biblical rules would seem familiar to other Christians around the world and many of them are in stark contrast or contradiction to the rules of the ghosts (although Old Testament research has revealed some equally striking similarities to those who seek them).

However, the European character of Kwara'ae Christian rules disguises some important differences between Kwara'ae and European understandings of Christian theology, for Kwara'ae see the rules as one kind with those of the ghosts, based on similar principles as part of essentially similar spiritual relationships. Hence the concept of tabu takes its place in Kwara'ae Christian theology as a translation of 'holy' although, as we have seen, the European and Kwara'ae concepts are actually rather different. As the rules of the ghosts ensured that they and the men who dealt with them were made tabu by being kept 'clean' and pure and protected in particular from defilement by women, so the observance of Christian rules is intended to keep a person tabu by being 'clean' in Christian terms. The criteria for cleanliness are different of course, since God has no aversion to women even during menstruation and childbirth, while he is offended by some behaviour which was accepted or even required by the ghosts. But in regarding God's rules as equivalent to those of the ghosts, Kwara'ae also see the 'sin' of breaking them as 'defiling' (*sua*) ('unclean' in the Biblical English familiar to Kwara'ae). In Kwara'ae terms the instruction "Be ye holy; for I am holy" (I Peter 1:16) is equally appropriate to the ghosts and to God, which is why when a child is dedicated to God or a pastor is ordained by the church, this is said to 'make him tabu' (*fa'aābua*). It is the Kwara'ae understanding of 'holy' which enables the 'tradition of the law' under the ghosts to be summarised in terms of 'ten commandments' resembling those of the Bible. In either case the 'commandments' are concerned with tabu, which is as central to Kwara'ae Christianity as it was to the religion of the ghosts.

RELATIONSHIPS WITH GOD

A person's behaviour affects his relationship with God in much the same way as it affects relationships with the ghosts, for God's support and protection is only given to those whose lives are kept clean and pure by following his rules. This is what it means to be 'true' (*mamana*) to God so that he will be 'true' in return, just as in a relationship with a ghost. In this relationship, God is usually represented by Jesus Christ and confers many of the same benefits as the ghosts. As explained by Philip Udua of Ubasi, Justus Ganifiri's brother and an experienced church elder,

> If I really live for Christ and am true to Christ, well, my family lives well, my garden grows well, and everything else; perhaps I'll get into some trouble, God will deliver me from it. It seems prosperity is like that, from God helping the man, because God's word says "Abiding in me ... and my words abide in you, you can ask what you will and it shall be done unto you." ... It's just the same, if a man is true for a 'devil', the 'devil' is true for him.

The evangelical doctrine of the SSEC, which emphasises 'accepting Jesus' and 'taking him as your personal saviour', has given new expression to the Kwara'ae talent for forming personal relationships with spirits. As with the ghosts, the relationship with Jesus requires not only observing rules of behaviour but also a mental and emotional committment to have faith in him, to believe in him or 'make him true' (*fa'amamanā*). This faith is rewarded and reinforced by spiritual experiences, miracles, dreams and visions and spirit possession, as it would be under the ghosts (although Christians prefer to compare these experiences to those in the Bible).

As with ghosts, God has power over those who depend on his support. When people break his rules or flout his authority they or their dependants may suffer sickness or other misfortune. In his autobiography, Michael Kwa'ioloa attributes a crisis in his marriage and threatening accusations of adultery to 'backsliding' when, after several years of pastoral work, he began to break SSEC rules on matters such as accepting restitution payments. "When I was in this state I almost died, because I already belonged to Jesus but I'd turned back." As in this

PLATE 48   *Celebrating Christianity. Michael Kwa'ioloa, as pastor, leads a*
                uniformed singing band from Mamulele in East Kwara'ae at the
                opening of a new church at Kobito, a Kwara'ae suburb of Honiara,
                in 1977. (Photo from Michael Kwa'ioloa)

case, God is concerned not only with the infringement of ritual rules but also with
the state of a person's human relationships, for people cannot be in the right
relationship with God if they are not in harmony with one another, 'loving'
(*alafea, kwaima*) one another as Jesus taught. Like spiritual relationships, this is
a matter of emotion as well as action and feelings of enmity themselves may
contribute to a person's problems. Hence it is sometimes suspected when children
fall sick that their parents may be involved in grievances or disputes between
themselves or with others, which they will have to admit and resolve in order for
the child to recover.

     In such situations opinions may vary as to whether God actually inflicts
punishment or merely withdraws his protection, leaving a person open to attack

by ghosts or Satan, or sorcery and other dangers. Those whose Christian education has encouraged them to see God as loving and forgiving, as described in the New Testament rather than the Old, may be reluctant to consider him as punitive and vengeful. But the effect is the same in either case and, as with the ghosts, it represents a reassertion of authority by a spiritual protector, analogous to the reactions of a human leader. Sickness or trouble is generally regarded as one of the ways in which God, like the ghosts, communicates with people by showing them signs or warnings. Kwa'ioloa recalls an incident when his wife was struck with stomach cramps for objecting to the time he was spending on pastoral work. People resist God's will only at great risk for, as Kwa'ioloa explains, God gives you life and can take it away. "The Bible says it's hard to kick against the pricks, and it's true. You don't kick against God."

But there are also some important differences between relationships with God and ghosts, which are regarded as the great advantages of Christianity. First, whereas ghosts require sacrifices, particularly of pigs, the rituals required by God involve no material offerings, only prayer and church services. Christians, especially women, are thus relieved of the work of feeding pigs to be eaten only by a few of the men and of the cost of sacrificing pigs whenever someone is sick. In any case, sacrifices do not always produce results and ghosts may be accused of failing or deceiving their dependants. Christians do make offerings at church services but these are for the benefit of the whole congregation, and when they provide pigs for church feasts they are eaten by men, women and children. These differences are often given as important reasons for conversion, for Christians can maintain a satisfactory relationship with God by following obligations which they regard as far less onerous. As Maefatafata contrasts life as a Jehovah's Witness with her upbringing as daughter of the priest Ramo'itolo of Latea, "The Master helps even a woman in childbirth or a menstruating woman to live and eat with the men. So nothing is tabu now, because the Master has smoothed things out."

The other great benefit of Christianity which the ghosts cannot offer is the promise of 'eternal life'. Unless a person has a satisfactory relationship with God, mediated by his son Jesus Christ, his 'soul' (*mangona* or 'breath') after death goes to the fiery Biblical Hell, whereas a Christian will go to Heaven or Paradise, to await the second coming of Christ and the resurrection of the dead. The separate 'spirit' (*anoanona*) recognised in the traditional theory of the afterlife is said to remain on earth or go to Hell, although inconsistencies with European Christianity on this point seem to make opinions rather ambiguous. 'Everlasting life' is often given as a critical advantage which has persuaded people to forsake the ghosts and dedicate their lives to Christ, and it also leads some to look towards the 'second coming' as a solution to the problems of the world. Its appeal may be the reassurance that, despite the fallibility of religious world views under the kind of social instability and change which Kwara'ae have experienced, all uncertainties and contradictions will be resolved after death.

In brief, as Kwara'ae are concerned the main difference between Christianity and tradition is that God is a more effective protector. In Udua's words:

> The power of a 'devil' deceives a man. You can follow him and give yourself to the power of the 'devil' and he won't help you ... to defend you from trouble or give you deliverance from trouble. But the power of God, why it is different from the power of Satan is because we have eternal life and we believe in God because of God's almighty power.

CHRISTIANITY AND THE POWER OF TRADITION

But despite the success of Christianity the ghosts are still a force to be reckoned with in Kwara'ae society, and if they are not the political threat to the churches that they were in the past, they are still a spiritual challenge. Even ghosts who have been formally abandoned generations ago may still have a hold over their Christian descendants as an alternative source of spiritual support and protection, for the Christian churches have been more successful in abolishing the traditional ritual system than in exorcising the ghosts whose power it acted to channel and control. For all the changes they have brought about, Kwara'ae are still heirs to much of the religious culture and spiritual power of their ancestors, and the traditional theology which has shaped Kwara'ae Christianity also continues to give them an alternative to it.

Under the traditional social order the priestly establishment would always have had difficulty in containing and channelling spiritual power. Personal encounters with ghosts and experiences of spiritual inspiration demonstrated that this power could not be confined by shrines and relics, nor reserved to those who inherited esoteric ritual knowledge. By the same token, abandoning shrines, destroying relics and breaking the rules of the ghosts may not in itself be sufficient to destroy the power they have for their descendants and over them. While people still identify themselves with their ancestors and inherit from them their relationships with their land and with one another, they inevitably evoke the ghosts into existence. The receptiveness to spiritual influences which has become one of the strengths of SSEC Christianity still enables people to have personal experience of ghosts as well as of Christian spirits, and the basic ritual knowledge to develop relationships with ghosts is still commonly available.

In Christian terms, dealings with ghosts are a consequence of 'backsliding'. Not everyone achieves a satisfactory relationship with God or manages to sustain it through all the distractions and difficulties of life which may lead them astray.

In the SSEC, parents take a child to be formally 'dedicated' when it is a few months old but although this is equivalent to baptism in other denominations, the SSEC reserves baptism for those who demonstrate their own committment to God as adults, which not everyone finds easy to do. Women and girls are probably less likely to go astray because they are more strictly supervised by their menfolk, who try to ensure their chastity and domestic virtues even if they sometimes seem less concerned for their own personal morality. But young men in particular usually have little concern for the restrictions and self-discipline required by God and accordingly many indulge in unruly behaviour, as their ancestors did under the traditional religion. This means wandering around in search of excitement, stealing, fornicating and fighting, enjoying tobacco and betelnut and getting drunk. Perhaps the main difference in recent generations is that instead of spending some years under the discipline of employment on a plantation, young men today are more likely to go to Honiara to work or hang around as idle 'wanderers' (*liu*). Here they can usually depend on material support from more settled relatives and experience the excitement of youthful rebellion and the pleasures and temptations of town life while avoiding the authority of their elders. This inevitably leads them into trouble and such young men are largely responsible for the reputation as agressive troublemakers which Malaitans in general have among other Solomon Islanders.

As 'backsliders' with little respect for the church or the authority of their elders, these young men come to depend instead on the support and protection of ghosts. They may have dreams and visions, possibly from the ghost of a 'father' or 'mother' who cared for them in childhood. These ghosts may offer power themselves and they may also introduce more ancient and powerful ghosts, including the famous warrior ghosts the men will have heard of from the stories of their ancestors. With the support of these ghosts many young men join fearlessly in the brawls, feuds and other criminal activities for which young Malaitans are famous. The power they receive is typically to fight, to steal, to 'creep' in pursuit of romantic liaisons, and generally to break the rules of God and the church as well as the government. Michael Kwa'ioloa, an active member of his local church, and Stephen Binalu, the fervent preacher, like many other devout and committed Christians, will cheerfully relate stories of a riotous and irresponsible youth when they depended on the power of ancestral ghosts. Like the youth of earlier times, they were prepared to forgo the protection of the established religion for the sake of avoiding its restrictive authority. But rebelling in this way against the church actually means following the rules of the traditional religion, making themselves tabu to women in order to benefit from the power of the ghosts.

Yet, as irresponsible and indisciplined (*dalafa*) young men in the past would eventually settle down to observe the rules and receive the support and protection of the ghosts, so these young men from Christian backgrounds sooner or later find themselves obliged to reject the ghosts, 'accept Jesus' and be 'born again'. For Kwa'ioloa this happened after he rejected the revival of 1970 and quarrelled with his family, which led to visions of divine retribution for 'backsliding', calling him by name into the church. Others realise the need for spiritual support after traumatic experiences such as illness or narrow escape from death, maybe with symbolic dreams or visions revealing the error of their ways. Such experiences often occur as men take on the responsibilities of marriage and settle into the stable domestic life encouraged by both tradition and Christianity. Binalu was 'born again' after his first child became sick due to a crisis in his marriage. Being 'born again' means renouncing anti-social behaviour and bad habits such as smoking, betelnut and beer, and diligently following the rules of a good Christian life. Some of the worst 'backsliders', men of strong personality who rebel against social conventions in their youth, seem to become the most devout and enthusiastic 'born again' Christians, and many who now receive Christian spiritual inspiration may have had their first experiences of spirit possession during drunken fights in the streets and bars of Honiara.

Being 'born again' thus has parallels in tradition, when young men became tabu and 'clean' enough to be acceptable to the ghosts and to partake of sacrifices. Even using the imagery of European Christianity (drawing on John 3:3), Kwara'ae explanations reflect the same religious perspectives. As Amasaia Unumaliu of Ubasi puts it, a chicken is born first inside an egg, "wet and dirty", but instead of dying there, if it is born again the egg breaks and "a small clean thing comes out. ... The man who is born again in the Lord Jesus Christ ... his life is clean, he is kind, he loves and everything in that man's life is very clean." Being 'born again' is necessary for a person to realise the reward of eternal life and avoid being consigned to Hell, and it is also the first stage towards becoming a fully participating 'member' of the church. In accepting the support and protection of God he will be supported by the congregation, and this means accepting obligations to God which are obligations to the local church, and acknowledging the authority of God, which underlies the authority of the church leaders. As in the traditional religion, personal spiritual relationships reach their full development through the ritual system which channels and directs spiritual power on behalf of the community as a whole.

SATAN IN KWARA'AE TRADITION

These continuities between tradition and Christianity form the foundations of the indigenous Christianity which Kwara'ae and other Malaitans have built through churches such as the SSEC. But in adapting Christianity to indigenous culture Kwara'ae have not thereby reconciled it with their concepts of tradition. On the contrary, it is because their new and their old religions both conceive of spiritual relationships in the same terms that some Christians are able to use traditional spiritual powers while others are persuaded that this is a serious challenge to the Christian order. The tradition-Christian opposition actually operates within the theology of indigenous Christianity.

Besides relationships with ghosts, various forms of magic for healing, for attracting lovers and other purposes are also apparently in common use in Christian communities. The role of ghosts in such magic is somewhat ambiguous, for it is sometimes said to operate by itself or by the natural properties of the materials used, and the attitude of the church may also be ambivalent. When people use traditional herbal medicine they may invoke God to give it power instead of the ghosts, although in general the SSEC tends to disapprove of traditional magic. Even so, when people recognise that the powers they use are legitimate in traditional terms they are quite willing to talk about their own transgressions of church rules. The same cannot be said for sorcery, by definition illegitimate in traditional as well as Christian terms, so although sorcery may well be as common in Kwara'ae today as it ever was in the past, its existence is as much a matter of suspicion as of proven fact. The question is what kind of challenge these powers actually pose to the churches. Irresponsible young 'backsliders' usually reform and are 'born again', while magic workers have quite limited and harmless objectives and sorcerers are a small minority of criminals. None form organised cults which could draw others away from the church, and the power of the traditional ritual system to do so has been effectively broken.

In Christian terms the continued existence of these powers represents the challenge posed to Christians everywhere by Satan, with whom the ghosts, sorcery and indeed all non-Christian sources of spiritual power are identified. In this sense Satan is ever present and people are constantly tempted or intimidated by him. Not only do ghosts still approach their descendants with offers of support but they are also a constant presence in the land which was once theirs. They are likely to be encountered at any time, especially around the shrines and other tabu places which Kwara'ae still remember and preserve as signs of their relationship to their land. They may wander around haunting the bush as 'wild ghosts', who some say include ancestral ghosts abandoned by their Christian descendants. Christian Kwara'ae still live in a world of non-Christian spirits and now that they have given their allegiance to God they are more than ever beset by unwanted intrusions from ghosts who tempt them with the alternative.

In identifying ghosts with Satan and calling them 'devils' or 'satans', the church seeks to discredit them and question their 'truth' and validity as a source of spiritual support and protection. The superiority of Christianity has been proved by its triumph over the ghosts, as a result of more effective protection and the promise of 'eternal life'. The traditional religion on the other hand, is sometimes said to have been devised by Satan, who modelled it on God's own work to deceive people into following his way instead. SSEC Christians often say that ghosts are not really the spirits of their ancestors, but only illusions created by Satan, who uses a dead person's 'spirit' (*anoanona*) to deceive his descendants into worshipping him, and hence Satan himself. Some say that ghosts derive from the dead person's 'bad spirit', as distinct from his 'good' one which goes to heaven, in another version of the traditional theory of multiple souls or spirits. The theory that ghosts are counterfeits or impersonations helps to explain why they are less reliable than God, demanding sacrifices and then failing to deliver the promised results. Such theories are supposed to free people from the power which ghosts may have for them and over them, since if people need no longer believe in them they will lose their reality and power. However, this does not make ghosts any less real and powerful to those who do continue to believe in them and seek their support, as those claiming to be non-believers would also agree. Even for these sceptics it is probably not as easy to deny the reality of ghosts as they would like to think.

Following their missionaries, Kwara'ae also refer to ghosts as 'evil spirits', and to followers of the traditional religion as 'wicked'. Some accounts of Melanesian Christianity seem to accept such definitions at face value in European terms and then have to explain why people do not always behave as if their traditional religion was indeed 'evil' (eg. Clark 1989). Others imply that Melanesian concepts of evil belong to a more relativistic morality than that of Western Christianity (eg. Barker 1990c), as seems to be the case in Kwara'ae. Kwara'ae have not wholeheartedly accepted their European missionaries' definition of 'good' and 'bad' as absolute and abstract values, but see them rather in terms of relationships between people. In the traditional morality which Kwara'ae Christians still tend to act upon today, whether an act is 'good' or 'bad' depends above all on its context, on who is doing it to whom. This reflects the values of a tribal social order which in the past recognised no central or absolute authority with the power to set universal laws, human or spiritual. For all the ideals of Christianity as a brotherhood under the fatherly authority of God, many Kwara'ae do not seem to share the European Christian conviction that the ghosts of their ancestors, or Satan himself, are intrinsically bad or the embodiment of evil. If they are 'bad', this is rather in the sense that they are a failed or discredited alternative to the superior power of God, by comparison unreliable, demanding and dangerous and in various ways less effective. But in the last analysis ghosts are only dead people, morally little different to the living, and even Satan is difficult to conceive of as other than a kind of ghost.

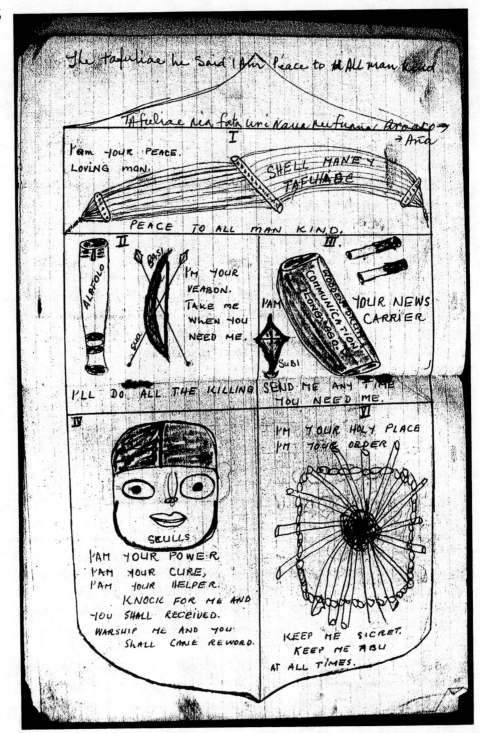

The tafuliae he said I Am Peace to the All man kind

Tafuliae Nia fata uri Naua Rufuana Broaro →
→ Ana

I

I am your peace.
loving man.

SHELL MANEY
TAFULIAE

PEACE TO ALL MAN KIND.

II

ALAFOLO

BASI

I'M YOUR
VEABON.
TAKE ME
WHEN YOU
NEED ME.

SUA

III

WOODEN DREM
COMMUNICATION
LONG AGO.

YOUR NEWS
CARRIER

I AM

SUBI

I'LL DO ALL THE KILLING

SEND ME ANY TIME
YOU NEED ME.

IV

SKULLS

I AM YOUR POWER.
I AM YOUR CURE,
I AM YOUR HELPER.
KNOCK FOR ME AND
YOU SHALL RECEIVED.
WARSHIP ME AND YOU
SHALL CAME REWORD.

V

I'M YOUR HOLY PLACE
I'M YOUR ORDER

KEEP ME SICRET.
KEEP ME ABU
AT ALL TIMES.

PLATE 49   'Our Kwara'ae Coat of Arms'. A Christian artist has created a
Western symbol of Kwara'ae traditional culture, featuring
weapons of war, wooden signal drum, ancestral skull and
sacrificial fire, under the heading of a tafuli'ae shell money as a
symbol of peace.
(From a book belonging to Adriel Rofate'e, about 1975)

KWARA'AE CHRISTIANITY AND CHRISTIAN TRADITION

Most Kwara'ae Christians would acknowledge that tradition and Christianity each have values essential to the society they would like to live in, and there have been some attempts to reconcile the two. Responding to the identification of traditional culture with 'heathen' religion, advocates of tradition have legitimated it in Christian terms by seeking a 'Christian tradition', which is aptly symbolised by the story of the first ancestor of Kwara'ae (see Burt 1982). This is only one of many Melanesian discoveries of indigenous antecedents for local Christianity (see eg. Chowning 1990, Smith 1990, Kaplan 1990). Many people, like Gwa'italafa whose account introduced this story in Chapter 2, say that this man did not worship his ancestors (who are unknown) but that he may actually have worshipped the 'true God'. According to Samuel Alasa'a of Tolinga, once a priest of the ghosts and an authority on Kwara'ae history and culture, who himself saw mission and government first arrive at Kwai, in the beginning at Siale there was no tabu and no sacrifice to the ghosts, for the people belonged to 'school' or 'church'. After the Biblical flood Malaita was uninhabited until God sent the angel Gabriel to tell the ancestors of Kwara'ae in Asia to go and settle there. It was only five generations later that they began to sacrifice to the ghosts and create the ritual system which endured until the advent of Christianity. It is generally agreed that, if the first ancestors were not actually Christian, they worshipped God in the tradition of the Old Testament and anyone who studies the Bible as thoroughly as Kwara'ae do will also find striking similarities between Kwara'ae religion and the ancient religion of the Jews. So it is that the story explaining the origin of Kwara'ae traditional culture, their rights to the land their ancestors first claimed, the authority of the laws they established and the brotherhood of all those descended from them, also shows the Kwara'ae people to be heirs to the Christian religion they now follow.

But recognising this religious heritage does not necessarily resolve the contradictions between the two religions. By continuing to define Christianity in opposition to the traditional religion, churches like the SSEC proclaim a spiritual threat which actually serves the purposes of the church, and the church may be suspected of provoking the struggle with tradition in the cause of its own authority. The continuing presence of the ghosts provides a challenge against which Christian devotion can be tested, as Satan does for European Christianity. The rules of the church and the authority of its leaders are legitimated by their claim to guard the whole community against these harmful spiritual forces, in much the same way that the ghosts' aversion to women upheld the traditional ritual and political establishment. In the church, as in other situations past and present, people may make rules of prohibition in order to claim authority and obedience to the rules confers power upon those who make them. Could it be that the uncompromising strictness of fundamentalist Christianity appeals to Kwara'ae for the same reasons that their traditional religion derived its spiritual power from the even stricter rules required by the ghosts?

It is interesting to compare the way Kwara'ae Christians attribute the religion of the ghosts to Satan with the theories of Anglican theology students from Isabel, who suggest that under their traditional religion God was 'behind' the ancestral ghosts (White 1991:247). Other Melanesians have even attempted to reinstate the ghosts once maligned by European missionaries within their own local visions of Christianity (see Macintyre 1990). But Kwara'ae Christians still agree with their fundamentalist missionaries in rejecting such possibilities, and in doing so they make the ghosts of their ancestors and much of the culture now symbolised by tradition into a real spiritual threat. It is not simple prejudice which leads SSEC Christians to oppose traditional practices such as wearing or keeping traditional heirloom ornaments, weapons or other relics, performing traditional songs and dances or passing on traditional oral history. Once the churches have decided that these things pose a threat to the Christian way of life, this becomes self-fulfilling. Those who follow the ways of their ancestors will indeed find themselves invoking ghosts and receiving dreams and revelations from them, whether they like it or not. However there are churches which have not tried to ban such practices, and Kwara'ae Anglicans may even celebrate Christian festivals with the same traditional costume and dances which were once devoted to the festivals of the ghosts. Such matters are still under debate in the SSEC, and congregations have recently begun to introduce variants of traditional music and dancing into singing-band performances and even church services. But their leaders recognise that such developments could hold serious spiritual risks and are not to be undertaken lightly.

In recognising that ghosts threaten the Christian way of life, fundamentalist churches like the SSEC inevitably confirm their power to do so, and actually confer power upon them as traditionists do, by giving them credence and hence making them 'true'. Kwara'ae themselves recognise the role of belief not only in empowering spiritual protectors but also in creating vulnerability to spiritual attack. Like the vulnerability of men and ghosts to the power of women under the traditional religion, this is the price paid to uphold the ritual system, which plays a central role in Kwara'ae social and political life under Christianity as it did under the ghosts. It is also the price of a firm ritual and moral framework for life in uncertain and rapidly changing times, as attested in the personal experiences of many Kwara'ae Christians who have been 'born again' into lives of moral rectitude, social responsibility and public esteem.

But the benefits of demonising the traditional religion also have other costs. In religious terms the rejection of the ghosts of their ancestors may deprive

Kwara'ae of traditional insights into the nature of persons and spirits which could enrich their Christianity as well as resolving some of the spiritual conflicts they now experience. Opposition to so much of the traditional culture created and passed down by these ancestors also takes a toll in social conflict, between people of different religious convictions, between fundamentalist churches such as the SSEC and more liberal ones such as the Anglicans, between second generation Christians and those brought up in the traditional religion and between 'back-sliders' and 'born again' Christians. Disputes arise over the honouring of traditional obligations such as bridewealth or restitution payments, indulgence in tobacco or betelnut, the use of traditional medicines or the performance of traditional arts, and over dealings with people who disagree on such issues. These conflicts may divide communities, families and even the hearts and minds of individuals, torn between their relationships with people, based on traditional values, and with God, based on the values of their church.

At another level there could be even more damaging long term consequences for Kwara'ae Christians who cut themselves off from traditional wisdom and values. As their history shows, the opposition between Kwara'ae tradition and Christianity has arisen from the deeper contradictions between the dominant world culture of capitalism which serves the interest of industrial countries, and the interests and aspirations of local people in the countries they once colonised and continue to dominate. If Kwara'ae allow their Christianity to deny a traditional culture which has served them well for hundreds of years and enabled them to survive a century of rapid colonial change, they may also be in danger of denying an alternative to the Eurocentric ideology of social and economic change which capitalism presses upon countries like Solomon Islands in the name of 'development'. In contrast to the exploitative, divisive and destructive economic system promoted by capitalist investment and advice, the 'tradition of the past' has the potential to inspire models for sensitive and equitable management of the island environment, based on communal control of natural resources and the values of community life. It also contains the basis for a legal system which could reflect the values of local people rather than of Western law, and for political organisations more responsive to local interests than Western styles of government have been. In brief, Kwara'ae tradition could provide a basis for economic, political and social developments which would respond to the people's own understanding of their society and environment and serve their own interests rather than those of the metropolitan countries overseas which advocate Western-style 'development' for Solomon Islands.

Many Kwara'ae, including devout members of the SSEC, recognise such possibilities in their concern for tradition, which still represents for them their land, their self-determination and their cultural integrity in a changing world. Kwara'ae continue to debate the distinctions between 'heathenism' and 'culture', between 'Christianity' and 'European tradition'. In a sense they have already created a 'traditional Christianity' by accepting as Christian much which has its roots in their traditional culture. But as Kwara'ae chiefs reaffirm the values of tradition by compiling books of genealogies and laws, as they set up committees and courts, plan local government reforms and cultural centres, they have still to resolve this contradiction within their own society by agreeing a Kwara'ae tradition which can also be Christian.

FIGURE 3   *A shell pendant and rings once belonging to Ramo'itolo, the last priest of Latea.*

Notes

CHAPTER 2

1 The analysis of tabu which follows in this and the following chapter has previously been summarised in Burt 1988. It has benefitted from detailed correspondence with David Akin and conversation with Pierre Maranda, although it does not necessarily represent their views on the subject.

2 On the European understanding of these concepts, Gordon Griffiths of the South Sea Evangelical Mission explained that in Biblical usage 'holy' implies to be separate or set apart and refers to things associated with God, while 'sacred' may refer to things associated with or dedicated not only to God but also to non-Christian spirits.

3 The negative implications of tabu explains why *ābu* is used as a negative prefix to certain verbs, as in *āburongo ana*, 'not listen to him'.

4 Kwara'ae translate *fa'aābu'a* as 'compensation', but this derives from another European misinterpretation of a Malaitan concept, in this case probably the result of a failure by the British administration to appreciate the function of *fa'aābu'a* in restoring relationships. 'Compensation' more accurately translates *du'unga'a*, which implies paying back or making a return for an offence.

CHAPTER 3

1 Some people distinguish *ngasingasi'anga* from *rigita'anga*, as a more specific term for the spiritual power of ghosts, although others regard this simply as the equivalent of *ngasingasi'anga* in the languages of North Malaita.

2 The role of women priests raises some interesting questions about these rules for the analysis of 'women's tabu' which follows. Like male priests, women priests were tabu to other women, men and children, and took the leading role in pig-sacrifices for the ghosts they were responsible for. But how women ghosts reacted to the defiling qualities of their priests is unclear, for they were not necessarily post-menopausal. Unfortunately lack of information makes it difficult to pursue the subject further.

3 An indication of the size of such congregations is given by the numbers of men

271

remembered as converting to Christianity together upon the death or conversion of their priests, from the second decade of this century onwards.

4 Opinion is divided as to whether men 'born of women' of a clan might also contribute to its festivals. They may have done so among the saltwater people, where women of the clan and their descendants, many living at a distance in other saltwater communities as far away as Lau and 'Are'are, would bring tabu pigs already dedicated to the ghosts of the festival shrine. It was probably less usual for men 'born of women' to contribute to festivals in the bush. Some men deny that it happened at all or say that it was forbidden to do so. Possibly only the sons of a woman of the clan would contribute, or those who were living with and dependent on the clan. But as a rule, men 'born of women' came to eat at festivals rather than to sacrifice.

5 In the Kwara'ae language, both skull and the husk and shell of the coconut are *lasi*. In view of the importance of this symbolism in Kwara'ae traditional ritual and in the cults which arose during the colonial period (see Chapters 5 and 6), it is interesting to note that quite different meanings are attributed to similar rituals of washing with coconut water in Kwaio (see Keesing 1982a:194).

6 There is also de Coppet's analysis of the political system of 'Are'are in South Malaita (1981, 1988), which focuses on the roles of "murderer" (*namo*, Kwara'ae *ramo*) and "peace-master" (*aaraha*). According to de Coppet (pers. comm. 1991), 'peace-masters' are also priests, but their fame as feast-givers seems to derive from the elaborate system of funeral exchanges rather than from sacrifice. And unlike Kwara'ae priests, 'peace-masters' and 'murderers' "are not inherited roles or stable status. They correspond to two hierarchically ordered ritual positions in the ceremonial exchanges" (1988). 'Are'are and Sa'a are known to have a tradition of chiefship more powerful than the language groups to the north, but de Coppet's material is difficult to compare because he does not describe the role of priests or the sacrificial system.

7 Although many Kwara'ae, including several writers, emphasise the title of *aofia*, its importance in recent times is questionable. *Aofia* is described by Lulute'e as "the Highess Man ... to give us rule" (Lulute'e c1936–8) and by Alasia as displaying "... most features of the 'Big-Man' type of leadership ... the feast-giver, 'maoma' [festival] organiser, and the political head of the society." (Alasia 1989:138). Like other peoples of North Malaita, Kwara'ae describe *aofia* or 'lord' as a kind of supreme secular leader ceremonially appointed to a position of absolute authority over his clan. But on investigation the last man to hold this title seems to have lived about ten generations ago, and only one or two such men are remembered, from a particular major clan.

CHAPTER 4

1 The story of these unfortunate 'recruits' has been confused by several authors with one of the other ships which visited the Solomons in 1871. This was the brig *Carl*, which became even more notorious after it returned to Fiji with about one hundred Solomon Islanders and Vanuatuans, having shot and thrown overboard about seventy men captured at Bouganville who had rebelled in the hold. The *Carl* also sailed up the east coast of Malaita on its way to the Western Solomons, but although the crew do not seem to have known exactly where they were for most of the time, the leader of the expedition could not recall capturing anyone there (Great Britain 1873:27–42,57–92, 226).

The accounts of the *Nukulau* and the *Peri* given by the British Consul for Fiji and Tonga, Edward March (Great Britain 1873:105–108,115, 213–220), and by the anonymous Fijian who recorded the story from the Kwai ("Leli") men in 1893 (Brewster 1937:230–236) and by Amasia himself in a statement to Woodford (Woodford 1901) are broadly in agreement. Anglican missionary accounts in the *Southern Cross Log* (Aug. 1900:19,20) and the diary of the photographer J. W. Beattie (1906:44) who visited Malaita with the missionaries in 1906, also supply information on the return of Amasia and Lau'a from Fiji. However, there are some important contradictions. The Fijian clerk names the ship which captured these men as the *Carl*, but March's reports on the *Nukulau* and statements by the culprits of the *Carl*, both published for a Parliamentary enquiry (Great Britain 1873) and corroborated by Woodford (1890:11), show this to be certainly a mistake and one which has unfortunately been perpetuated by recent authors such as Moore (1982:60, 1985:36,38) and Keesing (1986:270). It is most unlikely that the captives learnt the name of the ship which carried them until long afterwards, if ever, and Amasia told Woodford he could not remember it. Among other contradictions, Beattie heard that the survivors of the *Peri* were imprisoned for twenty one years in Fiji for murder (Beattie 1906:44) while Amasia and the Fijian told how they escaped from the warship in Fiji and lived among the Fijians (Woodford 1901, Brewster 1937:234). It may also be noted that March gives the total number captured by the *Nukulau* as 108 in his earlier reports, and that Brewster's map of the voyage is incorrect.

2 One such possibility is the case of the *Marion Rennie* which, after being "captured and all hands murdered" in the Western Solomons in about 1870, had disappeared altogether by 1882 (Great Britain 1873:208, 1883:118, Markham 1873:123–127). Another is the *Colleen Bawn* in about 1870 which, "after being spoken at Ugi in the Solomons, was never heard of again" (Woodford 1890:11). In addition, Rannie considered there was "ample proof" that vessels missing on the routes to China had been captured off Malaita (Rannie 1912:183).

3 This incident provides an example of the unreliability of some recruiters' accounts, for Wawn says that the *Borealis* was attacked off Kwai Island, which was then shelled by the *Emerald* (Wawn 1893:211–212). Maxwell's first hand description of the damage to Uru Island also contradicts Keesing's suspicions that the recruiters exaggerated the effects of their raid (Keesing 1986:291).

4 In his paper on the attack on the *Young Dick* at Sinalaagu in 1886, Keesing (1986) attributes both the *Borealis* and the *Janet Stewart* attacks to Maeasuaa of Uru Island, who is said by his Kwaio informants to have captured and burnt two ships, the first at Leri (Leili) Island and the second at Uru Island. Although the *Borealis* was not burned, it could well have been the second of these ships. This leaves a question as to the identity of the first. If it was the *Janet Stewart*, then all Keesing's informants have reversed the order of the two attacks; Keesing's own interpretation actually reverses their locations. But the burning of the *Janet Stewart*, the most spectacular success of all the attacks on Europeans in the area, may subsequently have embellished local stories of other ship attacks. While Keesing considers that the attack on the *Janet Stewart* casts doubt on the deterrent effect of the 1880 raid on Uru Island, the evidence of Captain Maxwell and Jack Mae would seem to cast the doubt instead on Maeasuaa's role in this attack. Possibly, like the heroes of ancient Kwara'ae stories, he could have been credited with the deeds of other less well known warriors.

In many respects the attacks on the *Borealis* and the *Janet Stewart* were remarkably similar; both were planned in advance and carried out while part of the crew were away in the boats and both left a single European survivor aboard undetected by the attackers. European accounts of the time also seem to confuse the two incidents; compare Rannie (1912:71), Wawn (1973:244) and the official report on the *Borealis* (Western Pacific 1880). The possibilities for confusion are further illustrated by Mae's recollections that another attack occurred between Ngongosila Island and the coast, giving details which actually match the attack on the *Young Dick* at Sinalaagu in 1886.

5 For some reason the cutlasses or 'bushknives' which are now a major agricultural tool, and which replaced wooden swords for clearing undergrowth and cleaning the ground, do not seem to occur in 19th century inventories of trade goods.

6 Such evidence contradicts Corris's conclusion that "Traditional religious practices and other customary observances seem ... to have fallen temporarily into abeyance" and that "There is no evidence ... of sorcery and other forms of magic being practiced among the Melanesians in Queensland". Despite his informant's opinion that "Queensland was a white man's country ... and the spirits weren't there", Corris himself describes how Malaitans there observed the rules of tabu

regarding defilement by women. These rules were far more than "latent beliefs" (Corris 1973:96–97) and they would have been observed as a condition for the support and protection of the ghosts, as they are by young Kwara'ae men in Christian communities who continue to depend on ghosts today. In fact, Malaitans who remained in Queensland were still making use of such powers as late as the 1930s, as Fatnowa recalls (1989 Ch. 2).

CHAPTER 5

1 Alfred Amasia's story is still remembered on Ngongosila, and so are the circumstances of Pauline's death, although she is said to have been Amasia's wife. That this is a mistake is clear from Amasia's own account, recorded by Woodford when Amasia reported Pauline's death in 1901 (Woodford 1901). Some Ngongosila people have also questioned some of the historical details given here, from a reading of the PhD thesis on which this book is based, but they have failed to provide alternative information. The archive sources for these incidents are also cited by Boutilier (1979) but his interpretation of them is somewhat misleading due to insufficient local knowledge.

2 The story of Lau'a's flight to Lau as recorded by Beattie could well have been confused with Amasia's experiences.

3 This figure is estimated from data given by Corris (1973:129–130,134)

4 Deck was preceded by Williams of the Melanesian Mission, who crossed from Fiu to Atā in 1901 (Fox 1962:139)

5 The contemporary sources cited here disagree as to the number of men shot and captured in this incident, except that three were hanged at Tulagi, and present day recollections are also vague.

6 According to Ivens (1930:135), in Lau, culturally similar to the saltwater people of Kwai, "Though the term *ano* is employed of the souls of the dead, they are more properly spoken of as *ano asa* (where *asa* = powerless, lost its cunning)." For Lau, these are the inhabitants of the afterworld island of Momolu, equivalent to the Kwara'ae Anogwa'u, although Kwara'ae say it is the soul (*mangona*) rather than the 'spirit' (*anoanona*) which goes there.

CHAPTER 6

1 Bell's omission of these incidents might throw doubt on Alasa'a's account, if Alasa'a's recollections were not so closely corroborated by contemporary reports of the Na'oasi incident and other events of the period. Alasa'a's remarkable

memory is attested in several cassettes of oral history which he recorded for his sons in the 1980s.

2 The three men whom Bell was pursuing after their escape from Tulagi are among several named by informants as those killed at Lama. Alasa'a names Refo, Maesala'a/Dausabea and Kisita: Lebekwau names Eofo and Dausabea: Bell names Suiasi, Maesala and Kisita. Unfortunately the Lama incident does not seem to be mentioned in Bell's reports.

3 These could be alternative names for Anogwa'u ('Empty-land'), possibly implying a place of yellow, dying leaves (sa'o).

4 Another cult described by Dausabea in his report to Allan serves to confuse the issue as far as *bulu* is concerned, although it provides important evidence for the antiquity of 'women ghosts' or 'women's cults' (*akalo kini*) with which *bulu* is associated. This occurred in the central Kwara'ae bush when Dausabea's father was a child, that is probably about 1870. Dausabea evidently regarded it as *bulu*, in comparing it to the 'new life' cult at 'Atori and 'Aisasale, but there is nothing in his account to suggest that this was anything more than his own interpretation. The cult began when an old woman began to promise the return of people's dead relatives if they carried out her instructions to build her a decorated house, clear wide paths to it (acts normally reserved for important ghosts) and make offerings of taro. Eventually her predictions failed and the people died in an epidemic attributed to sorcery (Allan 1974:182–184). Keesing, in dating this cult probably rather late to the 1880s or '90s, infers that it probably owed something to Christian preaching about the millenial resurrection of the dead, but it seems unlikely that an old woman would have been aware of this in the 1870s (Keesing 1978a I:258, II:61).

5 *Bulu* seems to be the focus for a whole complex of recurring symbolic associations in North Malaita. According to Tyhurst (pers. comm. 1986), in the Baelelea language of North Malaita the spirits of significant female ancestors are referred to as *abulu*. 'Bulu' refers to a type of malevolent magic usually controlled by women, from which protection can be sought by wearing a container of sea water on the body as, for instance, when entering a shrine-repository for women's bones. Ivens gives the meaning of *bulu* in Lau as an 'incantation' to immobilise sharks and crocodiles (identified with ghosts) and to cause enemies to sleep so that they can be killed (1930:163,140). He also notes that the "presiding ghost" of the Lau island of the dead is named after a black bird, "Kwadi bulu (The Black Whistler)" (1930:135). Fatnowa refers to *bulu* as a herb used by Malaitans in Queensland to protect a house from 'evil spirits' (1989:61). It is also curious to note that Āsufe, the original name of Buluanoasa of 'Aisasale, is a Kwara'ae word for 'rat'.

6 Bell's reports of this incident do not mention Ngwaki actually striking him;

perhaps, like his fall into the pigs' pool in 1919, he found it too embarassing to record. The fight is probably the same as that described by Keesing (Keesing 1978a I:255, Keesing and Corris 1980:94) from informants who had rather less background knowledge than Didi'imae and other Kwara'ae eyewitnesses.

CHAPTER 7

1 Fifi'i's book confirms the Kwara'ae accounts of the war and of Maasina Rule given here, but it was published after this chapter was written, so only passing references will be made to it. Colin Allan's account (1950), frequently cited in commentaries on Maasina Rule, has become largely redundant as a source of historical information as a result of access to formerly secret government reports in the Solomon Islands National Archives.

2 News of this story was recorded by the American Command in November 1945 (Holton 1945), but the only written record of Nori's meeting with a senior American officer seems to be when he and two others went earlier that year to enquire whether the Americans were going to take over from the British.

3 The variations of these names have been discussed exhaustively; it may well be, as Laracy suggests, that 'Māsing' derives from Malaitan attempts to Anglicise the original 'Maasina' (Laracy 1983:19–20, see also Keesing 1981.) But Kwara'ae also say that the movement 'marched' to them from 'Are'are; that it 'marched to rule', that is, for self-government or 'independence', and this in turn reflects the military symbolism which the movement developed. 'Māsing' could also have derived from the Kwara'ae habit of metathesising the words of their own and other languages. It is said that Kwara'ae changed the 'Maasina' to 'Māsingi', which loses its final 'i' in this process. Kwara'ae pronounciation was doubtless the cause for the initial British impression that the name derived from 'Marxian Rule' (Fox 1962:127), for 'Maasina' metathesises into 'Māsian'. For whatever reason, Māsing Rul is the name by which the movement became known in Kwai.

4 If, as Laracy states (1983:21) a £12 minimum wage was the main demand made, it is not recorded in these government reports of the meeting.

5 The full text of the letter is appended to the Acting Resident Commissioner's 'Report on Native Affairs', 1949.

CHAPTER 9

1 This account describes the SSEC as it was in the mid-1980s, shortly before several constitutional and organisational changes were made to the central administration of the Church.

CHAPTER 10

1 At the risk of causing semantic confusion, it should be noted that '*kastom*' is actually used by Kwara'ae to convey what Hobsbawm describes as 'tradition'; that is, usages which gain symbolic weight from real or supposed invariance or permanence. This Hobsbawm distinguishes from 'custom', describing the reality of precedent responding to changing circumstances (Hobsbawm & Ranger 1983:2). In Hobsbawm's terms, the present study uses 'tradition' to describe 'custom'. Although this contradicts the way Kwara'ae actually translate *falafala* (as *kastom*, English 'custom'), it conveys the sense in which they use these words. This should not of course obscure the fact that, in Hobsbawm's terms, what Kwara'ae represent as 'tradition' may actually be 'custom'.

2 Kwa'ioloa was the author of the letter of complaint from the self-styled 'Devil Priests' of 'Ere'ere to the SDA Director and pilot, which is cited by Keesing (1982a:236). We hope to publish his autobiography at a later date.

References

AKIN, D. 1984 *Social Distance and Dispute Management in East Kwaio, Malaita.* Unpublished research proposal, University of Hawaii.

ALASIA, S. 1987 The Case for Brideprice. *O'o* Vol. 1 No. 3: 59–68. University of the South Pacific, Solomon Islands Centre.

ALASIA, S. 1989 Politics. In H. Laracy (ed.) *Ples Blong Iumi: Solomon Islands, the Past Four Thousand Years.* 137–151 University of the South Pacific, Suva and Honiara.

ALLAN, C. H. 1950 *The Marching Rule Movement in the British Solomon Islands Protectorate: An Analytical Survey.* MA thesis, University of Cambridge.

ALLAN, C. H. 1951 *Notes on the Historical Background and Development of the South Seas Evangelical Mission.* Solomon Islands National Archives BSIP 1/III 23/9

ALLAN, C. H. 1957 *Customary Land Tenure in the British Solomon Islands Protectorate: Report of the Special Lands Commission.* Western Pacific High Commission, Honiara.

ALLAN, C. H. 1960 Local Government in the British Solomon Islands Protectorate. *Journal of African Administration* Vol. 12: 158–163

ALLAN, C. H. 1974 Some Marching Rule Stories. *Journal of Pacific History* Vol. 9:182–186.

ANNUAL REPORT 1931 Malaita District.
Solomon Islands National Archives BSIP 27/VI/1

ANNUAL REPORT 1933 Malaita District.
Solomon Islands National Archives BSIP 27/VI/1

ANNUAL REPORT 1934 Malaita District. (G. E. D. Sandars)
Solomon Islands National Archives BSIP 27/VI/1

ANNUAL REPORT 1940 Malaita District.
Solomon Islands National Archives BSIP 1/III F14/19B

ANNUAL REPORT 1941 Malaita District.
Solomon Islands National Archives BSIP 1/III 14/21

ANNUAL REPORT 1944 Malaita District. (D. C. C. Trench)
Solomon Islands National Archives, BSIP 1/III F14/9

ANNUAL REPORT 1945 Malaita District.
Solomon Islands National Archives, BSIP 27/VI/10

ANNUAL REPORT 1946 Malaita District. (G. E. D. Sandars)
Solomon Islands National Archives, BSIP 27/VI/11

ANNUAL REPORT 1947 Malaita District. (R. Davies)
Solomon Islands National Archives, BSIP I/LLL 14/36

279

ANNUAL REPORT 1949–1950 Malaita District. (C. H. Allan)
　　Solomon Islands National Archives, BSIP 27/VI/14

ANNUAL REPORT 1951 Malaita District.
　　Solomon Islands National Archives, BSIP 27/VI/15

ANNUAL REPORT 1952 Malaita District.
　　Solomon Islands National Archives, BSIP 27/VI/16

'*AUKI' LOG* 1925–7 Solomon Islands National Archives BSIP 15/IV 119a

AWDRY, F. 1902 *In the Isles of the Sea: The Story of Fifty Years in Melanesia.* Bemrose & Sons,
　　London.

BARKER, J. (ed.) 1990a *Christianity in Oceania: Ethnographic Perspectives.* Assocation for
　　Social Anthropology in Oceania Monograph NS 12, University Press of America,
　　Lanham.

BARKER, J. 1990b Introduction: Ethnographic Perspectives on Christianity in Oceania.
　　In J. Barker (ed.) *Christianity in Oceania: Ethnographic Perspectives.* Association for Social
　　Anthropology in Oceania Monograph NS 12: 1–24, University Press of America,
　　Lanham.

BARKER, J. 1990c Encounters with Evil: Christianity and the Response to Sorcery Among the
　　Maisin of Papua New Guinea. *Oceania* Vol. 61 139–155

BARNETT 1911 Letter to Edge-Partington 24 June. Solomon Islands National Archives

BARR, J. 1983 A Survey of Ecstatic Phenomena and 'Holy Spirit Movements' in Melanesia.
　　Oceania Vol. 54: 109–132

BARR, J. & TROMPF, G. 1983 Independant Churches and Recent Ecstatic Phenomena in
　　Melanesia: A Survey of Materials. *Oceania* Vol. 54: 48–72

BEATTIE, J. W. 1906 *Journal of a Voyage to the Western Pacific in the Melanesian Mission
　　Yacht Southern Cross.* Royal Society of Tasmania, Hobart Mss. RS. 29/3

BELL, W. 1916 Letter to Resident Commissioner, 3 July. Solomon Islands National Archives

BELL, W. 1917 Report to Resident Commissioner, 29 September.
　　Solomon Islands National Archives

BELL, W. 1918a Letter to Resident Commissioner, 19 February.
　　Solomon Islands National Archives

BELL, W. 1918b Deposition *In the matter of a charge against Galui.* 20 July
　　Solomon Islands National Archives

BELL, W. 1919a Report to Resident Commissioner on the Na'oasi incident, 17 May.
　　Solomon Islands National Archives

BELL, W. 1919b Letter to Resident Commissioner 19 May.
　　Solomon Islands National Archives

BELL, W. 1991c Letter to Resident Commissioner 1 December.
　　Solomon Islands National Archives

BELL, W. 1925a Report. Solomon Islands National Archives BSIP 14/58

BELL, W. 1925b Tour Report. Solomon Islands National Archives BSIP 14/59

BELSHAW, C. S. 1950 *Island Administration in the South West Pacific*. Royal Institute of International Affairs, London and New York.

BELSHAW, C. S. 1954 *Changing Melanesia: Social Economics of Culture Contact*. Oxford Unversity Press.

BENNETT, J. A. 1987 *Wealth of the Solomons: A History of a Pacific Archipelago, 1800–1978*. Pacific Islands Monographs, University of Hawaii Press, Honolulu.

THE BIG DEATH: Solomon Islanders Remember World War II. 1988 Solomon Islands College of Higher Education & the University of the South Pacific, Suva.

BERGER, P. 1967 *The Social Reality of Religion*. Penguin University Books (1973 ed.)

BOUTILIER, J. 1979 Killing the Government: Imperial Policy and the Pacification of Malaita. In M. Rodman & M. Cooper (eds.) The Pacification of Melanesia. *ASAO Monograph* No. 7: 43–87, University of Michigan Press, Ann Arbor.

BOUTILIER, J., HUGHES, D. T. & TIFFANY, S. W. (eds.) 1978 Mission, Church and Sect in Oceania. *A.S.A.O. Monographs* No. 6, University of Michigan Press.

BREWSTER, A. B. 1937 *King of the Cannibal Isles*. Robert Hale & Co, London.

BSIP 1911 *Handbook of the British Solomon Islands Protectorate, With Returns up to 31st March 1911*. Tulagi

BURT, B. 1982 Kastom, Christianity and the First Ancestor of the Kwara'ae of Malaita. In R. M. Keesing & R. Tonkinson (eds.) Reinventing Traditional Culture: The Politics of Kastom in Island Melanesia. *Mankind* Vol. 13 No. 4 (special issue) 374–399

BURT, B. 1983 The Remnant Church: A Christian Sect of the Solomon Islands. *Oceania* Vol. 53: 334–346

BURT, B. 1988 Ābu'a 'i Kwara'ae: The Meaning of Tabu in a Solomon Islands Society. *Mankind* Vol. 18: 74–89

BURT, B. 1990 Kwara'ae Costume Ornaments: A Solomon Islands Artform. *Expedition* Vol. 32: 3–15

BURT, B. 1991 Land Rights and Development: Writing about Kwara'ae Tradition. *Cultural Survival Quarterly* Vol. 15 No. 2: 61–64

CAMERON, A. R. P. P. K. 1947a *Reports of A. R. P. P. K. Cameron from Nafinua*, 3 June. Solomon Islands National Archives, BSIP 27 VII/I

CAMERON, A. R. P. P. K. 1947b Letter to G E D Sandars, 4 June. Solomon Islands National Archives, BSIP 1/III F14/33

CAMERON, A. R. P. P. K. 1947c *Travel Report, Kwai Sub-district*, 1 July. Solomon Islands National Archives, BSIP 1/III F14/33

CAMERON, A. R. P. P. K. 1947d *Report on Political Situation in Kwai Sub-District*, 2 July. Solomon Islands National Archives, BSIP 1/III F14/33

CAMERON, A. R. P. P. K. 1947e *Some notes on the holding of allegedly illegal courts in the Kwai area*, 3 July. Solomon Islands National Archives, BSIP 1/III F14/33

CAMERON, A. R. P. P. K. 1947f *A report on political conditions on the East Coast of Malaita, area from Oloburi to Kwai*, 8 August. Solomon Islands National Archives, BSIP 27/VII/I

CAMERON, A. R. P. P. K. 1947g *Report on Government Action at Sinerango, Kwai and Ata*, 20 September. Solomon Islands National Archives, BSIP 27/VII/1

CHOWNING, A. 1990 Gods and Ghosts in Kove. In J. Barker (ed.) *Christianity in Oceania: Ethnographic Perspectives*. Association for Social Anthropology in Oceania Monograph NS 12: 33–58, University Press of America, Lanham.

CLARK, J. 1989 God, Ghosts and People: Christianity and Social Organisation among Takuru Wiru. In M. Jolly & M. Macintyre (eds.) *Family and Gender in the Pacific: Domestic Contradictions and the Colonial Impact*. Cambridge University Press.

CODRINGTON, R. H. 1891 *The Melanesians*. Clarendon Press, Oxford.

COOPER, M. 1970 *Langalanga Ethics*. PhD thesis, Yale University.

COOPER, M. 1971 Economic Context of Shell Money Production on Malaita. *Oceania* Vol. 41: 226–276.

COOPER, M. 1972 Langalanga Religion. *Oceania* Vol. 43: 113–122

COPPET, D. de 1977 First Exchange, Double Illusion. *Journal of the Cultural Association of the Solomon Islands* Vol. 5: 23–39

COPPET, D. de 1988 *Bigmanship and the Socio-Cosmic Order*. Paper presented at conference on Rethinking Melanesian Models, London School of Economics.

COPPET, D. de 1981 The Life-Giving Death. In S. C. Humphries & H. King (eds.) *Mortality and Immortality: The Anthropology and Archaeology of Death*. 175–204 Academic Press, London.

COPPET, D. de & Zemp, H. 1978 *'Are'are: Un Peuple Melanesien et sa Musique*. Seuil, Paris.

COURT MINUTES, Government Station, Mala 1910–1912 Solomon Islands National Archives BSIP 15/II 30

CORRIS, P. 1973 *Passage, Port and Plantation: A History of Solomon Islands Labour Migration 1870–1914*. Melbourne University Press.

CROMAR, J. 1935 *Jock of the Islands: Early Days in the South Seas, Being the Adventures of John Cromar*. London, Faber & Faber.

DAVIES, R. 1947a *Tour Report, Kwai Sub-district, By District Commissioner, Malaita*, 1 December. Solomon Islands National Archives, BSIP 1/III F14/33

DAVIES, R. 1947b *Comments on tour reports by Mr. Marquand*. Solomon Islands National Archives, BSIP 1/III F14/33

DECK, J. 1927 Circular letter, 10 December, from Ngongosila. South Sea Evangelical Mission archive.

DECK, K. 1909 Diary-letter to her mother, June-July, from Ngongosila. South Sea Evangelical Mission archive.

DECK, Norman 1923a Letter to Florence Young, 17 July, from Ngongosila. South Sea Evangelical Mission archive.

DECK, Norman 1923b Letter to Florence Young, 30 October, from Ngongosila. South Sea Evangelical Mission archive.

DECK, Norman 1924 Letter to Florence Young, 2(?)November, from Ngongosila. South Sea Evangelical Mission archive.

DECK, Norman 1927a Letter to Florence Young, 29 July, from Ngongosila.
South Sea Evangelical Mission archive.

DECK, Norman 1927b Letter to Florence Young, 13 September, from Onepusu.
South Sea Evangelical Mission archive.

DECK, Norman 1928a Letter to Florence Young, February, from Ngongosila.
South Sea Evangelical Mission archive.

DECK, Norman 1928b Letter to Florence Young, 10 April, from Ngongosila.
South Sea Evangelical Mission archive.

DECK, Norman 1928c Circular letter, 18 May, from Ngongosila.
South Sea Evangelical Mission archive.

DECK, Norman 1928d Letter to Florence Young, 6 July.
South Sea Evangelical Mission archive.

DECK, Norman 1931 Letter to Mr Wallis, 26 November, from Ngongosila.
South Sea Evangelical Mission archive.

DECK, Norman 1932a Circular letter, 26 April, from Malaita.
South Sea Evangelical Mission archive.

DECK, Norman 1932b Letter to Florence Young, 26 September from Onepusu.
South Sea Evangelical Mission archive.

DECK, Norman 1933–4 A Grammar of the Language spoken by the Kwara'ae People of
Mala, British Solomon Islands. *Journal of the Polynesian Society* Vol. 42: 33–48, 133–
144, 241–256, Vol. 43: 1–16, 85–100, 163–170, 246–257

DECK, Norman n.d. *A Few Chronological Details Regarding the Rise of the Marching Rule*.
Typescript, South Sea Evangelical Mission archive.

DECK, Norman/HOGBIN, H. I. 1934–5 Correspondence on bridewealth in Malaita.
Oceania Vol. 5 : 242–245, 368–370, 488–489.

DIARIES 1910–1913 District Officer Malaita.
Solomon Islands National Archives BSIP 15/VIII 134

DIARY 1940 District Officer Malaita. Solomon Islands National Archives BSIP 15/VIII 157

DIARY 1949 District Commissioner, Malaita Office. (S. G. Masterman)
Solomon Islands National Archives, BSIP 15/VIII

DICKINSON, J. H. C. 1927 *A Trader in the Savage Solomons*. H. F. & G. Witherby, London

EDGE-PARTINGTON, T. E. 1910 Letter to Resident Commissioner re. raid on Ngorefou.
Solomon Islands National Archives

EDGE-PARTINGTON, T. E. 1911a Letter to Resident Commissioner, 26 June.
Solomon Islands National Archives

EDGE-PARTINGTON, T. E. 1911b *General Report on Mala* to Resident Commissioner,
7 July. Solomon Islands National Archives

EDGE-PARTINGTON, T. E. 1911c Letter to Acting Resident Commissioner, 15 July.
Solomon Islands National Archives.

EDGE-PARTINGTON, T. E. 1911d Letter to Resident Commissioner, 6 December.
Solomon Islands National Archives

EDGE-PARTINGTON, T. E. 1911e Letter to Resident Commisioner, 27 December.
  Solomon Islands National Archives

EDGE-PARTINGTON, T. E. 1912 Letter to Resident Commissioner, 15 February.
  Solomon Islands National Archives

EDGE-PARTINGTON, T. E. 1914 Letter to REsident Commissioner, 11 May.
  Solomon Islands National Archives

FATNOWA, N. 1987 *Fragments of a Lost Heritage*. Angus & Robertson, Australia.

FERNANDEZ, J. W. 1978 African Religious Movements.
  Annual Review of Anthropology Vol. 7: 195–234

FIFI'I, J. 1889 *From Pig-Theft to Parliament: My Life Between Two Worlds*. (translated and
  edited by R. M. Keesing) Solomon Islands College of Higher Education & University of
  the South Pacific, Honiara.

FORSTER, M. J. 1948 Letter to the Secretary to the Government, *Subject: District Headmen*.
  Solomon Islands National Archives, BSIP 1/III F14/8 PIB

FOSTER, R. J. 1992 Commoditization and the Emergence of *Kastom* as a Cultural Category:
  A New Ireland Case in Comparative Perspective. In M. Jolly and N. Thomas (eds.)
  The Politics of Tradition in the Pacific. *Oceania* Vol. 62 (special issue) 284–294

FOX, C. E. 1962 *Kakamora*. Hodder & Stoughton, London.

FUGUI, L. 1989 Religion. In H. Laracy (ed.) *Ples Blong Iumi: Solomon Islands, the Past Four
  Thousand Years*. 73–93 University of the South Pacific, Suva and Honiara.

FULBRIGHT, T. C. 1986 *The Marching Rule: A Christian Revolution in the Solomon Islands*.
  M A thesis, University of British Columbia.

GEGEO, D. W. 1991 Tribes in Agony: Land, Development and Politics in Solomon Islands.
  Cultural Survival Quarterly Vol. 15 No. 2: 53–55

GANIFIRI, J. J. n.d. *Na Taki ana Tua i Kwara'ae, Fanoa i Malaita*.
  Manuscript book in Kwara'ae language (in possession of A Rofate'e, Malaita.)

GOLSON, J. n.d. (c. 1980?) Agricultural Technology in New Guinea. In
  D. Denoon & C. Snowdon (eds.) *A Time to Plant and a Time to Uproot:
  A History of Agriculture in Papua New Guinea*. Ch. 3
  Institute of Papua New Guinea Studies.

GREAT BRITAIN 1872 *Further Correspondence respecting the Deportation of South Sea
  Islanders, In Continuation of Correspondence presented to Parliament*. [C.339–1871]
  Foreign Office Papers. (Museum of Mankind Library)

GREAT BRITAIN 1873 *South Sea Islands: Copies or Extracts "of any Communications of
  Importance respecting Outrages committed upon Natives of the South Sea Islands"* etc.
  Parliamentary Papers 1873 (Museum of Mankind Library)

GREAT BRITAIN 1881 *Solomon Islands, &c. (Punishment of Natives)*.
  Parliamentary Papers Vol. 60 (British Library)

GREAT BRITAIN 1882 *Reports of Proceedings of Her Majesty's Ships*.
  Public Record Office ADM1/6624

GREAT BRITAIN 1883 *Correspondence Respecting the Natives of the Western Pacific and the Labour Traffic.* Parliamentary Papers 1883 Vol. 47 (British Library)

GREAT BRITAIN 1891 Naval reports. Public Record Office ADM1/7112

GREAT BRITAIN 1894 *Correspondence Respecting Outrages by Natives on British Subjects, and other matters which have been under inquiry during the year 1894 by Her Majesty's Ships.* Public Record Office ADM1/7252

GRIFFITHS, A. 1977 *Fire in the Islands: The Acts of the Holy Spirit in the Solomons.* Harold Shaw, Wheaton Illinois.

GUIART, J. 1962 The Millenial Aspect of Conversion to Christianity in the South Pacific. In S. Thrupp (ed.) *Millennial Dreams in Action,* 122–138 Mouton, The Hague.

GUIDERI, R. 1980 *La Route des Mortes.* Seuil, Paris

HARWOOD, F. 1978 Intercultural Communication in the Western Solomons: The Methodist Mission and the Emergence of the Christian Fellowship Church. In J. Boutilier, D. Hughes & S. Tiffany (eds.) Mission, Church and Sect in Oceania. 231–250. *ASAO Monograph* No. 6: 201–208 University of Michigan Press, Ann Arbor.

HILLIARD, D. 1969 The South Seas Evangelical Mission in the Solomon Islands: The Foundation Years. *Journal of Pacific History* Vol. 4:41–64

HILLIARD, D. 1974 Colonialism and Christianity: The Melanesian Mission in the Solomon Islands. *Journal of Pacific History* Vol. 9:93–116

HILLIARD, D. 1978 *God's Gentlemen: A History of the Melanesian Mission 1894–1942.* University of Queensland Press.

HOBSBAWM, E. & RANGER, T. 1983 (eds.) *The Invention of Tradition.* Cambridge University Press.

HOGBIN, H. I. 1939 *Experiments in Civilization: The Effects of European Culture on a Native Community of the Solomon Islands.* Routledge & Kegan Paul, London.

HOGBIN, H. I. 1964 *A Guadalcanal Society: The Kaoka Speakers.* Holt, Rhinehart and Winston, New York.

HOLTON, R. G. 1945 *Memorandum to Col. R G Howie, Island Command,* 23 November. Solomon Islands National Archives, BSIP 1/III F19/8 part II

HORTON, R. 1971 African Conversion. *Africa* Vol. 41: 85–108

HUGHES, D. T. 1978 Local Level Missionary Adaptation: Introduction. In J. Boutilier, D. Hughes. & S. Tiffany (eds.) 1978 Mission, Church and Sect in Oceania. *ASAO Monograph* No. 6: 201–208 University of Michigan Press, Ann Arbor.

IFUNAOA, W. 1983 Implementing Provincial Government. In *Solomon Islands Politics.* 196–207 University of the South Pacific, Suva.

IMMIGRATION AGENT 1903 Letter to Dept. of Immigration, Pacific Islands Labour Branch, 1 April. Western Pacific High Commission IC 7/03 (University of Hawaii library)

IVENS, W. G. 1927 *Melanesians of the Southeast Solomon Islands.* Kegan Paul, London.

IVENS, W. G. 1930 *Island Builders of the Pacific.* Seeley Service, London.

JOHNSON, O. 1944 *Bride in the Solomons.* Houghton Mifflin, Boston.

JOLLY, M. 1982 Birds and Banyans in South Pentecost: Kastom in Anti-Colonial Struggle.
In R. M. Keesing and R. Tonkinson (eds.) Reinventing Traditional Culture: The Politics
of Kastom in Island Melanesia. *Mankind* Vol. 13 No. 4 (special issue) 338–356.

JOLLY, M. 1989 Sacred Spaces: Churches, Men's Houses and Housholds in South Pentecost,
Vanuatu. In M. Jolly and M. Macintyre (eds.) *Family and Gender in the Pacific: Domestic
Contradictions and the Colonial Impact.* Cambridge University Press.

JOLLY, M. 1992 Custom and the Way of the Land: Past and Present in Vanuatu and Fiji.
In M. Jolly and N. Thomas (eds.) The Politics of Tradition in the Pacific.
Oceania Vol. 62 No. 4 (special issue) 330–354.

JOLLY, M. & MACINTYRE, M. 1989 Introduction. In M. Jolly & M. Macintyre (eds.)
Family and Gender in the Pacific: Domestic Contradictions and the Colonial Impact.
Cambridge University Press.

JOLLY, M. & THOMAS, N. 1992 (eds.) The Politics of Tradition in the Pacific.
Oceania Vol. 62 No. 4 (special issue)

KAPLAN, M. 1990 Christianity, People of the Land, and Chiefs in Fiji.
In J. Barker (ed.) 1990 *Christianity in Oceania: Ethnographic Perspectives.*
Association for Social Anthropology in Oceania Monograph NS 12: 127–148,
University Press of America, Lanham.

KEESING, R. M. 1967 Christians and Pagans in Kwaio, Malaita.
Journal of the Polynesian Society Vol. 76: 82–100

KEESING, R. M. 1968 Chiefs in a Chiefless Society: The Ideology of Modern Kwaio Politics.
Oceania. Vol. 38: 276–280

KEESING, R. M. 1970 Shrines, Ancestors and Cognatic Descent: The Kwaio and the Tallensi.
American Anthropologist n.s. Vol. 72: 755–775

KEESING, R. M. 1978a Politico-Religious Movements and Anticolonialism in Malaita:
Maasina Rule in Historical Perspective.
Oceania (I) Vol. 48:242–262, (II) Vol 49: 46–73)

KEESING, R. M. 1978b 'Elota's Story: The Life and Times of a Solomon Islands Big Man.
University of Queensland Press

KEESING, R. M. 1980 Antecedants of Maasina Rule: Some Further Notes.
Journal of Pacific History Vol. 15: 102–107

KEESING, R. M. 1981 Still Further Notes on 'Maasina Rule'.
Journal of the Anthropological Society of Oxford Vol. 12: 130–134

KEESING, R. M. 1982a *Kwaio Religion: The Living and the Dead in a Solomon Island Society.*
Columbia University Press, New York

KEESING, R. M. 1982b Kastom in Melanesia: An Overview. *Mankind* Vol 13: 297–301

KEESING, R. M. 1982c Kastom and Anticolonialism on Malaita: 'Culture' as a Political
Symbol. In R. M. Keesing & R. Tonkinson (eds.) Reinventing Traditional Culture: The
Politics of Kastom in Island Melanesia. *Mankind* Vol. 13 No. 4 (special issue) 357–373

KEESING, R. M. 1984 Rethinking Mana. *Journal of Anthropological Research*
Vol. 40: 137–156

KEESING, R. M. 1985 Killers, Big Men, and Priests on Malaita: Reflections on a Melanesian
    Troika System. *Ethnology* Vol. 24: 237–252

KEESING, R. M. 1988 *Melanesian Pidgin and the Oceanic Substrate.*
    Stanford University Press.

KEESING R. M. 1986 The Young Dick Attack: Oral and Documentary History on the
    Colonial Frontier. *Ethnohistory* Vol. 33: 268–292

KEESING, R. M. 1989a Sins of a Mission: Christian Life as Kwaio Traditionalist Ideology.
    In M. Jolly & M. Macintyre *Family and Gender in the Pacific: Domestic Contradictions
    and the Colonial Impact.* Cambrige University Press.

KEESING, R. M. 1989b Creating the Past: Custom and Identity in the Contemporary Pacific.
    The Contemporary Pacific Vol. 1: 19–42

KEESING, R. M. & CORRIS, P. 1980 *Lightning Meets the West Wind: The Malaita Massacre.*
    Oxford University Press.

KEESING, R. M. & TONKINSON, R. 1982 (eds.) Reinventing Traditional Culture:
    The Politics of Kastom in Melanesia. *Mankind* Vol. 13 No. 4 (special issue)

KEESING, R. M. & Burt, B. 1990 Kwara'ae Conceptions of Abu: An Exchange.
    The Australian Journal of Anthropology. Vol. 1: 44–49 (review of Burt 1988, and reply)

KWAISULIA 1902 *Murder of Amisia 18th September 1902.* Statement to A. Mahaffy
    Western Pacific High Commission 7/03 (University of Hawaii library)

LARACY, H. M. 1971 Marching Rule and the Missions.
    Journal of Pacific History Vol. 6: 96–114

LARACY, H. M. 1976 *Marists and Melanesians: A History of Catholic Missions in the Solomon
    Islands.* Australian National University Press.

LARACY, H. M. (ed.) 1983 *Pacific Protest: the Maasina Rule Movement, Solomon Islands,
    1944–1952.* University of the South Pacific, Suva.

LARACY, H. M. 1988b War Comes to the Solomons. In H. M. Laracy & G. White (eds.)
    Taem Blong Faet: World War II in Melanesia. *'O'o* No. 4: 17–26, University of the
    South Pacific (Solomon Islands Centre), Honiara.

LARACY, H. M. 1988c Missionaries and the European Evacuation of the Solomon Islands,
    1942–43, In H. M. Laracy & G. White (eds.) 1988 Taem Blong Faet: World War II in
    Melanesia. *'O'o* No. 4: 27–36, University of the South Pacific (Solomon Islands Centre),
    Honiara

LARACY, H. M. & WHITE, G. (eds.) 1988 Taem Blong Faet: World War II in Melanesia.
    'O'o No. 4, University of the South Pacific (Solomon Islands Centre), Honiara.

LĀTŪKEFU, S. 1977 The Wesleyan Mission. In N. Rutherford (ed.) *Friendly Islands:
    A History of Tonga.* 114–135 Oxford University Press.

LĀTŪKEFU, S. 1978 Conclusion: Retrospect and Prospect. In J. Boutilier,
    D. Hughes & S. Tiffany (eds.) 1978 Mission, Church and Sect in Oceania.
    ASAO Monograph No. 6: 457–464 University of Michigan Press, Ann Arbor.

LINDSTROM, L. 1982 Leftamap Kastom: The Political History of Tradition on Tanna
    (Vanuatu). In R. M. Keesing and R. Tonkinson (eds.) Reinventing Traditional Culture:
    The Politics of Kastom in Island Melanesia. *Mankind* Vol. 13 No. 4: 330–337
    (special issue)

LONDON, C. K. 1910(?) *A Woman Among the Headhunters: A Narrative of the Voyage of the 'Snark' in the Years 1908–1909*. Mills & Boon, London.

LONDON, J. 1917 *Jerry of the Islands*. Mills & Boon, London.

LULUTE'E c1936–8 *Notes on Malaita Native Custom*. Manuscript ledger book compiled (and titled) by G. E. D. Sanders. Solomon Islands National Archives BSIP 27/I 1

MACINTYRE, M. 1990 Christianity, Cargo Cultism, and the Concept of the Spirit in Misiman Cosmology. In J. Barker (ed.) *Christianity in Oceania: Ethnographic Perspectives*. Association for Social Anthropology in Oceania Monograph NS 12: 81–100, University Press of America, Lanham.

MAENU'U, L. P. 1981 *Bib Kami Na Ano: Land and Land Problems in Kwara'ae*. University of the South Pacific, Solomon Islands Centre, Honiara.

MAHAFFY, A. 1902 Report to Resident Commissioner, 1 October. Western Pacific High Commission IC 7/03 (University of Hawaii library)

MALAITA DISTRICT JOURNAL 1940 Manuscript ledger (kept by Chief Magistrate, 'Aoke, Malaita).

MAETOLOA, M. 1985 The Remnant Church. In C. Loeliger & G. Tromph (eds.) *New Religious Movements in Melanesia*. University of the South Pacific and University of Papua New Guinea, Suva.

MARANDA, E 1974 Lau, Malaita: "A Woman is an Alien Spirit". In C. Matthiesson (ed.) *Many Sisters: Women in Cross-Cultural Perspective*. Free Press, New York.

MARANDA, P. & MARANDA, E. K. 1970 Le Crane et l'Uterus; Deux Theoremes Nord-Malaitans. In J. Pouillon & P. Maranda (eds.) *Echanges et Communications: Melanges Offerts a Claude Levi-Strauss*. Mouton, The Hague, Paris.

MARKHAM, A. H. 1873 *The Cruise of the Rosario Amongst the New Hebrides and Santa Cruz Islands*. Sampson Low etc., London.

MOORE, C. 1982 Malaitan Recruiting to Queensland: An Oral History Approach. *Bikmaus* Vol. 3: 57–71

MOORE, C. 1985 *Kanaka: A History of Melanesian Mackay*. Institute of Papua New Guinea Studies and University of Papua New Guinea Press.

NATIVE AFFAIRS BOOK, District of Malaita 1931–2. Solomon Islands National Archives BSIP 27/I/3

NATIVE AFFAIRS BOOK, Kwara'ae 1951–4. Solomon Islands National Archives BSIP 27/I/8

NGWADILI, A. 1977 *The Constitution of the Kwara'ae Chiefs*. Duplicated typescript (addressed to the Minister for Education and Cultural Affairs)

NIV (see NOT IN VAIN)

NOT IN VAIN (Annual report and later quarterly newsletter of the South Seas Evangelical Mission) Sydney. Mitchell Library, State Library of New South Wales (some early issues have no page numbers)

OJO, M. A. 1988 The Contextual Significance of the Charismatic Movements in Independent Nigeria. *Africa* Vol. 58: 175–192

OTTO, T. 1992 The Ways of *Kastom:* Tradition as Category and Practice in a Manus Village.
In M. Jolly and N. Thomas (eds.) The Politics of Tradition in the Pacific.
Oceania Vol. 62 No. 4 (special issue) 264–283.

OVEREND, R. 1990 *The Church and its Mission in the World.*
South Sea Evangelical Mission, Laurieton, NSW

RANGER, T. O. 1975 Introduction to Christianity and Central African Religions.
In T. O. Ranger & J. Weller *Themes in the Christian History of Central Africa.*
Heinemann, London.

RANNIE, D. 1912 *My Adventures Among South Sea Cannibals.* Seeley, Service, London

REPORT ON NATIVE AFFAIRS 1949 (Acting Resident Commissioner)
Solomon Islands National Archives BSIP 1/III F49/28

ROFATE'E, A. 1979 *Custom Book of Kwara'ae Taki, Halahala.* Manuscript book
(English version of Kwara'ae document based on Ganifiri n.d., in possession of A.
Rofate'e, Malaita.)

ROFATE'E, A. 1980 *Halahala ana Taki i Kwara'ae of Malaita.* Manuscript book
(listing traditional 'laws' and penalties, in possession of A. Rofate'e, Malaita.)

ROSS, H. M. 1973 Baegu: Social and Ecological Organisation in Malaita, Solomon Islands.
Illinois Studies in Anthropology No. 8

ROSS, H. M. 1978a Leadership Styles and Strategies in a Traditional Melanesian Society.
In Rank and Status in Melanesia *Publications de la Societe de l'Homme* No. 39: 11–22

ROSS, H. M. 1978b Competition for Baegu Souls: Mission Rivalry on Malaita, Solomon
Islands. In J. Boutilier, D. Hughes & S. Tiffany (eds.) Mission, Church and Sect in
Oceania. *ASAO Monograph* No. 6: 163–200

RUKIA, A. 1988 *Fulifera Abu Kami Ki: Ritual Sites in Some Solomon Islands Traditional
Socieites, Their Past, Present and Future.* Thesis for degree of Bachelor of Letters,
Australian National University, Canberra.

RUSSELL, T. 1950 The Fataleka of Malaita. *Oceania* Vol. 21: 1–13

SANDARS, G. E. D. 1943 Report on tour of duty in Malaita District.
Solomon Islands National Archives BSIP 1/III 19/9

SANDARS, G. E. D. 1946 Political Activity on Malaita, 9 October. Report appended to
Annual Report, Malaita District, 1946.
Solomon Islands National Archives, BSIP 27/VI/II

SAHLINS, M. 1972 *Stone Age Economics.* Tavistock Publications, London.

SAHLINS, M. 1981 Historical Metaphors and Mythical Realities: Structure in the Early
History of the Sandwich Islands Kingdom. *ASAO Special Publications* No. 1, University
of Michigan Press, Ann Arbor.

SAHLINS, M. 1985 *Islands of History.* University of Chicago Press.

SCARR, D. 1973 Recruits and Recruiters: A Portrait of the Labour Trade. In J. Davidson &
D. Scarr (ed.) *Pacific Island Portraits.* 225–251 Australian National University Press,
Canberra.

SCHEFFLER, H. W. 1964 The Social Consequences of Peace on Choiseul Island. *Ethnology* Vol. 3: 398–403

SCL (see SOUTHERN CROSS LOG)

SSEC (South Sea Evangelical Church) 1977 *Handbook for Pastors: Orders of Service for SSEC Meetings*. Honlit (SSEC), Honiara.

SIMONS, G. 1977 *A Kwara'ae Spelling List*. Working Paper for the Language Variation and Limits to Communication Project, No. 6. Summer Institute of Linguistics

SMITH, M. F. 1990 Catholicism, Capitalist Incorporation, and Resistance in Kragur. In J. Barker (ed.) *Christianity in Oceania: Ethnographic Perspectives*. Association for Social Anthropology in Oceania Monograph NS 12:149–172, University Press of America, Lanham.

SOLOMON ISLANDS 1986 National Census. Statistics office, Honiara.

SOLOMON ISLANDS 1987 *Provincial Statistics*. Statistical Bulletin No. 15/87. Statistics Office, Honiara.

SOUTHERN CROSS LOG Melanesian Mission, London (Newsletter of the Mission) (Melanesian Mission Archive and British Library)

SOUTH PACIFIC 1955 Education in the British Solomon Islands: An Historical Review. *South Pacific* Vol 8 No. 5: 99

THOMAS, N. 1991 *Entangled Objects*. Harvard University Press.

TIFFANY, S. W. 1978 The Politics of Denominational Organisation in Samoa. In J. Boutilier, D. Hughes & S. Tiffany (eds.) Mission, Church and Sect in Oceania. *ASAO Monograph* No. 6: 423–456

TIPPETT, A. R. 1967 *Solomon Islands Christianity: A Study in Growth and Obstruction*. Lutterworth Press, London.

TONKINSON, R. 1981 Church and *Kastom* in Southeast Ambrym. In M. Allen (ed.) *Vanuatu: Politics, Economics and Ritual in Island Melanesia*, 237–268 Academic Press, Australia.

TONKINSON, R. 1982 National Identity and the Problem of Kastom in Vanuatu. In R. M. Keesing and R. Tonkinson (eds.) Reinventing Traditional Culture: The Politics of Kastom in Island Melanesia. *Mankind* Vol. 13 No. 4 (special issue): 306–315.

TONKINSON, R. 1990 Sorcery and Social Change in Southeast Ambrym, Vanuatu. In M. Zelenietz (ed.) Sorcery and Social Change in Melanesia. *Social Analysis* No. 8 (special issue) 77–88

TOUR REPORT 1940 Resident Commissioner. Solomon Islands National Archives BSIP 1/III F19/11

TOUR REPORT 1948 District Commissioner Malaita (M. Forster), with covering memo from Divisional Commissioner's Office, Auki, to Secretary for Native Affairs, Honiara, 23 April. Solomon Islands National Archives, BSIP 1/III F14/33 part I

TISA, R. S. 1979 *Siale Customary Planning Organisation Constitution*. Duplicated typescript.

TROMPF, G. W. 1991 *Melanesian Religion*. Cambridge University Press.

WAISAKI 1902 *Murder of Bauleni (Fijian Woman) Wife of Waisaki.* (statement taken by A. Mahaffy) 18 September. Western Pacific High Commission 7/1903

WATSON-GEGEO, K. A. & GEGEO, D. W. 1986 The Social World of Kwara'ae Children: Acquisition of Language and Values. In J. Cook-Gumperz, W. Corsaro & J. Streek (eds.) *Children's Worlds and Children's Language.* Berlin.

WAWN, W. T. 1893 *The South Sea Islanders and the Queensland Labour Trade.* Swan Sonnenschein, London.

WEINER, A. 1976 *Women of Value, Men of Renoun: New Perspectives in Trobriand Exchange.* University of Texas Press.

WESTERN PACIFIC 1880 *Papers Relating to the Murder of a Part of the Crew of the "Borealis", at Malayta.* Western Pacific High Commission correspondence No. 13638 (University of Hawaii library)

WHITE, G. 1979 War, Peace and Piety in Santa Isabel, Solomon Islands. In M. Rodman & M. Cooper (eds.) The Pacification of Melanesia. *ASAO Monograph* No. 7: 109–139, University of Michigan Press, Ann Arbor.

WHITE, G. 1991 *Identities Through History: Living Stories in a Solomon Islands Society.* Cambridge Studies in Social and Cultural Anthropology, Cambridge University Press.

WHITEMAN, D. 1983 *Melanesians and Missionaries: An Ethnohistorical Study of Social and Religious Change in the Southwest Pacific.* William Carey Library, California

WILSON, A. 1942 Report on events at Tulagi on 14 December 1941. Typescript (in possession of Mrs A Bannatyne, London, copies in Museum of Mankind and University of Hawaii libraries)

WOLFERS, T. 1983 Centralisation and Decentralisation Until Independence. *Solomon Islands Politics,* 146–163 University of the South Pacific, Suva.

WOODFORD, C. M. 1890 *A Naturalist Among the Head-Hunters; Being an Account of Three Visits to the Solomon Islands in the Years 1886, 1887, and 1888.* George Phillip & Son, London.

WOODFORD, C. M. 1901 *Statement of Amisia at Tulagi 2nd. November* and *Story of Amisia. Told at Tulagi 3rd November.* Western Pacific High Commission archive WPHC 7/03 (University of Hawaii library)

WOODFORD, C. M. 1903 Letter to High Commissioner, 26 March. Western Pacific High Commission archive WPHC 7/03 (University of Hawaii library)

WORSLEY, P. 1968 *The Trumpet Shall Sound: A Study of 'Cargo' Cults in Melanesia.* Paladin, London (2nd edition).

YOUNG, F. H. 1925 *Pearls from the Pacific* Marshall Bros., London.

ZELENIETZ, M. 1979 The End of Headhunting in New Georgia. In M. Rodman & M. Cooper (eds.) The Pacification of Melanesia. *ASAO Monograph* No. 7: 91–108, University of Michigan Press, Ann Arbor.

ZELENIETZ, M. 1981 Sorcery and Social Change: An Introduction. In M. Zelenietz (ed.) Sorcery and Social Change in Melanesia. *Social Analysis* No. 8 (special issue) 3–14

ZINAMAMU 1901 letter to C. M. Woodford, 30 October. Western Pacific High Commission 7/03 (University of Hawaii library)

Index